ENDORSEMENTS

"Josephus was a reliable eyewitness to events in the land of Israel at the time of Jesus. His account has been an invaluable record to historians and scholars through the centuries. Now Miriam Maranzenboim has done us a great service by bringing Josephus into the 21th Century to give readers a deeper understanding of the turmoil and challenges the Jewish people continue to endure."

Dr. Christine Darg
Co-founder, The Jerusalem Channel

"Finally, a book that brings to life early Jewish/Christian history as recorded by a first century Jew.

In Prof. Bruce Metzger's class at Princeton Seminary, we students struggled through archaic translations of Josephus. What a pleasure to read Miriam Maranzenboim's modern condensation of Josephus' writings for English readers! A wealth of knowledge for any age reader is to be gained even about details of ancient life"

Pastor Kathleen Macosko, M.Div. (retired)

JOSEPHUS

THE HISTORY OF THE JEWS

CONDENSED IN SIMPLE ENGLISH

Miriam Maranzenboim

EDITED by Hannah Weiss

Illustrations by Mark A. Stephens
Cover Design and Timeline by Debbie O'Byrne

Hardcover ISBN: 978-1-944878-34-4
Softcover ISBN: 978-1-944878-32-0

"This book is dedicated to every person who recognizes his/her "chosenness" with the hope that we will fulfill our unique Divine callings and destiny."

INTRODUCTION

I wrote *Josephus – The History of the Jews Condensed in Simple English* in order to give average English speakers the opportunity to read an otherwise untouched book. The educated world recognizes Josephus as a reliable historical source of information. Those who study the Bible, including archaeologists and historians, are aware that his accounts have survived when others have been destroyed.

My aim has been simplicity. When you come to the name. "Jesus"; for example, don't just assume that this is the "Jesus of Nazareth" with whom you're familiar. Many people had the name "Jesus" in the time of Josephus.

I don't claim to be an expert in history, archaeology, or the Bible. However, I am good with words and love history. Therefore it wasn't difficult for me to draw out the main stories from William Whiston's translation done in 1700. I have given you a book-by-book and section-by-section summary of *Josephus – The History of the Jews Condensed in Simple English* which represents about one quarter of the original text.

In all of the various lectures I have listened to about Josephus, no one ever mentioned that Alexander the Great confronted the High Priest of Jerusalem, Jaddua. I find it a pivotal and believable moment in history. This is but one reason why I felt it was time to write up these events for our information.

I have been living in Israel since 1977; hence my life is intertwined with the history of the Jewish people. This book is an important testimony of their unfolding destiny.

If you would like more information about Josephus just do a quick internet search or visit your local library. The Haifa University library (near my home) has more than 90 books about him—and that is not an exhaustive list.

I hope you enjoy stepping back in time to the world Josephus wrote about.

Miriam Maranzenboim, Haifa, Israel

Josephus was born into a rich, religious Jewish family in the first century. In his teenage years he left home on a spiritual search that took him to the Judean desert. He later joined the strict sect of the Pharisees. A successful trip to Rome enabled him to free some Jewish priests. With them, he returned to Judea. Josephus then joined the army and became the commander in Galilee, fighting against the Romans. When around 40 years old, the Romans captured Josephus. He predicted to Vespasian that Vespasian would become the ruler in Rome. It sounded unlikely but it was proven true. As a result, Josephus was taken to Rome as both hostage and interpreter. Josephus returned to Judea with his Roman captors and witnessed the destruction of the second temple. Later after returning to Rome Josephus wrote about the wars in Israel. His book, *Antiquities of the Jews* was written when Josephus was 56. This book has been the second most important historical source for the 4,000 year period up to the first century; second only to the Bible.

My simplified version:

Caius made Petronius as president in Syria in place of Vitellius, and gave him an order to invade Judea. They were to put Caius's statue in the temple, and if the Jews would not allow it, there would be war. Petronius took two Roman legions with him and stayed for the winter in Ptolemais, planning to go to Jerusalem in the spring. But 10,000s of Jews came to him in Ptolemais begging him not to force them to break the law of their people. They would rather die than give in to this Roman order. Petronius said that he had no choice; he had to follow the orders of Caesar. The Jews answered that they feared the anger of God who was higher than Caius. Petronius saw that there was danger of war, and he went to Tiberias. Many thousands of Jews met him there also. They threw themselves on their faces and stretched out their throats, saying that they would not fight, but they would rather die than see Caesar's statue in their temple. They did this for forty days and left their farming, even though it was the time to plant crops.

King Agrippa's brother Aristobulus and other Jewish leaders came to Petronius, pleading with him to stop the plan. They said that Caesar would be wiser not to destroy the people. With no one to farm their land robbery would increase, and the people would have no money to pay their taxes. Tens of thousands of Jews were gathered in Tiberias, and Petronius said that he would send word to Caius of their request. He saw that they were telling the truth; they were being loyal to their God above all. He said that if Caius would be angry with him, he would rather suffer himself than to see so many people die who had been behaving well.

"Go back to your farming and I and my associates will go to Rome," he told the leaders of the Jews, and he encouraged them to be hopeful. As soon as Petronius finished speaking, there was a sign from God of His blessing. Suddenly heavy rain came down on a clear day, and this during a year that had seen almost no rain at all. Petronius saw that God was truly caring for his own people. Petronius wrote to Caius about this sign and pleaded with him not to bother this great crowd of people, for he would lose their taxes and would also be cursed by them for all time.

The original version from 1700s:

These thought they must run a mighty hazard if they should have a war with the Romans, but judged that the transgression of the law was of much greater consequence, and made supplication to him, that he would by no means reduce them to such distresses, nor defile their city with the dedication of the statue. Then Petronius said to them, "Will you then make war with Caesar, without considering his great preparations for war, and your own weakness?" They replied, "We will not by any means make war with him, but still we will die before we see our laws transgressed." So they threw themselves down upon their faces, and stretched out their throats, and said they were ready to be killed; and this they did for forty days together, and in the meantime left off the tilling of their ground, and that while the season of the year required them to sow it. Thus they continued firm in their resolution, and proposed to themselves to die willingly, rather than to see the dedication of the statue.....

And now did God show his presence to Petronius, and signify to him that he would afford him his assistance in his whole design; for he had no sooner finished the speech that he made to the Jews, but God sent down great showers of rain, contrary to human expectation; for that day was a clear day, and gave no sign, by the appearance of the sky, of any rain; nay, the whole year had been subject to a great drought, and made men despair of any water from above, even when at any time they saw the heavens overcast with clouds; insomuch that when such a great quantity of rain came, and that in an unusual manner, and without any other expectation of it, the Jews hoped that Petronius would by no means fail in his petition for them. But as to Petronius, he was mightily surprised when he perceived that God evidently took care of the Jews, and gave very plain signs of his appearance, and this to such a degree, that those that were in earnest much inclined to the contrary had no power left to contradict it... (pages 606-607)

CONTENTS

LIST OF ILLUSTRATIONS

TIMELINE

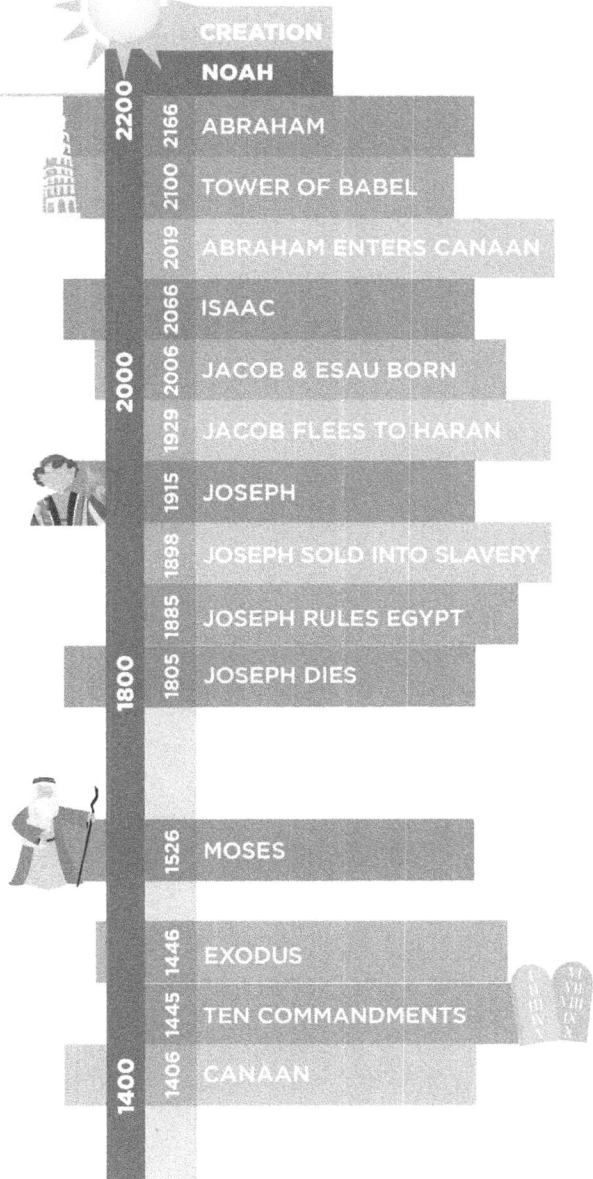

Noah's Ark

CREATION

NOAH

2200

2166 ABRAHAM

2100 TOWER OF BABEL

2019 ABRAHAM ENTERS CANAAN

2066 ISAAC

2000

2006 JACOB & ESAU BORN

1929 JACOB FLEES TO HARAN

1915 JOSEPH

1898 JOSEPH SOLD INTO SLAVERY

1885 JOSEPH RULES EGYPT

1805 JOSEPH DIES

1800

1526 MOSES

1446 EXODUS

1445 TEN COMMANDMENTS

1406 CANAAN

1400

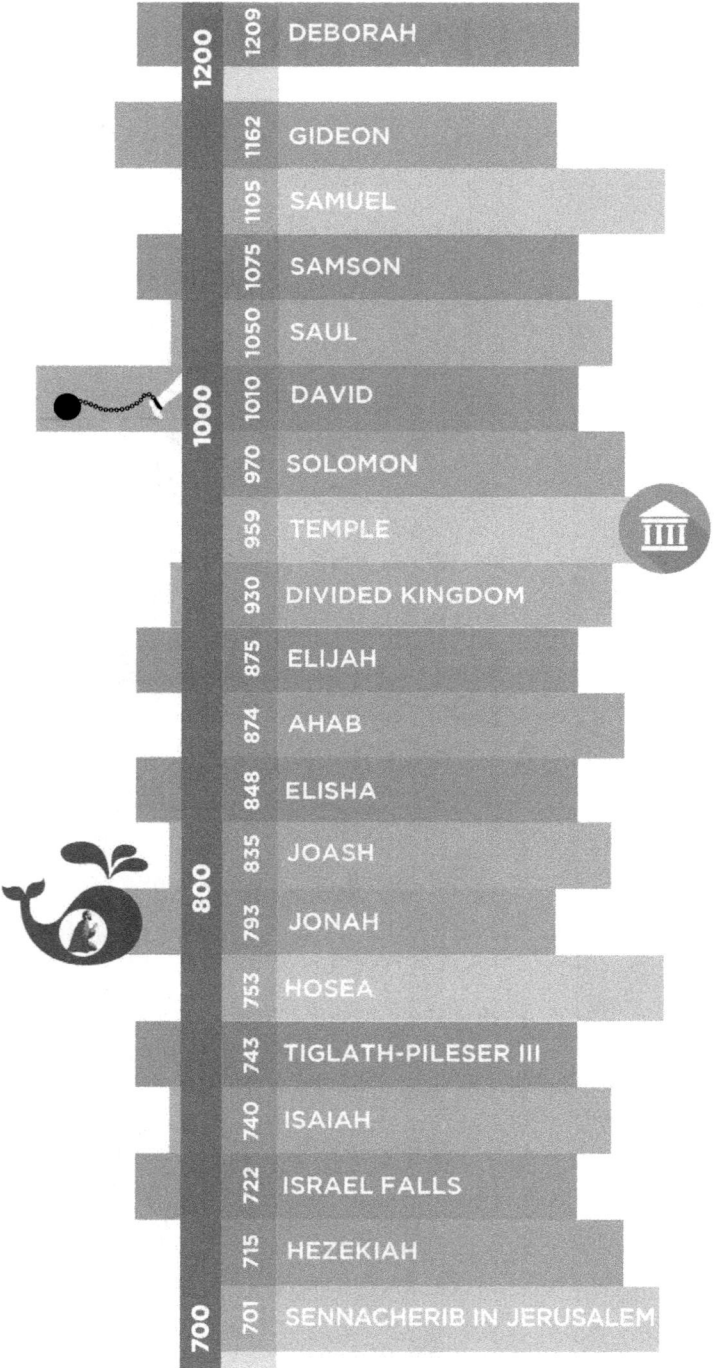

1200	1209 DEBORAH
	1162 GIDEON
	1105 SAMUEL
	1075 SAMSON
	1050 SAUL
1000	1010 DAVID
	970 SOLOMON
	959 TEMPLE
	930 DIVIDED KINGDOM
	875 ELIJAH
	874 AHAB
	848 ELISHA
	835 JOASH
800	793 JONAH
	753 HOSEA
	743 TIGLATH-PILESER III
	740 ISAIAH
	722 ISRAEL FALLS
	715 HEZEKIAH
700	701 SENNACHERIB IN JERUSALEM

640	JOSIAH
627	JEREMIAH
612	NINEVEH DESTROYED
605	DANIEL TO BABYLON
600	
586	JUDAH FALLS
539	CYRUS OVERTHROWS BABYLON
538	FIRST JEWS RETURN TO JERUSALEM
515	TEMPLE COMPLETED
479	ESTHER
458	EZRA
445	NEHEMIAH
430	MALACHI
400	
390	ARAMAIC
332	ALEXANDER THE GREAT IN JERUSALEM
330	PERSIA DEFEATED
255	SEPTUAGINT
200	
169	ANTIOCHUS IV
165	JUDAS MACCABEUS
100	JULIUS CAESAR

Date	Event
53-36	ARISTOBULUS III
31-7	ARISTOBULUS IV
51	CLEOPATRA
37	HEROD THE GREAT
25	MARY, JESUS' MOTHER
6/5	JESUS CHRIST BORN
4	HEROD DIES
5	PAUL
6/7	ROMAN PROVINCE - JUDEA
26	JOHN THE BAPTIST
26/27	JESUS MINISTERS
30	JESUS CRUCIFIED, ASCENDS. CHURCH IS BORN
40	HEROD AGRIPPA
54	NERO
64	ROME BURNS
68	QUMRAN DESTROYED
70	JERUSALEM DESTROYED
73	MASADA SUICIDES

0
25
50
100

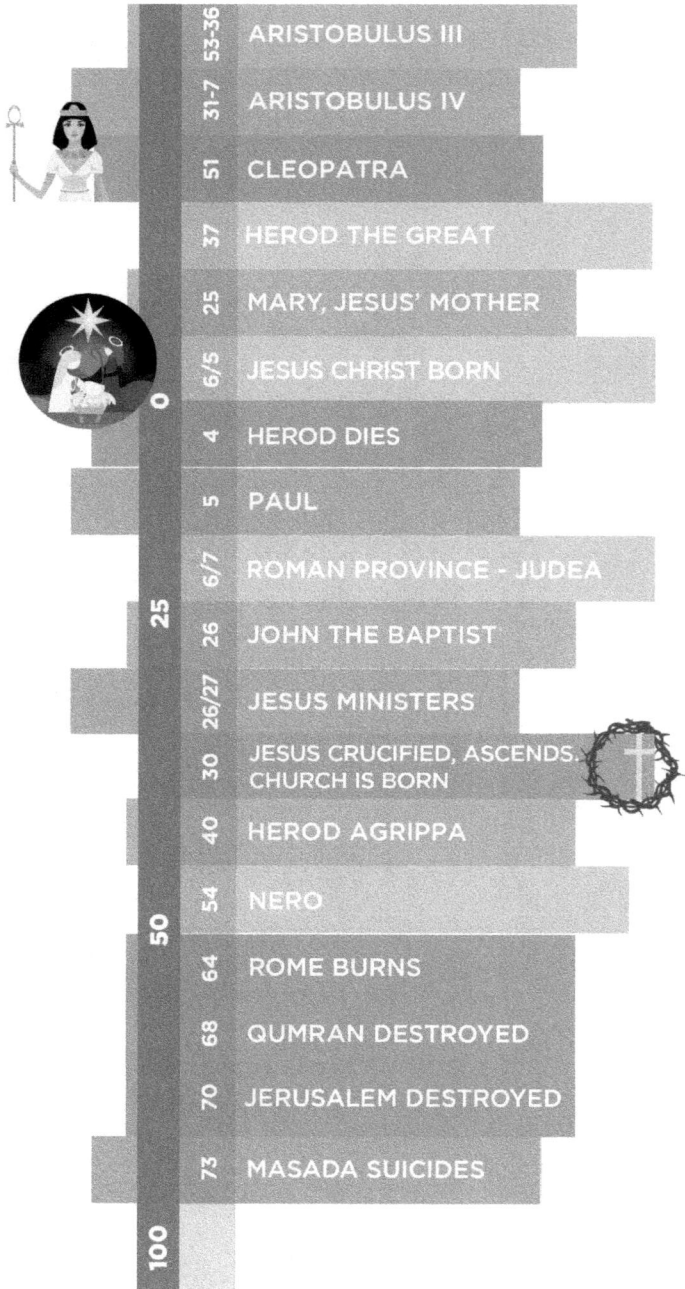

Note: Dates from Genesis can vary up to 200 years.

BOOK 1

FROM THE CREATION TO THE DEATH OF ISAAC

IN the beginning God created the heaven and the earth. The earth was covered with thick darkness, and a wind moved upon its surface. God commanded that there should be light. Then he separated the light from the darkness, calling the darkness "Night" and the other "Day." He further separated the beginning of the light and the time of rest into "The Evening" and "The Morning." Moses said that this was one day. I, Josephus, will write about this subject in another book.

On the second day he put the heaven surrounding the whole world, separating it from other parts. He also put a firmament around the earth which would provide moisture, rain and dew.

On the third day God appointed the dry land to appear, surrounded by sea, as well as the plants and seed which would spring out of the earth.

On the fourth day he decorated the heavens with the sun, moon and other stars, appointing them their routes and defining the seasons.

On the fifth day he produced the animals, sea life and birds of the air. He gave them their groups for reproduction so that they might multiply.

On the sixth day he created the animals with four feet, both male and female. He also formed man. Moses said that in six days everything in the world was made, and that on the seventh day

God rested. This is why we have a rest day to rest from our work on the seventh day. The word Sabbath in Hebrew means "rest."

After the seventh day Moses spoke of how man came about. He said that God took dust from the ground and formed him and put a spirit and soul into him. His name was Adam, which in Hebrew means "one that is red" since he was made out of red earth. It was unique, virgin soil. God showed Adam all of the living creatures, and Adam gave them names which have held to this day. When God saw that Adam was alone, he realized that like the male and female animals, something was missing. He put Adam to sleep and took one of his ribs and formed a woman out of it. Adam saw the woman and realized that she was taken out of himself. In Hebrew woman is "Isha", but this woman's name was Eve, meaning "the mother of all living."

Moses says that God planted a paradise in the east which contained many trees. One tree was the tree of life, and another of knowledge so that good and evil would be known. God brought Adam and Eve into the garden and told them to take care of the plants. The garden was watered by one river which ran around the whole earth but separated into four parts.

The 4 rivers:

The Phison flowed to India. The Greeks called it the Ganges.

The Euphrates, which means "dispersion" or "a flower".

The Tigris ran "swift with narrowness" to the Red Sea.

The Geon flowed through Egypt – "what arises from the east". The Greeks called it the Nile.

God told Adam and Eve that they could eat from all of the plants except the tree of knowledge. If they touched it, it would destroy them. All of the creatures had one language. The serpent was evil and persuaded Eve to taste of the tree of knowledge, emphasizing that she would obtain the knowledge of good and evil, thus having a happier life. Eve found the fruit tasty, and despite her disobedience to God's command she talked Adam into tasting it as well. They suddenly discovered that they were naked. They were ashamed, and since the tree gave them more understanding, they covered themselves by tying fig leaves around themselves. They were happier. God came into the garden and Adam, who had previously talked with him, feeling uncomfortable, walked away. God called him but Adam didn't answer. God said that he had intended for both of them the ideal life with no pain, worry or toil. He intended that they would live long, but now they had disobeyed God's commands. Adam's silence showed that his conscience was bothering him. Adam made an excuse and told God not to be angry with him, and blamed his wife. He said that she had fooled him. Eve blamed the snake. God punished Adam because he was weak and gave in to his wife's counsel. God said that they would have to work very hard in order for the land to produce fruit. And Eve would suffer when she was to give birth, since she gave in to the snakes' lies. The snake was afterwards unable to speak. God also put poison under its tongue, made him an enemy of people and suggested that man would strike the snake's head, and that he would no longer use his feet but rather drag himself along on the ground. Then God took Adam and Eve out of the garden.

ii

ADAM and Eve had two sons. The eldest was Cain, meaning "Possession." The younger was Abel, meaning "Sorrow." They also had girls. Abel was a good boy, who felt that God was part of his actions. He was a shepherd. Cain was not a good boy. He worked with the soil. Each were called to offer a sacrifice to God. Cain brought produce from his garden and from animals, but Abel brought milk and the first-fruits of his flocks. God was pleased only with Abel's offering, since it had grown naturally. Cain had forced the ground. Cain was very angry that Abel's sacrifice was preferred by God over his, so he killed Abel and hid his dead body.

God, who sees all, came to Cain and asked where Abel had been for many days. Cain said that he did not know, but God pushed the question again; Cain answered that he was not his brother's keeper, nor did he pay attention to his daily work. God said that he was surprised at how he would not know, since he himself killed him. God did not kill Cain since he had offered a sacrifice, but he did curse him up to the seventh generation. He sent Cain and his wife out of that place. Cain was afraid that he might be killed by wild animals. God told him not to worry and put a mark on him.

Cain and his wife journeyed through many countries and they built a city called Nod. They also had children. He was a self-centered man who walked over others in order to gain much for himself. He was wealthy but raped people and was violent. His friends were robbers. He was the originator of weights and measures. He was a crafty man. He determined boundaries around the lands and built a strong city. It had strong walls and his family lived inside. It was called Enoch after the name of his oldest son, Enoch. Jered was the son of Enoch. Malaleel was Enoch's son. Mathusela was his son. Lamech was his son and he had 77 children by two wives, Silla and Ada. Jabal, one son of Ada, built tents and loved the life of a shepherd. Jubal, another son, liked music and invented the psaltery and harp. (Maybe "Jobel" came from Jubal, the trumpet of jobel or jubilee; that large and loud musical instrument used in proclaiming freedom during the year of jubilee). Tubal, another son of Lamech, was strong in the martial (fighting) arts. He also invented the art of making brass. Lamech's daughter was named Naamah. Lamech knew that he was to be punished for Cain's murder of his brother, and he told this to his wives. Even while Adam was alive, it was known that Cain's descendants were trouble-makers and they would die one by one. They were warlike and robbed and exploited people for gain.

Adam, according to tradition, had 33 sons and 23 daughters. Cain had many children up to his age of 230 years old. He lived another 700 years. There are too many children to mention, but we'll speak of Seth. Seth was a good man and his descendants followed in his footsteps. They were happy people and prosperous up to their death. They knew about astronomy. Since Adam predicted that the world would be destroyed at one time by fire and another time by water, they made two pillars; one of brick, the other of stone. They inscribed their discoveries on them both; in case the pillar of brick would be destroyed by the flood, the stone pillar would remain. This pillar remains in the country of Siriad to this day. [this is debatable, due to the upheaval of the flood]

NOAH was not sure if God would send another flood, so he offered a sacrifice and pleaded with him. God sent the rainbow, together with the promise that man would never again be destroyed by flood, but he warned them that they were not to murder one another.

God gave the people longer life when they were virtuous They also had knowledge of astronomy and geometry, since they had many centuries to study these subjects.

Seth and his descendants believed in the God of the universe for seven generations. In time they left the ways of their forefathers and God, and became unfair in their dealings with other people. They saw God as an enemy and had intercourse with fallen angels, thus producing giants. Noah was very uncomfortable with this, but they were enslaved by their desires. Noah was afraid that they would kill him, so he left the area together with his wife and children and their wives.

God loved Noah since he was a good man. God intended to destroy all of mankind and to begin a new race of people who would not be wicked and who would have a shorter life span. They would live to be only 120 years. He turned the dry land into sea and only Noah was saved [with his family]. He was to make an ark as a way of escape.

The ark was four stories high. The cross beams braced it so that it wouldn't be overturned in a violent storm.

The flood occurred on the 17th day of Nisan. The Hebrews consider Nisan the first month for their festivals when God brought them out of Egypt. Moses says that this flood began 2,656 years from Adam; the time is written down in our sacred books with accuracy, along with the births and deaths of important people.

Seth was born when Adam was 230 years old and lived 930 years. Seth gave birth to Enos in his 250th year.

Methusela, the son of Enoch, lived to be 969 years old. We have the birth dates of men but not their death dates – don't look for the death dates here.

God gave the signal and it began to rain for 40 days. The rain stood 15 cubits* over the earth, covering all people and animals. Only 150 days after the flood the water began to be absorbed. This was on the 17th day of the seventh month. The ark rested on the top of a certain mountain in Armenia. Noah opened the door and was happy to see some land. In a few days he sent a raven out to see if the earth was dry elsewhere. The raven returned. After seven days he sent out a dove, which returned to him covered with mud and bringing an olive branch. They stayed another seven days, and he let the animals out of the ark. He and his family sacrificed to God and they feasted. The Armenians call this place "The Place of Descent". Parts of the ark are being shown by the local people to this day.

Even in primitive countries there is a flood story. Berosus the Chaldean writes that there is still a part of this ship in Armenia at the mountain of the Cordyaeans, and that some people took off pieces of the bitumen and used it as charms to avoid evil. Hieronymus the Egyptian writes about it in the Phoenician history and others. Nicolaus of Damascus wrote in his 96th book that there is a mountain in Armenia called Baris, and that many were saved from the flood. When the one who was saved landed on top of it, the wood of the ark was preserved for a long time. This could be the man Moses wrote about, the leader of the Jews.

Noah was afraid that God needed to destroy mankind, thinking he would drown the earth yearly, so he offered burnt offerings and begged God to hold off judgment. He hoped that man would be able to plant crops, build cities and live happily in them. He also hoped that they would have long life like before the flood.

God loved Noah and answered his prayers. The people had brought on their own destruction. He had not brought people into the world with the intent of destroying them; otherwise it would have been wiser not to have allowed them to live at all. "They repaid my holiness and virtue with wickedness, forcing me to punish them. On account of your prayers, I will no longer allow water to cover the earth. I will, however, require you not to shed men's blood, not to murder, and to punish those who commit murder. You may use all of the animals for food. You are in command over them, both those on the land, those in the sea and those that fly. You are not to drink their blood, since the life is in the blood. I am no longer angry, and the rainbow is my promise."

Noah lived happily for 350 years after the flood. He died after living 950 years. The ancient people lived longer, and there are reasons why. Noah lived long because he was righteous and their food was also more nutritious. They also made use of astronomy and geometrical discoveries, which enabled them to foretell the future. Other famous historians wrote that the ancient people lived a thousand years.

iv

NOAH'S three sons were Shem, Japhet and Ham, who were born 100 years before the flood. They had moved from the mountains and settled on the plains. Other people were afraid to live on the plains since they were afraid that another flood would occur. The plain was called Shinar. God had told them to spread around the earth so that they wouldn't fight among themselves. They could also work the soil and enjoy the fruit of their labors. They disobeyed God and instead of recognizing his blessing, they felt that their success was due to their own initiative. They also felt that if they were together they could resist oppression.

Nimrod, the grandson of Ham, was a bold, strong man. He did not fear God and became a tyrannical leader. The people depended on him. It was his idea to build a tower which would protect them in case of another flood. It would also be his revenge on God for destroying their ancestors. The people went along with this and worked on the tower with great motivation. It progressed more rapidly than expected. It was built of burnt brick, cemented together with mortar made of water-proof pitch. God saw what they were doing in defiance of him, and he caused them to begin to speak in various languages, so that one could no longer understand the other. The place where they built the tower is now called Babylon, since the word "Babel" in Hebrew means confusion. Sibyl wrote of this tower that it was destroyed by wind storms.

v

THE people went in various directions to live, with God leading them. Both inland and maritime countries were filled with people. Some went by ship to islands and lived there. Some of those original people stayed for centuries following. The Greeks gave names to some of the people groups and formed governments, claiming some of them as their own.

vi

NOAH'S three sons settled in the following areas:

Japhet with 7 sons - Asia, Europe, Scythia (Eurasia), Media (northern Iran), Greece, Phrygia (Anatolia, Turkey), Eastern Turkey and Cyprus.

Ham with 4 sons - Ethiopia, Egypt, Libya, Judea, Palestine (Canaan) and Lebanon. Nimrod stayed in Babylon.

Noah grew crops, including grape vines. After gathering the grapes when they were ripe and making wine from them, he offered a sacrifice to God, feasted and became drunk. He fell asleep and was unaware of his nakedness. His youngest son saw this and, laughing at him, called his brothers to see this. After Noah realized what had happened he cursed the sons of Ham. He prayed that his other sons would be prosperous. God himself cursed the children of Canaan.

Shem with 5 sons – from the Euphrates to the Indian Ocean, Persia, Assyria, Syria and Armenia.

By now man's lifespan was shortened before the birth of Moses. From now on human life was 120 years, since Moses lived to be 120 years old.

ABRAM did not have a son, so he adopted Lot, his brother Haran's son and his wife Sarai's brother. He left Chaldea when he was 75 years old and went by God's command to Canaan. He was a virtuous man and persuaded others to believe in God. He was the Creator of the universe and other gods had no power. He saw the order in the heavens and attributed it to God alone. He understood that God should be honored and thanked. The Chaldeans and other people of Mesopotamia were strongly against him, so by God's help he left and came to live in the land of Canaan. There he settled down and built an altar and sacrificed to God.

Nicolaus of Damascus, in his fourth history book, said that Abram was a ruler in Damascus who left together with an army from Babylon. He left for Canaan, which is now the land of Judea, and they multiplied into a great number of people. Abram is still famous in Damascus, since there is a village there called "The Habitation of Abram."

THERE was a famine in Canaan, and Abram was aware that the Egyptians had food. He wished also to converse with their priests regarding religious matters. He took Sarai with him but was afraid that the king would kill him and take his beautiful wife for himself. He pretended instead to be her brother. Pharoah was impressed with Sarai's beauty and would have taken her, had not God intervened. Pharoah became ill and there were also problems in the government. He asked the priests how he could free himself from these problems, and they said it was because he was lusting after the stranger's wife. He asked Sarai who she was. He then apologized to Abram and gave them a lot of money. Abram was able to speak with the most educated Egyptians, and he was known as a wise man.

Moses saw that the Egyptian customs were lacking truth and were contradictory. Abram, on the other hand, had wisdom on many subjects. He also taught them arithmetic and astronomy.

When Abram returned to Canaan, he and Lot needed to separate in order to have enough pasture land for their flocks. He let Lot choose, and Lot took the land of the plain near the river Jordan, not far from the city of Sodom. Abram lived in Hebron, a city seven years older than Tanis of Egypt. God destroyed the city of Sodom, which had been a good city.

ix

WHEN the Assyrians ruled over all of Asia, the people of Sodom were prospering. They were wealthy, and there were many young people. They had five different kings, each with his own army. The Assyrians came against them and won. They forced the people of Sodom to pay taxes. They paid taxes for 12 years but rebelled in the 13th year, so the Assyrians attacked them. All of Syria was destroyed. Descendants of the giants were killed. They set up their army camp at the Slime Pits near Sodom. God destroyed Sodom, and that area became Lake Asphaltites. The Sodomites fought with the Assyrians and many were killed. Others, including Lot who had assisted the Sodomites, were taken captive.

x

ABRAM cared about Lot and went quickly to help them against their enemy. On the fifth night he came to where the Assyrians were, near Dan, and he killed many while they were asleep. Others were drunk and escaped. Abram drove them into a suburb of Damascus, proving that even with a few courageous soldiers, large numbers of people can be conquered. He had only 318 on his side.

Abram saved not only Lot, but all of the Sodomites that had been taken captive by the Assyrians. The king of Sodom met

Abram at "The King's Dale" where Melchisedec, king of the city of Salem, received him. This name means "the righteous king," and he was a priest of God. Afterwards Salem was called Jerusalem. Melchisedec supplied Abram's army with provisions, and as they were feasting he began to praise him and to bless God for causing him to win the war. Abram gave him one tenth of his spoils, which Melchisedec received. The king of Sodom wanted his men back which Abram had saved from the Assyrians, but Abram did not agree to this. God told Abram that he would not lose the rewards which he had earned. He answered God that despite all that he owned, he was still lacking a son. God promised that he would have a son and that his descendants would be like the stars. Abram offered a sacrifice to God as he commanded him. He took a heifer of three years old, a female goat of three years, a ram of three years old, a turtle dove and a pigeon. He divided the larger animals into two parts but the birds he did not divide. He built his altar and the birds flew around it, since they were waiting to drink the blood. A voice from heaven told Abram that while his descendants would be in Egypt for 400 years, their enemies would envy them. They would suffer but afterwards would overcome their enemies. They would conquer the Canaanites in war and possess their land and cities.

Abram lived near an oak tree called "Ogyges" which belonged to Canaan, not far from the city of Hebron. Abram was concerned that his wife did not yet bear him a child, but God said that in addition to all of the blessings he had received since leaving Mesopotamia, he would have a child. Sarai brought to Abram one of her maids who was from Egypt. The woman was happy, but Abram set the order; she had to submit to Sarai. The woman did not get along with Sarai, so she tried to leave. She prayed for God to help her, and he sent an angel to her. While in the desert, the angel told her to return to Abram and Sarai, since she would have a better life; and that she needed to change her ungrateful and proud attitude towards Sarai. He also told her that if she disobeyed God that she would die. If she would return, she would become the mother of a son who would become ruler over that country. She therefore returned and was forgiven. Shortly afterwards she gave birth to Ismael, which means "Heard of God," since God had heard his mother's prayer.

Abram was 86 years old when Ismael was born. When he was 99, God promised him that he would have a son by Sarai, and said that the child's name would be Isaac. Isaac's descendants would become kings ruling great nations, and they would obtain all the land of Canaan by war from Sidon to Egypt. He was commanded to keep his descendants from intermarrying with others. The males should be circumcised in the flesh of their foreskin on the 8th day after their birth. Abram asked if Ismael would live, and God said he would live to be very old. He would be the father of great nations. Abram thanked God for these blessings. Abram and all his family and his son Ismael were circumcised, the son being 13 years old and he ninety-nine.

xi

THE Sodomites became very wealthy, after which they grew proud. They became unjust towards men, no longer feared God and hated strangers. They also engaged in filthy sexual practices (including men with men). God intended to punish them for their pride, to overthrow their city and to prevent the land from bearing any produce.

Abraham sat by the oak at Mambre, at the door of his tent. He saw three angels, and since they were strangers he greeted them and invited them into his tent. He ordered a meal to be made for them. He killed a calf and prepared it and served it to them under the oak. While eating, they asked him about his wife Sarah. He said that she was inside the tent. They said that they would visit again, and that she would have become a mother. Sarah heard this and laughed, saying that she was 90 years old and Abraham was 100 years old. Then the visitors said that they were angels from God. One was sent to inform them about the birth of their son, and the other two for the overthrow of Sodom.

Abraham was sorry for the Sodomites; he got up and began to pray that they would not all be destroyed. God said there was not even one good man among them. He said that if there were even ten good men, he would not punish them. Abraham was quiet. The angels came to Sodom and Lot invited them to stay with him for the night. He was a hospitable man, having learned this from Abraham. The Sodomites saw the young men as being extremely handsome, and they had wicked intentions to lie with them. Lot told them not to bother his guests. If they did, he would have to give them his daughters. They were not ashamed. God was so upset with them that he blinded them and condemned them forever.

God told Lot that he would destroy the city, so Lot left, taking his wife and two daughters with him. They were engaged to be married, but their future husbands did not accept the warning to leave. God sent a thunderbolt on the city and set it on fire. The city and surrounding country were burned. Lot's wife kept turning back to see the city, even though God had warned her not to look back. She was changed into a pillar of salt. I, Josephus, have seen it. Lot and his daughters stayed in a place called Zoar, which in Hebrew means "a small thing." He lived a lonely life and lacked basic provisions. His daughters thought that they should lie with their father in order to carry on the family. The older daughter gave birth to a son named Moab, meaning "one derived from his father." The younger gave birth to Ammon, which means "one coming from a relative." The Moabites and the Ammonites both became great nations and lived in the area of Celesyria.

xii

ABRAHAM moved to Gerar of Palestine, together with Sarah. Abraham was afraid of Abimelech the king, so he lied to him and said that Sarah was his sister. God allowed Abimelech to be ill, and the doctors did not know what was wrong with him. While asleep he dreamed about Sarah and was warned not to touch her. He understood that Abraham had lied to him, and he sent for Abraham. He told him how that God had protected them. He said that had he known that Sarah was Abraham's wife, he surely would not have had any evil intentions towards her. He wished to be at peace with Abraham. Abimelech even promised that if he wished to stay in the area that he would provide Abraham with all he needed. If he wished to leave, he would be escorted to safety. Abraham told him that Sarah was in fact his brother's daughter, and that he felt that he needed to lie for her safety. He decided to stay, and Abimelech gave him a plot of land and money. They swore to live together peacefully at a certain well. The well was called Beersheba which means "The Well of the Oath." This name is used to this day.

Soon afterwards Abraham and Sarah had a son as God had promised them, and they named him Isaac, which means "Laughter." He was called Isaac because Sarah had laughed when God told her that she would give birth to a son. Isaac was born when Sarah was 99 and when Abraham was 109. Isaac was circumcised on the eighth day. To this day the Jewish people circumcise their sons on the eighth day. The Arabians circumcise at age 13 because Ismael, the founder of their nation who was born to Abraham from the maid, was circumcised at age 13.

Sarah loved Ismael who was born by her maid, Hagar, and she thought he was to lead when his time came. But she did not want Ismael to be with Isaac, since he was too old for Isaac and might cause him harm after their father would die. She talked Abraham into sending Ismael and his mother far away. Abraham thought it was a heartless idea, since he was still young and no mention was made of provision for them. He agreed to it, however, since God was pleased with what Sarah had decided. Abraham told Hagar to take a bottle of water and a loaf of bread and to leave. Hagar's water was nearly finished, and she put the child who was almost dead under a fig tree and kept going, so as not to see him die. An angel came to her and told her that there was water nearby, and to take care of the child. She would be happy to see him alive. She was helped by shepherds, and they both recovered. Ismael grew up and married an Egyptian woman. They had twelve sons. They eventually lived in the country from the Euphrates to the Red Sea called Nabatene. They are an Arabian nation, and their tribal names are according to the sons' names. They were virtuous and bore the dignity of their father Abraham.

ABRAHAM loved his son Isaac. Isaac also respected his parents and worshipped God. Once God appeared to Abraham and spoke about how he had caused Abraham to overcome his enemies. His son Isaac was also his gift to him, and he required him as a sacrifice. He commanded Abraham to take him to the mountain Moriah, to build an altar and to offer him as a burnt offering on the altar. This was to test Abraham's faith in God which was to surpass his love for his own son.

Abraham could not disobey God since he is the supreme provider. He did not tell his wife or his servants, since he would have been prevented from obeying God's command. He took Isaac along with two of his servants, and saddled a donkey with what he needed for the sacrifice. The servants went with him for two days. On the third day, as soon as he saw the mountain, he left the servants and continued only with Isaac. This was the same mountain where King David built the temple. Isaac was 25 years old. Abraham was building the altar, and Isaac asked where the animal was for the sacrifice. "God will provide, since he is able to provide even from what man is lacking. He would even take from others if necessary, if they put too much trust in what they have." As soon as the altar was prepared and the wood had been laid on the altar, he spoke to his son. "O son, I prayed many prayers that you would be born. Your growth throughout these years has assured me that I have someone to whom to pass all that I own. It was God's will that I be your father, and now I need to give you up. I give you back to God, who requires this testimony of honor since he has blessed me as a supporter and defender. You will not die but be sent to God, the Father of all men. It seems he is sparing you from disease, war and other ways in which men usually die.

He will receive your soul with prayers and will take you near to himself, and from there you will support me in my old age. God will be my Comforter instead of you."

Isaac answered in a way which was suitable to a son of such a God-fearing father. He said that he was not worthy even to have been born if he should not obey God and his father. And even if his father alone had requested this sacrifice, he would have agreed. He went without hesitation to the altar to be sacrificed. God at this moment called loudly to Abraham by name and told him not to kill his son. He said that he was only testing to see if Abraham would be obedient to him. He was now sure that he was right in blessing Abraham, and he would continue to give him many descendants. Isaac would live to be very old. He would have a good life, be blessed and have many children. He said that Isaac's family would multiply and become many nations. The fathers would be remembered forever, and they would obtain the land of Canaan and be envied by all people. When God said this, he provided a ram which was used for the sacrifice. Abraham and Isaac, upon receiving the promises of these great blessings, hugged each other. After they sacrificed, they returned to Sarah and all were happy. God provided his help in all areas.

xiv

SARAH died shortly afterward. She lived to be 127 years old. They buried her in Hebron where the Canaanites sold them a place for burials. Abraham paid 400 shekels* to Ephron, one of the citizens of Hebron. Both Abraham and his descendants built their graves there.

xv

ABRAHAM married Keturah, and they had six sons who were strong and intelligent. There were many descendants, and they settled in the country of Arabia ("the Happy") up to the border of the Red Sea. One of Abraham's grandsons warred against Libya and took it. His grandchildren called it Africa which sounds something like Apher (mentioned by a historian other than Moses). Malchus wrote a history of the Jews which agrees with Moses's account. He writes that Assyria was ruled by the descendant named Surim. From two others Africa was named. After a war, Hercules married Aphra's daughter.

ABRAHAM wished that Rebeka, granddaughter to his brother Nahor, would marry his son Isaac, who was 40 years old. He sent his faithful servant to request her agreement to the marriage. Abraham sent presents, and it was a long journey through Mesopotamia. In the winter the clay was deep, and in the summer there was little water. Robberies were also frequent. The servant arrived at the outskirts of Haran and met many young women who were drawing water from a well. He prayed that God would give him a definite sign to help him to know which one was Rebeka. The sign was that she would offer water to him to drink. All of the women refused to give him water with the excuse that they needed it at home. One woman was upset with their behavior and offered him water. He thanked her and she drew water even though it was not convenient for her. He asked her who her parents were and said they should be proud of such a daughter. He even wished that she would be married to a good man approved by her parents and have children. She said, "They call me Rebeka. My father died and Laban is my brother. He and my mother tend to our family affairs and guard my virginity." When the servant heard this, he felt that God had brought him to the right woman. He gave her bracelets and other women's jewelry suitable for virgins to wear. He said that she deserved them, since she was helpful as opposed to the other women. She then invited him to stay overnight with them. He said that he would be able to pay for staying with them. She said that her parents would receive him, but without money. First she needed to tell her bother Laban, however.

Rebeka introduced her stranger, and Laban's servants brought all of the camels inside and cared for them. Laban invited the servant for supper. He then said to Laban, "Abraham was the brother of Nahor. They had the same father and mother, and he has sent me to you so that you would agree to let Rebeka marry his son Isaac. Isaac is his only heir. Abraham did not agree to have him marry any of the women in the area. Do you agree to this which God has arranged?" Rebeka's family understood that this was in God's will. Isaac married Rebeka and now he had an inheritance.

xvii

SHORTLY after this Abraham died. He was a righteous man. He lived to be 175 years old. He was buried in Hebron, where his wife Sarah was buried by their sons Isaac and Ismael.

xviii

AFTER Abraham died, Isaac's wife grew close to delivering a child. She was very uncomfortable and Isaac asked God about this. He answered that Rebeka would give birth to twins. The sons actually represented two nations, and the second child would be greater than the first. The firstborn child was rough and hairy. The younger one took hold of the heel of the first during the birth process. The father loved the oldest, named Esau, which means "roughness" in Hebrew. Jacob, the younger child, was loved by his mother. When there was no food in the land, Isaac wanted to go to Egypt; but instead he stayed in Gerar where God told him to stay. He was received by Abimelech the king since Abraham, Isaac's father, was his friend and had lived there before. In the beginning Isaac was treated well, but later Abimelech became jealous of him and no longer wanted him to live there. Isaac went to live in a place called "the valley" and dug a well. Shepherds fought with him, so he dug another one. The same thing happened. The king finally allowed him to dig a well peacefully, and this well was called Rehoboth which means "a large place." The names of the former wells were Escon ("strife") and Sitenna ("enmity").

Isaac was blessed and became rich. Abimelech began to fear him, since he thought Isaac might try to take revenge on former injuries he had received from Abimelech. Meanwhile, Esau was now forty years old and had wives belonging to important families of the Canaanites. Isaac was aware of this but did not interfere, preferring to keep the peace. When Isaac was old and blind, he called Esau to come to him. Due to his blindness and his very old age, he could no longer sacrifice to God. He therefore asked that Esau go hunting and bring him deer meat and prepare him a meal, so that Esau might support him until he would die.

Esau went hunting, but in the meantime Rebeka wanted the prayer for God's blessing to be given to Jacob. Rebeka told Jacob to kill young goats and she would prepare a meal. Jacob obeyed, and when the dinner was ready, he put goat's skin on his arm so that Isaac would be tricked into believing he was Esau. He was afraid but brought the meal to his father. Isaac felt that the voice was Jacob's, but after feeling his hand he accepted that it was Esau. After the meal, he prayed to God saying: "O Lord of all time and Creator of everything, you blessed my father and you have given me everything I own. You have promised to support my descendants with even greater blessings. Confirm these promises and do not forget me as I am weak, and I pray this in all seriousness. Be generous to my son and keep him from all evil. Give him a happy life and as many good things as you can give him. Cause his enemies to fear him, and make him honorable and loved among his friends." Isaac prayed to God, unaware that his prayers were being said for Jacob instead of Esau. When he finished, Esau came in. Isaac realized his mistake and was silent. Esau begged a blessing from his father, but it was not given. Esau was very sorry. His father was upset at his crying and said that he would succeed in hunting, be physically strong in work and would have strong descendants. In any case, they would serve his brother Jacob. Jacob's mother was afraid for Jacob, so she talked him into taking a wife for him from Mesopotamia. Isaac had not approved of any of Esau's wives.

JACOB'S mother sent him to Mesopotamia in order to marry her brother Laban's daughter. He went through Canaan on the way, but he would not stay with any of them since he hated those people. He slept outside and laid his head on some stones which he had gathered together. While sleeping he had a vision. He saw a ladder which reached into heaven with beings going up and down the ladder, and he saw God himself standing above it. God spoke to him saying, "O Jacob, the son of a good father and grandson of a righteous man: do not be downhearted but have hope. You will have everything by my help, the way I was with Abraham when he was driven out of Mesopotamia. I made your father a happy man. Take courage that I will bless you as well, and you will be married. You will have worthy children and so many descendants that they cannot be counted. They will prosper and you will rule over the land, and your descendants will fill the whole earth and sea as far as the sun rises and sets. Don't fear danger or the hard work which you must do, since I will direct you in the right time."

Jacob was very happy to hear what would be in the future. He poured oil on the stones and promised that he would offer sacrifices on them when he returned to this place. He would also give a tenth of his gain to God. He felt this was an honorable place and called it Bethel, which means "The House of God" in Hebrew.

Jacob continued on his trip to Mesopotamia and arrived at Haran. He met shepherds in the outskirts, with grown boys and young girls sitting around a well. He wanted a drink. He asked if they knew Laban. They said they knew him, and that his daughter would be coming to the well. She came shortly and Jacob met her. Jacob told her that he was a stranger, but he was interested to hear about her father. She asked who he was and tried to understand why he had come. She had hoped that her family could help him. Jacob was unable to control himself since she was beautiful. He said that they were related, going way back to the grandparents. He said, "My mother is sister to your father by both the same father and mother." Rachel began to cry. She hugged

Jacob and said that her father would be very happy to meet him, since she had heard about his family. Jacob was truly welcomed by Laban, but he needed to understand why Jacob came, and why he needed to leave his elderly parents. Jacob told them about the blessing he had received from his father. Laban promised to treat him well for his mother's sake. He would become the head shepherd of his sheep. When he should decide to leave, he would have many presents. Jacob was happy and said that he would work hard, but he wished to take Rachel with him to be his wife. Laban agreed with this, but said that he needed to stay and work with him for a while since he did not want his daughter living among the Canaanites. Jacob agreed to stay seven years. After seven years the wedding feast was planned. After everyone had feasted, Laban put his other daughter into bed with Jacob. She was not beautiful like Rachel. Jacob had become drunk, and because it was dark he did not know that he had slept with Lea instead of Rachel. Jacob was very upset with Laban in the morning. He loved Rachel, and had no choice but to agree to marry her after another seven years of work.

Both Lea and Rachel had servant women. Lea had Zilpha and Rachel had Bilha. Lea was upset knowing that her husband loved her sister. She asked God for children and Lea had a son named Reubel, meaning "God had mercy on her in giving her a son." Then she gave birth to Simeon, meaning "God has listened to her prayer." Later she had Levi, meaning "confirmer of their friendship." Afterwards Judah was born, meaning "thanksgiving." Rachel was unable to give birth and so she gave her servant Bilha, to Jacob. Bilha's child by Jacob was named Dan, meaning "a divine judgment" in Hebrew. Then Nephalim, "one who will not lose in war" was born. Rachel was trying to have more children than her sister by scheming. So Lea also gave her maid to Jacob. Gad was born, meaning "fortune"; and then Asher, meaning "a happy man" since Lea became happier. The oldest son of Lea, Reubel, brought apples of mandrakes to his mother. Rachel saw them and she wanted them, but Lea would not give her any.

Rachel argued and lost since Lea was able to sleep the same night with Jacob. She had Issachar, "one born by hire", and Zabulon, "one born as a pledge of benevolence towards her". She also had a daughter, Dina. Finally Rachel had a son named Joseph, "there shall be another added to him."

Jacob fed Laban his father-in-law's flocks. Twenty years had passed, and he wished to take his wives and leave. Laban would not let him leave, so he decided to leave in secret. He asked his wives what they thought. They agreed. Rachel took along little gods which they used to worship where she lived. All of the children and servants and belongings were gathered, and they left. Jacob took with him half of the cattle. They left without Laban knowing anything. Rachel had taken the gods in case she needed an excuse to give to Laban for their leaving without his permission. After the first day of travel, Laban went after them with some other men. On the seventh day he caught up with them resting on a certain hill. It was evening. God stood by Laban in a dream and told him to be at peace with them and to make a pact with Jacob. He said that if Laban fought them, God himself would resist him. Laban called for Jacob the next day and told him about his dream. He began to remind him of all of the good he had done for him when Jacob came to him empty-handed. "I have given you my daughters. You have treated me like an enemy, since you took away my cattle and talked my daughters into leaving me. You have also taken those gods which have meaning for us. You've done all this as a relative, my sister's son and the husband of my daughters. I was hospitable and fed you." Jacob answered, "You are not the only person in whom God planted the love of his native country. After such a long time I wanted to return. If someone were to judge between us, I would be the one in the right. I kept your cattle and increased them. I took only a few of them. My wives wish to follow me. I was worn out with your tough commands which held me here for 20 years." Laban had truly used Jacob, since he did not keep an agreement they had made regarding the cattle. Laban was envious and intended to delay paying his debt to Jacob for another year, which was a trick. As for the gods, when Rachel knew Laban would be looking for them she put them into the camel's saddle. She said that she could not get up since she was having her menstrual period. Laban gave up looking. He made a deal with Jacob and they agreed to be at peace, with Jacob loving and caring for Laban's daughters above all. They built a pillar in the form of an altar and called the hill Gilead. To this day the land is called Gilead. They feasted, and Laban returned home.

JACOB was on his way to the land of Canaan and angels appeared to him. They assured him that he would have a good future. He called the place the "Camp of God." He needed to know what Esau was thinking of him, since he was afraid, so he sent messengers. He told them to tell Esau that a long time had passed since they had seen each other, and now was the time for peace between them. He had his wives and children with him as well as his possessions. He had been blessed and wished to share something of what he had received from God with Esau. Esau was happy to hear this and came with 400 men to meet his brother. Jacob was afraid, however, when he heard that so many were coming; but he trusted God for his protection. Jacob divided his group into smaller parts so that in case they would be attacked, not everyone would be attacked at once. Those in front carried presents for his brother. The presents were cattle and other rare four-footed animals. They were walking at intervals to give the impression that they were more numerous than they really were. Hopefully Esau would be pleased, and the people were instructed to speak kindly to him.

Day and night they went along, and when they came to a river called Jabboc, Jacob stayed behind. He had a meeting with an angel and fought with him. He won the struggle, and the angel spoke to him and said that he had truly shown his strength and that he would be greatly blessed. His descendants would not fail and he would be able to overcome all men. This divine angel also changed his name to Israel, which in Hebrew means "one who struggled with the divine angel." Jacob asked the angel about the future, and after he related his message the angel disappeared. Jacob named the place Phanuel, which means "the face of God." Jacob felt pain in his large muscle and afterwards would not eat from the same animal sinew. The Jewish people also do not eat from it.

Jacob ordered his wives to go first to meet Esau together with their maids. Jacob came up to Esau and bowed down to him. Esau was interested in hearing about Jacob's family, and he said they would go together to their father. Jacob said that the cattle were tired, so Esau returned to Seir, which meant "Roughness" since he had rough hair.

xxi

JACOB came to the place called Tents ("Succoth") and then on to Shechem, which is a city of the Canaanites. They were celebrating a holiday and Dina, the only daughter of Jacob, went into the city. When Shechem, the son of the king, saw her, he raped her and wanted to take her to be his wife. He came to Jacob to ask to marry her. Jacob was afraid to deny him this wish, since Shechem was an important man. He held back, however, since Shechem was a stranger. Jacob told his sons about how their sister was ruined, and about Shechem, and asked them what they thought he should do. Dina's brothers by the same mother, Simeon and Levi, decided on a plan. The Shechemites were feasting, and while they were asleep these brothers entered the city and killed all the men, including the king and his son. They did not harm the women and they brought Dina back. Their father did not know about this.

Jacob was surprised at what they did and was blaming them, but God told him to make his tents clean and to offer the sacrifices which he had promised to offer when he first went into Mesopotamia and saw his vision. While cleaning up, he saw the gods of Laban, not knowing that Rachel had stolen them, and he hid them in the ground under an oak tree in Shechem. Then he offered a sacrifice at Bethel where he had had his dream.

They came to Ephrata and he had to bury Rachel, who died in childbirth. She is the only one of Jacob's family who was not buried in Hebron. After mourning her for a long time, he called the son who was born to her Benjamin, meaning "one born in the father's old age." The meaning of his name is debatable. In all, Jacob had twelve sons and one daughter. Eight sons were legitimate, six of Lea and two of Rachel, and four were from the maids (two from each).

xxii

JACOB came to Hebron where Isaac his father was living. Jacob did not find his mother Rebeka alive, and shortly afterwards Isaac also died. He was buried by his sons with his wife in Hebron. Isaac was a man whom God loved and who had experienced God's many blessings. He, like Abraham, lived to be very old – 185 years.

BOOK II

FROM THE DEATH OF ISAAC TO THE EXODUS OUT OF EGYPT

i

ESAU left Hebron and left it to his brother, Isaac. He went to Seir and ruled over Idumea [Edom in Greek, now in modern Jordan]. He was named Adom [sic, Edom] and so he named the country after himself. He called himself Adom ("red") due to the red soup which he had bought from Jacob in return for his birthright. He had five sons from his wife Alibama. Aliphaz, one of his sons also had five sons. A sixth, Amalek, was illegitimate, born to a concubine named Thamna.

ii

JACOB was a healthy, wealthy man with clever and wise sons, but Joseph surpassed them all. Here the trouble began; namely, jealousy. During the harvest time he told his brothers his dream about the wheat sheaves, but they pretended not to understand the implication. They prayed that it wouldn't come true. God, on purpose due to their envy, sent the second vision to Joseph about the sun, moon and stars.

Jacob didn't mind the dream, since to him it signified his son's future happiness. He was not aware of the reactions of his other sons. He felt that since the moon and sun were like mother and father: the one giving increase and nourishment to all things, and the other giving form and other power to them. Since the stars receive their power from the sun and moon, he had a positive response. Joseph's brothers, on the other hand, felt that they should be equal. So they set out to kill him. They went to good pasture land in Shechem without telling their father. He feared for them and sent Joseph to see what was happening.

THE brothers saw Joseph coming and plotted to kill him. Reubel [sic, Reuben], the eldest, tried to talk them out of it, knowing how upset their father would be. God was watching! He tried to wake up their consciences and to tell them that God would punish them for such a misdeed. It was argued that if they would kill the one who had been promised God's blessing, they would also miss out on what was intended for them. Reubel finally convinced them to allow him to put Joseph in a pit with no water in it. Judas [sic, Judah], one of Jacob's sons, saw some Arabians on the way to Egypt who were carrying spices and Syrian wares. After Reubel had gone, they drew Joseph up and sold him for 20 pounds (20 pieces of silver, a value which cannot be known today). Joseph was 17 at this time. When Reubel came to get him out of the pit, he was gone. Later he heard what happened. Joseph's brothers got the idea to dip Joseph's coat in goat's blood and tell their father that some wild beast had killed him. Jacob believed their lie, sat in sackcloth and refused to be comforted.

POTIPHAR, the Egyptian chief cook for Pharoah, discovered Joseph's faultless character and gave him many responsibilities in his household. Potiphar's wife tried to get Joseph to sleep with her, but he refused. The second time she threatened him. She said that if he refused her, she would accuse him falsely and say that he had chased after her. She used tears. He told her to keep her conscience clean and to sleep only with her husband. She could make better use of her authority over him than to give into evil and be ashamed afterwards.

She would not listen to reason. Potiphar's wife presented the crafty lie that she had been abused by Joseph, and she had Joseph's coat to prove it. She stressed how he had planned it before a festival, knowing that Potiphar would be away. "He was entrusted with governing your estate and the family, and he assumed that the privilege of abusing your wife was also included." Her tears convinced Potiphar of the truth of the incident. He mistakenly believed that she was a modest and chaste woman. He threw Joseph into prison.

V

JOSEPH trusted God. The keeper of the prison noticed this, and gave him better food than the others. The king's cupbearer noticed Joseph's wisdom and entrusted him with a troubling dream, complaining that God was adding to his already miserable state by giving him the dreams. The cupbearer told him about clusters of grapes from three branches which were being squeezed into a cup. Wine, symbolizing loyalty and confidence between men, helps to end their quarrels and takes away passion and grief, replacing them with cheer. The three branches signified three days, after which this man would return to his work. The chief butler shared his dream also; but it had the sad outcome that he was crucified after three days, and his flesh was eaten by fowls, as it was symbolized in the dream of the three baskets.

Finally after two years the king's cupbearer remembered Joseph. Potiphar had a troubling dream, and the cupbearer told him about Joseph, who was brought from prison to interpret his dream. We know that Pharoah believed his interpretation: he entrusted Joseph with the responsibility of saving up part of the corn harvest for the seven years of famine. He travelled in the king's chariot, carried his seal and wore purple. He left enough with the farmers for seed and for food. He did not tell about his reason for storage, the years of famine.

JOSEPH was now 30, and his Egyptian name was Psothom Phanech, meaning "revealer of secrets." He married an impressive woman, named Asenath. His oldest son was called Manasseh ("forgetful") because his present happiness caused him to forget his earlier misfortunes. Ephraim ("restored") meant that he was restored to the freedom of his forefathers.

Joseph sold corn to the Egyptians and also to the strangers in need. Joseph's brothers told him that they were 12 brothers from four different wives of Jacob. Joseph was trying to discover something about his father, who he learned was still alive. He put them in prison for questioning for three days. Afterwards he let them all go except for one. He said that when they should return, they must bring the youngest back with them to prove they were truthful. Joseph saw their distress, and because he understood their language, he broke down in tears and had to leave temporarily. Symeon had to stay behind.

Back in Canaan Jacob was very upset and couldn't be convinced to let Benjamin return with them to Egypt, even when Reuben offered his own sons as a guarantee. Finally when there was no choice, he let them return. They were also disturbed that the money they'd paid had been returned in their sacks. Judas [sic, Judah] said that if Jacob's two sons wouldn't come back, Judas would lose his own life. Jacob, knowing the price of corn in Egypt had doubled, finally let them go, together with Benjamin. He sent presents from the fruit of Canaan: balsam, rosin, turpentine and honey. He grieved for a whole day and then stayed behind.

When they arrived, they pleaded with Joseph's steward regarding the money which had been returned in theirsacks, but he didn't know what they meant by it. Judas threw himself at Joseph's feet, and was ready to be destroyed so that Benjamin's life would be spared. Joseph finally made himself known to his brothers. He promised that any guilt or hate would be forgotten. "Bring all the family to live here, so that we can be together." They feasted. The king heard about Joseph's family and gave them wagons of corn, gold and silver to take back.

WHEN Jacob came to Beersheva ("well of the oath"), he offered a sacrifice to God and made sure it was in his will to go to Egypt, since they could be destroyed there. God reassured him twice that he had control; even when his father Isaac would have taken it from him, he had been guided all along. "You will die in the arms of Joseph."

70 people arrived in Egypt. They didn't have to feed sheep as they were used to doing, but simply to care for their father (since sheep herding was not acceptable to the Egyptians). When the famine was over, with the rivers again overflowing and causing the ground to produce, people were allowed land for farming. Each one had to give one fifth of his produce to the king. This continued with later kings as well.

JACOB lived 17 years in Egypt. He prophesied over all of his sons before they died. He lived to be 150 [sic, 147] and was buried in Hebron at great expense. All the sons were present. After their father's death, the sons were afraid that Joseph might take revenge, considering how they had abused him, but he persuaded them not to be suspicious.

FROM 70 souls, the Hebrews now had 600,000 souls. The Egyptians became very abusive of the Hebrews. They forgot the benefits they had received from Joseph. They made them build walls for their cities and towers, and cut many canals from the river so that the water would not stagnate or run over its banks. They were forced to learn mechanical arts and to work very hard. A sacred Egyptian scribe told the king that one would come out of the Israelites who would cause them to rise, and that the Egyptians would be brought low. The king feared so greatly that he had all of the male babies thrown into the river. Even the midwives were commanded to destroy the males. Those families who saved their baby boys would be killed.

No one can go against God's purposes, even if 10,000 plans are thought up for this purpose. Amram, a wise Hebrew, was one who prayed often, and he understood God's plan to use someone to deliver the nation. He saw in a vision that this special one would also have a brother who would establish the priesthood. Amram told this vision to Jochebed his wife. She had an easy delivery, which was a sign of God's blessing, and she nursed her baby for three months. They made a cradle of river reeds and sealed it with slime (clay and tar), and put the baby in it, trusting God for the baby's care.

Miriam watched and the king's daughter, Thermuthis, who saw the basket, requested that a swimmer bring it to her. The baby was big and beautiful, and she loved him. The baby refused her breast as well as that of other women. Miriam, who was trying to appear "by chance", suggested that maybe a woman from among the Hebrews would succeed in nursing the baby. Unknown to others, the baby's mother came forth, and from then on she nursed him.

Thermuthis called him "Mouses" [sic, Moses]. The Egyptians called the water "Mo" and those who are saved out of it as "uses" Abraham was Mouses' ancestor by seven generations. Even at three years old, Mouses was tall and he was also brilliant for his age. He was stared at wherever he went.

Thermuthis took him to the king and since she had no child of her own, she stated that she hoped he would be the next king. The king hugged him and put a crown on his head. The child threw down the crown and stomped on it. The sacred scribe who knew the prophecy about a Hebrew deliverer saw this, and attempted to kill him. He told the king that if Moses were out of the picture, it would end the hope of the Hebrews and give the Egyptians more control. Thermuthis grabbed the child away.

Moses using a clever tactic to kill snakes.

Moses was guarded and properly educated. The Hebrews already depended on him, but the Egyptians were suspicious. They didn't kill him, however, since they didn't have any prophecy pointing to another future king.

THE Ethiopians attacked Egypt and were very successful, even to the point of capturing the city of Memphis. Things became desperate, so the king requested Thermuthis to allow Moses to lead the army. The king promised that no harm would come to him, and even the priest who had previously wanted Moses killed agreed that his help would be useful. Moses' tactic was to march by land and not come up the river. But that area had many snakes, which could also come out of the ground and fly. Moses' wisdom was seen in that he knew of a certain bird which could attack them. He held the birds in baskets and then released them to eat the snakes.

The Ethiopians were all killed, except for a few who retreated to Saba (Sheba), a royal Ethiopian city. It was a strong city, protected by a wall and three different rivers. Tharbis, the daughter of the Ethiopian king, saw Moses' success and courage as he was nearing the wall. She fell in love with him, and he accepted her on the condition that the city would surrender. In this case, love saved the day. Moses, together with his wife, returned to Egypt with his army.

THE Egyptian leaders and sacred scribes became jealous and fearful of Moses, thinking that he might start a revolt together with the Hebrews against them. Moses then escaped across the desert. Almost dead, he finally arrived at a well in Midian, near the Red Sea. He saw how people would fight for the water, some taking more than their share. He helped seven virgin sisters to get water by fighting off some mean men. The daughters of Raguel [sic, Reuel], a priest, invited him to their father's house. Moses remained there and was responsible for caring for the cattle. He married one of the daughters. The wealth of the barbarians at that time was in cattle.

xii

RAGUEL was also called Jethro. Moses tended to the flocks. He took them to a high mountain, Sinai, which had the reputation of God being there. Up to now the shepherd had not gone up there, although it was good pasture land. There God spoke to Moses from a thorn bush which burned and was not consumed. Calling him by name, God told him that he was appointed to boldly bring the Hebrews out from under the slavery which they were enduring. God promised that he would help Moses, and he revealed his name to him, which had not been known to anyone before. He also gave him supernatural signs.

xiii

MOSES took his wife and Zipporah (Raguel's daughter) and family by permission and went to Egypt quickly. On the way he was met by Aaron. The Hebrew leaders also came to meet him, and he told them about the supernatural signs and about his call from God to deliver the Hebrews from slavery. Moses came to the new king (the one from whom he'd fled earlier had died) and informed him of how he had helped the Egyptians in the war against the Ethiopians. He told them about the Sinai experience and also about the supernatural signs. He stressed the importance of not going against God's will.

xiv

THE plague of the water turning to blood affected only the Egyptians. When they drank it, they would have great pain and bitter torment. When the Hebrews drank, it was normal water. The second Egyptian plague was frogs, and the third, lice. People even died during this plague, and there was a lack of farmers. Some men also had distemper (a disease caught from animals).

The king finally allowed the men and women to go and sacrifice to their God, but said that the children were not permitted to join them. God then sent the boils and many Egyptians died. The king later agreed that the children could leave, but not the cattle which were needed for the sacrifices. So God sent darkness for three days, and some died because of the thickness of the air. The king threatened to cut off Moses' head.

When the 14th day of Nissan arrived, the people who obeyed Moses had offered their animal sacrifice, purified their homes with blood, ate the sacrifice and burned the rest, getting ready to leave. This is called "Passover", and the Hebrews left Egypt with many gifts - either to get them to leave quickly or because of friendly neighbors.

xv

THE Egyptians wept and repented that they had treated the Hebrews so badly. The Israelites lived for 30 days on the food they brought out of Egypt. There were 600,000 fighting men. Moses was 80 and Aaron was 83. They came out 430 years after Abraham came to Canaan. They had Joseph's bones with them.

Moses led them deliberately through the wilderness (not in the direction of the Philistines) since he wanted to see the Egyptians punished. He also went in the direction of Sinai in order to offer sacrifices. The Egyptians were coming close, and they were so angry at Moses that they started throwing stones at him. Moses told the people that God was their protector and could make small things great. "This mighty force against you is nothing but weakness. Don't be afraid! The mountains could be made flat ground for you or the sea could become dry land."

xvi

MOSES pleaded with God, taking his rod. He admitted that they were totally dependent on him. He asked him for a quick show of his power, suggesting that God could even fly them out of their dilemma if he so desired. He hit the water with his rod, and a road was created.

The Egyptians wasted time putting on their armor. They got into the middle of the sea and the water closed on them. There was rain, terrible lightning, thunder, and fire in thunderbolts from the sky. Not one Egyptian remained even to be a witness of the event. Moses wrote a joyful song about their deliverance in hexameter verse (a form of Greek poetry). The Hebrews collected weapons which had floated to shore. Moses then led them to Sinai to offer sacrifices for the salvation of the people as he had been commanded to do.

BOOK III

FROM THE EXODUS OUT OF EGYPT TO THE REJECTION OF THAT GENERATION

i

MOSES put a stick down a well at Mara, and prayed that God would make the water sweet to drink since it was bitter ("mar" means "bitterness" in Hebrew). They removed the first water and later were able to drink it.

Elim was a place of 70 palm trees, but there was very little water in that place. The people thought to stone Moses. As they held the stones in their hands, he urged them to remember what God had already done for them and to be patient. He went away to pray and when he returned to the multitude, he looked joyful and the people in turn changed their attitude.

God sent quails, which is a plentiful bird in the Arabian Gulf (more than elsewhere). Moses thanked God for this provision, which came sooner than he had promised the people. When Moses lifted his hands to pray a second time, dew came from heaven which stuck to his hands. He understood that this was food for them. Each one would gather one omer (around 3.6 liters or half a gallon) of this sweet food which tasted like coriander seed (a nutty, lemon flavor). The word "manna" means "what is this?" They ate this for 40 years in the wilderness.

They lacked water but Moses hit a rock and sweet drinking water came out. They gratefully sacrificed to God and admired

Moses as God's blessed servant. The scripture in the temple has the account of how God foretold to Moses that water would be taken out from rock.

RUMORS were out among the Amalekites about the strong Hebrews who had escaped slavery in Egypt. They decided that these Hebrews needed to be crushed before they would crush others. Moses gathered some soldiers who were strong and who believed in God. He put Joshua in charge. All night they readied themselves, and afterwards Moses went up on a mountain and gave the army to God and to Joshua. They fought hand to hand against the Amalekites. Aaron and Hur (Miriam's husband) held up Moses' hands, and only because of nightfall they didn't kill all of the Amalekites. Those Amalekites who had been killed couldn't be numbered. Not one Hebrew soldier was lost in the battle.

The spoil of war was taken, and this was the first proper food the Hebrews had received in the desert up to now. Neighboring people were in fear of the Hebrews after this great victory. There was also much silver and gold, many bronze vessels, embroidered cloth and furniture which they took. Their courage was greatly increased as they understood that there was a solution to every difficulty. Moses stripped the enemies' armor off and gave it to his men. Moses offered sacrifices at an altar called "The Lord the Conqueror." Everyone rested and feasted for a few days.

Three months after leaving Egypt, they came to Mt. Sinai (the place of the burning bush).

JETHRO, Moses' father-in-law, met him together with Moses' family and friends. They feasted, and Aaron and his family took Jethro and they sang hymns of praise to God for His faithfulness in delivering them from the Egyptians. Jethro even made a speech praising Moses in front of everyone.

JETHRO advised Moses on how to have different sized groups with someone over them, from small to large – from 10s to 20s to 50s to 100s, up to rulers over 1000s and 10,000s. This way Moses could spend more time hearing what God had to say in the largest matters. The small matters could be handled by others further down the chain of command. Moses informed the multitude about Jethro's advice so they wouldn't give credit to him for this wisdom.

MOSES went up the high, dangerous mountain. The people camped at the foot of the mountain, and prayed to God that he would favor Moses for their sake. They dressed in their best clothing, ate well, and didn't sleep with their wives for three days. On the third day, there was a huge storm. Moses returned and looked joyful. He told them the 10 commandments. He went up a second time and was gone for 40 days. They thought that perhaps a wild beast had killed him. He finally returned and showed them the two tablets, with five commandments written on each one by the hand of God.

MOSES told the people about the place of worship, called the tabernacle (a large tent), which needed to be built. The people willingly brought material, precious stones, wood, spices, etc. until Moses told them that it was enough. The whole temple [sic, tabernacle] was called the Holy Place, but the innermost part was called the Holy of Holies. The entrance appeared like a triangle in front. The outermost coverings were protection for summer and winter. The tablets with the commandments were placed in the gold-covered ark upon which sat two cherubim (angels made from gold). The ark was never to be moved on a cart by animals, but rather carried by men with the bars on their shoulders. The other items in the tabernacle are described in detail.

THE priests (Coheneem) had special clothing which is described. There was a certain cloth which was embroidered with multi-colored flowers. The 7-branched candlestick was divided into 70 parts, which were for the "Decani" or 70 divisions of the planets. Seven lamps on the candlesticks referred to the seven orbits of the planets. The veils were made of four things to remember the four elements. Fine linen represented earth (the origin of the flax). Purple symbolized the sea because purple dye comes from the blood of a sea shellfish. Blue means air and red indicates fire.

GOD appeared to Moses and told him that Aaron would become the priest. "He will intercede to God for the people." All the people were to give a half-shekel to care for the tabernacle (605,550 men between the ages of 20 and 50). Ointments were made for the priests and oil for the lamps. Three lights burned all the time, and the others only in the evening.

The tabernacle was dedicated two years after the Israelites had left Egypt. Besaleel was the most skillful of the workmen. He was Moses' sister's grandson. A deep, thick cloud rested over the tabernacle, a sign of God's presence. The priests and vessels all had to be purified by the blood of animals for seven days.

The fire which burned up the sacrifices on the altar was a supernatural fire, and the sight of it was like a flash of lightening. Nadab and Abihu, two of Aaron's four sons, were consumed by the fire because they did not bring the sacrifices which Moses had told them to bring. The people grieved but Moses said that they needed to seek God's honor first, and not their grief for these priests.

The jewels on the high priest's shoulders would shine out bright rays which could be seen far away. And his breastplate would shine to show God's presence with His people during battle. The Greeks called it "the Oracle." This breastplate lost its shine 200 years ago (i.e. 200 years before Josephus wrote his book), because God was displeased with the sins of the people.

Moses no longer went to Mt. Sinai once sins were atoned for by sacrifices in the tabernacle. There were twelve days of sacrifices; one tribe after the other brought 12 offerings.

ix

THERE are sacrifices for individuals, and sacrifices for all the people. The whole burnt offering of a bull, lamb or kid (young goat) is meant for feasting afterwards. Thank offerings use the same animals, but the roasted animals are given afterwards to the priests to eat and to those who offered the sacrifice. The sin offering is like the thank offering, but the poorer people could buy two pigeons or turtle doves, one of which is burnt and offered to God, with the other offered to the priests. Fine flour and oil must be added to the private and public sacrifices. Animals less than 8 days old cannot be offered. The blood must be drained from the animals before offering them.

x

A year-old lamb was to be offered twice daily (morning and evening), paid for out of public donations. On the Sabbath, two more are sacrificed. At the beginning of each month, other animals are sacrificed to atone for sins of ignorance.

On Atonement Day, two goats as well as other animals are offered. The scapegoat is sent out alive into the desert to symbolize the sins of the people being carried away. The blood of the bull which was killed and burnt, together with the second goat's blood, is sprinkled seven times toward the holy place. Later the blood is sprinkled on the altar, in the open court.

Many animals were offered during the eight-day period in the fall which is called Succot (Feast of Booths). The "four species" are carried in the hands at this time.

Passover (the Feast of Unleavened Bread) is celebrated in the spring by families or groups. The sacrifices have to be completely eaten on the same day. Barley offerings are brought to God, as well as many animal sacrifices during the week of Passover. Parts are burned up, and the rest is given to the priest. Following this, the people may reap their spring barley. At Pentecost (the Feast of Weeks), which is 50 days after Passover, a wheat loaf is offered as well as animal sacrifices.

Food for the priests is provided as well as for the people. The sacrifices make sure they have food to eat on days they have been commanded to rest. Bread is not baked on Sabbath; enough must be baked ahead of time.

Golden cups of frankincense will last for the whole week. The priests eat the holy bread with fresh frankincense poured on it. Priests offer sacrifices two times a day made with flour and oil.

xi

THE Levites were a special tribe who were purified. They were responsible for taking care of the tabernacle, the curtains and the vessels. They were not in contact with the other 11 tribes.

Moses told the people which animals could be eaten and which were forbidden. Blood was never to be used for food, since it contained soul and spirit. Dead animals could not be eaten. Lepers had to remain outside the city. Women would be pure only seven days after their menstruation. If people would be too long at a funeral, they would need to offer two lambs as a sacrifice; one for the fire and one for the priests. If lepers were cured by God, there was a way back into community which included sacrifices.

Some nasty people accused Moses of having leprosy when he left Egypt. So then wouldn't he have opposed such laws? On the contrary; he gave them these laws from God, and it can be pointed out that in surrounding nations in those times, even captains of armies and others of high office suffered with leprosy.

Women could come into the temple only 40 days after giving birth to a male child and 80 days after a female child.

If a man suspected his wife was guilty of adultery, he had to bring barley flour – a handful for God and a handful for the priest. The woman would sit at the gate facing the temple with her veil removed. God's name was written on a page of parchment. The priest had to make oaths to confirm her purity. If she was unjustly accused, she would bear a healthy child after 10 months. If she was unfaithful, the dust in the water cup which she had to drink would cause her to lose her thigh and to suffer a swollen belly, after which she would die.

xii

MOSES warned the people about incest, homosexuality, sexual acts with animals, and men having intercourse when a woman was menstruating. These deeds were all punishable by death. Priests could not marry prostitutes, slaves or divorced women. He preferred that they not marry a widow. High priests could not come to funerals. When priests were in their ceremonial clothing, they were not allowed to drink wine. All sacrifices had to be without defects.

Every seventh year the land was to rest. In the 50th year (the Jubilee year), all debts should be cancelled and slaves set free. Sold land should be returned to the original owner, and its value was set by a formula that measured the yield against the expenses. Houses that had been sold in villages and in cities were also estimated for value, and settlements were made with the owners. These laws had been set on Mt. Sinai.

Moses had to count all Israelites who could be soldiers. He found 600,000 between the ages of 20 – 50, besides 3,650 Levis who were excused from the army. Moses took Manessah, the son of Joseph, to be a leader of a tribe, and Ephraim in place of Joseph, since Jacob had adopted these two sons of Joseph to be like his own sons.

There were three tribes camped on each of the four sides of the tabernacle. There were roads between the tents, where shops were set up for buying and selling. Moses invented the silver trumpet. Two were made, and they were blown when the people needed to pack up the camp and move elsewhere. It was done in an orderly manner. Six tribes would lead the march, followed by the Levites carrying the tabernacles items. Six tribes would follow behind them. The trumpets would also be blown when sacrifices were offered, as well as on the Sabbath.

xiii

THE people of Israel left the area of Mt. Sinai and began to complain against Moses. He promised that God would give them fresh meat for many days. Someone asked where it would come from. He rebuked him and said that God and he would continue to take care of everyone. At that instant, many quail appeared, and the people began to eat them eagerly. God judged the people for their unbelief and many died. This place was called Kibroth-hattaavah, meaning "The Graves of Lust."

xiv

THE Hebrews arrived together with Moses at Paran, which is near the Canaanite border. Moses said to prepare for work, since the Canaanites would give up their land only after a fight. They chose twelve spies (one from each tribe). They were gone 40 days. Ten spies reported that the rivers were so large and deep that they couldn't cross over them. Also the mountains were too high to pass, and the cities had strong, thick walls. The people blamed Moses and Aaron and had a sleepless night. In the morning they set out to stone Moses and Aaron, planning to return to Egypt.

Joshua and Caleb calmed down the multitude, however, stressing that God was on their side, and with his help they would overcome all difficulties and conquer the cities. "Don't give up." Moses and Aaron fell on the ground and asked God to make order out of the chaos. A cloud appeared over the tabernacle as a sign of God's presence.

xv

MOSES came out of the tabernacle after he begged God not to punish the people. Remembering their unique calling, and aware of all God had done for them in the past, he had to tell the people that they would be punished by God - they would have to wander in the wilderness for 40 years. Only their children would be able to enter the Promised Land. It was not Moses himself who calmed tens of thousands of angry people; God was with him.

Moses had supernatural power even after he died. Some people would journey for four months to Jerusalem from beyond the Euphrates River, but because of something in Moses' laws, they could not eat from their own sacrifices. These laws were seen as divine. Moses was upright, and his writings are deeply respected to this day.

BOOK IV

From the Rejection of that Generation to the Death of Moses

i

THE people were uneasy, and they decided that with God's help they would start to fight the Canaanites without any help from Moses. They went to battle and lost many Hebrews. They understood that they had brought down God's anger, so when Moses decided it was wise to move further away from the Canaanites, they obeyed.

ii

CORAH was a rich man and a persuasive speaker. He was from the same tribe as Moses and was related to him. He was jealous that Moses had put Aaron in the position of high priest. He felt he was equal to Moses due to his family, and superior to him in riches and in age. He said that the office of priest should have been given to the older men of the Levites who were also wealthier.

The whole army began to believe the evil words of Corah. He had 250 supporters, including influential men. Again they tried to stone Moses. The people felt that they should have chosen the high priest, rather than Moses giving the office to his brother. Moses knew that he had done what God had desired, and he had even sensed their growing discontent over time. He spoke not to the multitude but rather to Corah. He told him to bring a censor (a pan for burning incense) from home, in order to offer a sacrifice to the Lord in the morning. God would then show who the rightful person was to offer sacrifices and to guide the religious matters of the people.

iii

THE multitude showed up with great anticipation. Moses invited Dathan and Abiram to come, but they refused. Moses went personally to them. They stood outside their tents with their wives and children. Their servants were ready to protect them in case Moses would use violence against them. Moses repeated all the great things God had done for them – releasing them from cruel slavery in Egypt and caring for them in supernatural ways in the wilderness up until this time. He prayed that if Dathan and Abiram were guilty of falsely accusing Moses in the appointment of his brother Aaron to the priesthood, that the very ground on which they stand would open up. Moses said this with tears in his eyes. The ground began to shake like waves of the sea. The rebellious group was swallowed up and when the ground returned, it was as if nothing happened. The people learned a great lesson from this, and they were not sorry, because they understood that these men had done much damage among the people.

iv

THE rebellion grew even worse after this. The people felt that God wasn't angry because of the wickedness of Corah; rather Moses was to blame for causing the severe punishment which cost the lives of many who were "zealous in divine worship." This prompted Moses to patiently listen to the people without opposing them. God gave him a solution.

He called the heads of all twelve tribes to bring their rods, each one with the name of their tribe on it. Everyone agreed that God would give a sign in one of the rods. They were put in the tabernacle overnight. In the morning when the rods were brought out, it was seen that Aaron's rod with the name "Levi" on it had almond buds and branches growing out of it. Aaron had been confirmed as the priest three different times, and finally the Hebrews calmed down.

The tribe of Levi was free from warlike activity, so that worship could be done in the tabernacle as God desired it. The Levites were given 48 good cities in Canaan; 13 out of the 48 would be for the priests.

The people were to offer a firstfruits offering to God. The firstborn of the four-footed animals would be offered as a sacrifice, or people could pay their value in shekels* according to male or female. Baked goods were also offered. Nazarites, who drank no wine, could dedicate their long hair and offer it to the priests to be burned in the fire. If animals were slain and eaten at home, certain parts of the meat would be taken to the priests.

Moses wanted to pass with the people through Idumea (Edom, now Jordan). He sent ambassadors to the king to ask permission, and to say he was willing to meet their demands – even to allow them to take hostages if necessary. He said he would order his army to buy supplies and pay for the water they would need. The king did not agree, so they had to go a different way.

Miriam died 40 years after leaving Egypt. She was buried on a mountain called Sin (in the Aravah Desert) at great expense. They mourned her for 30 days. They killed a red heifer, and the high priest sprinkled its blood with his finger seven times before the tabernacle. Then they had a purification ceremony for those who had touched a dead body, using the ashes from the burned heifer together with water.

Aaron gave his priestly clothing to his son, Eleazar, who would be the next priest, and then Aaron died and was buried at Petra (now in Jordan) in the presence of the people. He was 123 years old, and died in the month of "Abba" (the Hebrew month of Av).

THE people mourned for Aaron for 30 days. After this they moved on to the river Arnon, which comes down from the Arabian mountains. It runs through the wilderness and comes to Lake Asphaltitis (the Dead Sea). The Arnon marks the border between the land of the Moabites and of the Amorites. It is a very fruitful land, and their country was like an island since it was surrounded by three rivers.

Moses wrote to the Amorite king, named Sihon, requesting passage and promising that he would pay for any supplies and water. The king refused the offer. Moses saw that the people were eager to go to battle. In fact, they succeeded in killing many of the Amorites, including the king. The Israelites were very effective with slings and darts. It was summer, and the lack of water caused many of the enemy to be killed by the Hebrews when they came to drink at a river. The Hebrews gathered a lot of prizes, including much fruit. Remaining enemies were taken as prisoners by the Hebrews. In this way the Amorites were conquered.

The king of Gilead, named Og, came to help Sihon, but he found only a great slaughter; Og himself was killed and his entire army destroyed. Moses also conquered the kingdom of Og, the wealthiest area with soil that was very productive. Og was a tall, handsome king who had a giant-sized bed. The Hebrews conquered a total of 60 cities, all of which had strong walls. They gained great spoils of war from all of them.

THE Israelites took a few days to sacrifice and thank God for His goodness. They feasted and sent out one party of armed men to attack the Midianites. Balak, the king of the Moabites and a friend of the Midianites, feared for his own people's safety. He wanted to bring Balaam, a famous prophet, to curse the Hebrew people so that the Moabites wouldn't be attacked. Balaam was prevented by God from doing so, and the ambassadors returned to Balak to warn him not to fight the Israelites. Balak insisted a second time that the ambassadors should go back and urge Balaam to do as he requested. This time he yielded; but as he was on his way, his donkey, seeing an angel which was invisible to Balaam, refused to move forward. Balaam beat the donkey and it spoke with the voice of a man. Then Balaam could see that an angel was blocking him, and that it was God's sign that he was in error.

Balaam blessed the people of Israel from a high mountain and said they would be happier than any people under the sun. "Your descendants will spread out all over the world. God will bless you in times of peace, but also give you victory in times of war." Balaam explained to Balak that his words came directly from God and were not under Balaam's control. He asked that Balak offer sacrifices again in the same place, and he would see if a different word would come. Balaam then fell on his face and told what disasters would come to several kings and important cities of the nations. Balak then sent him away.

Balaam then explained to Balak and his men that God was the protector of the Hebrews. They might suffer minor setbacks, but they would always prosper again. He suggested to Balak's people that their daughters go and make themselves a temptation to the Hebrews near their camp. In this way they would cause the young men to leave their laws and worship of God and to begin to worship the gods of the Midianites and Moabites.

The men found the Midianite women irresistible and they began to eat their strange food and worship their gods. The whole army of the Hebrews became corrupted, including the leaders. Moses saw the sin of the people, so he called an assembly. He told them that they had lived soberly in the wilderness, but if they were to sin now that they were prospering, they were going to lose everything. The men, and one man in particular, Zimri, replied that Moses had deprived them of a sweet life. They didn't want to be ordered around, but rather be free to choose what they wanted to do. They claimed that Moses' slavery was worse than that of Egypt.

Phineas, the grandson of Aaron was angered by Zimri's insulting words. He realized that he needed to punish the ring-leaders before the situation got worse. He went to Zimri's tent and killed him with his spear. Others joined the killing of these sinful Hebrews. In addition, God sent a plague, and a total of 14,000 were killed who had refused to take a stand against the wickedness.

vii

MOSES gathered an army of 12,000 to fight against Midian, with Phineas as their leader since he was zealous for the laws of the Hebrews. All five kings of Midian fell in battle; and the name of one, Rekem, was the same as a city in the area which is now Petra in Jordan. The Midianites were very wealthy, so the Hebrews brought back a great amount of gold and silver furniture, as well as many cattle. They destroyed the people except for 32,000 virgins. Moses divided the spoils of war.

Moses was getting old, so he trained Joshua to take his place. The tribes of Gad, Reuben and the half-tribe of Manasseh were very prosperous. They came to Moses to request to settle in the land of the Amorites, because of their many cattle, but Moses felt that they were trying to get out of continuing with the army. After discussing their motives with Moses, things calmed down. Moses called in Eleazar the priest for advice, and he agreed with their request on the condition that they would do army service when needed.

Moses built ten cities out of 48 which would be for the Levites. Three would be cities of refuge. The leaders of the tribe of Manasseh came to Moses and explained that a certain man had no sons but only daughters. Moses said that if his daughters would marry within their own tribe, the man's inheritance would remain in it. If they married outside their own tribe, the inheritance of their father would be lost to them. This set a new law for inheritances and tribes.

MOSES spoke to all the people before his death, near the Jordan River where there were many palm trees, where the city of Abila stands (modern Jordan east of the Sea of Galilee). They had completed 40 years in the desert less than 30 days before this. Moses said to them: "You have been partners on this long and difficult journey. Now I'm 120 years old. The way to receive continued blessing is for you Hebrews to live in God's favor. It is the only source of happiness for you. And you must keep God's laws and never change them. Stick to worship of him, and you will have courage to face and defeat all your enemies, since God will be with you. Virtue (goodness) is the first reward. Eleazar the high priest and Joshua, together with the senate and chiefs of the tribes must be obeyed.

"You are aware that I was in danger of death from you, even more so than from our enemies. So when you became rich and possess Canaan, you must respect those in authority over you. Disobedience will cause you to be scattered around the world and to lose what God gave you. All enemies need to be killed; otherwise you yourselves will become wicked. Destroy all their altars and temples."

Moses passed on the entire book of the law to the people. They cried with bitter tears and were sorry for the times they had caused him great pain. He gave them more laws.

"You shall go three times a year up to the temple to thank God for his goodness. In this way you will also continue to live in peace with one another. You are to bring 1/10 of your produce besides what you give to the priests and Levites, and you may sell these in the country in order to celebrate before God. Every seven years at the Feast of Tabernacles, these laws need to be read out to the people at the temple."

The people are to pray twice a day, put portions of scripture on their mezuzot (their doorposts), and wear the phylacteries (the Karaites did not take these three commands literally). Each city would have seven judges, and under each would be two Levites.

Decisions which couldn't be decided at this level would have to be decided at the temple. The judges were not to take bribes or pervert justice. Each case must be decided by hearing two or three witnesses. Women and slaves would not be able to testify in court. If a witness was discovered to have lied, he would be punished with the punishment which had been intended for the accused person.

If in time the Israelites would appoint a king, it should be done with the high priest and votes of the senators. He should not have many wives, nor gain too much riches and horses. Let the countries' boundaries remain stable in order to avoid wars. Keep God's landmarks. Fruit is to be eaten from a tree only after its fourth year, and this only after the fruit has been offered at the temple. Seeds aren't to be two or three kinds mixed together. Beasts should be yoked together only with their own kind. Some of the crop yields must be left for the poor. Foreign workers can be used to help reap harvests, but if they are treated wrongfully, the guilty one should be whipped 39 times.

Besides the tithes already mentioned, a third tithe every third year should be collected for widows and orphans. Ripe fruit should be given to the temple and the firstfruits to the priests. Before leaving the temple the worshiper who brought the fruit must thank God for his deliverance from Egypt, testify that he's given his tithes (one-tenth), and pray that God will be merciful and gracious to him and to the whole house of Israel.

It is preferable to marry a virgin, not another man's (divorced) wife. Do not marry prostitutes; they are to be stoned. If a daughter of a priest does not live righteously up to the time of marriage, she is to be stoned. If a man has two wives with sons, and he prefers the younger son for whatever reason, the double-portion inheritance must still go to the older son. If a virgin is violated, but the man who did this doesn't want to marry her, he must pay her father 50 shekels*, the price of a prostitute. If a woman's husband does not give her children and dies, the man's brother can marry her in order to keep the family line going. If he doesn't wish to, he is cutting off the memory of the dead brother, and the matter has to be settled with the senate. The refused widow loosens the sandal of the brother, spits in his face and says that he has refused to continue the family line. He will bear the shame all his life, and she is free to marry someone else.

If a man takes captive from a war a woman who is a virgin or who had been married, she is to shave her head and put on mourning clothes and be sorrowful for 30 days for those lost in battle or otherwise died. Afterwards she can feast and be married.

Young men who show disrespect to their parents even after they have been warned are to be taken outside the city with the people and stoned to death. The body is left there all day and buried in the evening. All enemies who have fallen in battle must be buried.

No one is to take a loan for food or drink. God will reward you for giving these things freely. Don't keep a man's clothing overnight for a guarantee of payment since he might need it to keep warm. If cattle are stolen, they must be restored four times as much. If it's an ox, the fine is five times as much. Slaves are to be freed after seven years. If gold, silver or cattle is found on the road, an effort should be made to find the true owner, rather than a person rejoicing in another's misfortune. Beasts in distress must be helped. Correct directions should be given to those asking for them. Blind or dumb people are not to be ridiculed. If a man kicks a pregnant woman he must pay. If she dies, he must be put to death – a life for a life. Poison is unlawful to keep. Children are not to be punished for the faults of the parents. Men who have made themselves eunuchs have deprived themselves of manhood and the seed which God has given men for the increase of their kind. They are to be driven away.

Don't make war outside of your own country. Try to make peace before taking up arms. God has been merciful, and we don't wish to fight or take what others have. If there's no choice, God is your supreme commander but you must have a lieutenant, the most courageous man among you. The army must be made up of the strongest people physically and emotionally. If the soldiers have owned a home less than one year, or planted vineyards and have not yet eaten from them, or are newly married, they do not need to fight. If you need wood for war machines, don't use fruit trees. Kill off your enemies, but keep some alive so they can pay taxes. But when you fight the Canaanites, kill them all.

Moses had already delivered the laws in writing. He read a poetic song to the people, which contained both history and a prophecy. He told them not to forget the harm done by the Amalekites and to continue to make war with them. They should build an altar facing the sun not far from Shechem, between Mount Gerizim on the right and Ebal on the left. Six tribes should stand on each of the two mountains together with the Levites and priests. Those on the Gerizim side should pray for those involved in worship and faithful in keeping the law. The other group wished all kinds of happiness for them. Those who broke the law would be cursed. The two groups answered each other in agreement of the blessings and curses. In this way by much repeating, the people would remember these important points.

They sacrificed and offered burnt offerings. This was the last day they offered sacrifices on this altar east of the Jordan River. Moses wrote out the blessings and cursings next to the altar. The next day the people promised that they would obey all of God's laws. Moses taught them about the sacrifices. He also told them how they would receive direction in wartime by using the stones in the high priest's breastplate. Joshua also prophesied in the presence of Moses. Moses' prophecy spoke of their enemies' victories over the Israelites, the overthrow of their cities, the burning of their temple and that they would be sold as slaves if they did not keep worshipping God. Moses encouraged Joshua to lead the army against the Canaanites. He hoped that Joshua would never cause God's anger, which could result from neglecting God's laws, which the Creator had given to him. Moses gave commands to each tribe individually.

The whole multitude cried and the women beat their chests. Even the children cried so much it was like a competition between the adults and the children. The old folks feared for the future of the young, who had not experienced enough of Moses' virtue. Moses himself wept. Moses waved the people away from where he was going, but a few went with him. They came to a high mountain near Jericho called Abarim, from where one could see Canaan. He sent away members of the senate who were following him. As he was speaking to Eleazar and Joshua, a cloud suddenly stood over him and he disappeared in a certain valley. He wrote in the book that he died, so that people wouldn't say that because of his great virtue he went to God.

Moses died at the age of 120 on the 1st day of Adar (February or March). About one third of that time, he ruled the Hebrews. He was greater than all men in understanding. He had a graceful speech before the multitude. He was an outstanding general and prophet. You would think you were hearing God himself. He was mourned for 30 days.

BOOK V

FROM THE DEATH OF MOSES TO THE DEATH OF ELI

i

JOSHUA was in charge of the Hebrews now. He called together the rulers of Reuben, Gad and half of the tribe of Manasseh. He told 50,000 soldiers to prepare to march from Abila to the Jordan River.

The spies reported to Joshua on what they had seen in Jericho, particularly the weak parts through which they might enter the city. While the king of Jericho was at supper, someone reported that they thought some Hebrew spies had arrived. Some messengers arrived at Rahab's house, and she said they had eaten there but had already left. The Hebrew spies promised that Rahab and her household would be saved since she was kind enough to keep them safe. She only had to put a red cord in the window so that the soldiers would know which house was hers. The spies then brought back word to Joshua about this oath they had made with Rahab.

Joshua had to cross a swift, deep river, but God had promised to move on their behalf. After two days the priests with the ark went first, then the Levites with the tabernacle and its furniture. The people followed behind according to the tribes and their families. When the priests entered the water, the water became shallow so that everyone, including the small children, could pass safely. The priests remained until everyone had passed. When they left the river, the current ran strongly like before. The prophets said to take 12 stones out of the river, and Joshua built a memorial with them. The people celebrated Passover there and had plenty of corn which they took from the Canaanites. The manna which had fed them for 40 years stopped.

The priests carried the ark around the city of Jericho for one day, while blowing seven trumpets. They were followed by the senate. Then they returned to the Hebrew camp. They did this for six days. On the seventh day, Joshua told the army that God would cause the walls to come down with no effort on their part. He told them to kill everyone in the city, including the animals, but not to take anything. They were to bring only gold and silver as a firstfruits offering to God. After they finished walking around the city walls seven times, the walls fell down. Everyone in the city was killed except Rahab and her family. The city was burned, including the surroundings. Rahab was held in high esteem by the Hebrews for the way she had helped the spies, and she was immediately given some land.

Joshua pronounced a curse on anyone who tried to rebuild Jericho: whoever would try would lose his firstborn son; and upon finishing it, he would lose his youngest son. Joshua delivered the pile of gold, silver and brass to the priests.

Achar (in our Bible, Achan) of the tribe of Judah hid clothing and a gold brick under his tent. Joshua sent 3,000 armed men to capture the city of Ai, but they were defeated, losing 36 men. They were good men, so the people mourned for them all day and fasted. Joshua prayed on his face, asking for wisdom. God told him that there was a sinner in the camp who had stolen from him (God). They cast lots and it was shown that someone from the tribe of Judah was guilty. They discovered that Achar from the family of Zachar [sic, of Charmi and Zebedias] had stolen something. He showed them what he had hidden and he was immediately put to death. Joshua again planned to take Ai, and this time the strategy worked. The Hebrews took spoil in the form of women, children, servants, furniture, cattle and lots of money, for it was a rich country.

The Gibeonites, together with 20 other neighboring peoples, came to Joshua with a plea for the Hebrews to accept them. Claiming not to be Canaanites, they said they lived far away and wished to live in peace. They had deliberately made their clothes look old. Eleazar and the senate made a covenant with them. After the lie was discovered, they agreed to make them servants.

The king of Jerusalem saw how the Gibeonites had joined Joshua, and he decided to join three other kings to fight against the Gibeonites. They asked Joshua to help them. Joshua brought his soldiers out to battle and they were successful. God even helped him by sending thunder, thunderbolts and large hail stones. The day was even made longer. Joshua also killed kings who had hidden in a cave.

Joshua went to the mountains of Canaan and killed many people. He took the spoils of war and returned to the camp called Gilgal. Neighboring people heard about the courage of the Hebrews. Many were frightened of them. When Joshua heard about Canaanites in the Galilee he was afraid, since they had many horses and chariots. God had to reassure them that he would help them overcome their enemies. Joshua went out against them suddenly. After five days of marching, he arrived and killed almost all of them and burned their chariots.

After the fifth year there were no Canaanites left, except in very strong places. Joshua moved his camp to the mountains and set up the tabernacle in Shiloh. He also built an altar at Shechem where Moses had told them to do this. He divided the army, placing half on Mt. Gerizim and half on Mt. Ebal. The tribe of Levi and the priests were standing by the altar. They offered sacrifices and returned to Shiloh.

Joshua was getting old. A total of 31 kings had been defeated and their capital cities captured. Other cities remained, and the sieges were longer since those inside knew about the victorious Hebrews and they had strengthened their defenses. Some of the Israelite warriors wanted to go back to their homes and families. Joshua decided to send one of every tribe to explore the land, and then come back with a report on the land, its residents, and how much land was good for farming. After seven months, the experts (including those in geometry, who measured the fields) returned with a full report. Joshua took Eleazer, the senate and the heads of the tribes, and he divided the land according to the population of each tribe. (See the map)

Six nations which were called Sons of Canaan were possessed by 9 ½ of the tribes. Joshua was getting too old to carry out some of his instructions. The Levites were promised 38 cities. Joshua gave a thank-you speech to these 50,000 armed soldiers who had settled in the land of the Amorites east of the Jordan River. He warned them not to reject God's laws. It was hard for them to separate from the rest of the Hebrews, and they did so with tears in their eyes.

These tribes built an altar on their side of the Jordan after they had crossed over. The tribes on the other (western) side misunderstood the intention of this altar, and they almost started a war. It wasn't intended for worship but only as proof of their relationship with the other tribes. Phineas, the son of the priest, commended the people for their pure motives, and when Joshua received this report he praised God that the matter had been settled and there was no reason to start a war between brothers.

Joshua died at the age of 110 years, 40 of which he had lived with Moses. He commanded the Hebrews for 25 years. He was buried in Timnah, located in the land of the tribe of Ephraim. About this time Eleazar, the high priest died, leaving the job to his son Phineas.

ii

PHINEAS prophesied that the tribe of Judah would destroy all of the Canaanites. The Canaanites were very rich, and they did not believe the Israelites would be able to destroy them now that they were without Joshua. The tribes of Judah and Simeon together destroyed 10,000 of the Canaanites, and they took the city of Bezek and their king named Adonibezek ("Lord of Bezek"). They cut off his toes and fingers. He admitted that he had dared to do the same to 72 other kings, and he died next to Jerusalem.

Map of the Twelve Tribes

The Israelites moved to Hebron and killed the giants who had strange faces and were frightening to listen to. One can still see their bones today (in the time of Josephus). The Levites received this city as well as 2,000 surrounding suburbs. Caleb and Jethro's family settled there also. Judah and Simeon's tribes took Askelon and Ashdod near the sea, but Gaza and Ekron, having many chariots and mean soldiers, were not successfully taken.

The tribe of Benjamin in Jerusalem permitted the Canaanites to pay them taxes, so the ground was farmed and they lived together in peace. The tribe of Ephraim took Bethel successfully when they found a man whom they bribed with a promise, that if he would help them he and his family would be saved. As in the case of Jericho, only this one family survived.

The Israelites grew lazy since they had the Canaanite money, and they didn't remember God's laws. They didn't even build a good government, but only cared about farming the fields and having pleasures and luxury. They began to fight among themselves.

A Levite who lived in Ephraim was having problems with his wife. She went home to her parents in Judah after four months, and he went after her. After five days, they made peace and headed back home. But they didn't want to stay overnight in a Canaanite city. They came to the house of an old man from Ephraim who lived in Gibeah (a city of the tribe of Benjamin). The old man was bothered all night by Gibeanites, who wanted to abuse the man's wife. She ended up being taken by force, and she was abused so terribly that she died afterwards. The Levite put her on his horse and took her back home. He cut her dead body into 12 pieces and sent them around to the 12 tribes, together with the story of the abuse by the Gibeanites.

The people were very disturbed about this, so they gathered at Shiloh and thought to start a war against the Gibeanites. The senate, however, said that they needed to talk to the Benjamites first, to see if they would be willing to hand over the Gibeanite evildoers for punishment. When this idea was presented, they refused.

The Benjamites fought with the other Israelite tribes and actually won twice.

At Bethel the Israelites fasted and were encouraged by Phineas that God would help them to overcome their enemies. They divided their soldiers into half against the city of Gibeah and the other half against the army of Benjamin. The Israelites destroyed all the cities in Benjamin, including Jabesh Gilead since they didn't help to fight against the Benjamites. In the end, only 400 virgins were left alive in Jabesh Gilead, and 600 men in the tribe of Benjamin who had managed to escape.

The Hebrews afterwards regretted the slaughter of their own brethren, the Benjamites. They all met together at a rock called "Rimmon", and the Israelites gave the Benjamite survivors compensation in lands and the 400 virgins of Jabesh Gilead. But there were 200 Benjamites left without wives, and the Israelites had taken an oath that none of them would give his daughter to marry a Benjamite. A certain person had an idea. The families of Israel would be in Shiloh three times a year at the festival times. At this time a man of Benjamin could rush in and steal a daughter from the Israelites without causing them to break their oath. In this way they obtained wives, worked on the land of Benjamin, and increased in wealth and in numbers.

iii

THE tribe of Dan suffered from the Canaanites so much that they felt forced off the farm land given to them by Joshua. They found a new spot to settle in the midlands (between the mountains and the lowland), and they built a city called Dan. At the same time the Israelites began to leave their worship of God and to do evil like the Canaanites around them. God became angry and allowed the Assyrians to make war against them, so that the Hebrews had to pay heavy taxes to them for eight years.

Othniel, of the tribe of Judah, was a courageous man who stood up to the enemy. He destroyed the fort which Chusar, king of the Assyrians, had built to rule over them. More Israelites joined Othniel, and they were able to defeat the Assyrians, chasing them to the other side of the Euphrates. Othniel became their judge and he ruled the people for forty years.

AFTER Othniel died, the Israelites again left their belief in God and his laws. Eglon, king of the Moabites made war against them and conquered them, demanding taxes from the Hebrews. Eglon built himself a royal palace in Jericho. For 18 years, the Hebrews were poor and suffering. Hope came, however, when God raised up Ehud, a young man from the tribe of Benjamin. He won the friendship of King Eglon and would bring him gifts. One day he entered the king's presence, together with two servants. Ehud had hidden a knife under his clothes. It was very hot and the king's guards were at dinner. Ehud told the king that God had given him a dream. The king was excited, and stood up from his throne, and then Ehud thrust the dagger into the king's heart. All was quiet. Ehud told a few people about what happened. In the evening the king's guards finally discovered that the king was dead. The Israelites immediately came in and began to kill the Moabites. More than 10,000 were killed, some of them near the Jordan River. The Israelites were no longer slaves to the Moabites, and Ehud governed them for 80 years. Shamgar ruled after Ehud but only for one year, and then he died.

SINCE the Israelites still didn't return to God and his laws, they were again taken as slaves by the king of the Canaanites, Jabin. He was from Hazor, a city located near Lake Semechonitis (Hulah Lake, north of the Sea of Galilee). It was very strong. The Israelites had no choice but to pay taxes for 20 years. They began to listen to a prophetess, Deborah ("bee" in Hebrew) and to pray to God again. God delivered them and appointed Barak ("lightening" in Hebrew) of the tribe of Naphtali as general. Deborah told Barak to form an army of 10,000 to fight against the Canaanites. Barak said he wouldn't go unless Deborah came along as a second general. She went, and they set up camp at Mount Tabor, where Sisera (Jabin's general) met them. Barak wanted to leave after seeing the size of the enemy's army, but Deborah persuaded him to fight right away. The battle began. God sent rain, hail and bitter cold so that the Canaanites couldn't even see to aim their arrows and slings. The storm didn't bother the Israelites, since it blew at their backs and not into their eyes. The Israelites killed many of the enemy, and others were killed by their own horses or chariots. Sisera escaped to the tent of a Kenite named Jael. She gave him sour milk to drink, so much that he fell asleep. Jael took an iron nail and drove it through Sisera's head with a hammer. Later when Barak came, he saw that the victory was won by a woman, as Deborah had foretold. Barak then fought with Jabin at Hazor and killed him. He overthrew the city to the foundation and ruled Israel for 40 years.

vi

BARAK and Deborah died about the same time. Then the Midianites, Amalekites and Arabians joined forces against the Israelites. They burned everything and took spoils of war for three years. Because of this, the Israelites moved to the mountains. They also guarded things in caves to keep the Midianites from robbing them, especially at harvest time. They were left alone to plow and plant in the winter, because the Midianites wanted to have something to take away later on.

Gideon, son of one of the leaders of the tribe of Manasseh, was threshing corn [sic, wheat] in the wine press, because he didn't want the enemy to see him at the threshing floor. A being like a young man appeared to him and said that he would lead the Israelites to victory. Gideon told him that he was too young and from a small tribe. But Gideon repeated this message to some friends, and they were quickly able to gather an army of 10,000 men.

God told Gideon in a dream that he was to bring this army to the river and to choose only the humble men from among them.

The ones who bent down on their knees to drink were to be seen as men of courage, who would give God the credit for the victory. These totalled 300, and the rest were sent home.

Gideon's army set up camp at the Jordan River, intending to cross it the next day. Gideon had been told by God that they were to attack the enemy at night. God told him to take one of his soldiers and to go near the Midianite tents. He obeyed and overheard a conversation about a dream one Midianite soldier had. He had seen a barley cake, which wasn't even good to eat, rolling through the camp and destroying the king's tents and all the other tents. The barley cake represented a "bad seed" just like the Israelites were thought to be the worst of all the people of Asia. The other soldier said, "I'm afraid that God has given this Gideon the victory over us." Gideon was really encouraged to hear this and passed this information on to his men. They were ready to fight.

Gideon made three groups of 100 men each, and attacked during the fourth watch of the night (just before dawn). Each soldier had an empty pitcher covering a lighted lamp in their left hand, and a ram's horn in their right hand. The Midianites were in a circle surrounded by camels. On the signal, the Israelites shouted, "Victory to Gideon, by God's help!" The Midianiates were half asleep since it was night. As God has said it would be, more of them killed each other than were killed by Israel. This was partly because they didn't speak the same language and there was chaos.

The Israelites ran after those who tried to escape and reached a blocked place. Oreb and Zeeb, two of their kings, were killed. Another 18,000 escaped but Gideon chased them also and killed them all, taking their leaders Zebah and Zalmuna captive. About 120,000 were killed in all, and the Hebrews took gold, silver, clothing, camels and donkeys. When Gideon returned to his own country of Ophrah, he killed the Midianite kings.

The tribe of Ephraim was very upset with Gideon, since they weren't involved in the battles, and they began a revolt against him. Gideon was wise and explained that he was carrying out the order which God had given him. This tribe afterwards suffered for their unfair uprising against Gideon. Gideon enjoyed being governor of the people. He ruled them with justice for 40 years.

GIDEON had 70 legitimate sons. One illegitimate son, named Abimelech, was not honorable and lived in Shechem. Later he came back to his father's house and killed all of his brothers, except Jotham who escaped. He took over and ruled unjustly. Jotham went boldly and gave a speech at Shechem using a parable about trees in order to warn the people that Abimelech was undoing all of the blessing which Gideon's rule had brought to them. He then left and lived in the mountains for three years since he feared Abimelech.

The Shechemites regretted having killed the sons of Gideon. They chased Abimelech away, but they were afraid that he would be back to trouble them during the grape harvest. A strong man named Gaal came to help them, and they were able to catch some of Abimelech's men and kill them. Zebul, a Shechemite leader who had sided with Abimelech, urged Gaal to fight Abimelech who was waiting for him. Gaal fought him but lost, and Zebul and the men of Shechem chased Gaal out of the city. But Abimeleck attacked Shechem, and in the end all the Shechemites were killed. The city was totally destroyed and its ruins were covered with salt. A few escaped, but Abimelech set fire to wood around a wall they were building for protection, and all died in the fire – 1500 men, women and children. Abimelech then went to Thebes. As he was on his way to attack the tower, a woman threw a millstone down on him. He asked his armour-bearer to kill him so that no one would know a woman had killed him. He obeyed and Abimelech's army went home. Jotham had predicted the slaughter of the Shechemites.

Jair, a Gileadite from the tribe of Manasseh, became ruler. He had 30 good children who rode on horses. He ruled for 22 years. But because the Hebrews did not fear God or keep his commandments, the Ammonites and Philistines took all of Perea. The Israelites then prayed to God and offered sacrifices.

The new leader was Jephtha, whose father had a good reputation. Some said Jephtha was illegitimate, however, so he became their leader only after the leading men begged him. He led the people to war from his camp at Mizpeh. He sent a message to the Ammonites, telling them to leave his land, but the Ammonites said the land was theirs. Jephtha said that Moses could have taken the Ammonite land along with the Amorite land but he didn't. And in any case, the Ammonites had no complaint for 300 years while Israel was on the Amorite land. They would not listen but went to war.

Jephtha promised that he would offer a sacrifice to God after the victory: the first thing that would meet him after the battle. He took many of the Ammonite cities and spoils of war, and he freed his people from 18 years of slavery. His only daughter, a virgin, came to meet him. He blamed her for being so bold to meet him, but she didn't know about his vow to God. She cried for two months, and after that he sacrificed her.

The tribe of Ephraim fought against Jephtha because they were left out of the battle and he did not share the spoil with them. He blamed them for not being willing to come quickly and help him. He sent for extra soldiers out of Gilead and defeated about 42,000 of them. His rule lasted for six years.

After that, Ibzan from Bethlehem of Judah became the new ruler. He had 30 sons and 30 daughters. He ruled for seven years. Then Helon ruled for ten years, but both of these rulers did nothing worthy of note. After him was Abdon, the son of Hilel, from the tribe of Ephraim. He enjoyed his family and there was peace, but he didn't do anything notable. He had 40 children and 30 grandchildren. They were all good horsemen. He had a big funeral.

viii

AFTER Abdon died, the Philistines ruled over the Hebrews for 40 years and took taxes from them. A righteous man called Manoah, together with his beautiful wife, used to come often to the Great Plain (there might have been a place of prayer there). They begged God to give them a child since they had none. The woman saw a vision of a young man who told her that she would give birth to a son. She was not to cut his hair and he was not to drink wine. Her husband also wanted to see the angel. She asked the angel to come again, and he did. This time she called Manoah. He asked the angel to explain his message again, because Manoah was jealous. He pressed the man to tell his name, so that they could give him a present after the baby's birth. He also wanted him to stay with them awhile. The angel stayed and food was prepared, but then he told them to put the bread and meat on a rock, after which the angel touched it with a rod. A fire burned up the food and the angel went up to heaven riding in the smoke. Manoah was afraid, but his wife told him that this was a sign of God's blessing. She gave birth to Samson (meaning "strong") and he was clever. His family visited Timnath, a Philistine city, for a festival. There Samson fell in love with a woman, and he asked his parents to bring her to him to be his wife. They refused, but he talked them into it because the idea was from God. Samson continued to visit the girl, one time killing a lion that got in his way. Later, when passing by the dead lion, he saw that the bees had made honey in the body of the lion. He gave this honey to his wife-to-be as well as to her family. At the marriage ceremony, there were 30 young men sent to guard him, since the people feared him. Samson told them a riddle and told what prizes he would give at the end of seven days to those who guessed it. His wife cried and nagged him for days for the answer. These 30 young men said they would burn her if they did not find out the answer to the riddle. In the end he told her, and she told them Samson took the prizes he had promised from some Askelonites (who were also Philistines). He divorced his wife, and she married his friend who had been their matchmaker.

Samson was out for revenge. He caught 300 foxes, joined lighted torches to their tails and sent them into the ripe fields of the Philistines, destroying everything. When the Philistines learned the reason for this, they sent their rulers to Timnath and burned his ex-wife and her family.

Samson killed many Philistines and came to Etam where there was a strong rock of the tribe of Judah. So 3,000 armed men of Judah came against him and complained that because of him the Philistines were making trouble for them. They asked him to surrender, and he was tied with ropes. They were on the way to bring him to the Philistines when he broke the ropes and picked up the jaw bone of a donkey which was at his feet. With this he killed 1000 Philistines and chased away the rest.

Samson was very proud and did not give credit to God for his victory. But when he became very thirsty, he repented and asked God to deliver him. God provided a fountain of sweet water for him to drink. He went to an inn in Gaza, and when the people realized who he was they surrounded the inn. Samson knew their plan. He got up at midnight and tore off the gates of their city, carrying them on his shoulders to a mountain by Hebron.

Samson then fell in love with a Philistine woman named Delilah. The leaders wanted her to discover the secret of Samson's strength. A few times they tied him with ropes, but he broke them each time. Delilah nagged him to death until he revealed the secret – his long hair was the reason for his strength. And so she told the leaders.

After Samson's hair was cut, they put out his eyes, put chains on him and led him around. By the time the Philistine festival was held in a large room supported by two pillars, his hair had grown back. He asked the boy who was leading him around to let him rest against one of the pillars. He suddenly pushed the pillars over and the whole temple fell down, killing 3,000 men including himself. This was the end of 20 years of his rule over Israel. Samson had extraordinary virtue except for the time he was trapped by Delilah.

ix

AFTER the death of Samson, Eli the high priest led the Israelites. Due to a famine, a family from Bethlehem of Judah moved to Moab. There Elimelech and Naomi, together with their two sons, settled down, and their sons married two Moabite women. All three of the men died within ten years, leaving Naomi with her two daughters-in-law. Then Naomi heard that the famine in Israel was over, and she returned to Bethlehem. Orpah stayed in Moab but Ruth came with her mother-in-law.

Ruth went to the fields to gather food for herself and her mother-in-law by going behind the reapers and picking up what they dropped. She came upon the field of Booz [sic, Boaz], a man who was a relative of her father-in-law. Booz told the servants to give her dinner and to let her to drink when the other reapers drank. She brought corn [sic, barley] back every day for her mother-in-law. After they were finished gathering barley, Booz would be sleeping on the threshing floor to guard it. Naomi advised Ruth to lie down next to him so that they could talk things over. He was surprised but glad, and early in the morning he woke her up and gave her as much barley as she could carry. He was careful that no one saw this. He told her that he needed to ask a closer relative if he wanted to marry Ruth - if not, Booz would marry her himself.

The next day Booz gathered the senate of the city, together with Ruth and the other relative. The other man said that he had a wife and family and that he didn't want to marry her. Booz told Ruth, in the presence of witnesses, to loosen his shoe and spit in his face according to the law. Afterwards she married Booz, and within a year they had a baby boy. Naomi nursed this baby and the women said to call him "Obed" ("servant" because he could help Naomi in her old age). Obed was the grandfather of David. This shows that God can raise up a person as important as King David from a line of common people.

X

THE two sons of Eli the high priest were very wicked. They feared neither God nor man. They forced women to sleep with them, bribed people and were unjust judges.

Elcanah, a Levite who lived with the tribe of Ephraim, had two wives, Hannah and Peninnah. He loved Hannah more than Peninnah, but Hannah had no children. Once when they were in Shiloh to sacrifice in the tabernacle, she became very unhappy. She was sad when she saw the second wife happily celebrating the feast with her children. She begged God to give her a child and promised that she would give him back to serve him. Eli the high priest thought that she was drunk, but she said she was only very sad. He then told her that she would bear a child.

She came to her husband hopefully and enjoyed the meal. After they returned home she became pregnant. They named the boy Samuel ("asked of God"). When he was old enough, she brought him to the tabernacle to offer sacrifices, and to pay their one-tenth. Elcanah and Hannah gave the boy to Eli to raise, so that he might become a prophet. He was to let his hair grow long and was to drink only water. Later Elcanah had other sons by Hannah, and three daughters.

When Samuel was twelve, he began to prophesy. Once when he was sleeping, God called him to pass on a message to Eli. At first he didn't understand that it was God speaking, so he went to Eli to ask what he wanted. Eli understood that God had a message for Samuel. Samuel didn't want to tell Eli what God said, since it wasn't good news. Eli's sons would both die in one day, because Eli loved them more than he loved to worship God and refused to punish them. Up to now, all that Samuel had prophesied had come to pass.

xi

THE Philistines made war against the Israelites and killed more than 4,000 of them. The Hebrews thought it would be good to bring the ark of God into the battle, together with the sons of Eli. His son Phineas was already serving as high priest because Eli was too old. Their father didn't agree with the idea and told them not to come to him again.

The ark did not help them in battle - they lost about 30,000 men, including the two sons of Eli, and the enemies carried away the ark. A Benjamite came to Shiloh with a message about the ark and the losses. Eli was sitting on a high throne at one of the city gates. He understood from the crying that something terrible had happened. He expected to hear that his sons had been killed, since it had been prophesied. Then he heard that the ark was taken, which he did not expect, and he fell down from where he was sitting and died. He was 98 years old and had been a leader for 40 of those years.

Phineas's wife died on the same day as her husband, while she was in labor with their son. The son was only seven months in the womb but he lived. He was named Icabod ("disgrace") since the army had been disgraced.

Eli was the first of the family of Ithamar, the other son of Aaron. First Eleazar, the son of Aaron, had been high priest, then Phineas. Abiezer his son took the honor and gave it to Bukki his son, and then to Bukki's son Ozi. When Solomon reigned, the family of Eleazar again took the priesthood.

BOOK VI

FROM THE DEATH OF ELI TO
THE DEATH OF SAUL

THE Philistines took the ark to Ashdod and put it next to their own god, Dagon (said to look like a man above the navel and like a fish below it). In the morning when they came to worship Dagon, they saw that he had fallen down as if he was bowing to the ark of the God of Israel. Then God sent all the people in the city and country of Ashdod a kind of dysentery which caused sudden death. The people were vomiting up their intestines. In addition mice came and bit them and ate all of the plants and fruit. They understood that it was because of the ark of God, so they sent it to the people of Askelon. When the people of Askelon received the ark, they had all of the same disasters. They sent the ark away and the ark went around to five Philistine cities, all of which were affected by these disasters.

The leaders of the five cities - Gath, Ekron, Askelon, Gaza and Ashdod - met to decide what to do with the ark. Some were not willing to believe that God was punishing them, for they said that sometimes there were natural causes that happened in the bodies of men, which they should bear with patience. Other men who were thought to be wise said that they should dedicate five golden images of mice, one for each of the five cities, to put them in a bag and to attach cows full of milk to a cart. The cows, which were missing their calves, would choose to go either on the road toward where the Hebrews live or elsewhere. This way they would know whether or not the ark was the reason for their suffering.

The cows went to Bethshemesh, a village of the tribe of Judah. The people were harvesting their summer crop and they were glad to see the ark. They took it off the cart, and offered the cows as a sacrifice to God and then feasted. The Philistines saw this and went home. But around 70 people of Bethshemesh who touched the ark died, because only priests were allowed to touch it. There was much crying in that village. They took the ark to Kirjathjearim, where a Levite named Abinadab lived. His sons were able to serve God properly and they took care of the ark for 20 years. The ark had been a total of four months with the Philistines.

ii

NOW that the ark was restored to the Hebrews, they gathered together to offer sacrifices to God. Samuel the prophet encouraged them to worship God with all of their hearts. If they did, he would bless them with prosperity, they would be a free people and they would gain victory over their enemies. "God has promised that he would bless you, not through weapons of war or by your own physical strength, nor by numbers of warriors, but by being good and righteous men." Samuel was applauded. They gathered at Mizpeh ("watch-tower"), drew water and poured it out to God. They fasted all day and prayed.

The Philistines saw what they were doing and decided that they would attack the Hebrews while they were totally unprepared. Samuel promised the Hebrews that God was on their side, and he offered a young lamb as a sacrifice. He prayed that they would not have another defeat. While the lamb was still not burned by the fire, the enemy came near to them. God caused the ground under the Philistines to shake so hard that they couldn't stand. Cracks in the earth opened up, swallowing some of them, and the weapons even fell out of their hands. In addition there was a noise of thunder and fiery lightning which could burn their faces. They ran away naked, and Samuel with his people chased them to Bethcar (one of their cities). The Israelites set up a stone as a memorial of their victory, calling it the "Stone of Power".

This ended the fighting of the Philistines against the Hebrews. Samuel led one more battle against them, killing many, and they took the country from the borders of Gath to the city of Ekron. The Canaanites who still remained within these borders were friendly with the Israelites at this time.

iii

SAMUEL the prophet visited each of the cities in Israel twice a year just to keep the order. As he was getting too old, however, the job passed to his sons. Joel, the older son, and Abiah, the younger, became judges in the cities of Bethel and Beersheba. But these sons were terrible leaders - unjust, taking bribes and living in luxury. They went against the will of God and their father, the prophet, who had tried to lead the people in righteousness. When their behavior was reported to Samuel, the people asked for a king.

Samuel was very upset and couldn't eat or sleep all night. God appeared to him and told him that it was himself who they rejected, and that since leaving Egypt they had wanted a king. "They are actually being ungrateful towards me and your prophetic office," God said. Nevertheless he would give them what they wanted. Later they would be sorry, but it would be too late.

Samuel gathered the Jews early the next morning and told them that he was to set up a king for them, but first he had to explain the disadvantages of having a king. Even after hearing the problems, the people insisted that Samuel give them a king. They felt that it would be better if they had a king to help them fight their battles, since they were fighting enemies who had one. Samuel said he would call them together after he knew God's choice for a king.

iv

THERE was a good family in the tribe of Benjamin, whose father was Kish. He had a son who was tall, handsome and wise. His name was Saul. Saul and his servant were out looking for a couple of lost donkeys. When they couldn't find them, someone suggested that there was a prophet in the city of Ramah who might be able to help. Some young women in the city told them which house was Samuel's, and also that he had a big feast about to start. Samuel had called this feast because God had told him that the future king would be coming.

Saul came to the prophet's house. Samuel knew that he was the man he was waiting for, and invited him to supper, telling him that the lost donkeys were already found. The prophet told Kish that he had some good news to tell him which he would not want to believe. Saul said that he was from a small tribe and a small family. "You must be joking," he said. Seventy people were at the feast, and everyone left except Saul and his servant, who stayed overnight with the prophet. The next day Samuel woke up Saul and walked with him out of the city. The servant was told to go ahead so that Saul and Samuel would be alone. Samuel took a jar of oil and poured it on Saul's head and kissed him and said: "Be now a king, by the order of God, and fight against the Philistines to get revenge for what the Hebrews have suffered from them." Samuel then told him different things that would happen to him on the way back to his home, and it all happened exactly as Samuel had prophesied.

Abner, Saul's favorite relative, was very friendly and tried to hear all the details of where Saul had been. But Saul was wise and didn't speak about it, since such matters can cause jealousy and ruin the trust between good friends or family.

Samuel called the Hebrews together at Mizpeh and repeated that their best choice of a ruler was God himself. When a man is king, he can make his people into slaves, be greedy for power and not care for men in the same way as God would. "Go ahead, however, since you have made up your minds." They cast lots, and the lot pointed to the tribe of Benjamin. By the end, the lot showed that Saul, the son of Kish, was to be the king. Saul hid himself, and it took some time until Samuel heard from God where to find him.

A man was sent to bring him out to the people, and they saw that he was taller than everyone and handsome. The people shouted, "God save the king!"

The prophet wrote down all that he had said, and it was kept in a book inside the tabernacle to remind future generations what Samuel had foretold. Samuel returned to Ramah, his home country, and Saul went to Gibeah, his birthplace. Not everyone was pleased with Saul - some rejected him and didn't bring him presents.

V

NAHASH, the king of the Ammonites, warred against the Israelites who lived on the east side of the Jordan River. He made them slaves by force and violence, and poked out the right eyes of some of them. He commanded the Israelite city of Jabesh to surrender, giving them seven days to decide what to do. These Israelites sent ambassadors to ask for help from the other tribes. The Hebrews were very sorry to hear about the terror in Jabesh, but they themselves were too afraid to do anything. Saul was angry and promised to attack the enemy by the morning of the third day. Saul cut the sinews of his oxen, and said he would do the same to people who refused to join him in battle. He gathered 77,000 at Bezek, including the tribe of Judah, and they headed out toward the Jordan. The Ammonites were totally surprised and many were killed, including Nahash. Those who had been against him immediately gave him the honor which was due. The army gathered a lot of spoils of war, which was divided among everyone, and they all feasted. Samuel asked the people to gather at Gilgal, and he again anointed Saul as king in front of everyone.

Moses and Joshua had been notable leaders. For 18 years there was chaos, and then Israel was ruled by various judges. Samuel was justified before the people, who said that he had taken care of them in a holy and righteous way. He again told them it was not good that they had asked for a king. "Remember the oppression of Egypt? God himself delivered his people without a king. After coming to this land, you betrayed God's worship and laws. In spite of this, you overcame the Assyrians, Ammonites, Moabites and Philistines under the leadership of Jephtha and Gideon. What madness is causing you to run from God? I will prove to you by signs that God is upset: he will send a winter storm in the middle of harvest time to prove it." God sent thunder and lightning and hail. The people were terrified and confessed their sins. Samuel urged them to be righteous and to remember the misery which comes from walking away from God. He said that if they would grow careless of keeping Moses' laws, great punishment would come on them and their king. Then he sent them home.

vi

SAUL chose 3,000 men, 2,000 to be his body guards in Bethel and 1,000 to guard Jonathan, his son, in Gibeah. The Philistines had taken all the weapons of the Hebrews away, and even their farming tools they could get only from the Philistines. Jonathan attacked some of the Philistines not far from Gilgal. They were in a rage and so they came to battle against the Jews with 300,000 soldiers, 30,000 chariots and 6,000 horses. They camped at Michmash. Saul heard about this and went out to meet them in war. Many of the Israelites were so afraid they hid in caves and holes in the ground. Most ran away into the land beyond the Jordan which belonged to Gad and Reuben. Saul needed the prophet Samuel to ask God what to do.

Samuel said he would come there to offer sacrifices in seven days. But when Samuel was late, Saul didn't wait for him. For this the king was strongly rebuked. The prophet said that his reign would be cut short because he disobeyed.

Jonathan came home with only 600 men and mostly without weapons. Jonathan agreed, together with his armor carrier, to attack some Philistines at night by themselves. They had to climb up a high rock, but they succeeded in killing about 20 Philistines. Due to having different languages, the rest fought one another, and some were killed climbing down from the rock. Saul's watchmen reported on the battle, and the soldiers found out that Jonathan and his armor carrier were gone. Saul told the high priest to put on his priestly clothing and to prophesy to him if they should go out to fight against the Philistines. After this 10,000 Hebrews came to Saul and they chased the enemy.

Saul put a curse of death on the Hebrews if any of them should eat food before the battle was over. Jonathan did not hear this curse, and he broke off some honeycomb in a forest. He said that this food had given him more strength to fight the enemies. They killed tens of thousands of Philistines and took much spoil. But the people ate the meat with the blood in it. Saul ordered a large stone to be rolled into the area and made the people bring their meat to sacrifice it on the stone, so that they would eat it without the blood. This was the first altar Saul built, and they offered sacrifices to God on it.

The next day the king asked the high priest Ahitub if they should continue against the enemy. There was no answer. Saul knew there was a reason for the silence. He promised that even if his own son had committed a sin, he would kill him to turn away God's anger. They threw lots and it pointed to Jonathan. Jonathan admitted that he had eaten the honeycomb. He was willing to die since the Hebrews had been victorious and that was his comfort. But the people wouldn't allow it, and they protected Jonathan from danger.

Saul had slain about 60,000 Philistines. He came home, reigned happily and continued to fight against the Ammonites, Moabites, Philistines, Edomites, Amalekites and also the king of Zobah. Saul's bodyguards were good-looking and tall. The Hebrews became rich and were greater than other nations.

vii

SAMUEL came to Saul reminding him that God had chosen him above others and made him king. He must obey God, submit to his authority and go to war against the Amalekites. Because they troubled Israel many times, their name was to be entirely erased.

Saul immediately gathered 40,000 soldiers at Gilgal and 30,000 from the tribe of Judah. They were ordered to kill the Amalekites of all ages, and to destroy their cities and all of their cattle. They trapped the Amalekites their cities by using war machines, by digging tunnels under the ground, and by building walls on the outside. Some died from lack of food. The Israelites fought without mercy, since it was a direct command of God.

They captured the Amalekite king Agag, who was a tall, handsome man. They also kept the cattle, even though God had commanded to destroy them. Saul was happy that he had conquered all of the Amalekites from Pelusium in Egypt to the Red Sea. Samuel heard that God was sorry that he had made Saul king, since he did not obey him. All night Samuel prayed that God would not be angry with Saul, but it didn't help. In the early morning Samuel came to Saul. Saul ran and hugged him and said "I give thanks to God, who has given me the victory, for I have done all that was commanded of me to do." Samuel said, "Why do I hear the sounds of sheep and cattle in the camp?" Saul promised that they were to be used for sacrifices to God. The prophet said that God was not pleased with sacrifices, but with good and righteous men who follow his will and his laws and obey him. "It doesn't matter if impressive sacrifices are offered. Even if they are made of gold or silver, they are a symbol of wickedness to him and they will be rejected."

Saul then said that the soldiers couldn't be controlled – they wanted to keep the cattle and he let them. "I ask your forgiveness," he said to Samuel, "and I will not disobey in the future." He wanted the prophet to come back with him to offer a thank-you offering, but Samuel turned to go home. He saw that God would not forgive Saul. Saul reached for Samuel's coat as he was leaving and it tore. The prophet said that in this way the kingdom would be torn from him, and a good and just man would rule in his place. What is agreeable to man's passion is not agreeable to God.

Saul admitted his wickedness, but he still begged Samuel to come back with him to make a sacrifice in front of the people.

Samuel went with him and worshipped God. Then King Agag was brought out. Samuel said said to him, "As you have made many Hebrew mothers sorrow for the loss of their children, your own mother will also cry." He gave the order to kill Agag immediately at Gilgal. Samuel then returned to Ramah.

SAUL went up to his royal palace at Gibeah ("hill") and no longer went to see Samuel. Samuel cried for Saul, but God told him not to be sad, but rather to go and anoint a new king. God told him to take holy oil and to go to Bethlehem to Jesse, the son of Obed and to anoint one of his sons king. Samuel was afraid Saul would find out and kill him either secretly or openly. God told him to take a sacrifice with him, which would be his reason if anyone would ask why he was coming. Samuel called Jesse's family to sacrifice with him and he saw Jesse's six sons. God told him that those handsome ones were not what he had chosen. Instead it was one with a good soul, who was righteous, strong in character and obedient to God. The prophet asked Jesse if he had another son. He answered, "Yes, but he's a shepherd." Samuel asked Jesse to bring him home, otherwise they wouldn't even start the meal. David came and he had a yellow (golden) complexion. He had sharp eyesight and was good-looking. They began to eat, and Samuel took oil and anointed him. He whispered in David's ear that God had chosen him to be the next king. Samuel told him to be obedient to God so that his reign would be long, he would be successful and he would be known around the world. He would also overthrow the Philistines and all other enemy nations. His good name would continue for generations.

At this time, God's power left Saul and moved to David. David began to prophesy, but Saul suffered from a choking condition which the doctors could not help. He was attacked by evil spirits, but Saul's servants found that singing and playing on the harp would calm him. Saul commanded that they find someone to play and sing songs about God.

Someone standing by had seen a shepherd boy in Bethlehem, who played the harp well although he was a child. They sent for Jesse, who gave his permission for David to play for Saul. Jesse also sent some gifts for King Saul. Saul greatly valued David and his playing - it was the only thing that helped to bring him back into his right mind again. Saul asked if David could stay with him. Jesse agreed, because he didn't want to say no to the king.

ix

NOT long afterwards, the Philistines made war against the Israelites. They moved camp and gathered to face the Israelites from across a valley. Their hero was Goliath of Gath, a huge giant. He carried a spear on his shoulders and also had a lance (a spear that was thrown). He had many servants following after him, carrying his armor. He said to the Israelites, "Let's avoid a battle. Just send me one man to fight me, and the loser's side will become servants to the winner's side." He came day after day for 40 days. The Israelites were terrified. They put on their armor to fight, but they didn't dare to answer Goliath's call.

While the war was going on, Jesse sent David to visit his brothers who were with Saul's army. He fed his sheep and then went to look for them. After a short time, David found his three brothers and gave them the food supplies which Jesse their father wanted them to have. While talking with them, he heard the Philistine's abusive words to the Hebrews. David said that he wanted to fight this Goliath. He was rebuked by his oldest brother, who told him he was too young and he needed to go back to his flocks and his father. David left them, but when he heard other soldiers talking, again he said that he wanted to come against this giant.

Word got to Saul and he called for David. He said to the king not to be afraid. He said he would win the fight, that people would laugh at Goliath and Saul's army would get the victory by someone who is not a warrior or a commander, but only a child. David told King Saul that although he was not being trained as a warrior like Goliath, he had already killed a lion with his bare hands. He took the lamb from its mouth, jumped on it, caught its tail and threw it on the ground. David said, " I did the same with a bear. This Goliath will die like those animals - God will bring him under my power."

Saul put his armor on David, but David could hardly move with it. He decided he would be better off with his staff and five stones in his shepherd's bag. With a sling in his right hand, he went towards Goliath. Goliath saw by his weapons that David acted like he was coming after a dog. David said, "I'm not after a dog, but after an animal worse than a dog." Goliath got angry and cursed David, and said he would give his flesh to the beasts and birds to be torn apart. David said, "You are coming to me with a sword, spear and breastplate, but I have God as my armor. God will destroy you and all your army by my hands. Today I'll cut off your head, and the dogs will eat the rest of your body. Everyone will know that God is protecting the Hebrews and that without him all war is useless."

Goliath came slowly towards David, due to the heaviness of his armor, but David was fast. David took one stone and threw it with his sling, and the stone struck the giant's forehead, sinking into his brain. He was stunned and fell face down. David ran and stood on him and cut off Goliath's head with his own sword. The Philistines all ran away, but Saul and his whole army shouted and chased them to the borders of Gath and the gates of Ekron, killing 30,000 of them.

Saul returned to the Philistine camp and burned everything. David carried Goliath's head to his own tent but dedicated his sword to God at the tabernacle.

X

AFTER the victory over the Philistines, there was great rejoicing among the Israelite women. They sang with cymbals and drums that Saul had killed thousands - but David had killed 10,000s. When he heard this, Saul was very afraid and suspicious of David. He stopped using David as his armor carrier, and he made him a captain over a thousand soldiers. It was a good position, but Saul was hoping that he would be in a dangerous battle and be killed. Instead David succeeded in everything he did.

Saul's daughter loved David, and Saul agreed to the match because he thought he could use it against David. David understood that it was a great honor to become the king's son-in-law, but he felt that he was unworthy. The king assured him that he didn't need to bring a rich present, but only to show his character by killing some Philistines. Saul said that David could marry his daughter, if he brought him 600 heads of the enemies. David agreed and he immediately went out and began killing many Philistines. He came to Saul and showed him the 600 heads which he had gathered. Saul didn't want to break his word, so he gave his daughter, Michal, to David for a wife.

xi

SAUL was more and more jealous of David, but Jonathan, Saul's son, loved him. Jonathan couldn't understand his father's hatred. Once he told David to stay away the next day while he tried to find out the reason behind it. Jonathan came to his father when he was in a good mood and reminded him about all that David had done in killing Goliath, his deeds in the army and how he killed more Philistines so that he could marry Michal. Jonathan said it would be very unfair to make Michal a widow when they had been married only a short time. Apart from this, he said, "David helped your problem with the evil demons by playing soothing music, and afterwards you would always feel better." Jonathan told David that he felt his father would receive him again.

David was ordered to fight another battle against the Philistines. He succeeded and returned to Saul. But Saul was attacked by demons and, in spite of David's harp playing, he got angry and threw a spear at David. David moved out of the way in time and he went quickly to his home for the rest of the day. King Saul wanted David to be watched all night so that he could be killed the next day. Michal understood the plan and told David that he needed to escape, which he did by climbing down a rope hanging out of the window. She then made the bed look as if he was still in it. She put a jerking goat's liver in the bed, which moved like a person who had asthma. The officers were told to bring David to Saul, even after hearing that he was sick. When Saul saw that Michal had tricked him, he forgave her because she told him she had no choice.

David came to Samuel in Ramah and told him how Saul tried to kill him with the spear. Samuel took David with him to Naioth for his safety. Saul heard about this and sent some soldiers to bring David back. There were prophets there, and the soldiers also started prophesying. Two more groups of soldiers were sent, and the same thing happened. Even Saul himself came and he became mentally unstable - he lay on the ground all day and night in front of Samuel and David.

David left there and came to Jonathan in a field. He told Jonathan that he was sure his father wanted to kill him. David said that if Jonathan saw sin in him, then Jonathan could kill David himself. Jonathan did not think so, but he was ready to help. David asked Jonathan to explain to Saul that he needed to go to Bethlehem to be at a family event, and so he would be missing at the usual new moon supper with the king. Saul's reaction about David being gone would show Jonathan Saul's true intentions about David. Jonathan in return asked that if something should happen to him, that David would be kind to Jonathan's children. Then they went to a place where they used to practice shooting arrows. David said that after Jonathan knew his father's real feelings, he should shoot three arrows. If he told his servant that they were in front of him and that he should take them away, this would mean that there was nothing to fear from Saul. If he told his servant the opposite, it would mean that David was in danger.

The next day at the new moon, after the king had purified himself, he came to supper. Jonathan sat on his right and Abner the captain on the other side. David's place was empty. The following day it was again empty, and Saul asked about David.

Jonathan explained that he was attending a family feast and that even he, Jonathan, had been invited. Saul became very angry and called him an enemy in partnership with David. He said the Jonathan had no respect for his father or mother, and that his kingdom would not be safe until David was dead. Saul even took his spear and jumped on Jonathan to kill him. He didn't succeed because his friends stopped him but Jonathan plainly saw Saul's hatred for David. Jonathan left the table immediately. He could not eat and cried all night about the attack on himself, and also because of Saul's hate for David.

In the morning he went out to where David was and gave his message with the arrows. He sent his servant home, and David and Jonathan spoke together. David fell at Jonathan's feet, saying that he had saved his soul. Jonathan lifted him up and they hugged and cried a long time. They cried because they were too young to die. They cried because envy was separating them, and the separation would be no better than death itself. They made promises to each other.

xii

DAVID had to run for his life from Saul. He came to the city of Nob to the priest, Ahimelech. The priest wondered why he was alone, and David said he was on a secret mission and was on his way to meet his servants. The priest gave him something to eat and asked if he had any weapons. He answered that he had none, so Ahimelech gave him the sword of Goliath. Doeg, a Syrian who was a keeper of the king's mules, saw everything.

David then went to King Achish in Gath, Philistine territory. Some of the king's servants knew who he was, and they told him how many Philistines David had killed. David was afraid he would be killed so he pretended to be crazy by drooling saliva from his mouth. The king of Gath became angry that they brought David to him, and he sent him away. David then came to the tribe of Judah and stayed in a cave by the city of Adullam (near modern Beit Shemesh). He let some of his people know where he was, so they came to him, together with their families. There were about 400 who were willing to let him lead and protect them.

David came to the Moabites and asked them to take care of his parents, which they did. David then left the desert and went with his people to Hareth, a city in the tribe of Judah near Adullam. Saul heard about this and was afraid that David would harm him. He gathered some of his friends and commanders from his tribe, and he reminded them how he had given them land, and good positions of authority as soldiers. He said, "Do you think that David will give you more than what I have given you? I know that my son Jonathan favors him, but I don't know what promises they made between them. I know that Jonathan is helping those who are against me, and you are not telling me anything." Doeg then told the king about David receiving food and the sword of Goliath from Ahimelech, who safely sent David away. Saul then sent for the high priest and his family, and questioned him about this action. "Were you not aware of how David hates me?" The priest did not deny that he helped David, but he said that he did not think that David was his enemy. "I knew he was a captain over a thousand of your soldiers and also your son-in-law. These are not awards given to an enemy. He told me that he had a job he had to do quickly for you."

Saul was in fear and did not believe the priest, and so he told his soldiers to kill him and his family. They did not want to touch the high priest, so Saul ordered Doeg the Syrian to kill them. Doeg killed 385 people. Saul then ordered that all the priests in Nob be killed along with their families. Nob was totally burned, but one son of Ahimelech, Abiathar, escaped. This was the fulfillment of the prophecy given to Eli that his family would be destroyed because of his two wicked sons.

The city of Nob was a unique place for priests, where they were educated. The people there were holy and humble. By murdering these families, King Saul had done a terrible crime. Abiathar, the one who escaped, went to David and told him how his father and all of those of the priesthood were killed by Saul. David was not surprised, remembering that when he was with the priest, he saw Doeg and expected that he would be falsely accused before Saul. Then David hid Abiathar.

DAVID heard that the Philistines had robbed the country of Keilah. He asked the prophet to find out from God if he should fight against them. The prophet said God answered to go ahead, and so David suddenly attacked them, taking a lot of prisoners and gathering a lot of grain and fruit. Saul heard about his success and thought that it would be a good time, while David was inside a fortified city, to attack the city and kill David. David heard about the plan and escaped with his 400 men to the desert near a city called Engedi. David then moved on to the "New Place" which belonged to Ziph. There Jonathan visited David and encouraged him, happy that David would be the next king and repeating that they would keep their promises to each other. Jonathan made David feel better.

But when Jonathan left, the men of Ziph sided with Saul. They offered to betray David to Saul, but they failed, because David was a man who God loved and they were unjustly wanting to put him to death. David heard that Saul was coming and he left the area, going to a great rock in the desert of Maon. Saul was very close to David and was about to catch him, but just then Saul heard that the Philistines were troubling his people. David escaped and went back to Engedi.

Saul took 3,000 soldiers to Engedi, and he happened to stop by a large cave. He didn't know that David was hiding in the cave with his 400 men. While he was relieving himself in the cave, one of David's friends told him that now was David's chance to get rid of his enemy. David went up behind Saul quietly and cut off a piece of Saul's clothes, but later he felt bad about it. Afterwards he came out of the cave and shouted to Saul, bowing in front of him and asking him why he was listening to wicked men. "No men should be suspicious of their friends! You should believe actions and not pay attention to words. You have been listening to many lies. I never wanted to kill you. Why then are you unjustly chasing me? You see: I could've killed you just now, but I didn't. If I cut this garment, I could just as well cut off your head. May God judge between us." Saul cried and admitted that David would someday be king over all the Hebrews. "Please promise me that you will not kill all my family," he begged. David promised that he would save Saul's family.

Samuel died and was buried in Ramah, his city. He was a gentle, righteous man, and the people cried many days for him. He had served as priest and leader of Israel 12 years after Eli. He served another 18 years together with King Saul.

Nabal, a Ziphite of the city of Maon was very rich with many cattle. Nabal was a wicked man, but he had a wise and beautiful wife. David sent ten of his men when Nabal was cutting the wool of his sheep, asking for some supplies for his soldiers. Nabal asked who their leader was. When he heard that it was David, son of Jesse, he ridiculed David as a servant who had left his master. David was very upset with this answer, since he and his men had been careful not to touch anything of Nabal's. David gathered 400 of his men to attack Nabal and destroy his entire house and family. A shepherd told Nabal's wife that Nabal had been mean to David's men in spite David's good actions.

Abigail, Nabal's wife, loaded some donkeys with many presents and went to meet David. She didn't tell Nabal since he was drunk at the time. When she came to David with his large army, she jumped down from her donkey and bowed before David. She explained that Nabal ("folly") was a fitting name for her husband and she apologized for his bad behavior. She had not seen his servants when they came to Nabal. David accepted the gifts and told her that she had come just in time - he would have killed everyone in the city that same night. He said that God's mercy had brought her to him and he saw that God wanted this meeting. "Nabal has escaped punishment for now, but his evil conduct will someday be his ruin."

Abigail came home to find her husband feasting with many people. Abigal told him only in the morning about bringing supplies to David's army, and he reacted like a dead man. He lived for only another ten days. After David heard about Nabal's death, he understood that God had paid Nabal for his wickedness and had kept David's hands clean. David invited Abigail to come and marry him, because she was wise and righteous and David saw this as well as her beauty. She came, together with her servants and told him that she wasn't worthy to touch even his feet. Then she became his wife.

Saul heard from the Ziphites that David was in their country, and this would be another chance to catch him. Saul came with 3,000 armed men and stopped for the night in Hachilah. David heard about this and sent spies. Then he took Abishai his sister Zeruiah's son, and Ahimelech the Hittite, and went to find Saul. Saul and his armed men were asleep, even Abner the commander. Abishai wanted to kill Saul, but David said that God had anointed him to be king and no one should hurt him. Instead, he took Saul's spear and water jug. Suddenly David shouted out, waking up the men. "It's me, the son of Jesse, whom you have turned into a wanderer. Why isn't your body guard taking care of you, Saul? He deserves the punishment of death. Here's the king's spear and water jug. We could easily have killed King Saul." Saul realized that he owed David thanks for saving him and told him that he would stop chasing him. He at last understood that David loved Saul more than he loved himself. He was sorry that he had made David run in fear for his life, living away from friends and family, and Saul saw that in the end he was losing a good friend. David told Saul's soldiers to come and get the king's things, and that God would be their judge.

Saul had now escaped from David's hands twice, and he went back to his royal palace. David went to the land of the Philistines to be safe from Saul. David had 600 men with him when he came to Achish, the king of Gath, one of the five Philistine cities. David's two wives, Ahinoam and Abigail were were also with him. Saul did not go after David again when he heard where they were.

Achish gave them a place to live. David asked to live in the country instead of the city, so they would be less of a burden, so Achish gave him a village called Ziklag. David's sons later liked Ziklag very much. David and his family were there about five months, and during that time he went out secretly to attack the Geshurites and Amalekites, neighbors of the Philistines. They always won the battles and took much spoil in animals and camels. David sent presents to the king of Achish, but he didn't tell him where he got them. When Achish asked, David told him they were from the Jews in the south, and in this way David got the Philistine's approval. The king hoped to keep David with him all his life, thinking that he had fought against his own people.

xiv

THE Philistines decided to make a surprise attack on the Israelites near Shunem. Achish, the king of Gath wanted David to help them and to be his body guard. David agreed. Saul heard about the plan, so he gathered his soldiers near Shunem. He saw that the Philistine army was too large for him, so he went to the prophets for advice from God. But he didn't get an answer. He knew God had left him, so he looked for a fortune teller to ask if he would win the battle. Saul went to the fortune teller in Endor in disguise, together with two of his servants, and asked her to call up someone from the dead. The woman was not willing; she was afraid of punishment (all fortune tellers in the land had been banned). Saul promised that her act would be kept secret. He asked her to call up Samuel and she did so, not knowing who Samuel was. She was shocked when she suddenly found out that she was doing this for King Saul. Saul pressed her to describe the person who she saw. It was clearly Samuel, and he did not like Saul bothering him. He repeated what had already been said when he was alive; it was about to happen. Saul hadn't obeyed God with the Amalekites, nor had he obeyed God's commandments. "The people will be slaves to their enemies, and you and your sons will fall in battle tomorrow and be with me."

Saul fell on the floor, either because he was upset or because he hadn't eaten for many hours. The woman begged him to eat and wanted to be rid of him quickly so that she wouldn't be discovered. She took her only calf, which she fed herself, and prepared it for Saul and his servants. Saul arrived back at his camp that night. This woman should receive some favor from God, since she risked her life to feed the king, although he had banned fortune tellers like her; she showed compassion and received no payment for it. As for Saul, he remained brave even with the prediction of death hanging over him and his sons. He went out to war without telling anyone of the doom which he had heard from the prophet Samuel.

The Philistines organized their army and marched to the battle field, together with King Achish, who was followed by David with his 600 men. They didn't like this. How could David's men fight against Saul? The other soldiers didn't trust David and said he would betray them, so they sent his soldiers back to guard Ziklag. But while David had been marching with the Philistines, the Amalekites came and burned down Ziklag, taking spoil and prisoners with them. David's wives and children had been taken and he tore his clothes and cried. His companions had the same sorrow, and they almost stoned David because they blamed him for this. He went to Abiathar, the high priest, to ask what to do. The priest told them to go after the Amalekites, and David took 400 men. While they were on the way, they met an Egyptian who was very weak and hadn't eaten for three days. They fed him and he told them that he was with those who had destroyed Ziklag and other Judean cities. David used him as a guide to find the Amalekites. David's army found them easy to overcome, since they were naked, drunk and sleeping. David's army killed them from morning until evening, and only 400 Amalekites escaped by riding their animals and camels. David gathered much spoil, as well as his wives and all the captured families. Then they returned to the 200 men he left guarding the camp. The 400 fighters didn't want to divide the spoil with them. David said that they needed to share God's blessings with those who had watched the camp. It became a law that those who stood guard would get the same reward as those fighting on the front lines. David even sent some of the spoil from the Amalekites to family and friends in the tribe of Judah.

The Philistines killed many Hebrews in battle. King Saul and his sons fought with all their might, knowing that their hope was lost anyway, and all three sons of Saul died. After Jonathan, Abinadab and Malchisua were killed, the Hebrews ran away. Saul had many soldiers around him, but he was too weak to stand from so many wounds. He asked his armor carrier to kill him before the enemy would take him alive, but the man refused. Saul tried to kill himself with a sword but he did not succeed. He then called a young man nearby who was an Amalekite. Saul asked him to kill him, and he did, taking Saul's bracelets and royal crown and running away. When Saul's armor carrier saw that Saul was dead, he killed himself. The king's guards all fell dead on Mount Gilboa. When the Hebrews heard that Saul and his sons had fallen in battle, and that the army was destroyed, they left for stronger and safer places. The Philistines took over the empty cities.

The next day, the Philistines took everything from the dead soldiers. They stripped Saul and his sons and cut off their heads. They then sent messengers around the land to tell about their victory, and they dedicated the captured armor in the temple of Astarte. The bodies of Saul and his sons were hung on crosses on the walls of the city of Bethshan. When the people of Jabesh-Gilead heard that the bodies of Saul and his sons had been treated this way, they could not allow such a thing. The most courageous of them walked all night, took down the bodies and brought them to Jabesh. The people cried and buried the bodies in the best place in their country, called Aroura, and mourned for them for seven days, whole families together. They beat their chests and fasted until the evening.

Saul's death was a fulfillment of Samuel's prophecy. He disobeyed the commandments of God regarding the Amalekites, and he destroyed Ahimelech the high priest, as well as his family and the whole city of the high priests. Saul had reigned while Samuel was alive for 18 years, and another two years after Samuel died.

BOOK VII

FROM THE DEATH OF SAUL TO THE DEATH OF DAVID

DAVID returned to Ziklag after the battle with the Amalekites. A couple of days later, a man escaped from the battle with the Philistines and came to him. David heard about the battle and the tens of thousands of Israelites who had been killed. David was very sad for both Saul and Jonathan, in spite of Saul's attempts to kill him. The man said that he was there when Saul was wounded and was too weak to kill himself. He brought out the gold bracelets which Saul had been wearing and his crown. David found out that this man was an Amalekite and he ordered him to be killed. David wrote some sad songs for Saul and Jonathan, which are still with us.

David asked the prophet of God which city of Judah he should live in. The answer was Hebron, so he left Ziklag, together with his two wives and his soldiers. The people of Judah crowned him king there in Hebron. The people in Jabesh-Gilead had buried Saul and his sons were honored by David and were promised a reward. He told them that he was king in Judah. Abner, Saul's general, when he heard that Saul and his sons were dead, quickly took the remaining son, Ishbosheth, and made him king over the other tribes of Israel. They set up camp in Mahanaim ("The Camps"). Abner was angry that the tribe of Judah had crowned David as their king, and he decided to fight. He was met by David's general Joab (the son of Zeruiah, David's sister). Joab had his brothers Abishai and Asahel with him, as well as his soldiers. The two generals agreed to have twelve soldiers from each side fight against one another, but in the end all 24 died together. It was a horrible fight: they caught each other by the head and ran swords into each other's sides and groins. The rest then started a battle, and Abner's men were beaten. Joab kept chasing Abner, along with young Asahel, who was so fast he could even outrun a horse. Abner turned back to look at him and told him to stop following him. Asahel would not leave, so Abner killed him with a back stroke of his sword.

The other soldiers stopped and gathered around the dead Asahel. But Joab and his brother Abishai kept chasing after Abner. Abner climbed a hill and cried out from there, saying that men of the same nation should not be fighting this way against one another. So both sides quit. Joab stayed there and Abner went back to Mahanaim. Joab counted all the dead and gave them funerals. Abner lost about 360 men and David's army lost 19. Asahel's body was carried to Bethlehem, where he was buried with his fathers. The battles between Saul's men and David's men continued, but Saul's men became weaker.

David had six sons by six wives. Abner went to Saul's maid and Ishbosheth started rumours about him. Abner thought it might be better to join David. He sent some of his men to David to ask him to agree to an alliance. David asked them to bring back his first wife, Michal, to him. Abner's men were accepted, and Abner also urged the tribe of Benjamin (body guards for Ishboshet) to join David, which they did.

Abner left Hebron after meeting with David. Joab, David's general, was afraid that he would lose favor with David. He spoke bad things about Abner, but David didn't listen to him. Then Joab sent some men to run after Abner and say that David had forgotten something and that he needed to speak with him again. As Abner was coming back, Joab met him and spoke kindly to him until they moved away from the others. Only Joab's brother, Abishai was with him. Joab drew his sword and killed Abner in the groin as punishment for killing Joab's brother Asahel in the last battle. But his real reason was to keep his own authority with David. So this reminds us that there are 10,000 evil ways to gain money and authority. And when they are afraid it might be lost, they will do even more wicked things.

When David heard that Abner was killed, he was very upset. He mourned in public and said that he was not involved in Abner's death. He commanded the people to mourn for Abner, to rip their clothes and wear sackcloth and to follow the body to its burial. He followed the body himself with tears. Abner had a very grand burial in Hebron. David's friends tried to get him to eat, but he refused. No one believed that David had anything to do with Abner's death. He said that Joab, his killer, would not go unpunished by God who judges men's actions. David complained that he was not able to change any of the three sons of Zeruiah [including Joab] who were more strong-willed than he was.

ii

ISHBOSHETH was very upset about Abner's death. Shortly afterwards, some Benjamites snuck into an upper room where he and his female body guard were asleep on a hot day, and they killed Ishbosheth and cut off his head. They brought the head to David, thinking he would be pleased to see his enemy dead. David was very upset with them, even more upset than he had been with the man who had killed Saul. He said to them, "You have killed a righteous man in his bed, and you will be punished!" He tormented them in various ways and then killed them. He buried the head of Ishbosheth in the grave of Abner.

After this, all the leading men of the Hebrews came to David. They had a great feast. He told how God had chosen him and given him power to overcome the Philistines. In answer, 6,800 strong men from the tribe of Judah came to him with shields and spears, 7,100 came from the tribe of Simeon and 4,700 from the tribe of Levi. The high priest Zadok came, together with 22 captains. Other tribes also joined them. They brought corn, wine and other food, and David's kingdom became sure. After rejoicing in Hebron for three days, they all went to Jerusalem.

JERUSALEM was inhabited by the Jebusites [Canaanites]. They shut their gates and put the blind, lame and maimed people on the wall, laughing at David and saying that even they could block him from coming in. David began to capture Jerusalem, taking the lower city first. He promised a reward for whoever would first climb through the ditches under the city to capture it. Joab stopped them, however, and he took over.

David threw the Jebusites out of the city and rebuilt Jerusalem, calling it "The City of David." He reigned only seven years and six months in Hebron before moving to Jerusalem. God blessed and prospered him in Jerusalem.

The king of the Tyrians, Hiram made a trade agreement and he supplied David with cedar trees, mechanics, and builders and architects. They built many buildings in the lower city, which was joined to the upper city. Joab was told to take care for their safety. During Abraham's time Jerusalem had been called Salem or Solyma (Hebrew: "shalema" or "security"). From the time of Joshua to this time when David took the city was 515 years.

Araunah, a wealthy Jebusite, was good to the Hebrews and got along with David. David had many wives and concubines. He had a total of 11 sons.

THE Philistines again came with a huge army to attack David in Jerusalem. They waited in a valley called "The Valley of the Giants" not far away. The Israelites always consulted a prophet and God's will before going out to battle. The high priest told them that they would win in spite of the great numbers of the enemy. They were told to wait in a forest called the "Grove of Weeping" and not to move until the trees would move without the wind blowing. When this would happen, they were to run against the enemy. The Israelite army chased them to the city of Gaza, took great wealth from their camp, and destroyed their gods.

David consulted with the elders, rulers and captains to send the best men to Kirjathjearim to bring the ark of God to Jerusalem. He wanted it to be there when the people were offering sacrifices. When they had done this in Saul's time, they did not lose battles with their enemies. The king came with them, and they set the ark on a cart to be drawn by oxen. They sang hymns and danced and played musical instruments. When the oxen shook the ark, Uzza put out his hand to steady it, and God struck him dead. David was afraid that the same could happen to him, so instead of bringing it to Jerusalem he went to the house of a righteous man named Obededom, who was a Levite. The ark stayed with him for three months. Obededom's house was very blessed during this time.

The ark was then taken to Jerusalem with much singing, and harp playing by David. Michal, Saul's daughter, saw David doing this and laughed at him. He put the ark in the tabernacle and offered expensive sacrifices to God. They he passed out bread, cake, another cake in a pan and a piece of meat to everyone. After the feast everyone went home.

Michal, David's wife, wished him much happiness and God's blessing when he returned home. But she accused him of dancing in an improper way among the servants and maids. He said that he wasn't ashamed to dance before God, who had preferred him over her father, and he didn't mind what others thought. Michal had no children from David but had five children from her other husband.

David had a tall house made of cedar, but the ark was in a tent, so he wanted to build a temple for God. Also Moses had predicted that a temple would be built someday. David spoke with Nathan the prophet, who urged him to go ahead since God was with him. That night, however, God appeared to Nathan and told him that although he approved of David's desire (the first time someone had this idea), he did not want David to build his temple, because he was a man of war. The temple would be built by his son instead, whose name would be called Solomon. This son should be careful not to sin, however, otherwise he would be punished by disease and barren land. David received a promise that he would become famous. He came to the ark, bowed down and began to thank God for all of his goodness in raising him from the shepherd's field up to a position of honor. He thanked God for the freedom which the Hebrews now enjoyed. He sang a hymn of praise to God and went home.

IN order for David's children to live in peace, he realized that it was time to go to war against the Philistines. He won those battles, and more land was added to the Hebrews. He then went against the Moabites and overcame two thirds of their army, taking the last third captive and collecting an annual tax from the people. Then he went against Hadadezer, the son of Rehob, king of Sophene (near the Euphrates River). He destroyed 20,000 footmen, 7,000 horsemen and most of the chariots, keeping only 100 of them. When Hadad, king of Damascus and Syria heard that David fought against his friend, he came against David and lost. But Hadad's children were strong, and the third king after him defeated the Jews in Samaria when Ahab was king of Israel.

David went up against Damascus and other parts of Syria and captured them. He kept guards there who would collect taxes. He dedicated some of the Syrian army's armor to God in Jerusalem, as well as other wealth which was in later days taken from Jerusalem. David took another three cities by force, destroyed them and brought home much gold, silver and brass to be used. One kind of brass, said to be more valuable than gold, and was later used for the "Bronze Sea," a giant washing pool for the temple.

The king of Hamath heard about Hadadezer's defeat and he decided to make friends with David before he would come against him. He brought David many presents, such as special items made of gold, silver and brass. David dedicated them to

God. God also gave Abishai, the brother of Joab the general, success in battle over the Idumeans (Edomites). They had men staying there who gathered taxes from the people. David appointed a record keeper, a high priest, a scribe and the body guards. He ruled with justice and truth.

David also remembered the promises he made to his friend Jonathan, and he asked if there were any of Saul's family still alive. He still felt that he should do something in memory of his friendship with Jonathan who was dead. He heard of a son named Mephiboshet who was still alive and who was lame. When his nurse heard that the baby's father and grandfather had died in battle, she picked him up to run away with him, but he fell off her shoulders and his feet were severely injured. David sent for him from the city of Lodebar. Mephiboshet bowed down before David but David urged him to expect better times. He gave him Saul's house and invited him to eat with David. David ordered his servant Ziba to take care of Saul's land and to bring the profits to Jerusalem. Ziba, who had 15 sons and five servants himself, all promised to do what David asked. Mephiboshet lived like David's own son. Mephiboshet also had a son named Micha.

NAHASH, the king of the Ammonites died. He had been David's friend, so David sent messengers to his son to comfort him. David also sent a message that he hoped the same kindness would be in him as in his father. Some Ammonite princes felt that the Israelites were just spying and they told the new king not to be fooled. So Nahash's son treated David's ambassadors very badly, cutting off half of their beards and half of their clothes. This really upset David and he decided to go against the Ammonites in battle. The Ammonites paid the king of Mesopotamia to help them in the war, along with another two kings. David ordered Joab to attack Rabbah, the great Ammonite city. Joab sent his brother Abishai to lead the army on one side while Joab and his men fought on the other. They won and returned joyfully to Jerusalem.

The Ammonites were still not quiet and they paid the Syrians to help them against the Hebrews. David crossed the Jordan River and led his army against the Ammonites by himself, without his generals. He killed 40,000 of the enemy's foot soldiers and 7,000 of their horsemen. He wounded the Syrian king, who later died. The people of Mesopotamia surrendered to David and sent him presents. It was winter and David returned to Jerusalem. In the spring he sent Joab to fight the Ammonites again, and he defeated them.

DAVID was a righteous man who kept God's laws. Late one evening while walking as he was used to doing, he saw a woman washing herself in her house. She was very beautiful and her name was Bathsheba. He couldn't control himself and he sent for her and slept with her. She told David that she was carrying a child from him. Those who committed adultery were supposed to be punished by death.

The king sent for Joab's armor carrier, named Uriah, who was this woman's husband. He asked Uriah about the army and what was happening. He ate with David and then David sent him home to sleep with his wife. But Uriah slept near the king with the rest of his armor carriers, saying that it wouldn't be right to sleep with his wife while the other soldiers had to sleep on the ground in the camp and in an enemy's land. The next evening David again invited him for supper, and the king caused him to drink until he was drunk. But again he slept on the ground with his fellow soldiers. David was angry and wrote to Joab that Uriah had offended him. He said Uriah should be punished without saying why. David asked Joab to put Uriah in the most dangerous place in a battle, so that he would likely to be killed.

Joab told Uriah that he would be given good soldiers to help break down part of the wall and enter the city. Uriah was grateful that he, being a brave soldier, was chosen to do this job. He gave orders to his companions. The Ammonites brought their best soldiers, opened the gates suddenly and ran violently upon the Hebrews. Uriah's soldiers let him meet the enemy alone as Joab had ordered them. Uriah killed many but he was killed at last, along with some other soldiers.

Joab sent word back to David that they did their best to take the city but there were great losses, including the death of Uriah. First David was very angry and told them that they should not have attacked the wall. He reminded them that when Abimelech, the son of Gideon, was taking the tower in Thebes, he was killed by a large stone thrown down on him by an old woman. They had used the wrong strategy. But David felt better when he heard about Uriah's death. He told the messengers to return to Joab and tell him that this is a common tragedy in wartime and that they should use protection and machines in attacking the city. They should destroy everyone inside.

Bethsheva mourned for her husband Uriah many days. Then David took her to be his wife and she gave birth to a son. God was very angry at David and appeared to Nathan the prophet in his sleep. Nathan told David a parable about a sheep in order to give God's message to David. David understood that just as the one sheep of a poor man had been stolen wrongfully, so he had stolen Bathsheva from another man and then caused his death in the battle. He had been a righteous man up to now, and he realized his sin. Because he confessed his sin, God promised that he would keep his life and his kingdom.

The baby who was born became very sick. David fasted for the baby for seven days and wore a black cloth and lay on the floor. David knew by watching the servants that something was wrong: the baby had died. He got up, washed himself, dressed in white and came to the tabernacle of God. He also began to eat. His servants were puzzled, and he explained that it was worthwhile to fast only when he wasn't sure if God might heal the baby or not. They were impressed with the king's wisdom. He slept with Bathsheba again and she had another son. Nathan the prophet had said that his name should be Solomon.

Joab cut off the water supply of the Ammonites. Joab wrote to the king, asking him to come and finish the battle so that David might have the honor of the victory. The king came and destroyed Rabbah and his soldiers took the spoils of war. David himself took the king's crown which had a sardonyx stone in the middle. Afterwards David wore this crown. He found many valuable things in the city. He tormented the people and then killed them. He took other cities of the Ammonites by force as well.

viii

AFTER David had returned to Jerusalem, a very sad event took place with Tamar, David's unmarried daughter who was very beautiful. Tamar had the same mother as Absalom. David's oldest son (from a different wife), Amnon, loved her. He couldn't eat and began to be thin and pale. Jonadab, a friend of his, suggested a plan to get Tamar alone so that Amnon would get what he wanted. Amnon followed this advice and raped Tamar. After this Amnon lost his love and instead hated her. He threw her outside in the daytime, so people came to know what happened. She tore her loose coat which virgins of those times wore tied at the hands and down to the ankles, hiding their inner coats. She put ashes on her head and went into the middle of the city, crying because of what had happened. Absalom met and asked her what had happened. He comforted her and told her to be patient and not to consider it an injury. She stopped crying and lived as a widow with her brother Absalom.

David especially loved Amnon, but Absalom wanted revenge. Two years passed, and Absalom invited his father and family for a feast at the time of the sheep shearing. David asked to be excused but the others came. Absalom told his servants to watch when Amnon would become sleepy from the wine, and when he gave them a signal, they were to kill him.

When it happened, the other brothers were afraid for their lives and left on horseback, riding back to David. But before they got home, a false rumor went out that Absalom had killed all of his sons. David tore his clothes and lay on the ground crying for all of his sons. Jonadab told him that he didn't believe the sons had all been killed. Then many horses showed up with David's sons, and they cried together for the one son who had been killed. Absalom ran away to Geshur, to his grandfather on his mother's side who was king there, and he stayed there three years.

Time passed and David sent for Absalom, after Joab sent an old lady to speak a sort of parable to King David, so that he would agree to receive Absalom. David heard her parable and made a merciful decision, and then she pressed him to follow through in real life in the same way with his son Absalom. David understood that he had been tricked by Joab, but it worked. So Joab went and brought Absalom back to Jerusalem. Absalom was in Jerusalem two years and became the father of three sons and one daughter. His beautiful daughter married Rehoboam, the son of Solomon.

Joab was asked to do Absalom a favor and contact David, but because he did not do it, Absalom set fire to his field. When Joab came running, Absalom explained to Joab that staying in Geshur would be better than to be here when David did not agree to see him. So Joab spoke to the king for him. They finally met and Absalom threw himself on the ground before David. David raised him up and promised to forget his evil deed of revenge against Amnon.

ix

AFTER Absalom gained David's favor, he began to quickly collect many horses and chariots. He had 50 body guards, and every day he would come to the king's palace. He talked with many people and told those who lost their cases in court that they should have won – he would be more just than the king's counselors. He became popular, and after four years, he asked his father David if he could go and make a sacrifice in Hebron. Many people came with him, including Ahithophel, one of David's counselors, and another 200 men who only came for the sacrifice. While there, they made Absalom king.

When word reached David, he was very upset – he had only recently forgiven Absalom, and now his son was trying to take not only on the kingdom but his own father's life. David left with his closest friends and crossed the Jordan River. He left the palace with his ten concubines. The same 600 armed men joined him who had been with him when he fought Saul. He told the priests to stay behind with the ark, and he hoped that he would manage without them. He was upset that Ahithophel had chosen to be with Absalom, and David prayed that God would cause Absalom not to trust him. Hushai, David's faithful friend, saw David's sadness and comforted him. David asked Hushai to return to Absalom as a spy, to understand what Absalom was planning, and hopefully convince him not to listen to Ahithophel's advice.

David met Ziba, Mephibosheth's servant, who came with many supplies for David and his men. David asked about Mephibosheth, and Ziba said that Mephibosheth was hoping to become king. David was upset, and he gave to Ziba everything that belonged to Mephibosheth, which made Ziba very happy.

As David was leaving Israel, a relative of Saul, Shimei, threw stones at him and spoke badly to David, calling him a bloody man. He said God was punishing David by taking the kingdom away because he had done harm to Saul. Abishai wanted to kill Shimei, but David stopped him. He said, "I will not worry about this dog. I trust in God. I will have to put up with this abuse, since I am getting the same treatment even from one of my sons." When they came to the Jordan River, David allowed his men to rest.

So Absalom and Ahithophel came into Jerusalem. Hushai showed up and praised Absalom. Absalom asked why someone who was on David's side had suddenly come to his side. Hushai replied, "We ought to follow God and whoever God favors. Besides, most of the people are with you." Absalom believed him.

For advice, Absalom called Ahithopel, who urged him to sleep with his father's concubines, which would show that he was against David. He stayed in a tent on top of the royal palace where everyone could see, and he slept with his father's concubines. Nathan had prophesied that this would happen.

Absalom then asked Ahithophel if he should go to war against David. Ahithophel said that with 10,000 of the best soldiers he would kill David. Absalom asked Hushai's advice as well. Hushai pointed out how successful David had been in many battles, and how he was good at surprising the enemy. He advised Absalom to gather many men to fight with David, with himself as the general. "David will be in some city, and then we will attack it and take him." God caused Absalom to take Hushai's advice over Ahithophel's.

Hushai sent word to the high priests, who went to warn David of the plan. Some riders saw them and they looked for a place to hide. A woman hid them in a well. When the riders asked her, she said they had come there and already left. The priests finally reached David and told him of the plan, so they quickly crossed the Jordan.

Ahithophel, after seeing his advice rejected, rode on his donkey to Gilon, his country and called his family together. He told them that he would soon die when David would return and be king again. He felt it was best that he take his own life rather than to be punished by David. So he went into an inner room of his house where he killed himself by hanging.

David came to Mahanaim, a nice and very strong city. The leaders all received him kindly and gave him all the supplies he and his men needed. They had beds, blankets, plenty of meat to eat, wine and bread.

X

ABSALOM gathered a huge army together, and crossed the Jordan River to be near David and his army. He chose Amasa to be captain.

David had about 4,000 men and he divided them into three parts. Joab led one part, Abishai Joab's brother led another, and Ittai commanded the third. David was not allowed to be in the battle. So David asked them to not kill Absalom.

Joab and Absalom fought with much courage. David's men began to win, taking some prisoners, and killing around 20,000 in all. David's men ran after Absalom, who got on the king's mule and escaped. But his hair got tangled in a huge spreading tree, and his mule kept going. One of David's soldiers saw Absalom hanging by his hair. Joab said, "If you had shot and killed him, I would've given you 50 shekels*." The soldier answered, "Even if you would give me 1,000 shekels* I wouldn't have killed him, because he is David's son." Joab asked where he was, and he shot Absalom in the heart. Joab's armor-carrier took down the body and threw it into a pit, and put many stones over it. After this they stopped chasing Absalom's army.

Absalom had already set up a marble pillar close to Jerusalem called Absalom's Hand, saying that if his children were killed, his name would still be remembered. He had three sons and one daughter, Tamar, who later married David's grandson, Rehoboam and had a son, Abijah, who became a king.

Ahimaaz went to Joab and asked to tell David of the victory which God had given them. Joab sent Cushi instead. Ahimaaz said that he would not tell David about Absalom's death, only about the rest. So Ahimaaz was allowed to go, and he took a quicker road than Cushi. David was waiting for news of the battle. The watchmen recognized Ahimaaz, the high priest's son. First he bowed to David, then he said that as soon as the enemy was defeated, he left the battle and came to David. Meanwhile, Cushi arrived and bowed to David. He said, "May our enemies be like your son, Absalom." David knew that Absalom was dead.

David went up to the highest part of the city and cried for Absalom, beating his chest and tearing his hair, tormenting himself. He said that he wished he had died instead of Absalom. He especially loved Absalom above the other sons. Joab saw his extreme sorrow and told him that he was giving the impression to everyone that he hated those who loved him, and loved those who hated him. "We see now that if we had all died and Absalom were still alive, you would only want him. Please come out to your soldiers and thank them for this victory - otherwise, I myself will tell the people to leave you and choose another king!" David came to his senses and changed his behavior. He sat at the gate and properly greeted the people.

xi

THE Hebrews from the tribe of Judah who had followed Absalom realized that they now needed to return to David, since Absalom was dead. David sent word to them through the high priests: since he was from the tribe of Judah, they ought to come - all was forgiven. Amasa was to be their leader. They crossed the Jordan River and met David.

Shimei also came with 1,000 men from the tribe of Benjamin. Ziba and his sons and servants also came. Shimei held David's feet and begged for David's forgiveness, which was given. Abishai, Joab's brother, said that he should die for cursing the king. David calmed him down and said that he didn't need any new trouble. All past events would be forgiven.

Then Mephibosheth came. He had been in mourning since David left his throne, and had not been taking care of himself. David asked him why he didn't come away from Jerusalem with him. It turned out that Mephibosheth had been treated like a slave by Ziba at the time, and Ziba had lied about him. David did not punish Ziba or Mephibosheth, but he gave back to Mephibosheth half of the estate which had mistakenly been passed to Ziba. Mephibosheth refused it, saying that he was only thankful that David had come back as their king.

David wanted Barzillai the Gileadite, a good and important man who had provided for him at Mahanaim, to join him and to live in Jerusalem. But Barzillai said that he was 80 years old and preferred to remain where he was, in spite all of the advantages he would have received. David asked for Barzillai's son to come with him instead, and he agreed to that. David arrived in Gilgal with about half of the people of Israel and the whole tribe of Judah.

The leaders of the other eleven tribes complained to the leaders of Judah that they had come first to David in a secret way. They said that David didn't belong only to them but to all of Israel. The leaders of Judah said that they had not received any gifts from David for coming first.

Then Sheba from the tribe of Benjamin, a known troublemaker, saw his chance. He shouted out, "We have no part in David!" He blew a trumpet and declared war against David, and gathered all the tribes to himself except the tribe of Judah.

David was settled back in Jerusalem. He moved his concubines to another house and provided well for them but no longer slept with them. He appointed Amasa as captain (in place of Joab) and ordered the army to report to him within three days. They would fight this Sheba. But after three days, David didn't want to wait any longer. He told Joab that they needed to put down Sheba's rebellion, or it would be worse than the damage Absalom had caused.

Joab took 600 men and went quickly to find Sheba. He met Amasa's army on the way. Joab dropped his sword on purpose when he got near Amasa; then he grabbed Amasa's beard and thrust the sword into his stomach. He had killed Abner for the same reason – jealousy – but because Abner had killed Joab's brother, people understood. This time he killed a relative who hadn't done him any harm.

He then went off to kill Sheba, who was inside of a strong city. Joab wasn't allowed in, so he was going to tear the city down.

A woman, who was not important, but who was wise, spoke to Joab and urged him to spare all of the innocent people in the city. He agreed and asked the people only to turn Sheba over to his army because he had rebelled against King David. The woman urged the people to cut off Sheba's head, reminding them that David had only done them good and should not be opposed. After Sheba's head was given to them, Joab's army left the city in peace. He returned to Jerusalem and became general of all of the people. David also appointed some new officials for the tax collecting, recording and for the priesthood.

THERE was a bad famine in the land, and David asked God why. The prophets answered that God wanted them to make things right with the Gibeonites. King Saul hadn't kept Joshua's promise to them, and many had been killed. The king went to them and asked what they wanted. They wanted to have seven sons of Saul given to them for punishment. David found seven to give them, but he saved Mephibosheth. After these sons of Saul were killed, God sent the rain, and the country again had crops and fruit.

David made more wars against the Philistines and won. One time, when he was alone and tired, a son of the giants saw him. He ran at David, but Abishai, Joab's brother saw him in time and the king was protected by his shield and saved. The commanders, after seeing that David was in danger, told him not to join them in battle again.

There were three more battles with the Philistines. In the first one, a Hittite, a brave soldier, killed many sons of the giants. In a second victory, some strong Philistines were forced to run away. In the third, there was a man coming against the Israelites who was six cubits tall (9 feet or almost 3 meters), with an extra finger on each hand and an extra toe on each foot, but the Philistines still lost. This was the end of their battles against the Israelites.

During the time of peace, David wrote songs and hymns to God. He taught the Levites to sing them for the Sabbath and other festivals. They played on musical instruments. The viol had 10 strings and one used a bow. The psaltery had twelve musical notes and was played with the fingers. The cymbals were large and were made of brass.

David had 38 brave men who went everywhere with him. The most famous of them are these five:

Jessai, an expert in surprise attacks, did not stop until he had killed 900 of the enemy.

Eleazar, son of Dodo, was with the king at Arasam. He fought alone against many Philistines, killing so many of them that his sword stuck to his hand. Later the army came and helped him take the spoils.

Sheba, son of Ilus, also single-handedly killed many and chased the others.

These three brought David water from the pit near the gate in Bethlehem, because David was talking about how good that water was. They dared to walk right past the Philistines, who were so surprised they let them alone. David refused to drink it because they had risked their lives. Instead he poured out the water to God, thanking him that they had come back safe.

Abishai, Joab's brother, killed 600 in one day.

Benaiah, from the priestly line, overcame two important Moabites. He also killed an Egyptian with the enemy's own spear. Once when snow was on the ground, a lion fell into a pit and was roaring, because he couldn't escape. Benaiah jumped in and killed him with a sharp stick which was there.

David's other 33 men were also very brave.

xiii

MOSES had told the Hebrews that if the people were counted, each must pay to God a half shekel. David forgot this and commanded his captain Joab to count everyone. Joab thought it was a bad idea but he obeyed. He took the tribal leaders and the scribes with him, and returned to David after nearly ten months. He didn't number the tribe of Benjamin or Levi. But the others numbered 900,000 men who were able to be soldiers. Judah alone had 40,000 men.

The prophets told David that God was angry at him for counting the people. Nathan told him to choose one of three ways in which God would judge them: Famine would come for seven years, there would be war for three months, or a fatal disease would break out on the people for three days. The king thought famine would be a bad choice, since he had food stored up and the people would see that he and his family did not suffer from it. If he chose war, he wouldn't be affected since he had body guards.

He also knew that it would be better to fall into the hands of God than those of men. Nathan declared to God that he had chosen the disease.

It was so bad that people suddenly died with great pain. Some were so thin there was hardly a body to bury. Some died while they were burying a family member. Some were choked, and saw only darkness. In this manner, 70,000 died in one day. David put on sackcloth and lay upon the ground, begging God to stop this disease. He said that he and his family should be punished but not the innocent people.

God caused the disease to stop and commanded the prophet to go to David. David was to go right away to the threshing floor of Araunah, the Jebusite, and build an altar to God and offer sacrifices. When Araunah saw David and his servants, he ran ahead and bowed to him because he was a friend of David's. This is how he as a Jebusite had survived. David said that he wanted to buy the threshing floor to offer a sacrifice. Araunah said that he would give it to David for free, as well as the plows and the oxen for the burnt offering. The king thanked him but said that he would not offer a sacrifice which didn't cost him anything.

So David paid 50 shekels* for the threshing floor. He built an altar, offered a burnt offering and a peace offering. This was the same place where Abraham had offered his son Isaac for a burnt offering, but a ram appeared and was offered instead of Isaac. When David saw that God had heard his prayer, he called that place "The Altar of All the People." He would later build a temple to God there. The prophet later told him that it would be his son who would build it.

xiv

DAVID counted the strangers in his kingdom, and they were 180,000. Some worked in stone, some carried the stone, and others were the foremen. They used a lot of iron, brass and cedar trees from Tyre and Sidon. All of this would wait for when his son would start the work of building the temple. David told his son that due to all the wars he had fought, God had told him not to build the temple. It would be built in a time of peace [Solomon's name had been given by God and meant "peace"]. Solomon would rule in a time when there would not be rebellions either, the greatest of all blessings. David told his son that even before he was born he had been chosen by God for this job, so he was to be religious, righteous and brave. "Keep the laws of Moses, and do not allow the people to break them. Do not be afraid of the size of the task, since I have prepared the material ahead of time." He listed how much gold, silver and other materials were gathered. David told the rulers of the people that they should help Solomon in building the temple, and be religious and righteous. Then God would bring them peace and success. "After the temple is built, the ark will be put inside and all of the holy things. We should have had a temple long ago, but your fathers neglected God's commands."

David was old and cold and suffered from numbness. The doctors agreed that a beautiful virgin should be chosen from the whole country, who could keep him warm. They found Abishag who succeeded in warming him, but David did not sleep with her.

The fourth son of David was very tall and handsome, named Adonijah. He gathered many chariots and horses and had fifty body guards running in front of him. His father didn't question him. Joab, the captain of the army, and Abiathar, the high priest, helped Adonijah. Those who opposed him were Zadok the high priest, Nathan the prophet, Benaiah captain of the guards, and David's friend Shimei. Adonijah prepared a feast but didn't invite Solomon and the others in the opposition. Nathan told Bathsheba about this, and said that David was not aware that Adonijah was rising in power. Nathan urged her to speak right away to David, because she was aware that Solomon was to be the next king, and he promised to go to David after her. After she bowed to David, Bathsheba told him all that Nathan had told her to say. She told him about Adonijah's feast and who had been invited. She said that all were looking up to David to know who he would name as the next king. If Adonijah would be king, she and Solomon would be killed. David's guard came as they were talking and said that Nathan was outside. Nathan asked David if he had passed the kingdom to Adonijah. David asked for Bathsheba to return to the room. Then David swore by Almighty God that Solomon would be king as he had promised before. "And he shall become king today." Bathsheba bowed down to him and wished him a long life.

The king sent for Zadok and Benaiah, and he ordered them to take Nathan the prophet and all the armed men around the palace, to set Solomon on the king's mule and to carry him out to the Gihon fountain, and to anoint him with holy oil and make him king. He was then to be brought through the city with trumpets blowing. David charged his son to rule over all the Hebrews and especially the tribe of Judah, religiously and righteously. They did as David had commanded. Solomon was set on the throne, and there was much joy and celebration. The people danced to musical pipes and the earth and air echoed with the music.

When Adonijah and his guests heard this, they became very upset and no one ate. A messenger told them what had happened, and they left the feast and ran home. Adonijah was frightened and ran to God's tent and took hold of the horns of the altar (asking to be saved from death). Solomon was told that he was afraid and that he wanted a promise that he wouldn't be punished. Solomon answered that he was forgiven, but if he tried any further rebellion, he would be punished for trying to take the kingdom. Solomon raised him up and told Adonijah to go home and show that he was a worthy man.

David called all the people together and appointed those who would be responsible for taking care of the temple, and those who were to be judges, scribes, porters and musicians. The priests served for eight days at a time. There were 24 courses of priests in all, and the timing was determined by lots. The Levites kept the treasures and the donations. They served together with the priests in the temple day and night, as Moses had ordered.

The army was divided into twelve parts, with their captains of hundreds and commanders. They would wait on Solomon in shifts of 30 days. Some would watch the treasures, and some would be assigned to the villages, the fields or the animals. David told about his desire to build the temple, a job which was passed to his son. He said, "Jacob had 12 sons, but Judah was appointed to be king [sic]. I was chosen over my six brothers. I want none of my sons to go against Solomon, since we all know that God has chosen him. The brothers will all receive the benefit. If you, Solomon, continue to be a religious and righteous man and observe God's laws, you will know happiness. If not, expect trouble."

David continued explaining details of the temple building project, like the measures and weights of the dishes. He said that the work should be easy, since he had already gathered the materials for Solomon, including stonecutters and carpenters. The people were willing and gave more rich gifts for the temple, including precious stones.

David then blessed God, calling him in a loud voice, "the Father and Parent of the universe, and the Author of human and divine things," which he had given to Solomon, the leader and guardian of the Hebrew nation, and of its happiness, and of that kingdom which he had given his son. He prayed for the happiness of all of the people. He told the people to bless God. They all fell down on the ground and worshipped him. They gave thanks to David for the time of his reign. The next day they offered tens of thousands of sacrifices. The king feasted all day, together with the people, and they anointed Solomon a second time with oil as king, and Zadok as the high priest for everyone. Solomon sat on the throne and the people obeyed him.

David called Solomon to himself when he felt he was about to die. He reminded his son to be righteous towards the people and God-fearing, and to keep God's laws and commandments in order to keep the kingdom in their family line for all time. "Be aware of Joab, who killed two generals out of envy. I did not punish him, but you may do so. The son of Barzillai deserves continued honor, since we owe a debt to his father. Shimei I forgave, but he does deserve punishment for an act of betrayal against an anointed king." David gave some more advice about public affairs and about his friends. He then died at age 70. He had reigned 7 ½ years in Hebron over the tribe of Judah, and 33 years in Jerusalem over all Israel. He was a virtuous king. He went into danger and motivated his subjects to act in the same way without being a tyrant. He judged matters well and made wise decisions. The only mistake he made was with the wife of Uriah. He left behind him greater wealth than any other known king.

He was buried with a grand funeral. Much wealth was buried with him. We know this because 1300 years later, during a siege by Antiochus (the Greek king), the Jewish high priest opened one room of David's tomb and took out 3,000 talents* in order to end the siege. Then many years after this, Herod, the king of Judea, opened another room and took out much money. But no one reached the actual coffins of the kings since they were cleverly buried and were not found.

BOOK VIII

FROM THE DEATH OF DAVID TO THE DEATH OF AHAB

i

SOLOMON was very young when he became king. It was hoped that he would also reign until old age as David had done. Adonijah, the son who had tried to be the king while David was alive, came to Bathsheba and said that he still felt he should have become king, since he was older than Solomon. He would be contented, however, to be a servant under Solomon. He wished to ask his brother a favor: He wanted to marry Abishag, who had slept next to David but who was still a virgin. Bathsheba agreed to ask Solomon for this. Bathsheba entered the throne room, and a throne was set for her as well. She started out by saying that she only had one request, and that she hoped Solomon would grant it. Solomon replied that he meant to always agree to anything she would ask, and he wondered why she talked as though he might say no.

When Solomon heard that Adonijah wanted to marry Abishag, he was very angry and sent his mother away. He understood that not Adonijah had greater things in mind and could even take the kingdom. Adonijah also had strong friends like Joab and Abiathar the priest. He called for his captain and ordered him to kill Adonijah. He told Abiathar that he would not be killed, but he must stay in his home town and not come to Jerusalem anymore. From then on, the house of Ithamar did not continue in the priesthood, just as God had foretold to Eli, the grandfather of Abiathar. The priesthood was transferred to Zadok from the family of Phineas.

When Joab had heard that Adonijah had been killed, he was afraid since he was a closer friend to him than to Solomon. He ran to the altar in God's tent, and felt he would be safe there. Solomon ordered Joab to come to him, but he refused to leave. He said he would rather die there than elsewhere. Benaiah told the king his answer, and Solomon commanded that his head be cut off there. After Benaiah killed him he became the chief army captain in Joab's place.

As for Shimei, Solomon told him to build a house in Jerusalem, and he was not to leave the city or he would die. He even forced him to make an oath. Three years later, two of his servants ran away to Gath and he ran after them. The king heard of this and became very angry. He reminded him of the oath. "You had abused my father, and now you don't keep your word to me." When a crime isn't punished immediately, the punishment grows with the passing time. The king commanded Benaiah to kill Shimei, which he did.

ii

SOLOMON was married to the Egyptian Pharaoh's daughter. The Hebrews had won the battles against their enemies, and now they were building the walls of Jerusalem larger and stronger than before. Solomon ruled with wisdom and success greater than a normal man his age. He went to Hebron to offer sacrifices on the bronze altar which Moses had built. He offered 1,000 burnt offerings. God appeared to him in his sleep that night, and asked him to choose a reward. Solomon pleased God because he didn't ask for riches as most people would have. He asked for a quick mind and good understanding to be able to judge the people with truth and righteousness. God gave him his request – and also riches and victory over his enemies. As long as he acted like his father in doing good, God said, he would rule for a long time. When Solomon woke up, he again worshipped God and returned to Jerusalem, where he feasted with his family.

Once he had to make a difficult decision about two 3-day-old babies born in the same house. One baby had died because his mother rolled over him in her sleep; the other was alive and well. Both women said the live baby was theirs. Solomon discovered that the true mother was the one who was willing to give the live baby to the other woman, rather than to see him die. The people understood that God had given Solomon special wisdom.

Solomon chose army captains and officers for the different parts of the country. The tribe of Judah was especially rich in farming, because there was peace in the country and they could work without anyone bothering them. The land became more valuable. Solomon's kingdom reached from the Euphrates River to Egypt. In these areas they paid money to Solomon, and they sent many supplies for Solomon's family and his workers. Solomon had 40,000 chariots and horses, and 12,000 horsemen.

The Egyptians at this time were famous for their knowledge, but Solomon was even wiser than that. He wrote 1,005 songs and many parables. He knew about many subjects, and understood trees, animals and fish. He also knew how to chase demons out of people. I (Josephus) saw a man named Eleazar use a cure that Solomon invented. He put a ring into the nose of a demon-possessed man and pulled the demon out. The man fell down and Eleazar repeated some verses that Solomon had written. Eleazar proved to the Romans who were watching that the demon had come out by putting a dish of water at a distance. If the demon knocked over the dish, it showed that it left the man for good. This made Solomon very popular as a man who truly heard from God.

Hiram, the king of Tyre, had been a good friend of David. He sent messengers to congratulate Solomon. Solomon told him about his desire to build a temple for God and asked to buy wood from Tyre. He was willing to pay whatever was needed. Hiram answered that he would send wood by floating the logs down the sea to Israel. "Then your people will carry them to Jerusalem. In exchange we need corn [sic, wheat], since we live on an island."

The copies of these letters are still kept by the Jews and the people in Tyre.

As soon as Solomon received the reply, he began sending wheat, oil and wine to the king of Tyre every year. King Solomon had 30,000 workers who worked on building the temple in three shifts. They went to work cutting trees in Tyre for one month and had two months off. There were tens of thousands of foreign workers who carried stones and other materials. Large stones were cut in the country and fitted together, and later brought into Jerusalem. Some of Hiram's workers also worked in Jerusalem.

iii

SOLOMON began to build the temple 592 years after the Hebrews left Egypt. It was the fourth year of his rule. Hiram had already been king of Tyre for eleven years.

The foundation was laid very deep in the ground with the strongest possible stones. White stones were used for the visible part of the temple, which stood sixty cubits* high. Another building was built on top of this one, which was also sixty cubits.* The doorway faced east. There was a porch, and around the temple were thirty small rooms which had passages between them. The roof of the temple was made of cedar wood. The middle walls were made strong by very long cedar beams. Gold plates with carving on them were nailed on the beams, causing the entire temple to shine. There were many precious stones in the walls, and they were set into the walls without using hammers. Boards of cedar inside and out were held together by thick chains, which made a very strong building.

The center room of the temple had cedar doors covered with gold. The curtains which hung in front of the door were made of blue, purple, and red cloth, and soft linen with flower designs. There were two solid gold angels (cherubim) inside the temple, and their wings touched the ends of the room on one side and covered the ark on the other side. The floor was of made of plates of gold. The inside of the temple was all gold.

Hiram of Tyre was from the tribe of Naphtali on his mother's side. He was an expert craftsman in gold, silver and brass. There were two hollow brass pillars eighteen cubits* high. Their tops had lily and palm designs. On this network 200 pomegranates were hung in two rows.

There was a brass washing pool which was called a sea because it was so large. In the middle under it was a pillar, and ten spirals surrounded it. There were twelve oxen looking up, three in each of the four directions, which looked like they were holding up the pool. The priests would wash their hands and feet here as they entered the temple.

There were other smaller washing pools, standing on small pillars and having carvings of lions, bulls and eagles. These could be moved on wheels. They were for washing the animals for sacrifice.

The altar was made of brass, as well as tools for sacrifices like pots, shovels, bowls, candle trimmers and tongs. They shone brightly like gold. There was a table made of gold to hold the bread. There were 10,000 smaller tables which held gold and silver jars and cups. There were 10,000 candlesticks to keep Moses' command have candles lit in the daytime.

There were 80,000 pitchers and 100,000 golden jars, and twice as many silver jars for the offerings made of flour. There were 20,000 golden pans for carrying incense to the altar and others for carrying fire from the large altar to the smaller one. The high priest had 1,000 pieces of clothing, along with a long robe, an oracle (the plate that was used to ask God questions) and its precious stones. There was only one crown, on which Moses had written the name of God. There were many fine linen garments for every priest, made with a purple belt. There were 200,000 trumpets made, and 200,000 garments for the singers who were Levites, and many musical instruments. Psalteries (an ancient guitar) and harps were made of the finest brass.

Solomon did not write down the cost since it all was for the honor of God. He put a fence around the temple 3 cubits* high to keep the people from coming inside. Only the priests were allowed inside.

SOLOMON'S temple was built over a period of seven years, a very short time. He ordered all of the Hebrews to gather in Jerusalem to see the temple and to be there when the holy things were moved from the tent to the temple. This was the same time as the festival of Tabernacles which lasted for one week. The priests and Levites offered many sacrifices, and much incense was burned. The sweet incense could be smelled from far away. The people sang hymns and danced on their way to the temple. The ark was carried into the holy place by the priests, and the cherubim covered the ark like a tent covering. The ark contained only the Ten Commandments written on the two tablets of stone. The candlestand, table and golden altar were placed in the temple. The bronze altar of sacrifice was placed near the door of the temple, together with its tools.

After this, a thick cloud covered the temple, making it dark so that the priests could not see each other. This was a sign of God's presence in the temple. Solomon reminded the people that God is found also in the heaven, air, earth and sea. He said to God, "We have built this temple for sacrifices, so that we can pray and know your presence from this place day and night." He then spoke to the people about how God's power had been revealed, how David had done what God wanted, and how the temple would be built after David's time. Because they saw that God kept his promises, they could trust his promises for their future.

King Solomon then lifted up his right hand and said, "Man is not able to thank God properly for his blessings. He needs no reward, but since we are higher than the animals, we will give him thanks for blessing us as a people. We will praise with our voices. God, you have promised to bless the family of David for 10,000 generations. May your Spirit come and sit in this temple. Keep it safe from our enemies. If we sin and suffer the results of sin, let this be a place where we can find mercy and forgiveness from you. And this is the same for all men in any part of the world; that the blessing of this place would come to non-Hebrews as well."

Solomon then fell on the ground and worshipped for a long time. He sacrificed on the altar, and he knew that his offerings were accepted when God sent a rushing fire which burned up everything. All the people knew that God was there, and they fell on the ground and worshipped him. Solomon prayed that they would be pure and continue to keep God's laws which he had given to Moses, so that they would be the most blessed nation on the earth.

Solomon sacrificed 22,000 oxen and 120,000 sheep, and all the families had a great feast. They stayed there for a second week, and were then Solomon sent them to their homes. They prayed for Solomon's protection and sang hymns as they traveled home.

Solomon had a dream that the tribe of Judah would continue to reign if the people would continue to be righteous. But if they started to break God's law and worship other gods, his family line would be cut off and the people of Israel would be destroyed with 10,000 wars. They would also be cast out of the land of their fathers and live in strange lands. The temple would be destroyed by their enemies and the city overthrown. The world would wonder why such a great and rich people would have come to such an end.

V

SOLOMON began building a palace, and it took 13 years because it was not as important as the temple. It had many pillars of cedar and was a place where trials would take place. It was 100 cubits* long, 50 wide and 30 high. The roof was built in a Greek style with folding doors. There was another very beautiful house inside where the king would sit. There was a special place for the queen as well. There were rooms for eating and sleeping after the meetings were over. The floors were made of cedar. The walls were built of 10-cubit* stones, and some were carved with designs of trees and plants. Near the ceiling the walls were decorated with pictures. He had a beautiful dining room full of gold, special furniture and dishes of gold. There were many small rooms, each one leading outdoors to the trees for shade. Solomon's throne was made of ivory and had six steps. There were lions on the sides and the throne was in the form of a bull.

Solomon received much sold, silver, cedar and pine wood from Hiram. In return he sent corn, wine and oil to him; things they didn't have because they lived on an island. Solomon gave Hiram twenty cities in the Galilee which were not far from Tyre, but he was not happy with them. Hiram went to visit them and called them Cabul which means "what does not please" in the language of the Phoenicians. In Tyre there was once a temple of Hercules and of Astarte. There was a youth who could solve some of the problems which Solomon sent to him through Hiram. When he could not, they had to pay Solomon a large fine. And Solomon had to pay a large fine to Hiram when he could not solve the riddles. Hiram sent hard sayings to Solomon to explain, and he was able to solve them all.

vi

KING Solomon saw that the walls of Jerusalem needed to be made stronger, so he did that. They were repaired, made higher, and large towers were added. He also built the strong cities of Hazor, Megiddo and Gezer. Gezer had belonged to the Philistines, but Pharoah of Egypt had destroyed it. He also built Beth-horon and Balaath. These cities had good weather for farming and good water. Solomon built a large city where he found some water. It was two days away from upper Syria and one day away from the Euphrates River.

In Egypt the kings were called Pharoahs. The kings of Alexander, after gaining a kingdom were called Ptolemies, and the Roman emperors were called Caesars. Herodotus said there were 330 kings of Egypt after Menes who built Memphis, but we don't know their names – only that they were called Pharoahs. One exception was a queen named Nicaule.

King Solomon collected taxes from places in Lebanon. Some would be his servants and some would take care of cattle. They did jobs which the Hebrews did not do. The Hebrews built the army and took care of the chariots and horses. There were 550 Hebrews who ruled over the Canaanite slaves.

Solomon built many ships in the Egyptian bay of the Red Sea close to the city of Eloth (Eilat). Hiram, king of Tyre, sent many captains who were good in steering ships. Solomon wished that they would bring him gold from Ophir in India, and they did.

The queen of Egypt and Ethiopia (actually of South Arabia) heard about Solomon's amazing kingdom and wished to see it for herself. She had many questions which she expected him to answer. She came with camels loaded with gold, sweet spices and precious stones. Solomon was able to quickly answer all of her questions. She was amazed at the palace, the food, the clothes, the order of the workers and the sacrifices in the temple. She said that she was impressed by the wisdom, care and happiness everyone showed. "I see that the Hebrew people, including the servants, are happy and are rich from hearing your wisdom every day. Everyone must bless the God who loves this people." She gave Solomon many gifts and he gave her all that she desired. Then she returned to her kingdom.

vii

FROM a country called Aurea Chersonesus, precious stones and pine trees were brought to Solomon for the temple and for making musical instruments. This was the best wood ever used up to this time. The wood was white and shining. Much gold was also brought, including some from the kings of Arabia. Solomon made many shields and put them into the house which was called the "Forest of Lebanon." He also made many cups of gold and precious stones. Many ships on the sea of Tarsus (the Mediterranean) would carry gold, silver and other items to faraway countries, and he would receive ivory, Ethiopians and apes in return. This was a round trip taking three years.

Many kings wanted to visit Solomon after hearing of his fame. They brought many presents with them, including purple garments, spices, horses and chariots. The horses were not only beautiful but were the fastest in the world. Their riders were tall young men who had long hair and were dressed in purple. Gold dust was sprinkled on their hair to give them a sparkling appearance. The king rode on a chariot wearing white, along with these men who were wearing armor. He would go out in the morning and go to Etham near Jerusalem which had beautiful gardens and water springs. Solomon built roads of black stone leading to Jerusalem. He kept chariots in every city, and these were called the "cities of his chariots". He also planted cedar trees in the plains of Judea, which had not grown there before. He bought chariots and horses from the Egyptians and sent them to the kings of Syria and to kings beyond the Euphrates.

In spite of his fame and favor from God, Solomon wandered away from the laws of God and died an unhappy man. He married many wives, including many from foreign countries who caused him to worship their gods. He had 700 wives and 300 concubines, many of them daughters of important people. He got old and began to lose his wisdom. He had already sinned when he made the images of the oxen which supported the bronze sea, and the images of lions near his throne. His father had been an example of virtue, but although God appeared to him twice in his sleep urging him to be like his father, David, he did not listen. A prophet also came to him and told him that the kingdom would be taken from him, but not during his lifetime (in honor of God's promise to David). God would give ten tribes to one of Solomon's servants, and leave two tribes to one of his sons, for David's sake because he loved God, and for the sake of Jerusalem.

Solomon was sad, and God raised up an enemy against him named Ader (sic, Hadad). Ader was from the Edomites, and he ran to Egypt when David's army came through. He was received well in Egypt and even married the Pharoah's niece. They had a son who grew up with the Pharoah's children. When Hadad heard that David and Joab were dead, he asked to return to his own country. When Solomon's problems got worse, Hadad came to Edom by Pharaoh's permission. He did not succeed in getting the Edomite people to rebel against Solomon, so he went to Syria. There he met a band of robbers, and they made Hadad king of Syria. They bothered Israel by robbing the people.

Jeroboam also tried to take Solomon's throne. He was given the job of watching the walls in Jerusalem. Once when he was leaving Jerusalem, a prophet met him and showed him an object lesson by ripping his robe into pieces. In this way the prophet told Jeroboam that he would rule ten tribes of Israel. "Solomon has sinned against God and his son will rule only two tribes. You must honor God as David did." Jeroboam was so encouraged that he persuaded the people to leave Solomon. Solomon was aware of this and tried to kill him, so he ran to Shishak in Egypt and stayed there until Solomon's death. Solomon reigned 80 years and lived for 94 years. He was buried in Jerusalem and had been higher than all other kings in riches, wisdom and happiness. In his later years he was ruined by women and didn't keep the law of God, and for this the whole nation suffered.

viii

SOLOMON'S son Rehoboam (whose mother was an Ammonite) was chosen to be king after Solomon. The people sent for Jeroboam to return from Egypt. They all met together in Shechem. The rulers advised Rehoboam to be gentler than their father was, and to tax them less. He said he would give them an answer in three days. Rehoboam asked advice of his father's friends. He did not like their advice, and he turned to the young men. They told him that he should be even harder than his father. Rehoboam spoke to them roughly, and the people felt as if they'd been hit by an iron hammer. Ahijah the prophet had foretold that this would happen. They then shouted that they would no longer have anything to do with David's sons. They said Rehoboam could keep the temple.

When Rehoboam sent Adoram, the tax collector to calm them down, they stoned him to death.

Seeing this, Rehoboam left quickly in his chariot for Jerusalem. He became king of the tribe of Judah and Benjamin. He formed an army and went against Jeroboam in order to make slaves of all of the other tribes. But Shemaiah, God's prophet, told them not to go to war against their brothers. He said that it was God's will that they be separated.

Jeroboam built palaces in Shechem and Penuel, but lived in Shechem. When the feast of Tabernacles was coming near, Jeroboam wanted to keep the people from celebrating in Jerusalem, because he was afraid that he would lose them to Rehoboam. He also feared for his own life. He made two golden calves and built two small temples for them; one in Bethel and the other in Dan. He gathered the people and reminded them that God is not limited to only one place. "He can be worshipped here without taking the long trip to Jerusalem, which is an enemy city. A man built the temple there, and I have also dedicated these statues to the same God. I will choose priests and Levites from among you. He who wants to be a priest can bring a bull and a ram, the same things which Aaron the first priest offered." By doing this he misled the people and caused them to leave the worship of their fathers and break their laws. God later allowed them to lose wars against foreigners and to be led captive.

So Jeroboam celebrated the feast of Tabernacles in Bethel at the same time the two tribes, Judah and Benjamin, were celebrating in Jerusalem. He made himself a high priest and went to the altar, surrounded by his own priests. A prophet of God, Jadon, came from Jerusalem, and in the hearing of the king he prophesied that a certain man of David's family would kill all these false priests. He said the sign would be that the altar of sacrifice would immediately be broken and the fat of the sacrifices would pour on the ground. After he said this, Jeroboam stretched out his hand to order the man's death, and his hand became limp as if dead.

Then the altar broke as the prophet had said. The king begged for his hand to be restored. The prophet prayed and God granted his request. Jeroboam invited Jadon to stay and eat with him, but he said that God had forbidden him to do so. He was also to return home a different way from the way he came.

ix

JEROBOAM highly esteemed a certain false prophet in the city. He was old and stayed in bed, but he heard about Jadon whose prophecies had come to pass. This wicked man felt that he would be less honorable in the eyes of the king, so he ordered his sons to saddle his donkey, and he rode on it to catch up with Jadon. He found him and complained that Jadon had not come to his home. The prophet said that God had forbidden him to taste anything in the city. The man replied that he was also a prophet, he worshipped God in the same way, and God had sent him to invite him to his home. Jadon believed the lying prophet and went home with him. God appeared to Jadon and told him that he would die in a lion attack on his way home, because he disobeyed him. Jadon would not be buried in the graves of his fathers. These things came to pass, so that Jeroboam might not pay attention to the words of Jadon. Jadon died from the lion, and then the lion and the donkey stood by the dead man. The false prophet heard what happened, and they brought Jadon's body and had a big funeral for him. He said that he also wanted to be buried with Jadon. He then went to Jeroboam and told him that this silly Jadon did not speak the truth. He said that Jeroboam's hand had become limp from the hard work of lifting the sacrifices, and that the altar had fallen down from the weight of what had been laid on it. The false prophet also told him about the death of Jadon, and in this way he persuaded the king not to do what was righteous and holy.

x

REHOBOAM, the son of Solomon who was king of the two tribes, built many large cities, including Bethlehem, Lachish and

Hebron. He built some in the tribe of Judah and others in the tribe of Benjamin. He put walls around them, making them into fortresses and supplying them with corn, wine and oil. He also gave them shields and spears. Many priests, Levites and other righteous men gathered in Jerusalem to worship. Rehoboam had 18 wives and 30 concubines. He had 28 sons and 60 daughters. One of his wives was the daughter of Absalom by Tamar. Her name was Maachah, his favorite. He appointed Abijah, Maachah's son to be the next king.

As the kingdom became richer, the people went away from the worship of God. So God sent Shishak, the king of Egypt, to punish them. Tens of thousands of men came with chariots and horsemen, most of them Libyans and Ethiopians, and they easily captured the strong cities. The last city left for them to capture was Jerusalem. Shemaiah the prophet told them that God had left them because they had stopped worshipping him. They understood their sin and confessed it to God. God told the prophet that he would not destroy them, but that they would become servants of the Egyptians. When the Israelites gave up, Shishak did not keep his promise to leave them in peace. Instead, he ruined the temple, stole the treasures and carried away all of the gold and silver. He also stole the shields which Solomon had made and the golden quivers which David had dedicated to God. He returned to Egypt. Shishak fought against Syria as well, taking prisoners. He left pillars with writing on them, telling of his victories and with drawings of women's private parts. The Ethiopians learned from the Egyptians about circumcision.

When Shishak left, Rehoboam made shields of brass instead of gold and fixed the king's palace. He ruled the people quietly, but in fear of Jeroboam who was his enemy. He died at 57, having ruled for 17 years. He was a proud, foolish man who did not take advice from his father's friends. He was buried in Jerusalem in the graves of the kings, and his son Abijah was king after him. By then Jeroboam had been king for 18 years.

GOD would soon punish Jeroboam's wickedness. Jeroboam's son Abijah was sick. He asked his wife go to Ahijah the prophet, pretending to be someone else, and ask what would happen to the boy. Ahijah had foretold that Jeroboam would be king. God had told Ahijah that Jeroboam's wife was coming. The blind prophet shouted to her, "Come in, wife of Jeroboam! Why are you pretending to be someone else?" He said to tell her husband, "God made you great and gave you a kingdom from what belonged to David's family. But since you have forgotten God and have worshipped other gods, I will destroy all of your family and make them food for the dogs and birds. All the people will also suffer - they will be scattered beyond the Euphrates River, because they have done the same wicked deeds as their king and did not sacrifice to God. Tell your husband this. As for your son, he will die when you get home. But the people will cry for him, because he is the only good person in the family."

Jeroboam paid no attention to what he heard. He gathered a large army to fight against Abijah, the son of Rehoboam. He thought Abijah was weak because he was young. Abijah heard about the planned attack, and he also gathered an army out of his two tribes. He had 40,000 soldiers, but the enemy had double this number.

Abijah stood up on a high place to speak. He said that God had given David and his family to be rulers for all time. "Now you are here trying to take this away. My father Rehoboam was good to the people, and if he did not speak kindly to you, it was only because he listened to bad advice. But you have chosen to go away from God and his laws. The hard words from Rehoboam which disturbed you should have been forgiven, since he was young and didn't know how to be a king. And how will you succeed now? Will those calves and the altars which you have set up give you a victory? There is no strength in an army even of tens of thousands, when the war itself is unjust. We have continually worshipped only the true God, not one made by human hands. I offer you a chance to repent and call off the war. Think about where your happiness of today comes from."

While he was still speaking, Jeroboam sent some people to surround Abijah, which made his army afraid. Abijah told them to trust God. The priests blew the trumpets and shouted, and they ran at their enemies. Abijah's army had a greater victory than any war in history. They killed 500,000 soldiers from the ten tribes, and the strongest cities were taken and destroyed. They captured Bethel and its surrounding towns.

Jeroboam never got over this loss while Abijah was alive. But Abijah died soon after that - he was king for only 3 years. He was buried in Jerusalem in the graves of his fathers. He had 22 sons and 16 daughters. Abijah's son Asa became king in Jerusalem, and for the next ten years, there was peace in all of Israel.

Jeroboam was king for a total of 22 years. When his son Nadab was king, Nadab's friend Baasha killed him and all his family. The whole house of Jeroboam was destroyed just as the prophet had foretold.

xii

ASA was a God-fearing king who kept God's laws and got rid of wickedness in the kingdom. He had an army of hundreds of thousands. After he had reigned ten years, Zerab, the king of Ethiopia, came to Mareshah, a city in Judah, to fight against the Hebrews. They had more than double the number of soldiers and also 300 chariots. Asa cried out to God to help them kill many ten thousands of the enemy; God was the only one who could help them against this strong army. While he was still speaking, God helped them to kill many Ethiopians, and the enemy ran away. Asa's army took much gold and silver, and many camels and cattle from one of the Ethiopian camps, then they returned to Jerusalem.

A prophet named Azariah told them that they had won because they were following God's will. They would continue to do well if they continued to worship him. But if they turned away from God, there would no longer be a true prophet or priest to speak God's word to them. Their cities would be ruined, and their nation would be scattered around the world, where they would live like strangers and homeless people. The people listened and lived righteously. Asa made sure that the word of the prophet also got to the people who lived far away from Jerusalem.

Baasha, the king of the ten tribes, was king for 24 years and was very wicked. He was warned by a prophet named Jehu to change his ways, or he would not be king for long - but he did not repent. He took his army and captured Ramah, a city 40 furlongs* from Jerusalem. He made it strong in order to have a base for attacking Asa's kingdom in the south.

Asa knew about this move and sent messengers to the king of Damascens (Damascus in Syria) with gold and silver, and asked for his help. The Syrian king agreed and broke his friendship with Baasha. His men went to Israel and burned some of the northern cities and robbed others. When the king of Israel heard about it, he stopped his work in Ramah and went home to help his own people. Asa used the materials which Baasha had left and built two strong cities.

Baasha died, and his son ruled for two years until he was killed by his own army captain, Zimri, when the king didn't expect it. Then Zimri killed Baasha's whole family. This fulfilled the prophecy that Baasha's wicked house would be destroyed the same way that Jeroboam's house had been destroyed.

Zimri reigned only seven days, however, because Omri was made king by the army. Omri attacked the city where Zimri was. Seeing that he couldn't defend himself, Zimri set the palace on fire and killed himself. Omri ruled for 12 years; half in the city of Tirzah, and the rest in the city of Samaria. This city was on a mountain, called Semareon because it was bought from a man named Semer. Omri was wicked and died in Samaria. The throne was taken over by his son Ahab.

Many kings of Israel were wicked and were killed along with their families. Asa, king of the two tribes was a good king and reigned 41 years, living to an old age. Those who ruled with courage and righteousness from David's seed were blessed.

AHAB, the king of Israel, lived in Samaria and was a very wicked king. He ruled for 22 years. They continued to worship the calves which Jeroboam had made, in addition to other strange things which they worshipped. Jezebel, his wife, was the daughter of the king of the Tyrians and Sidonians. She brought her gods as well. She built a temple for them, planted groves of trees and chose people to be priests and false prophets for the god, Belus of the Tyrians.

A prophet of God named Elijah came to Ahab and warned him that there would be no rain or dew for a long time. This Elijah went south and was able to drink water from a brook in order to survive. God also sent birds to bring him food every day. After the brook dried up, he walked north and met a woman from a city near Tyre. She gave him the last of her food, and by a miracle it lasted for a long time.

This woman's son grew and suddenly died. She thought it was God's punishment on her. She came to the prophet beating her chest and crying. Elijah brought the son back to life after pleading with God that such a woman who had helped him should not have her son cruelly taken away. God pitied the mother and brought the child back to life, so that she would not think that the prophet came in order to hurt her. She understood then that Elijah was truly someone who knew God.

Elijah came to tell King Ahab that there would soon be rain. Not only were people suffering, but the cattle were dying. Ahab had looked everywhere for Elijah but couldn't find him. The king then called his servant Obadiah, who took care of the cattle, to try to find some grass for the animals. Obadiah took one road and the king took another one.

When Obadiah was alone, Elijah met him. Obadiah bowed to Elijah, who told Obadiah to go to King Ahab and to tell him that

Elijah wanted to talk to him. Obadiah was afraid to do this; he worried that Elijah might disappear. He told Elijah how he saved some of God's prophets after Jezebel had killed the others. Obadiah had hidden 100 prophets and fed them with bread and water. Elijah said not to worry - he would talk to Ahab that same day.

Ahab and Elijah met. Ahab was angry and asked if Elijah was the one causing all the suffering in the land. Elijah answered that Ahab himself was the cause. Everyone was suffering because they were worshipping strange gods and not the only true God. Elijah told Ahab to meet him on Mount Carmel, and to bring his prophets and his wife's prophets.

At the meeting, Elijah cried out, asking the people how long they would keep changing their minds about who was the true God. The people did not answer. Elijah told the 400 false prophets to kill a calf and make a sacrifice. He would do the same, and whichever sacrifice would be burned by fire from heaven would show who the true god is. The prophets of Ahab called on their gods from morning until noon, and cut themselves with swords and knives according to the customs of their countries. After this, Elijah prepared his sacrifice and made sure the people came close, so that no one would think a fire had been secretly put under it. He took twelve stones as a symbol of the twelve tribes of Israel and built an altar with a ditch of water around it. The whole sacrifice had four barrels of water poured on it. Elijah began to pray, and a fire suddenly came from heaven and fell on the altar, burning up everything.

When the Israelites saw this they fell on the ground and worshipped God, calling him the great and only true God. Elijah told them to kill all of the false prophets, which they did. He told Ahab to go and have dinner before the rain would start. Elijah then went to the top of Mount Carmel and sat on the ground, leaning his head on his knees. He had his servant go to see if there was a cloud rising out of the sea. He went time after time and didn't see anything. After the seventh time he said that he saw a small black thing in the sky not larger than a man's foot. When Elijah heard this, he told Ahab to go to the city before the rain would begin. Ahab came to Jezreel, and in a short time there was a huge storm. The prophet ran alongside the king's chariot to Jezreel, a city of Izar (the tribe of Issaachar).

When Jezebel heard how her prophets had been killed, she promised to kill Elijah. Elijah was so afraid he went to Beersheba, very far south, belonging to the tribe of Judah. He left his servant and went into the desert. He prayed to die, saying that he was no better than his fathers. He slept under a tree and when he woke up, he saw that food and water had been given to him, and he ate and drank. He felt stronger and walked all the way to Mount Sinai. He went into a cave. A voice spoke and asked why he had left the city. He said that he had told the people that they should worship only the true God, and Jezebel was going to kill him for this. The voice told him to come out of the cave the next day, which he did. There was an earthquake, a fire, and a still Divine voice telling him that his enemies would not have power over him. He was to anoint Jehu to be king and Hazael of Damascus to rule over the Syrians. He was to prepare Elisha to be a prophet in his place. Through these men, the rebels among the people would be killed. Elijah returned and found Elisha plowing a field. He left his parents and followed Elijah, becoming his disciple.

There was a man named Naboth who lived in Jezreel who owned a field next to the king's land. Ahab wanted this field and offered Naboth other plots of land in a trade, but Naboth said that the field belonged to his family and he would not accept a trade. This made the king so upset he wouldn't wash or eat. Jezebel asked what was bothering him, and he told her. She said she would fix the problem and make sure that Naboth was punished. She wrote letter in Ahab's name telling the men of Naboth's town to call a fast and then a gathering with the well-known Naboth sitting in front. Three bold men would testify that Naboth had cursed God and the king, and then he was to be stoned.

Jezebel's plan succeeded, Naboth died, and the king went to see the vineyard. God was angry and sent Elijah the prophet to meet Ahab in Naboth's field. Elijah told him that he would die, and in the same place where Naboth had died and dogs had eaten his body, Ahab, and his wife would die, and his whole family would be killed. King Ahab put on sackcloth and went barefoot and refused to eat, confessing his sin. So God told the prophet that he would delay the punishment of Ahab's family; it would come during his son's reign.

xiv

THE king of Syria, Benhadad, made an agreement with 32 kings beyond the Euphrates River to fight against Ahab. Ahab had made the cities strong and he himself lived in Samaria. Benhadad's army surrounded the city, but first he wanted to see if Ahab would give up instead of going to war. The Syrian wanted Ahab's riches, wives and children as the price for peace. He wanted the right to take anything he wished from the palace and from the king's friends. Ahab answered that Benhadad could have all of this, but the Syrian king sent a new demand. This time he said that to make peace, all of the people would have to give up their wives and children and anything good that they owned. The people told Ahab to say no to this. Benhadad was so angry he came to close up the city in order to starve them out. A prophet came to Ahab and told him not to be afraid, because God would fight their enemies. He was to take the 232 sons of the princes, and with this army they attacked the Syrian army by surprise while they were feasting. Many were naked and drunk and they ran away. The rest of the Hebrews joined the princes and had a great victory, gathering up the armor which their enemy left behind. Ahab took lots of spoil from their camp, where was much wealth. He took gold, silver, chariots and horses. The prophet told the king to be ready for another attack from Benhadad the next year.

Benhadad got advice from his friends to fight against Israel the next time on flat land, and not on the hills where Israel's God was strong. Also he should send the 32 kings home but keep their armies. The next spring he came to the city of Aphek on the flat plain, and Ahab went to meet him in battle. After one week, the battle started. Ahab's army chased the enemy in a great victory. The enemy was being destroyed by one another, and even by their own chariots. Another 27,000 soldiers were killed when a city wall fell on them.

Benhadad escaped with some friends and stayed in a cellar. These friends put on the clothes that showed they were giving up, and they came to Ahab. They brought a promise that Benhadad would be his servant. Ahab allowed Benhadad to come to him, and they made an agreement and treated each other like friends. Benhadad said he would give back the cities of the Israelites which the earlier kings had taken, and that Ahab was welcome in Damascus. Ahab gave him presents and Benhadad returned to Syria.

A prophet named Micaiah came to one of the Israelites and told him to hit him on the head. When the man refused, Micaiah said a lion would kill him. The first man died, and he went to a second one. This one hurt his head, and the prophet put a bandage on it. He told the king that he had been a soldier in this battle, and was taking care of a prisoner who had escaped. He was in danger of death for losing the prisoner. Ahab said this punishment would be just. The the man took off the bandage and the king saw that it was Micaiah the prophet. He warned Ahab that because he had allowed Benhadad, a man who cursed God, to escape, that Ahab would be killed by this man. Ahab was very angry and demanded that Micaiah be put in prison.

XV

JEHOSHAPHAT kept God's laws. He was liked by the other kings, who gave him presents. He was wealthy and respected. In the third year of his rule, he sent priests and rulers around the country to teach the people in every city the laws of Moses and how to worship God. The Philistines paid him taxes, and the Arabians supplied him every year with 360 lambs and goats. He also made all the cities strong and had a huge army gathered from the tribes of Judah and Benjamin. Some were good with bows and arrows.

Jehoshaphat took the daughter of Ahab to be his son's wife. When he went to visit Ahab's family in Samaria he was treated well, and so were his soldiers. Ahab hoped that Jehoshaphat would join an attack on Syria and help him get back the city of Ramoth which had belonged to his father. Jehoshaphat agreed, but he was used to getting advice from God's prophets before going to war. So Ahab called his 400 prophets to ask them about the planned attack. They reported that God promised to help them win against the Syrians. Jehoshaphat did not believe them and asked if there was another prophet they could ask. Ahab said there was Micaiah, but he hated Micaiah because he prophesied bad things about Ahab. The man who went to call Micaiah the prophet told him what the other prophets had foretold. Micaiah said he would speak only what God told him to say. He came to Ahab and said that God had shown him that the Israelites would be chased by the Syrians and would be scattered like sheep whose shepherd was killed. He said that in spite of losing the battle, the people would come home and only Ahab would die.

The king was upset, and Zedekiah, one of the false prophets, came and told him that Micaiah was lying. He said that Elijah, a better prophet than this one, had said that the dogs would lick Ahab's blood where they had licked the blood of Naboth, and not on a battlefield three days away. Zedekiah then hit Micaiah and said, "If he is a real prophet, he should hurt my hand just like Jadon caused Jeroboam's hand to dry up." But nothing happened to him. So Ahab took courage and decided to lead his army against the Syrians. Zedekiah made horns of iron and said that God is giving this as a sign of victory. Micaiah answered that in a few days Zedekiah would hide in a secret room to run away from his punishment for lying. Micaiah was taken to prison and given bread and water.

Ahab and Jehoshaphat set out against Syria, and when the Syrian king heard this, he told his soldiers to kill no one but the king of Israel. Jehoshaphat wore Ahab's royal clothes so that Micaiah's prophecy would not come to pass. The battle went on from the morning until evening but they didn't kill anyone. They couldn't find Ahab. A young man wounded Ahab by accident, but he kept quiet in his chariot and suffered until sunset, and then he died.

The Syrians heard that Ahab was dead, they went home. The Israelites took Ahab's body to Samaria. They washed the chariot in the fountain of Jezreel and the dogs licked the blood as Elijah had prophesied. But he died at Ramoth as Micaiah had foretold. The true prophets should be listened to, because God wants men to know what to stay away from. Ahab was deceived, but even if he didn't believe those who had foretold his defeat, that did not change what happened. Ahab's son Ahaziah was king after him.

BOOK IX

FROM THE DEATH OF AHAB TO THE CAPTIVITY OF THE TEN TRIBES

KING Jehoshaphat went home to Jerusalem after helping Ahab fight against the king of Syria. Jehu the prophet said the king was wrong for helping such a wicked man, and God was not pleased. But he was saved from the enemy himself, because his heart was good. The king thanked God and offered sacrifices. He went around the country teaching the people the laws of Moses and how to worship God. He chose judges in every city and told them to do justice and not take bribes or pay attention to rich leaders or princes. God is aware of all secrets. If the judges in the cities could not make a decision, they would be brought to Jerusalem where the priests and Levites would decide.

The Moabites and Ammonites came against Jehoshaphat, along with many Arabians. They camped at Engedi, a city on the lake Asphaltitis (the Dead Sea), which is 300 furlongs* from Jerusalem. There were many palm trees there. Jehoshaphat heard about these enemies and prayed to God in the direction of the temple that he would be able to win against them. He cried, and all the people prayed. A prophet named Jahaziel cried out that God had heard their prayers and would fight for them. He said that they should bring out the army the next day and that they would find the enemy at a place called "The High Place" between

Jerusalem and the road coming up from Engedi. But they would only need to stand still, and God would defeat their enemies. The people thanked and worshipped God, and the Levites kept singing hymns and playing their instruments.

The people came to the desert, and the priests and Levites sang as if they had already been saved from the enemy. God caused the Ammonites to be so confused that they started killing one another. Not one man from this huge army escaped. Jehoshaphat saw many dead men and allowed his army to take spoil from their camp and from their dead bodies. They gathered spoil for three days, and on the fourth they blessed God for his power in a place they called the Valley of Blessing ["Berachah"].

When they came back to Jerusalem, the people feasted and offered sacrifices for many days. The countries around them were afraid when they heard about this victory. Jehoshaphat was blessed because he feared God and acted justly. He had an agreement with Ahab's son for ship building, but they were too big and not built right, so they were destroyed.

ii

AHAZIAH, the son of Ahab, was king of Israel, living in Samaria. He was wicked like both of his parents, and like Jeroboam who had misled the people. In the second year of his rule, the king of Moab stopped paying the taxes he had paid to his father Ahab. As Ahaziah was coming down from the top of his house, he fell and had to stay in bed. He asked for help from the god of Ekron, "the Fly", to know if he would get well. The God of the Hebrews appeared to Elijah and told him to go and meet the messengers who going with Ahaziah's request. He said to tell the king that he would suffer.

When the messengers came back, the king asked how they could return so quickly. They said that a man met them and told them to tell Ahaziah that his sickness will end in death. They described the man: he was hairy and wore a belt of leather. The king understood that this was Elijah. He sent a captain and 50 soldiers to Elijah, telling him to come to the king. He refused to come down from the top of a hill. He told them that if he was a true prophet, they would see fire coming from heaven to destroy all of them. He prayed and a whirlwind of fire fell and destroyed all of them. King Ahaziah heard about this and sent another captain with 50 men. The same thing happened. A third group was sent, but this captain spoke with more wisdom, and Elijah said that he understood he was just carrying out the king's orders. Elijah came with him and directly spoke to the king. He prophesied that since Ahaziah had not asked for help from the true God, and instead wanted to hear from "the Fly," he would die.

The king died within a short time. Since he had no children, his brother Jehoram became the next king. He continued like his father Ahab in wickedness during the 12 years of his rule. The people worshiped foreign gods. Elijah disappeared, and Elisha, his disciple, continued as a prophet. Elijah and Enoch both disappeared and no one knew for sure that they had died.

iii

JORAM (Jehoram) gathered his army to fight against the king of Moab, named Mesha. He asked for help from Jehoshaphat since he had been his father's friend. He also asked for help from the king of Edom. Joram came to Jerusalem, was well received, and the kings planned their attack. It was a 7-day journey through the desert of Edom. They had no water and cried out to God to deliver them from the king of Moab. Jehoshaphat asked if there was a prophet of God who could tell them what to do. Someone had seen Elisha, so the kings asked him what to do.

Elisha told Joram to go to his father's and mother's prophets. He said he would answer them only because of Jehoshaphat, who had been a holy man. He asked someone to play music, and then the Divine Spirit came upon him. Elisha told them to dig many ditches in the valley. "God will send water and you will also win against your enemies and cut down their fruit trees." [This was forbidden in the Law of Moses, but because the Moabites were to be punished in a strong way, it was allowed this time]. They were also told to cut off the Moabites' water supply. The next day before sunrise God sent a storm and the ditches filled up with water. The king of Moab saw the water from far away and thought that it was blood, since it looked red. They came expecting to rob their enemies, but they were wrong. The Israelites cut them to pieces and the enemy ran. All of the cities of Moab were torn down and ruined. They filled them with stones from the brooks and cut down the best trees. All the walls were broken down. The king of Moab, together with 700 men, tried to attack on horseback but they did not win. Then he took his oldest son who was to be king after him and lifted him up on a wall and offered him as a burnt offering to God, which made everyone feel so bad they stopped the war. Jehoshaphat returned to Jerusalem and died at age 60 after being king for 25 years. He had a grand burial because he had been righteous like David.

iv

JEHOSHAPHAT had many children and he chose his oldest son, Jehoram, to be king after him. His mother's brother, son of Ahab, was also named Jehoram. When the king of Israel came back from Moab to Samaria, Elisha the prophet was with him. The widow of Obadiah, Ahab's servant, came to Elisha and reminded him that her husband had kept 100 prophets safe from Jezebel who would have killed them. To feed them, Obadiah had to borrow money, and now that she was unable to pay it back, she and her children were going to be sold as slaves. She needed help right away. The prophet asked what she had in the house. She had only a little oil. He told her to borrow many empty jars and jugs from her neighbors, shut her door, and pour oil into them. God filled them all with oil. She told Elisha that they had all been filled, and he told her to go and sell the oil and pay what she owed and keep what was left for their own needs.

Elisha sent a message to Joram that Syrians were hiding and waiting to kill him. So the king stayed away from that place. When

Benhadad, the Syrian king, heard that his plan failed, he wanted to kill his servants for telling the king of Israel, because only they had known the secret. They told him that it was Elisha's fault, so he then wanted to kill Elisha. Benhadad's soldiers came at night with many horses and chariots and surrounded the city where Elisha was staying. Elisha's servant was very afraid, but Elisha told him to trust in God. Then Elisha prayed that God would show the young man that he was there with them. Elisha's prayer was heard, and the servant saw a large number of chariots and horses which were on Elisha's side to protect him. Then Elisha prayed that the enemies would not be able to see him, and God answered this request.

Elisha came out and talked to them, but they didn't see that it was Elisha. He promised to lead them to the man they wanted, if they would follow him, and they did. He led them to Samaria and ordered Joram the king to shut the gates and gather his army around these people. Elisha then prayed that God would let them see again, and the Syrians saw that they were surrounded by enemies. Joram asked if he could kill them. Elisha told him not to hurt them, because they hadn't done any harm, and it was by Divine Power that they had come to this place. The Syrians were given all the food they could eat, and then they were sent back to King Benhadad.

When they told Benhadad their strange story, he knew that the God of Israel was with Elisha, and he stopped trying to kill the king of Israel. He decided instead to go to war against the Hebrews openly. Joram shut himself up in Samaria behind strong walls. Benhadad tried to win by sitting in front of the gates until the people starved. The situation got worse and worse, and every day Joram went around among the guards to make sure no one would give the city to the enemy. A lady cried to him for help. He said that he didn't have any food to give her. She said she wanted justice, and told him that she had made an agreement with another woman to kill their children and eat them; hers would be eaten the first day and the other woman's the next day.

The other woman broke her agreement and was hiding her son. Joram was very upset and tore his clothes. He blamed Elisha because he did not pray to God to stop this awful suffering of the Hebrews. He wanted to have someone cut off Elisha's head. But Joram changed his mind and ran to save Elisha at his house. Elisha told his servants to not open the door for the man sent to kill him, because the king was coming right behind him to change the order, which he did.

Joram accused him of not praying for help, and Elisha promised that within 24 hours there would be plenty of food. Joram was very happy and believed him, since former predictions had come true. The captain of the third group, a friend of the king, said that it was impossible for God to pour down bags of barley and fine flour from heaven. The prophet told him that he would see these things, but that he would not get any of them.

In Samaria there was a law that those who had leprosy had to stay outside the city. There were four lepers who sat by the gates, and since they were starving just like the people in the city, they decided that they had nothing to lose if they gave themselves up to the enemy. At night they entered the enemy camp. But the Syrians had been scared away by the noise of chariots and armor in their ears which God had caused them to hear. They ran to Benhadad and said that Joram and the king of Egypt and the king of the Islands were coming after them. Benhadad believed them since he heard the same noise, so they left their horses, animals and many riches in the camp, and ran for their lives. The lepers came and saw that the camp was totally empty. They ate and drank in one of the tents and took many clothes and much gold and hid them. They continued in tent after tent, but then they understood that they needed to tell Joram and the people about this. They came to the walls of Samaria and called loudly to the watchmen.

Joram heard the news and said that it was a trap to get them to open the gates - then the Syrians would come back and fight them. He told his soldiers,"Guard the city carefully." Someone said that this was a good idea, but it would still be worth it to send a couple of riders to see where the Syrians went. The two found many supplies thrown down by the road, and even weapons. Joram sent out many people to take things from the camp, and they found much gold, silver and many cattle. There was also wheat and barley, and the price was very low, just like Elisha had foretold. The captain of the third group was killed by the crowd stepping on him as they ran out the gate. Elisha had foretold his punishment when he didn't believe what Elisha had said about God bringing them food.

When Benhadad got home to Damascus, he understood that God had caused his army to lose. Then Benhadad got sick. He sent Hazael, his most faithful servant, to meet Elisha and give him gifts, and ask if the king would get well. Hazael bought Elisha 40 camels loaded with the best fruit. The prophet said that the king would die, but not to tell him. Then Elisha cried because he knew how the Israelites would suffer after Benhadad's death. He said that he, Hazael, would tear down the strongest cities and kill women and children. Hazael asked how he would do such things. The prophet said he would be the next king. Hazael told the king he would get well, and the next day he took a wet cloth as if to help Benhadad, but instead he smothered him to death. Hazael became king. He built many temples and Damascens (Damascus) was beautiful. The Syrians still honor these kings as gods, even though they lived not so long ago. When Joram, the king of Israel, heard that Benhadad was dead, he was at peace.

V

JEHORAM, the king in Jerusalem, (who had the same name as the king of Israel) killed many of his family and his father's friends who were under him. He was no better than the kings of Israel, who no longer worshipped God but went after foreign gods. His wife, Athaliah the daughter of Ahab, caused him to be wicked. God allowed one person to remain in the family line due to His promise to David. Jehoram made the people stop their good ways and learn wicked ways. The Edomites had killed their king who served Jehoram's father and set up a king of their own, so Jehoram went out with his horsemen and chariots to attack them by night. He lost and became angry, and so he forced the people to go up to the high mountains and pray to foreign gods. Elisha the prophet sent him a letter of warning that God would punish him for killing his brothers and other good men, and also because he had led the people against God's laws and ways. Jehoram would die from a terrible disease that would make his guts fall out.

Not long after this, Arabians who lived near Ethiopia and the Philistines attacked Jehoram's country, including his home. They killed Jehoram's sons and wives, leaving only one son, Ahaziah. The king got very sick, and in the end his insides came out as Elisha had foretold. The people felt that it was God's punishment on him, so they did not honor him when he died. He was buried as a common man. He had lived to the age of 40 and was king for eight years. Ahaziah became the king in Jerusalem.

vi

JORAM, the king of Israel, hoped to take Ramoth, a city of Gilead, from the Syrians after Benhadad died. During the battle with his large army, he was shot by an arrow. He returned to Jezreel, leaving the army with a general named Jehu. Elisha gave one of his disciples some oil to anoint Jehu to be the next king. He found Jehu sitting with his captains as Elisha had foretold, and the prophet and Jehu went into another room. The prophet said that when Jehu was king he needed to destroy the house of Ahab for all of Jezebel's wickedness in killing God's prophets. The servant then left quickly so the soldiers wouldn't see him. Jehu came out, and when his soldiers asked what this young man came for, Jehu said that he was crazy: he had brought a message from God that he was the next king. When they heard this, each one took his coat and put it on the ground (an Eastern custom), blew trumpets and called out that Jehu was king.

Afterwards Jehu gathered the army and set out against Joram who was getting well from his wound in Jezreel. Ahaziah, king of

Jerusalem, was also there for a visit. Jehu had to make sure that Joram didn't hear about him having been anointed king. So his soldiers guarded the roads. The king at Jezreel sent his watchmen to ask who these riders were, but when they met Jehu, they stayed with him and didn't come back. Joram knew something was wrong, and in spite of being sick he went out in his chariot with Ahaziah. He met Jehu. Jehu told him that his mother Jezebel was a witch and a harlot. The king turned his chariot and called to Ahaziah that Jehu was betraying them. Jehu then drew his bow and killed Joram. His body was thrown into the field of Naboth, as Elijah had prophesied after Naboth had been cruelly killed by his father. Ahaziah was afraid for his life and tried to run away. Jehu followed him and wounded him. A short time afterwards, he died and was buried in Jerusalem. He had ruled only one year and was more wicked than his father.

When Jehu came to Jezreel, Jezebel was all dressed up and standing on a tower. Jehu looked up and asked who she was, and ordered her to come down to him. Finally he ordered the servants to throw her down, which they did. Her blood was sprinkled on the wall and the horses stepped on her body. When Jehu came into the palace, he ate with his friends. He sent his servants to bury Jezebel, but all they could find were a few pieces of her body. Elijah had prophesied that she would die in Jezreel in this way.

Ahab had 70 sons who grew up in Samaria. Jehu sent two letters; one to those who raised his children and one to the rulers in Samaria. He told them to choose one of Ahab's children as king, and let him fight against Jehu to punish him for the murder of Ahab (sic, Ahab's family). The rulers were afraid, because they knew about the victory of Jehu. They said that they would do whatever Jehu wanted. He told them to cut off the heads of all Ahab's sons and send them to him. They did this, and put the heads in baskets and sent them to Jezreel. When Jehu was at supper with his friends, the heads were brought in and put in two piles. He told all the people the next morning that he had killed Joram but he had not killed these sons. He reminded them that Elijah had prophesied that all of Ahab's family would be destroyed.

Later on the road he met relatives of Ahaziah, king of Jerusalem, who said they were coming to honor Joram and their own king Ahaziah. They didn't know that Jehu had already killed them. He ordered his men to catch these 42 people and kill them, so they did.

Jehu met an old friend named Jehonadab, who was righteous. He began to praise Jehu for destroying the house of Ahab. Jehu invited him to join him in his chariot and come with him to Samaria. He was going to punish the false prophets and priests who had misled the people and made them worship foreign gods. He had a plan. He invited all the priests to come and worship Ahab's god and promised that many sacrifices would be offered. If any one of them would be missing, that one would be punished by death. Messengers were sent out to bring all of the priests of Baal to Jehu. They were given special clothing. He and Jehonadab made sure there were no strangers in the room. He put 80 of his men outside to kill all of these prophets inside and not to let any escape. They were all killed, and the temple of Baal was burned. So there was no more idol worship in Samaria. Jehu wasn't completely righteous, however, because he allowed the people to still worship the golden calves. But he did enough good things, so the prophet said that his sons would be kings in Israel for four generations.

vii

WHEN Athaliah, the daughter of Ahab, heard that her brother Joram and her son Ahaziah had been killed, she set out to kill all of the family of David. She almost succeeded, but one of Ahaziah's sons was saved by his aunt, Jehosheba. She was married to the high priest Jehoiada. This child was only one year old and was hidden in the temple for six years.

The high priest felt that the time had come to gather some soldiers against Athaliah and make the child Jehoash king.

Messengers went out and gathered all the priests, Levites and the heads of the tribes to Jerusalem. They all took an oath that they would be quiet, and then he showed them the child from David's family. He said that God had promised that David's family would sit on the throne forever. "I want one-third of you guard him in the temple, one-fourth guard the temple gates and that the rest of you guard the gate which leads to the king's palace. Only the priests will be allowed in the temple. The king should be guarded at all times by soldiers with swords, and only people without weapons will be allowed in the temple square." The high priest then opened David's room of weapons and gave out spears, arrows, and other weapons to the captains, priests and Levites. They crowned Jehoash and anointed him with oil and made him king. Everyone shouted "God save the king!"

When Athaliah heard the noise, she quickly called her own guards and came into the temple. The priests let her in but stopped those who were with her. When she saw the child standing on a pillar with the royal crown on his head, she tore her clothes and cried out to kill him. Jehoiada called for his captains and ordered them to kill Athaliah in the valley of Cedron so as not to pollute the temple. Anyone trying to save her would be killed. They took her to the gate of the king's mules where she was killed.

The young new king took an oath that he would worship God and keep the laws of Moses. Then some of the people went to the house of Baal built by Athaliah and her husband, Jehoram, and destroyed it. The priests offered burnt offerings twice a day and incense offerings in the temple. Jehoash appointed some of the Levites and servants to guard the temple from unclean people.

All of the people brought the king to his throne and were very happy and feasted for many days. There was peace after Athaliah's death. Jehoash was careful to keep God's laws, and when he was old enough he married two wives and had children.

HAZAEL, the king of Syria, fought against the Israelites and their king Jehu and took over the parts of the country beyond the Jordan River (to the east). Jehu did not try to defend these cities because he had gone against God and his law. He died after being king for 27 years. His son, Jehoahaz, was the next king in Israel.

Jehoash, king of Jerusalem, decided to repair the temple. He asked the priests and Levites to collect a half-shekel of silver from every person in his kingdom. Jehoram and Athaliah and her sons had ruined the temple. Jehoiada didn't agree to this plan, because he didn't think the people would pay that much; so the project was delayed for many years. When Jehoash had reigned for 23 years, he started the collection idea again. He made a wooden box with a small hole in it, set it in the temple beside the altar and asked everyone to put in whatever amount of money they wished in order to rebuild the temple. Every day the priests counted the gold and silver which was brought until there was enough. Stonecutters and carpenters were hired and large pieces of wood were bought. Lots of dishes and tools were made from the leftover gold and silver. Many valuable sacrifices were offered to God every day.

Jehoiada was a righteous high priest who lived to be 130 years old. Part of the reason is because he had restored the kingdom to the family of David. But after Jehoiada, the king and the people became wicked again, and even Jehoiada's son was stoned to death in the temple. This was because he told the king and the people to act righteously, and that if they did not, God would punish them. He suffered and died a violent death, in spite of the good that his father had done for Jehoash.

Punishment soon came from the king of Syria. He overthrew Gath and then came against Jerusalem. Jehoash was afraid and emptied out all the temple treasure to pay off this king, and he called off the war. Then Jehoash became very sick, and some of his friends came against him in order to pay him back for the death of Zechariah, the son of Jehoiada. Jehoash was trapped and killed. He was buried in Jerusalem, but not in the graves of his fathers since he was wicked. He died at age 47, and his son Amaziah became king.

Meanwhile, Jehoahaz, the son of Jehu, ruled over the Israelites in Samaria for 17 years. He was very wicked and the king of Syria fought against him and killed most of his army. Jehoahaz also lost strong cities. Elisha had foretold that this would happen. Jehoahaz cried out to God that Hazael would not kill him, and God answered. The kingdom again became quiet and prosperous.

After Jehoahaz died, his son Joash became king in Samaria. He had the same name as the king in Jerusalem (Joash is the same as Jehoash), he ruled 16 years. Unlike his father, he was a good king. Elisha was old and ill and Joash came to visit him. The king cried when he saw him, and called him his father. Joash said that he had won his wars not with weapons but by Elisha's prophecies. Now they would be conquered by the Syrians and other enemies – it would be better to die along with Elisha.

Elisha told him to shoot some arrows out of the window, and the king shot three. Elisha said that if he had shot more arrows, he would have won against Syria completely. "In the future you will win against them only three times." The king left, and soon Elisha died. He had performed many miracles and the Jews held him in high honor. He had a grand funeral. Later some robbers threw a dead man into his grave, and when the body touched Elisha's dead body, the man came back to life. Elisha had God's power in life and even after his death.

After Hazael the king of Syria died, Joash the king of Israel made war with Adad, Hazael's son. He won three battles and took back the cities and villages which Adad's father had taken from Israel.

ix

IN the second year of Joash's reign in Israel, Amaziah was ruling over the tribe of Judah in Jerusalem. He was righteous when he was young, but as he got stronger he wanted to pay back the men who killed his father Jehoash. He killed all those who had been responsible, but he did not kill the children, because Moses wrote that the children should not be punished for the sins of their fathers. He then formed an army from the young men around 20 years old from the tribes of Judah and Benjamin. When he had 30,000 of them, he organized them into groups of 100 with captains over them.

In addition Amaziah paid men from Israel to join this army, since they would be fighting against the Amalekites, Edomites and Gebalites. A prophet came and advised him to send the Israelites home. They were not good men and because of them, Amaziah's army would lose. God would allow them to win with a smaller army. So Amaziah sent them home, paying them even though they never went to battle. He won the battle with his own men. He brought back many prisoners and threw them down from a high rock in Arabia. He also brought great riches from those nations. But the Israelites who had been sent home decided they had been insulted by the king, so they began to ruin Amaziah's country, stealing cattle and killing 3,000 men.

Amaziah became very proud after his victories and began to worship the gods of the Amalekites. A prophet warned him about this, but he became very angry and told him to be quiet or he would punish him. The prophet said that God would judge him.

Amaziah then wrote a letter to Joash, the king of Israel, saying that all the people should obey him as in the days of David and Solomon. If they did not, he would fight against them. Joash answered by a parable about a thorny weed giving orders to a tall tree in Lebanon. It was a clear warning to keep down his pride and not put his kingdom in danger.

Amaziah went to war, but as soon as he led his army against Joash, they became so confused that they scattered, and Amaziah was left alone and captured. Joash said he would kill him unless the gates of Jerusalem were opened to receive him and his army. Amaziah surrendered and Joash tore down 400 cubits* of the city wall and drove his chariot through the hole. He then took over Jerusalem, stole all the temple and palace treasures, freed the king and returned to Samaria. Amaziah's friends made a plan against him and he was killed. There was a royal funeral held for him in Jerusalem. He was 54 and had ruled 29 years.

IN the fifteenth year of the rule of Amaziah, Jeroboam the son of Joash became king over Israel in Samaria. He ruled for 40 years. Jeroboam worshipped idols and caused much sorrow to the people of Israel by not obeying the true God. The prophet Jonah foretold that he would fight against the Syrians and push out the borders of his kingdom as Joshua had commanded Israel to do.

Jonah was also sent to warn the kingdom of Nineveh that they would lose their status as a powerful nation. Jonah disobeyed God and went to Joppa, got on a ship and sailed to Tarsus. The ship hit a storm at sea and they decided that someone on the ship was the cause of it. They threw dice and the dice pointed to Jonah. He told them that he was a Hebrew and a prophet of God, and that he was running away from what God had told him to do. If they would throw him into the sea, the storm would stop. The sailors felt this would be a terrible thing to do to a stranger who had entrusted his life to them, but in the end they agreed since they had no choice, and they threw him overboard. The sea suddenly became calm. Jonah was swallowed by a whale and stayed inside of it for three days and nights. After that the whale vomited him out on the Euxine Sea (the Black Sea). He was forgiven by God for his sin of disobedience. He went to Nineveh and foretold to them that they would soon lose control of Asia.

Jeroboam ruled happily for 40 years and was buried in Samaria. His son Zechariah became king. Uzziah, the son of Amaziah, began to rule over the two tribes in Jerusalem during Jeroboam's 14th year of rule. Uzziah was a careful and good king who won a battle against the Philistines. He took over Gath and Jabneh, breaking down their walls. He also won against the Arabs near Egypt. He built a strong city on the Red Sea, and from there he attacked the Ammonites and gathered taxes from them. He ruled over all the land as far south as Egypt, and he cared for Jerusalem for the rest of his life. All of the city walls were rebuilt, including the part torn down by the king of Israel when he had captured his father Amaziah. Uzziah built many towers 150 cubits* high and he dug many water canals. He had many animals for work and many cattle. He was good in farming. He had a strong army of 370,000, led by 2,000 captains and officers. They had good swords, armor, bows and slings. They used war machines to win against cities which could throw stones and arrows at them.

Uzziah's power and wealth made him go bad, and he began to sin as his father had done. On a holiday, he put on a holy priest's robe and went into the temple to offer incense on the golden altar. This was a job which only the sons of Aaron could do, so the high priest came with 80 priests and told Uzziah to leave. He said he would punish them with death if they didn't keep quiet. A great earthquake suddenly shook the ground and made a crack in the temple. The sun's bright rays came in and fell on the king's face and gave him leprosy. Half the mountain broke off on the west and moved four furlongs* to the east, ruining the king's gardens. When the priests saw that the king's face had leprosy, they made him leave the city, as all people with this disease had to be kept outside of the city. He lived a private life of suffering outside the city due to his disobedience to God. Jotham became king in his place. Uzziah lived 68 years and was king for 52 of them. He was buried in his own gardens.

xi

WHEN Zechariah, the son of Jeroboam, had reigned six months in Israel, he was killed by a man named Shallum, who reigned for only 30 days. Menahem, the army general, heard what happened while he was away. He returned to Samaria and killed Shallum, then made himself king. He came to the city of Tiphsah, but the people would not open their gates to him. To pay them back, he burned the land around them and took the city by force, killing everyone, including the babies. He was a cruel king and ruled for

10 years. When Pul, the king of Assyria, came down to fight him, Menahem gave them 1,000 talents* of silver in order to avoid war. He took money from everyone in his kingdom in order to collect enough. He later died and was buried in Samaria. His son reigned for only two years and was as cruel as his father. He was killed at a feast by the keeper of his horse, named Pekah. This Pekah ruled for 20 years and was very wicked. The king of Assyria, Tiglath-Pileser, took many of Pekah's people in the land of Gilead and east of the Jordan River. He took prisoners and made them part of his kingdom.

Jotham, the son of Uzziah, ruled over the tribe of Judah in Jerusalem. He was righteous and he honored God. He fixed all that was broken in the temple and the walls. He built strong towers for defense. He led a battle against the Ammonites and won, taking taxes and making them give him wheat and barley every year.

Nahum the prophet spoke of the overthrow of the Assyrians and of Nineveh. They would lose their money and flee from the city. "Their faces will be black with fear. Your lions will no longer give their laws to the world." This prophecy was fulfilled 115 years after it was given.

JOTHAM died when he was 41. He ruled for 16 years and was buried in the graves of the kings. Ahaz his son reigned and was very wicked. He built altars in Jerusalem like they had done in Israel, and he even offered his son as a burnt offering in the way the Caananites did. Rezin the king of Syria and Pekah the king of Israel, who were friends with each other, fought against him. They tried to capture Jerusalem but it was very strong, so they went to other places. The king of Syria took Elath on the Red Sea, killed all the people and filled it with Syrians. He took other cities and returned with his army to Damascus.

Ahaz knew that Rezin had gone home, so he gathered his army to attack the king of Israel. He was beaten, because God had to punish him for his wickedness. He lost 120,000 men. The general of the Israelite army killed Zechariah, the king's son, as well as the governor. He captured the general of the army of Judah, and he also took the women and children of the tribe of Benjamin as prisoners to Samaria.

Obed, a prophet in Samaria, met the army before they entered the city, and he told them that they had not won by being strong, but because of God's anger against King Ahaz. He told them to let go of all the prisoners or they would be punished by God. The leaders gathered the people together and talked about what to do. One named Berechiah, who was a leader, said that it would be best to listen to the prophet, and the people agreed. They gave the prisoners supplies and sent them home.

Ahaz had great losses from that battle, and he begged the king of Assyria to help him fight the Israelites, and promised to send him money. After receiving many gifts, the Assyrian king helped Ahaz. On his way, he fought against the Syrians. He ruined their country and the city of Damascus, and he killed their king Rezin. All the people of Damascus were moved to Upper Media (Persia) and he brought Assyrians to live in Damascus. He took many people prisoner from the land of Israel.

So Ahaz took all the gold and silver that was in the king's treasury, and other valuable gifts, and he gave them to the king of Assyria in Damascus. He then returned to Jerusalem. He continued to worship the Syrian and Assyrian gods even though he had been beaten by them. He closed the temple, stopped all the sacrifices from being offered, and took away all the gifts which had been given. He died at age 36 and had ruled for 16 years.

xiii

PEKAH, the king of Israel, was killed by Hoshea, a friend of his who became king for nine years. He was wicked, and the king of Assyria, Shalmaneser, won a battle against him. They had to pay a tax to Assyria. In the fourth year of the rule of Hoshea, Hezekiah began to rule in Jerusalem. He was a righteous king who worshipped God. He called together the priests and Levites, and he told them that they had suffered because his father had gone against the worship of God. He told the people to make themselves clean and that the temple sacrifices would start again. The temple was opened and cleaned. The sacrifices started again, and everyone in the whole country was invited to celebrate the Feast of Unleavened Bread (Passover) in Jerusalem. He also invited the Israelites to come and keep the old ways of worshipping God in the temple. In this way they would be united, and they would be blessed. The Israelites laughed at the king's messengers, and at the prophets who warned that they would suffer if they did not return to worship of the true God. They even caught some of the messengers and prophets and killed them. But many from the tribes of Manasseh, Zebulon and Issachar obeyed the prophets and returned to the worship of God in Jerusalem.

When these men arrived, Hezekiah stood with the rulers and the people and offered many offerings for himself and the people. The priests kept offering many sacrifices, and the Levites stood around playing musical instruments and singing songs to God as in the time of David. The king and the people got down on the ground and worshipped God. Hezekiah offered many sacrifices and the people had a feast. They continued celebrating for one week, and then for another week. Such a celebration had not been done since the time of Solomon.

After this the people went out and destroyed all of the idols. The king ordered that sacrifices should be offered every day. Tithes (one-tenth offerings) and first-fruit offerings should be given by everyone to the priests and Levites, so that they could do their job for God. The people brought much fruit to the priests and Levites, so they and their families had plenty to eat. After these matters were settled, the king fought against the Philistines and won. He took all of the enemy's cities from Gaza to Gath and made them part of Judah. The king of Assyria came and told Hezekiah to pay the tax which his father had been paying, but Hezekiah refused to be afraid. He trusted God and Isaiah the prophet, who told him about the future.

SHALMANESER, the king of Assyria, heard that Hoshea, the king of Israel, had asked for help from So, the king of Egypt, to fight against him. Shalmaneser was very upset and came to Samaria in the seventh year of Hoshea's rule, but they would not let him into the city. He fought against the city for three years and finally took it by force. He moved the Israelite people to Media and Persia, and he took Hoshea as a prisoner. The Assyrian king brought into Israel people from Persia called Cutheans, since they lived near a river called Cuthah. All ten tribes of the north were taken from their land 947 years after they had left Egypt. This was punishment for rebelling against Rehoboam the grandson of David, and for making Jeroboam their king. They also refused to keep God's laws and did not listen to the prophets' warnings to stop their evil deeds.

The king of Assyria invaded all of Syria and Phoenicia. The history books of Tyre (in Lebanon) tell us that after the invasion there was peace and he went home. Tyre then rebelled against the Assyrian king, so 60 ships were sent out with 800 men to row them. The Tyrians had only 12 ships but they won the battle and took 500 prisoners. The king of Assyria came back again and put guards at their rivers and water bridges, and the Tyrians could not draw water. This kept on for five years, but they found water inside their city by digging some wells.

The Cutheans who lived in Samaria brought their gods with them, and God caused them to be sick. They discovered through one of their priests that they should worship Almighty God. They sent messengers to the king of Assyria asking him to send them priests from Israel who had been taken captive. These priests taught them the law of God and how to worship, and after that the sickness stopped. These are the Samaritans. They want to be accepted as part of the Hebrew people when the Jews are doing well. But when the Jews have trouble, the Samaritans don't want to be related to them, or do anything kind for the Jews.

BOOK X

FROM THE CAPTIVITY OF THE TEN TRIBES TO THE FIRST YEAR OF CYRUS

IN the fourteenth year of Hezekiah's reign over the southern kingdom, Sennarcherib, the king of Assyria, came against him with a huge army and took all of the tribes of Judah and Benjamin. He was preparing to come against Jerusalem, but Hezekiah sent ambassadors and offered to pay whatever was required rather than go to war. Sennacherib demanded 300 talents* of silver and thirty talents* of gold in return for leaving the city in peace. The Assyrian king did not keep his promise, however. He went to war against the Egyptians and Ethiopians, but left behind his chief commanders with their army to destroy Jerusalem. They camped outside the walls and called Hezekiah to come and speak with them. He sent three of his friends to speak with them. Rabshakeh, the Assyrian commander, wanted his whole army to enter the city and said that God was behind this mission. The general spoke in Hebrew, and he was asked to speak in Syrian so as not to disturb the people. The general spoke even louder, urging the people to surrender. He offered them 2000 horses if they had enough people to ride them (he knew that they didn't).

The ambassadors brought the message to Hezekiah, and he put on sackcloth and fell on his face asking for God's help, because they were without hope. He also sent some of his friends and some of the priests to the prophet Isaiah, asking him to pray to God and offer sacrifices for their deliverance. Isaiah did this and God spoke, saying that their enemies would be beaten without a battle. He said that Sennacherib would not win the battle in Egypt, and that when he went home he would be killed by the sword. At the same time, the king of Assyria wrote to Hezekiah to make him afraid, bragging about all of his successes in other nations. He ordered Hezekiah to open the gates of Jerusalem to his army. Hezekiah rolled up the letter and put it in the temple. Isaiah said that there would be a time of peace and the crops would be successful.

The king of Assyria returned home because he heard that the Ethiopians were coming to aid the Egyptians. Herodotus wrote that the Egyptian priest prayed to God, and God defeated the Assyrians by sending mice to chew up their armor. When Sennacherib came to Jerusalem, he saw that many captains and generals were destroyed by sickness together with the soldiers. He took the army which survived and went home to Nineveh. He was killed by his oldest sons in his own temple. These sons had to run away, and they settled in Armenia.

ii

HEZEKIAH was delivered by God through a miracle and he and all the people thanked him. The rest of his enemies were afraid and they left Jerusalem. But in spite of Hezekiah's devotion to God, he had a serious disease and was expected to die. He was very upset because he had no child who could rule the kingdom after him. He begged God to let him live until he could have a child. God sent him Isaiah the prophet, who told Hezekiah that he would get well within three days and that he would live another 15 years and father a child. Hezekiah asked Isaiah to give him some sign so that he could believe him. Hezekiah asked that the shadow of the sun which had gone down ten degrees in his house would return again to the same place as before. The prophet prayed to God and this sign was granted. Hezekiah then went to the temple and worshipped God and made vows to him.

The king of Babylon, Baladan, sent ambassadors to Hezekiah with presents, wanting to make friends with him. Hezekiah received them gladly, made them a feast and showed them all of his treasures. They saw the armory, the gold and precious stones and he gave them presents to take back to Baladan. Isaiah came to Hezekiah and asked about the guests. He replied that they were from the king of Babylon, and that he had showed them everything he had. The prophet said, "In a short time all of these riches will be taken away to Babylon, and your descendents will lose their manhood and will grow up in Babylon." Hezekiah was very upset. Isaiah as well as 12 other prophets wrote down all of their prophecies, so that the events could be checked against what was foretold. Whether good or bad was prophesied, the events came true according to what had been said.

iii

HEZEKIAH lived another 15 years in peace and died at age 54, having reigned 29 years. He was followed by his son, Manasseh, who was very wicked. He copied the sins of the Israelites (the northern kingdom) for which they had been destroyed. He made the temple of God, the city and the whole country unclean. He cruelly killed all the righteous men and the prophets. Jerusalem was filled with blood. God was angry and sent prophets to him and to the people warning them of God's judgment, but they were not believed.

God caused the king of Babylon and Chaldea to attack Judea. The country was destroyed and Manasseh was brought to the king to be punished. Manasseh realized that he was to blame for all of the nation's misery, and he asked God to forgive him. He was released and returned to Jerusalem. He cleaned the temple, and for the rest of his life he thanked God for his deliverance. He convinced the people to worship God according to Moses' laws. He rebuilt the altar and sacrifices were offered. He repaired the old walls and added another one to make them stronger. He built high towers and provided everyone with all that they needed. He was not only a happy man but an example for others. He lived to be 67 years old, and was king for 55 years. He was buried in his garden, and his son Amon became the next king.

AMON was not a righteous king – he acted like his father in his younger days. Amon's own servants killed him at age 24, only two years after he became king. The people punished the killers, and Amon was buried with his father. Josiah was eight years old when he began to reign. He was an honest king like King David and a good example for everyone. When he was twelve, he urged the people to stop their idol worship and to worship the true God. He had wisdom beyond his years, learned from the mistakes of those who had ruled before him, and he listened to the wisdom of older men. He went around the country and cut down all of the groves of trees which had been devoted to false gods and destroyed their altars. Any gifts which had been dedicated to them by his ancestors were destroyed. He offered sacrifices and burnt offerings on the altar in Jerusalem. He set up judges and officers to decide matters in a just way, the same that they would want for themselves. Much gold and silver was brought to repair the temple. There were four men responsible for handling the money so that the work could be done right away. Everyone realized that the king had done an important and righteous thing.

When Josiah had reigned 18 years, he ordered Eliakim the high priest to use the the leftover money to make cups, dishes and jars for the temple worship. While they were bringing gold out of the temple they found the holy books of Moses, which were given to Shaphan the scribe. He read them, and then he read them to Josiah, and when Josiah heard what was written, he tore his clothes. He gathered his friends and sent them to Huldah the prophetess to ask her to pray to God for them. She said to tell Josiah that God had already decided to punish the people and throw them out of their country. Prayers could no longer help, because the people didn't listen to the warnings of the prophets.

The punishment would be delayed, however, since Josiah was a righteous king. When the king heard this, he sent for all the people, including the children, to gather in Jerusalem, together with the priests and Levites Josiah began to read the books to them, standing on a platform in the center. He urged them to make a covenant that they would worship God and keep the laws of Moses. They were willing. They offered sacrifices and asked for God's mercy. The high priest was told to take out any dishes or tools from the temple that had been dedicated to idols. These were burned, the ashes were scattered, and the priests of the idols, who were not of the family of Aaron, were killed.

Josiah went on and destroyed all of the buildings around the country [of the northern kingdom] which had been built when Jeroboam was king which had been dedicated to false gods. He burned the bones of the false prophets on the first altar which Jeroboam had built. This was in fulfillment of a prophecy that had been given 361 years before.

Josiah also sent a message to the Israelites who had escaped capture and slavery under the Assyrians and urged them to worship only the true God and to trust him. He searched all of the houses, villages and cities and made sure there were no idols left in them. He took away the chariots of the Sun which were in his royal palace. He and the people returned to Jerusalem and celebrated the feast of unleavened bread, called the Passover. They offered 30,000 sacrifices and 3,000 oxen for burnt offerings. Many lambs were sacrificed. The priests taught the people, explaining the meaning of what they were doing. There had not been such a celebration by the Hebrews since the time of Samuel the prophet. Josiah lived after this in peace, in wealth and with a good reputation.

V

NECO, the king of Egypt, marched with his soldiers to the Euphrates River in order to fight against the Medes and Babylonians who had conquered the Assyrians. When he came to the city of Mendes, which belonged to the kingdom of Josiah, Josiah stopped him from passing. Neco said that he wanted only to pass Mendes peacefully. Josiah was in his chariot and organizing his soldiers when he was shot with an Egyptian arrow. He returned to Jerusalem badly wounded and he later died. The people gave him a grand funeral. He had lived 39 years and reigned for 31. Jeremiah wrote a lament for him which has been kept to this day. This prophet also predicted the destruction of Jerusalem. Ezekiel before this wrote a prophecy about the destruction of Jerusalem in two books. These two prophets were priests by birth, but Jeremiah lived in Jerusalem from the thirteenth year of the reign of Josiah until the city and temple were destroyed.

When Josiah died, his son Jehoahaz, age 23, reigned in his place. He was a wicked king. When the king of Egypt returned, he wanted Jehoahaz to meet him in Hamath which belongs to Syria. He made Jehoahaz a prisoner and gave his brother, Eliakim, the throne, changing his name to Jehoiakim. He had to pay a tribute of 100 talents* of silver and a talent* of gold to Neco. Neco took Jehoahaz to Egypt where he died. He had reigned only three months and ten days.

vi

IN the fourth year of the reign of Jehoiakim, Nebuchadnezzar became ruler over the Babylonians. He went to war against Neco who was ruling over all of Syria. Neco lost tens of thousands of soldiers. Nebuchadnezzar took all of Syria but did not take Judea. After four years, he demanded a tax from Jehoiakim. This tax was paid for two years, but not in the third year; Jehoiakim thought that the Babylonian king would be beaten by Egypt in a battle. But Jeremiah the prophet warned them not to depend on Egypt. Jehoiakim and the Jews would not escape the destruction of Jerusalem in any case. The people would not believe Jeremiah's words, and they brought him to court. The elders didn't want to harm him, saying that other prophets, including Micah, had also foretold the destruction of Jerusalem. Those prophets had been honored under the kings of those times. The prophet Jeremiah wrote everything down, while the people were fasting and gathered at the temple, in the ninth month of the fifth year of Jehoiakim's reign. The book was read, and when the rulers heard it they took it from him and told him and his scribe, Baruch, to hide. The book was taken to the king. When the king heard it he became angry and tore it and threw it into the fire. He wanted to punish Jeremiah and Baruch, but they escaped.

Shortly afterwards the king of Babylon came to Jerusalem in battle, and Jehoiakim opened the gates, thinking that if he didn't try to fight, he would not be harmed. As soon as the Babylonian king entered the city, he began killing people in every direction, regardless of age or rank. Jehoiakim was killed and not buried. His son, Jehoiachin became the king. Nebuchadnezzar took the best people as captives, leading 3,000 away to Babylon. Ezekiel, the young prophet was among them. Jehoiakim had lived 36 years and reigned for eleven years. Jehoiachin reigned for only three months and ten days.

vii

THE king of Babylon was afraid after giving the kingdom to Jehoiachin, thinking that since he'd killed his father, Jehoiachin would rebel against him. He sent an army to Jerusalem. But Jehoiachin was gentle and didn't want a fight. He gave up his mother and family to the commanders which Nebuchadnezzar sent, because they promised him that his family and the city would be spared. The promise was not kept; instead the army was ordered to take everyone captive, both the youth and those men skilled in work, and bring them to Babylon. There were 10,832 in all, including Jehoiachin. They were kept under guard and the uncle of Jehoiachin, Zedekiah, was made king. He had to promise that he would not rebel or make a deal with the Egyptians.

Zedekiah became king at age 21. He had the same mother as Jehoiakim but he was very wicked. Jeremiah often warned him to repent, and not to listen to the wicked rulers or to false prophets who said that the Babylonians would not make war against them.

Zedekiah would agree, but then his friends would convince him to reject the prophet's advice. Both Jeremiah (in Jerusalem) and Ezekiel (in Babylon) prophesied what would happen to Jerusalem. But while Jeremiah said that Zedekiah would be taken to Babylon, Ezekiel foretold that Zedekiah would not see Babylon. Zedekiah did not believe them since they didn't agree. But both were right in the end.

Zedekiah kept the agreement with the Babylonians for eight years. He then asked for help from the Egyptians against the Babylonians. When the king of Babylon heard this, he came with his army, ruining the country and shutting up Jerusalem in a siege. The Egyptians came to help, and the king of Babylon left. The Babylonians chased the Egyptians and drove them out of Syria. False prophets came to Zedekiah and said that the Babylonians would no longer make war against Jerusalem or take any more captives. They said the prisoners already taken would come back along with the temple dishes which had been taken. Jeremiah prophesied the opposite. He said that the Babylonians would return and that there would be a famine in Jerusalem. He said that all of the remaining riches would be taken and the rest of the people would be taken captive. The entire city would be burned. They would be in Babyon for 70 years, until the Persians and the Medes would overthrow the Babylonians. Only then would some return to this land to rebuild the temple and restore Jerusalem.

Most of the people believed Jeremiah, but the rulers and wicked people hated him and thought he was crazy. Jeremiah went to his home in Anathoth, but when he was on his way he was arrested and accused of deserting to the Babylonians. He said he was only going home. They took him back and tortured him unjustly.

In the ninth year of the reign of Zedekiah, the king of Babylon returned to Jerusalem and surrounded it for eighteen months. The people inside had nothing to eat and disease broke out. Though Jeremiah was in prison, he told the people to open their gates in order to stay alive. He said that if they did not do this, they would die of famine or be killed by the sword. The rulers did not believe him but they told the king of the prophet's words. The king did not think that Jeremiah was crazy. The king was on Jeremiah's side, but he didn't want to upset the rulers, so he let them do to Jeremiah what they wanted. They took him from prison and put him in a muddy pit to die. He was up to his neck when one of the king's servants, an Ethiopian, told the king that his friends and rulers had done a very evil thing. This kind of death was a crueler death than that in prison. The king let the Ethiopian take 30 of his men and ropes to bring Jeremiah out of the pit as soon as possible. He was returned to the prison.

The king called him to hear a word from God. Jeremiah said that he didn't want to speak since the king's friends already decided to destroy him as if he was guilty of some wickedness. "And where are those men who deceived you, saying that the king of Babylon would no longer come against us?" The king gave a promise that he would not kill Jeremiah. So Jeremiah told him that he should give the city up to the Babylonians, and then the city would not be destroyed nor would the temple be burned. But if the king disobeyed, everyone would suffer. Zedekiah was willing to obey, but he was afraid that the people who had gone over to the Babylonians would say bad things about him. The king let Jeremiah go, and told him not to tell any of the rulers what they had discussed. "Just tell them that you were begging to be released from prison." The rulers did question him, and he replied as the king had told him to.

viii

THE Babylonians piled up dirt against the walls of Jerusalem and used war machines against those inside, but the Hebrews weren't discouraged by famine or disease. They continuously sent their darts and other weapons to beat back the Babylonians. It became a war of skill between the people of Jerusalem and the Babylonians. This went on for 18 months, and the city was finally captured in the eleventh year of Zedekiah's reign. The king of Babylon stayed in Riblah in Syria and his seven generals led the attacks. The Babylonians entered the city at midnight and went into the temple. Zedekiah heard of it, so he took his wives, children, captains and friends and got out of the city through a big ditch which ran out to the desert. Someone found out, and the Babylonians chased them and caught them not far from Jericho. The friends and captains ran away to save themselves, but Zedekiah was captured. Nebuchadnezzar called him wicked and a promise breaker. He said that he had given Zedekiah the kingdom after having taken it from Jehoiachin and he should have been grateful. All of his sons and friends were killed with Zedekiah watching. Then they put out his eyes. He was brought to Babylon as Jeremiah had prophesied, but he did not see it as Ezekiel had prophesied. God's prophecies are fulfilled perfectly in time, showing men how foolish they are.

Thus the kings of David's line ended, a total of 21 kings. The line lasted 514 years. Saul, the first king was not from the same tribe as the rest.

The king of Babylon sent Nebuzaradan, the army general, to rob and burn the temple in Jerusalem. The royal palace was also burned and the entire city was torn down to the ground. All the people were taken captive and brought to Babylon. The Babylonians carried off gold and silver dishes, the large washing pool which Solomon had made, along with the pillars of brass, the golden tables and candlesticks. The temple was burned 470 -1/2 years after it had been built. It had been 1,062- 1/2 years after the Hebrews had left Egypt.

The high priest and his helper were taken to Babylon. The three rulers guarding the temple, the eunuch who was over the armed men, seven friends of Zedekiah, his scribe and sixty other rulers were all taken to the king of Babylon, to Riblah, a city in Syria. The heads of the high priest and the rulers were cut off there.

There is a list of all of those who served as high priests up to now [the time of Josephus] beginning with Zadok from the time of Solomon. The sons received the priesthood from their fathers.

King Zedekiah was kept in prison until he died. He had a grand funeral. The dishes which were taken from the temple were dedicated to Nebuchadnezzar's gods. Nebuchadnezzar also freed the high priest (the son the one he had killed).

THE Jews carried into Babylon were led by the army general, Nebuzaradan. Some of the poor people were left near Jerusalem and Gedaliah, a kind man from a noble family, was left in charge to make sure the king received his tax. The people worked on their farms. The general took Jeremiah out of prison, but he refused the offer to go to Babylon. He didn't mind living among the ruins of the country. The general gave him supplies and asked Gedaliah to look after him. Jeremiah asked the general to free Baruch the scribe, who was excellent at language, which he did. The general left for Babylon, and some of the Jews who had been scattered after Jerusalem fell joined Gedaliah and Jeremiah in Mispah. There were four rulers over the people, and one wicked man named Ishmael, from the king's family. Gedaliah encouraged the people to spread out and to use the season to grow corn, wine and oil. He told them there was no need to worry about the Babylonians. Some of the people sensed that Ishmael, who had lived for a time with Baalis, the king of the Ammonites, had come as a spy and intended to kill him so that he could rule over the Israelites. They wanted permission to kill Ishmael, but Gedaliah felt that because he had treated Ishmael well, the man would not do such a wicked thing. He said he would rather die than to kill a man who had come to him for safety.

These informers went away, and in 30 days Ishmael came to Gedaliah again, together with ten men. They feasted with him and Gedaliah gave presents to them. Gedaliah became drunk and fell asleep. Ishmael and his ten friends killed Gedaliah and all who were at the feast, and went on until they had killed all of the Jews in the city, including the soldiers who were left by the Babylonians. The next day 80 men came from the country to give presents to Gedaliah, not knowing what had happened. Ishmael invited them in to see Gedaliah, and when they were inside the court he shut them in and killed them all, throwing their bodies down into a pit. A few of these men escaped death by bringing Ishmael their riches which they had hidden in the fields, including furniture, clothes and corn. All of the wives and children in Mispah were taken captive, including the daughters of King Zedekiah who were also with Gedaliah. Ishmael returned to the king of the Ammonites.

When Johanan and the rulers heard what Ishmael had done at Mispah, and of the death of Gedaliah, they chased after Ishmael and found him at the fountain in Hebron. The people captured by Ishmael came gladly to their side, and Ishmael escaped to the Ammonites with eight friends. Johanan took care of the people and thought about taking them to Egypt. He then came to ask Jeremiah what to do. After ten days God appeared to Jeremiah and told him that he should inform Johanan and the other rulers and all the people that he would protect them from the Babylonians. They were to stay in the country and not go to Egypt. If they would go to Egypt, they would be punished. Jeremiah's word was not believed. They all went to Egypt, and they took Jeremiah and Baruch with them.

While in Egypt, God revealed to Jeremiah that the king of Babylon was coming against them in Egypt. Some would be killed and some taken captive to Babylon. This came to pass.

Twice the Hebrews were carried beyond the Euphrates. The ten tribes were taken out of Samaria by the Assyrians in the days of King Hoshea. The two tribes that remained after Jerusalem was taken were carried away by Nebuchadnezzer, the king of Babylon and Chaldea.

Now after the Israelites were removed, they were replaced by the Cutheans who had formerly lived in Persia and Media. They were called Samaritans. Judea, Jerusalem and the temple became deserted for 70 years. From the captivity of the Israelites to the carrying away of the two tribes totaled 130 years.

NEBUCHADNEZZAR, the king of Babylon, took some talented and good looking young Jews along with Zedekiah's family, and he put them in the care of teachers. Some were forced to be eunuchs (losing their manhood). The king wanted them to eat well and have a Chaldean education. Four from the family of Zedekiah were called Daniel, Ananias, Misael and Azarias. The king changed their names to Baltasar, Shadrach, Meshach and Abednego, respectively. These four wanted to eat only vegetarian food, which the king's servant agreed to allow for ten days as a test. They ate a sort of cereal and dates. After the test, they looked healthier than those who were eating the king's food, so they were allowed to continue in this way. They were able to learn more easily and could work harder as well. Daniel was especially wise and was also able to interpret dreams which God revealed to him.

Two years after the destruction of Egypt, King Nebuchadnezzar had a dream. By morning he forgot it, however, and when he asked for the meaning he expected the Chaldeans, magicians and prophets not only to interpret his dream but to even remember it for him. They all said this was asking too much. The king said he would kill them all. Daniel heard about this and realized that he and his three friends were also in danger. He went to Arioch, captain of the king's guards, and when he heard the problem, he requested that Arioch tell the king to wait for one night and see if Daniel might get an answer from God. God revealed the dream to Daniel that night and by morning he and his friends were joyful. They thanked God and told Arioch that Daniel wanted to see the king.

Daniel confessed to the king that he wasn't better than the other Chaldeans and magicians, but that God had pity on those who were in danger of being killed. The king's dream was about those kingdoms that would come after Babylon. There was a high statue with a head of gold, shoulders and arms of silver, belly and thighs of brass, and the legs and feet of iron. A stone was broken off a mountain, which landed on the statue and broke it into pieces. The pieces were like dust which was all blown away by the wind. The stone grew and grew and seemed to fill the earth. Daniel said: "The gold represents your kingdom, including the kings of Babylon who came before you. The silver means that your government will be dissolved by two kings, and then that one will be taken by another king from the west armed with brass. Yet another king like iron will end the power of the brass kingdom. Since iron is stronger than gold, silver and brass, it will rule over the earth." Daniel also told him about the stone, but I [Josephus] will not explain that part, because it is still future.

The king was amazed that Daniel had such wisdom, and he fell on his knees and saluted him in the way men worship God. He commanded that Daniel be given sacrifices as if he were a god. He gave the name of his own god to Daniel [Baltasar] and made him ruler of his whole kingdom; his kinsmen were also given high positions. The enemies of these men became jealous. The king made a high image of gold (60 cubits*) and set it in the great plain of Babylon. He asked the rulers to come for the dedication of the image. When they would hear the sound of the trumpet they were ordered to fall down and worship the image. Those who did not bow down would be thrown into a fiery furnace. Daniel's three friends could not go against the God of Israel, so they did not bow down to the image. They were thrown into the fire but were saved by God. The fire did not touch them. The king continued to highly regard these men.

Nebuchadnezzar had another vision which showed that he would fall from power and eat his food with the wild beasts. After seven years he would again become king. He called his magicians to explain this dream but they could not. Only Daniel could explain it. It came to pass.

I, Josephus, have not added anything here. I've simply translated the Hebrew books into the Greek language.

xi

NEBUCHADNEZZAR reigned forty-three years and died. He was an active man and more fortunate than the previous kings.

When his father heard that the governor he had set over Egypt and in other places revolted against him, he was too old to go to battle, so he sent his son instead. He won the war, but about the same time his father died in Babylon. He settled affairs, appointing leaders over the captive people who were to be taken to Babylon, together with weapons and supplies. He went ahead of them over the desert with a few people to Babylon. He received the whole kingdom of his father and sent the captives to different places in Babylonia. He decorated the temple of Belus and the other temples in a grand way from the spoils of war. He rebuilt an old city since it was important for protecting the water supply. He built three walls around the inner city of Babylon using burnt brick. The gates were beautiful. He built a palace which was attached to his father's palace. It was very large and expensive but took only 15 days to build [sic – this could be a mistake, as noted in the footnote]. He built elevated walking trails to resemble mountains, and he planted trees along them. His wife grew up in the palaces of Media so he built a special paradise with things she had known. One author wrote a book about India, and he wrote that Nebuchadnezzar was greater than Hercules. He also conquered a great part of Libya and Tyre.

After Nebuchadnezzar died, Evil-Merodach was king. He freed the Jewish king Jeconiah and became his good friend. He honored him over the rest of the captive kings, because his father had not treated him fairly. Jeconiah had given himself up trying to save Jerusalem, together with his wives and children. Evil-Merodach reigned 18 years. His son Niglissar reigned for 40 years. Niglissar's son reigned only nine months, and after that Baltasar became king. Cyrus, the king of Persia, and Darius, the king of Media, warred against him.

Baltasar had a vision while he was having supper in a large hall and his concubines and friends were with him. They were drinking from many silver cups, which had been taken from the temple in Jerusalem, and they were making fun of Israel's God. Then Baltasar saw a hand come out of the wall and write some letters on the wall. He called for the magicians and Chaldeans to know the meaning of the writing. They could not explain, so he promised gifts to the one who could interpret the writing, which included one third of the kingdom. The king's grandmother, seeing how upset he was, told him that there was a Jewish captive from Judea who had come when Nebuchadnezzar had destroyed Jerusalem – he could probably read the writing for him. They called for Daniel. He didn't want the gifts. "Divine wisdom is free", Daniel said. But he warned that the king had forgotten the punishment Nebuchadnezzar received when he left God out of his life, which was life among wild animals for seven years. He said that God was angry at Baltasar for using holy cups with his concubines. The first word, "Maneh" meant "number" because his days were numbered. "Thekel" meant "weight": the kingdom was weighed and the scales went downward. "Phares", meaning "fragment", meant that the kingdom would be broken in pieces and divided among the Medes and Persians.

Baltasar was very upset, but he kept his promise, and even though the news was very bad for himself, he gave all the gifts to Daniel. In a short time, Cyrus the king of Persia fought against Baltasar and took him and conquered the city. Baltasar had been king for 17 years. Cyrus, the friend of Darius was won against Babylonia when he was 62 years old. He carried Daniel the prophet to Media, and Daniel became one of the three presidents over his 360 provinces.

Daniel had much favor with Darius and others were jealous of him. He couldn't be tempted to take bribes, and they had trouble finding anything wrong to accuse him of doing. He did pray to God three times a day, and so they made this into a problem before King Darius. They asked to make a law for 30 days not to allow someone to pray to anyone apart from the king. The punishment would be to be thrown into a lion's den. The king had no idea that this was a plot against Daniel, so he agreed to it. Daniel prayed to God as usual, and his enemies saw this. They immediately reported it to the king and said that Daniel was the only one who didn't keep the law. The king wanted to forgive Daniel but the rulers said that the law must be kept. Darius hoped that Daniel would be protected by his God. The stone over the top of the den was sealed. All night the king couldn't sleep or eat. In the morning he opened the seal and called to Daniel. Daniel said that he was not hurt. The king ordered to get him up out of the den. Daniel's enemies did not admit that God had protected Daniel. They said that the lions were not hungry. The king ordered lots of meat to be given to the lions. Then he ordered Daniel's enemies to be thrown into the den, to see if they would be eaten or not. All of these princes were torn to pieces, so this was a sure sign that God had protected Daniel. Darius sent letters all over the country praising the God of Daniel. He was the only true God and had all power.

Daniel became well known, and he built a tower in Media. It was a beautiful building, and it is still well preserved today. Kings of Media, Persia and Parthia are buried in this tower, which is cared for by a Jewish priest.

This man, Daniel, was a great prophet and one who talked with God. He not only knew of future events but knew the timing of some of them. When he was in Susa, a city of Persia, he was with his friends in a field. Suddenly he fell on his face and on his two hands, and his friends ran away. He saw a vision of a ram and a goat fighting with each another. The ram he saw was a symbol of the kingdoms of the Medes and Persians, and the horns were the kings who would reign. The last horn would be the last king who would be the richest and most glorious. The goat with one horn was one who would come from the Greeks who would fight twice with the Persian king and overcome him. Four kings following the Greek king would take over that kingdom which would spread in four directions in the world, but they would not be the first king's children. A certain king would take over the Jewish nation and ruin the temple, forbidding the sacrifices. Antiochus Epiphanes did exactly this. Daniel also wrote of the Roman government which destroyed our land. All of these prophecies were fulfilled.

The Epicureans are mistaken in the way they leave God out of everything. God is indeed a ruler and manager, not leaving mankind like a ship without a pilot, destined to drown. Those who do not see God's power over human affairs are mistaken.

I have described these matters as I found them, and those who don't see them as truth have a right to their own opinion without blame from me.

BOOK XI

FROM THE FIRST YEAR OF CYRUS TO THE DEATH OF ALEXANDER THE GREAT

CYRUS was called "God's Shepherd" by Xenophon as well as by Isaiah (Isa. 44:28). Jeremiah foretold that after 70 years, the Jews would be restored to their land and would rebuild the temple. In the 70th year from the day the captives were taken from Jerusalem to Babylon, God stirred up the mind of Cyrus to write to everyone in Asia, "Since the Almighty has appointed me to be king over the habitable earth, and since he is the God the Israelites worship, and my own name was mentioned 140 years previous by the prophet Isaiah, I will fulfill what is written." He gave the prominent Jews in Babylon permission to return to Jerusalem, and he offered his assistance by writing to their rulers and governors in Judea to contribute gold and silver for the building of the temple and animals for the sacrifices.

The rulers of the two tribes of Judah and Benjamin, with the Levites and priests, went quickly to Jerusalem. Some remained in exile because they did not want to give up their possessions. Gold, silver and many cattle and horses were gathered by the king's friends. Cyrus gathered up the vessels which had been stolen from the temple so that they would be returned. They would be safeguarded by Sanabassar in Judea and kept until the temple was built.

Cyrus wrote a letter to the governors in Syria. He said that he had given the Jews permission to return to their country and to rebuild their city and the temple in the same place where it was before. He sent his treasurer and Zorobabel, the governor of the Jews, to lay the foundations of the temple. "It will be 60 cubits* high. There will be polished stones on three walls and one wall of wood. I will pay for this." He then listed the many specific items to be returned: cups, large vessels, jugs, etc. Small animals were to be sent, along with wine and oil. Samaria would also contribute towards the expenses. He wrote, "The sacrifices will be offered as before according to the laws of Moses. They will pray to God for me and my family. Those who disobey these instructions will be hung on a cross and their goods brought into the king's treasury." The number of those returning to Jerusalem was 42,462.

ii

THE Jewish people were highly motivated regarding the building of the temple in Jerusalem. The king of Assyria had settled some people in Samaria who were from Persia and Media. They began to make trouble. They had money and they allowed the Jews to borrow it when needed, but they charged high interest for the loans. Cyrus was not checking on the Jews' progress, since he was involved in wars, including one against Massagetae. (It could be that Cyrus died in this war, which was near the Caspian Sea; but another account says that he died peacefully in his own country of Persia.) The son of Cyrus, Cambyses, became king, and the governors of Syria, Phoenicia, Ammon, Moab and Samaria wrote him a letter, with help from a historian, a scribe and judges.

The letter described the Jews who had returned from Babylon as rebellious. They said that once these Jews were settled, they would refuse to pay taxes to him. They would try to rule over others instead of being ruled. "We thought, O King, to warn you since the building project is going quickly. Do a search of their history books, and you will see how they were enemies to the surrounding kings. Once they finish the city wall, you may not even be able to pass through the area."

Cambyses read the letter and he wrote back to those in Samaria and Phoenicia. He said that he had looked at the history books of the Jews. "I saw that they have had some powerful and cruel kings who took taxes from Syria and Phoenicia. I order that the Jews be forced to stop building their city."

The men got on horseback and rode to Jerusalem right away, bringing many people along, and they stopped the Jews from building the city and the temple. Everything was at a standstill for nine years, until the second year of the reign of King Darius. Cambyses reigned six years, and during that time he took over Egypt. He returned and died in Damascus.

iii

MAGI (wise men) who ruled in Persia for one year after Cambyses died were all killed. The leaders of seven families of the Persians chose Darius to be their king. While he was still a private citizen, he made a vow to God that if he would become king he would make sure that all of the items which had been taken from the temple in Jerusalem would be returned. A Jewish governor named Zorobabel came from Jerusalem to Darius. He had known him from years before. He and two others were honored as the king's bodyguard. In the first year of Darius' reign he gave a large feast. His family, the rulers of the Medes, princes of the Persians and the top leaders of India and Ethiopia were there. His army generals who watched over his 127 provinces were also there. After the feast, everyone went home and Darius could not sleep. He woke up and talked to three of his bodyguards, and he promised a reward to them if they could give a wise argument about which is strongest: wine, kings, women or truth. The reward would be great riches, a ruling seat next to Darius, and being called a "cousin of the king". In the morning he sent for his top men, princes and rulers of Persia and Media, to hear what the three guards would say.

The first began to tell how strong wine is. "It fools the mind, making the king the same as an orphan. The slave thinks he is free, the poor man believes he is rich. Those who are suffering are not sad. Those who owe money forget their debts, and people forget that they need to obey the king. Men forget their families and even fight against them. In the morning they don't remember anything they have done. Therefore wine is the most powerful thing."

The second spoke about the strength of a king. "They force the earth and sea to bring them riches. They can send men to war and make them go through danger without refusing. They order men to bring down mountains and to pull down walls and towers. Their armies kill when told to kill, and they bring the spoils of war to the king. Those who work hard in farming bring part of what they grow to the king. They don't refuse, even knowing that the king has no lack of food or pleasure and sleeps in peace. He is carefully guarded by a man who thinks of nothing else. The king must then be the strongest."

Zorobabel began to speak about the strength of women. "A woman brings the king into the world. Women raise the men who plant the vines and make the wine. We receive everything from them, even our clothes. They keep us alive, and we can't live without them. If we gain riches, we will leave them all for a woman. We leave father and mother and even our best friends for the sake of a woman. We even die for them. We bring to a woman or mistress the fruit of our labor which we have gained at great sacrifice by land or sea. Once I saw the concubine of a king slap him in the face, taking his crown and putting on her own head. He was patient, and when she smiled he smiled, and when she was angry he was sad. He let himself be disgraced to please her."

The princes and rulers looked at each other, and Zorobabel began to speak about truth. He said, "In spite of the power of women and of the king himself, truth is stronger. God is true and righteous and all the evil in the world cannot do anything to stop it. All other things will die, but truth never dies. It doesn't get old like beauty or get lost like riches."

After Zorobabel finished, the people agreed that he had the wisest argument. The king said Zorobabel would sit with him and be called his cousin. Zorobabel had already promised God that if he would rise in the kingdom, he would rebuild Jerusalem and the temple, and bring back the items which Nebuchadnezzar had taken to Babylon. The king was willing to grant these wishes, and he rose and kissed Zorobabel. He wrote to the leaders and governors to support this new project. He ordered the rulers in Syria and Phoenicia to cut down and carry cedar trees from Lebanon to Jerusalem and to help Zorobabel rebuild the city. Darius also wrote that all of the Jewish captives who wanted to go back to Judea should be freed. He ordered that no more taxes should be collected from the Jews. They could have all the land in Judea that they needed, without being taxed. Villages which had been taken should be given back to the Jews and they should be given 50 talents for building the temple. They would be free to offer their sacrifices, and the king would pay for everything needed by the priests. He would also pay for the musical instruments which the Levites needed for singing hymns to God. Plots of land would be given to the guards of the city and temple, and they would be given money to keep everything in order. All that Cyrus had promised to do regarding Jerusalem would be continued by Darius.

Zorobabel received all of this from the king, and as he left the palace he looked up to heaven and gave thanks to God for the wisdom he had received from him and the victory it brought. He did not think that he was worthy of these, but it was the Lord's favor to him. He prayed for favor for the future, and after he told his people in Babylon, they also gave thanks to God for giving them the land of their fathers again. They had a feast for seven days and chose rulers from the different tribes who would go to Jerusalem, together with their families and cattle. They sang along the way, making music with pipes and cymbals. Darius sent some of his men along to keep order.

There were people from the tribes of Judah and Benjamin, as well as Levites. All together there were about 42,462 people, as I wrote before. There were some who had married foreign women, so they could not be priests, and their names were not recorded in the family tree. The camels and other beasts were numbered. Zorobabel, the son of Salathiel [Shaltiel, of David's line], and Jeshua, the son of Josedek the high priest were the top leaders. Mordecai and Serebeus also came back with them, rulers who gave 100 pounds of gold and 5,000 of silver. These came to Jerusalem with part of the Jews, but many of the others returned to their own lands.

IN the seventh month after the exiles from Babylon had returned to Jerusalem, Jeshua the high priest and Zorobabel the governor invited everyone in the country to gather to offer sacrifices to God. This was done in the place where sacrifices used to be offered. They also celebrated the Feast of Tabernacles. They began to build the temple, and much money was given to the stone cutters and wood workers. The Sidonians brought the cedar frees from Libanus [Lebanon] tied together in a raft, which they floated to Joppa. As Cyrus had first ordered, now Darius made it happen.

The second year after coming to Jerusalem, the Jews laid the foundations of the temple. The Levites who were 20 years old or above, and some of the priests were in charge of building the temple. It was finished sooner than expected. The priests had special clothes and trumpets, and the Levites and sons of Asaph stood and sang hymns to God in the way which had been arranged by David. Most of the people were pleased that they had a place to worship God, but a few cried because they remembered that the original temple was far more beautiful. Those who cried were old men and priests, and their sound blended in with the sounds of the music and the joy of the others.

The Samaritans, who were enemies of the tribes of Judah and Benjamin, came to Zorobabel, Jeshua and the heads of the families, saying that they wished to help build the temple. They were allowed to worship in it, but they could not be partners with the Jews, because they were not given the job in the beginning by Cyrus, and now by Darius. When the Cutheans heard this, they were upset and persuaded the nations of Syria to ask their leaders to stop the temple building. The governor of Syria and Phoenicia and others came to Jerusalem to ask about this building project; they said that it was more like a royal city than a temple. They asked why they needed such strong walls around the city as well.

Zorobabel told them about the history of the first temple. He told how the Babylonians and Chaldeans had ruined it and taken their people captive. He explained that Cyrus had allowed them to come and rebuild the temple quickly. He said that they could check with King Darius to see that this was true. The men then wrote to Darius right away, and the Jews were afraid that he might change his mind about supporting them. Two prophets, Haggai and Zechariah, urged them not to be upset but to keep on building. Darius received the letter saying that the temple was more like a royal city. They also showed him the letter from Cambyses that stopped them from building the temple. So Darius asked to look at the royal records. The original book included Cyrus's letter which gave the measurements of the temple. Three walls were to be built of polished stone, and one from the stone of their own country, paid for by the king. The temple dishes and tools would all be taken back to Jerusalem, and men were chosen who would protect these items. The Jews would be given supplies, and there would be animals for sacrifices. The Jews would pray for God to keep the king and the Persian nation safe. If any of these orders were not followed, the offender would be hung on a cross and their possessions given to the king. God would strike dead anyone stopping the building of the temple.

Darius wrote his answer to Sisinnes and his partners, telling them to do everything in Cyrus's letter. They agreed to help the leaders of the Jews and the princes of the Sanhedrim [sic, Sanhedrin, the judges]. The temple was built in seven years, and finished in the ninth year of the rule of Darius. Many sacrifices were offered. The priests and Levites set gatekeepers at every gate according to the laws of Moses.

In the month of Nisan, all of the people gathered to celebrate the Passover feast. This lasted for seven days, and many sacrifices at great cost were offered. They were grateful that God had restored them to the land of their fathers and to their laws. They were also grateful that the king of Persia had shown them favor. The high priests ruled as judges until a kingly rule was set up by the Asamoneans (Hasmoneans, the Maccabees). Judges had ruled the people after Moses and Joshua for more than 500 years. Then kings ruled over the people for the next 532 years.

The Samaritans were supposed to pay a tax to the Jews, but they refused. Darius wrote a letter to them to remind them that they needed to pay for sacrifices being offered on their behalf, as well as for the daily sacrifices and prayers for himself and the Persians.

V

AFTER Darius died, Xerxes his son became king of Persia. He feared and worshipped God and was friendly to the Jews. Jeshua, also called Joacim, was high priest. The main priest, however, was Esdras [Ezra], who was greatly respected by everyone. He knew the laws of Moses well and was friends with King Xerxes. He wanted to go up to Jerusalem together with some others, and he asked the king to write a letter to the governors of Syria about him. The king agreed that Esdras and some of the priests and Levites should go to Jerusalem. He wrote to the governors of Syria, telling them, "My seven counselors are coming to see if everything is being done according to the law of God in Judea." He gave silver and gold to pay for sacrifices. Besides the holy items which had been sent back, Xerxes gave them more to be taken to Jerusalem, paid for by the king. He wrote to the treasurers of Syria and Phoenicia to support Esdras so that God would be pleased with Xerxes and his family. He also gave a hundred cori* of wheat. He gave Esdras the right to choose judges in all of Syria and Phoenicia and to teach the people the law of God. Those who would not listen would be punished by death or have to pay a fine.

Esdras was very happy to receive this letter, and he thanked God because he knew the king's favor was God's work. He read the letter to the Jews in Babylon and sent a copy of it to those Jews in the country of Media. Some of them came to Babylon with their things, asking to join him. Many stayed in Babylon, and this is why there are only two tribes under Roman rule. The other ten tribes are still beyond the Euphrates River, and they are so many people they can't be counted.

Many priests, Levites, gatekeepers, singers and servants came to Esdras, and he stayed with them beyond the Euphrates for three days. They fasted before they left, and prayed that God would protect them on their trip to Jerusalem. They left Euphrates in the first month of the seventh year of the reign of Xerxes, and arrived in Jerusalem in the fifth month. Esdras gave the money [650 talents* of silver] to the treasurers as well as many dishes of gold and costly brass. Many sacrifices were offered for sins. Esdras gave the king's letter to the governors of countries they passed through, which gave them what they needed.

After some time some people came to him, accusing some of the priests and Levites of marrying foreign women. They urged that this matter be fixed so that God would not punish everyone. This sin was done even by the top leaders of the people. Esdras tore his clothes when he heard this and pulled out hair from his head and beard and fell on the ground. Some people came running to him, also crying. Esdras got up and stretched out his hands to heaven, saying that he was ashamed to look up because of the sins of the people. They had forgotten how God had punished them in the past for their sins. He asked God to forgive them – they were already a small group which had seen disaster and captivity, and they were on their way to the restored Jerusalem and their own land. They had asked for mercy while under the King of Persia, and it was granted. Jechonias, a leader from

Jerusalem, came to him and advised him to send away the wives and children who were not Jewish. Esdras listened to this advice and after he made the people promise that they would do this, he went into the house of Johanan to eat, because he had not tasted food all that day. An announcement went out that everyone should gather in Jerusalem within two or three days. Those who would not come would no longer be part of the people, and their possessions would be taken to be used in the temple. The elders were sitting in the upper room of the temple and it was very cold. Esdras stood up and told the priests and Levites who were guilty that they would have to decide whether or not to obey God in relating to their marriage. They agreed, but they said this would take time. They took one month to find all the priests who needed to send their wives away, and many left their wives and children and offered sacrifices to please God. The line of priests was then made pure, and it stayed that way for some time.

The Feast of Tabernacles (Booths) was celebrated. Esdras read the laws of Moses the whole morning. They cried because of their sins, knowing that they would not have suffered if they had kept God's laws. Esdras told them that it was not lawful to cry because it was a holiday. They should be more careful in the future. So they celebrated in their booths for eight days and then returned home, singing hymns to God and thanking Esdras for making things right. He died an old man and had a grand funeral in Jerusalem. Joacim the high priest also died and his son, Eliasib, was the priest after him.

One of the Jews who had been a captive in Babylon was the cupbearer for King Xerxes, Nehemiah. He was walking in Susa, the capitol of the Persians, and he heard some strangers speaking Hebrew. He learned that they had traveled from Judea, and he began to ask how things were there. They told him that the walls were broken down, and even in the daytime, the nations around them stole from them. Some people were captured at night, and during the day the roads were full of dead men. Nehemiah cried and looked up to heaven, asking God how long he would let the

Jews be victims of these injustices. Someone came to tell him that the king was ready to eat, so he had to go on his way without washing himself. The king was in a good mood and noticed that Nehemiah was not his usual self. Nehemiah prayed that he would gain the king's favor. He told him what he had heard about Jerusalem. He said that the tombs of his fathers had been destroyed and that the gates had been burned. "Could I be allowed to go build the walls and finish the building of the temple?" The king freely granted him this request, and he also said that he would give Nehemiah a letter to the governors to help him. Nehemiah worshipped God and thanked the king. The letter was ready the next day to take to the governors of Syria and Phoenicia and Samaria. They were ordered to give him anything he would need for the building project.

He came to Babylon and others joined him who wanted to help. He told them that first of all they would have to trust fully in God in order to stand against those who would try to stop the work. The work was divided among the people.

The Ammonites, Moabites, Samaritans and those who lived in Syria heard about the building and tried to stop it. They killed many of the Jews, and hired some of the foreigners to kill Nehemiah. Rumors were spread that the Jews would be attacked. They almost stopped building, but Nehemiah took body guards and kept working. He felt that if he would die, the work would stop. He ordered the builders work with their armor on. The stone cutter would have his sword on, and so would those carrying the building materials. He said that their shields should be close beside them. He placed trumpeters at every 500 feet to let the workers know if enemies were coming. He went around the city at night, even missing his own food and sleep.

This went on for two years and four months. The walls were finished during the 28th year of the rule of Xerxes. The people offered sacrifices and feasted for eight days. The Syrians were angry, but Nehemiah urged all the priests and Levites to move into the city. He built them houses which he paid for himself.

Those who were working in farming were to bring tithes (one-tenth) of their produce to Jerusalem so that the priests and Levites would have enough to eat. Jerusalem had more people than ever before. Nehemiah died an old man. He was a good, righteous man who worked hard to make his nation happy. The walls of Jerusalem were a lasting reminder of Nehemiah.

vi

AFTER the death of Xerxes, his son Cyrus (whom the Greeks called Artaxerxes) became king. He had governors over 127 provinces from India to Ethiopia. In the third year of his rule, he invited the Persian governors as well as his friends to a costly feast. He showed them his riches for 180 days. For the next seven days other nations were invited to Shushan. He pitched a large tent which was supported by pillars of gold and silver. These pillars were covered with curtains of linen and purple, and ten thousands could sit down. The cups were of gold and had precious jewels in them. He ordered his servants not to force the guests to drink, but to make sure enough was available. He ordered that the people take a vacation from work with pay. Vashti, the queen, gathered her guests for a feast in the palace. The king wanted to show his wife to the guests, but the Persian law forbids the wives to be seen by strangers, so she refused. She refused more than once, and he finally left his party, and after consulting with seven men who were experts in law, he accused his wife of rebelling against him. One of the lawyers, Memucan, said that the queen's refusal to obey the king would be a bad example for other women, who would also look down on their husbands. The king ordered that she be punished by sending her away. He felt bad about this decision afterwards, but by law he could not reverse it.

Artaxerxes was told by his friends to try to forget her and his love for her, and to find someone from the virgins to take her place. He took this advice and virgins were chosen. One of these girls was an orphan of the Jews in Babylon, who was raised by her uncle Mordecai of the tribe of Benjamin. Mordechai was one of the

Jewish leaders in the community. This woman, Esther, was more beautiful than all of the others. One of the king's guards took care of her. She needed to bathe in costly oils for six months. There were 400 virgins and each would be called one at a time to go to the king's bed for one night. The king was pleased with Esther; he fell in love with her and married her. There was a wedding feast in the seventh year of his rule. The marriage feast was also celebrated in the other nations. The Persians and Medes and leading men of the nations celebrated for an entire month. Esther came to the royal palace and was crowned. The king did not know that she was part of the Jewish nation. Her uncle Mordechai moved from Babylon to Shushan to hear how she was doing, since he loved her like his own daughter.

The king made a law that people could come to him only if they were called. Those who stood by him held axes in order to punish any who were not called. The king held a golden scepter in his hand which he would hold out to someone, giving permission to come close to him.

After this time two guards, Bigthan and Teresh, plotted against the king, and a certain Jew knew about this plot. He told Mordecai about it. The king hanged the two evil men, but he forgot to reward Mordecai who had saved his life. His name was just recorded in the books, and he was allowed to live in the palace as the king's friend.

There was a man named Haman, an Amalekite who used to go in to the king. Foreigners and Persians bowed down to him, but Mordecai refused. Haman, knowing that Mordechai was a Jew was very angry, thinking that Mordechai was no better than a slave. Haman asked the king to give him permission to punish Mordechai, and in fact the whole Jewish nation. Haman knew how the Jews had destroyed his Amalekite nation. So he told the king about this nation which did not mix with other nations and did not worship the gods like the others. He said that they were always arguing with others in their manners and practices. If the king would give an order to destroy them, rather than making them slaves, nothing would be lost. Haman said he would give the king 40,000 talents* out of his own riches whenever he needed it, in order to rid Persia of the Jewish people.

The king refused the money but allowed Haman to do what he wished. A decree was written: "Haman, second to the king, has ordered that a troublesome nation which opposes our laws and does not obey the kings be destroyed, together with their families. This will take place on the 14th day of the twelfth month of this year. Then there will be peace in our land." In Shushan they were quick to spread the news about this plan. The king and Haman feasted together, but the city was in an uproar.

Mordecai was told of this decree, and he tore his clothes and put on sackcloth. He sprinkled ashes on his head and went around the city crying out that a nation which hadn't hurt anyone was going to be destroyed. He was not allowed to enter the king's palace dressed like this, so he stood outside. In several other cities the crying began. Esther heard about Mordecai and urged him to change his clothes. Mordechai knew that Haman promised to give the king money to destroy the Jews. He had a copy of the decree to give to Esther, and he told her to ask the king to do something. Esther told Mordecai that she would lose her life if she were to go into the king without being called, and he did not hold out the golden scepter to her. Mordecai urged her to think of saving her own life and that of her nation. God would help his people in any case, but she should take this chance to save her own family which otherwise would be destroyed. Esther told her servant to tell Mordecai to gather the Jews in Shushan to fast for her. She and her maids would also fast, and then she would try to see the king. The people fasted and prayed to God to save his people. Mordechai said that this danger came about because he had refused to bow down to Haman. They asked God to deliver the Jews from this evil plot. Esther lay on the ground in mourning clothes and refused all food and drink for three days. She prayed that her words would persuade the king and that she would be more beautiful than ever. After three days, Esther dressed in her queen's clothes and took two of her maids with her. She leaned on one, and the other carried her long dress which swept along the ground. She was blushing when she came to the king. His clothes were woven with gold and precious stones which made him appear fierce, and he looked at her with anger. Her legs failed her and she fell down sideways, but the king seemed to change his mood – he came quickly from his throne and took her in his arms, and she felt stronger. He spoke nicely to her and told her not to be worried about the law which was for common people, for after all she was the queen. He put the scepter into her hand and laid his rod on her neck because of the law. She was no longer afraid. She explained in a low voice why she felt sick, and the king said not to worry – if needed, he would give her half of the kingdom.

Esther only asked that he and his friend Haman would come to a dinner which she would prepare. The king agreed. Esther didn't tell him what she wanted, but put it off until a dinner which he and Haman would come to on the next day.

Haman was very happy that he was invited to a dinner with the king and queen. When he saw Mordecai in the court, however, he became upset since Mordechai still did not bow to him. He told his wife Zeresh how he had been honored until Mordecai upset him. She said that Haman should order a gallows of 50 cubits* be built, and in the morning Mordecai could be hanged on it. Haman took her advice and had it built in the court. That night the king could not sleep. He decided to use the time and asked the scribe to bring him some old records. He read about Mordecai's good deed in saving his life by stopping the evil plan of his two guards. The king asked what reward had been given to Mordechai, and he heard that nothing had been done. He asked what time it was from the servants who watched the time, and they said it was morning.The king told them to see if any of his friends were in the court. Haman had come early in order to have Mordecai killed. The king, calling Haman his only true friend, asked what could be done to honor someone whom the king greatly loves. Haman said that the man should ride through the city on horseback in the king's robe with a gold chain around his neck. Someone should shout out to everyone that this is someone the king wants to honor. The king was pleased with this advice, and he told Haman to do this, as the king's friend, for Mordecai the Jew. "This will be his reward from us for saving my life." Haman took a horse and did as he was told. Mordecai did not know why Haman was doing this, and he called Haman names for making fun of him. But when he understood it was the king's order, he put on the robe, got on the horse and let Haman lead him around the city. Haman went home ashamed and crying. He told the family what happend. They said that God was with Mordecai and that he could never get revenge on him.

Esther's servants came to bring Haman to the dinner, and they saw the gallows. One asked why it was built, and when he was told he kept quiet. The king asked Esther what gifts she would like. Esther told him how her nation was about to be destroyed. If they had only been made into slaves, she said, she would not have bothered the king. The king asked who was behind this idea. She said that Haman was the one who wanted to kill all of her people. The king was very upset and went outside to the garden. Haman was inside, trying to beg forgiveness from Esther so that he would not be punished. He fell on her bed, and when the king saw this he was even more upset – he asked Haman if he was trying to hurt his wife. Haman could think of nothing to say. Then the servant told the king about the gallows in Haman's court. The king ordered that Haman be hung on his own gallows. God showed his wisdom by punishing a wicked person in the same way he had planned for someone else. The lesson is that when someone plans evil against another person, without knowing it, he prepares evil against himself.

Haman was hung and his house was given to Esther. The king learned that Mordecai was in her family, and he gave Mordecai the ring that the king had given before to Haman. Esther gave Haman's house to Mordecai and begged the king to save her nation from death. She showed him the decree and said that if her people were killed she would not want to live. She wrote up a new decree, and the king signed and sealed it and sent it to all parts of his kingdom. The letter stated, "Those who receive great honor can sometimes use their power to do evil. They think that they can lie before God and avoid his punishment. They can be angry even at those who have done them no harm. Punishment must be done justly, and favors should be granted only to the innocent. We took in an Amalekite, and we were very generous with him. I, the king, called him 'my father' but his success caused him to lose his mind. He plotted against Mordecai who had saved my life, and he tried to kill my life's partner, Esther. The Jews, dedicated to worshipping God who has given me the kingdom, are hereby free from the evil decree which Haman sent out. I have hung Haman and his family here in Shushan. The Jews may continue to live in peace with their own laws and are to be protected. The 13th day of Adar is their day of salvation, when they are allowed to defend themselves from anyone who tries to harm them. Anyone who does not obey what is written here will be killed by fire and sword."

The horsemen went quickly with the new decree. Mordecai appeared in a parade in Shushan where there was great joy. Many men in the other nations circumcised their foreskins in order to be safe. The Jews in Shushan killed 500 of their enemies in the city on the 13th of Adar, the same day on which they would have been destroyed. The ten of Haman's sons were hung on the gallows. On the 14th day of the month 300 more enemies were killed in Shushan, but the Jews did not take their property. In the country 75,000 enemies were killed. In Shushan there was a feast. The Jews still celebrate the victory to this day, sending food portions one to another, because Mordecai wrote to the Jews who lived in the kingdom of Artaxerxes to observe these days so that it would be remembered for all times. These days are called Purim. Mordecai became a very influential person, helping the king during his reign. The Jews lived better than ever before.

AFTER the high priest, Eliasib died, his son Judas took his place. When he died, his son John became the high priest. The general of Artaxerxes' army defiled the temple and put a tax on the Jews. They were to pay 50 shekels* for every lamb offered as a sacrifice. John had a brother, Jesus, who had favor with this general. He had been promised the priesthood. Jesus and John fought so fiercely that John killed his brother right in the temple. Even the Greeks and barbarians would not have done such a terrible thing. This is why God punished the people by allowing them to become slaves, and the temple was ruined by the Persians. The general was angry about the murder, and he came into the temple although they tried to keep him out. He punished the Jews for seven years for the murder of Jesus. After John died, Jaddua became the high priest. He had a brother, Manasseh. Sanballat, who was a Samaritan, was sent by Darius, the last king of Persia into Samaria. He knew that the Jews had caused trouble to the Assyrians and others, so Sanballat let his daughter Nicaso marry Manasseh so that he would stay on good terms with the Jews.

PHILIP, the king of Macedon, was killed and his son Alexander became king. He won against the generals of Darius's army and also conquered Ionia, Caria and Pamphylia.

The elders in Jerusalem were not happy that the brother of Jaddua the high priest, Manasseh, was married to a foreign wife, since he was one of the priests. They felt that this would open the door to too many foreigners, a habit which had caused trouble in the past. They gave Manasseh a choice: either to divorce or to stop his work in the temple. He went to his father-in-law, Sanballat, who urged him to stay with his wife. He would make Manasseh governor of all the places he himself ruled and he would build him a temple like the one in Jerusalem on Mount Gerizzim, the highest mountain in Samaria. Sanballat said he would get Darius's approval for this as well. The people in Jerusalem were upset about this offer, because many of the priests and Levites who also had foreign wives went with Manasseh. Sanballat gave them money and lands.

Darius had heard about Alexander's victories and he gathered an army to stop him from taking over all of Asia. He crossed the Euphrates and waited for the enemy at Issus of Cilicia. Sanballat was glad that Darius was on his way and felt that he could soon keep his promises to Manasseh. But to the surprise of all, Darius lost much of his army to the Macedonians. His mother, wife and children were taken prisoner and he fled to Persia. Alexander took Damascus, Sidon and Tyre. He wrote to the Jewish high priest to send him soldiers and supplies to his army. He promised to send presents in return if the Jews would come over to the side of the Macedonians. But the high priest had already promised Darius not to fight against him. Alexander was upset and decided to go and punish the Jewish high priest as soon as he took over Tyre. He then went to the city of Gaza and besieged it and its governor, who was named Babemeses.

Sanballat disowned Darius as king, took 7,000 of his people and came to Alexander in Tyre. Alexander received his people kindly, and so Sanballat asked Alexander to let him build another temple; he agreed. Manasseh was the priest, and Sanballat was happy that his daughter's children would have honor. But after the seven-month siege of Tyre was over, and the siege of Gaza had gone on for two months, Sanballat died.

After Alexander took Gaza he started off to Jerusalem. Jaddua the high priest was afraid to meet the Macedonians, so he told everyone to pray and offer sacrifices to God and ask him to protect their country. God told Jaddua in a dream to have courage and decorate the city. The people should appear in white and the priests in their priestly clothes. He opened the gates of Jerusalem as God had told him to, and the people marched out to meet Alexander. They reached Sapha, which was a place where one could see Jerusalem and the temple. The high priest was dressed in purple and red with the head turban and the golden plate which had

Alexander and his soldiers meet the High Priest and Jewish people in Jerusalem

God's name on it, a name which Alexander honored. Alexander saluted the high priest. The Jews in one voice saluted Alexander. Alexander's people thought that he had lost his mind. One asked him how he could show honor to the Jewish high priest. He said he was honoring the God who had given him this position, and that he had seen this very scene in a dream when he was in Macedonia. He felt that this step was needed in order to win against the Persians. He was welcomed by all of the priests, and he offered a sacrifice to God. They showed him the book of Daniel, in which was written that one of the Greeks would destroy the Persian Empire. Alexander felt that he was that person. The next day he asked the priests what he could do for them. They asked to be free from paying taxes in the seventh year. Alexander agreed to this. They also asked that the Jews in Babylon and Media would be free to keep their Jewish laws. Alexander also promised them this. He then offered any Jewish soldiers who wished to join him that they would be free to keep their own Jewish laws while in his army.

Alexander went to other cities, including those in Samaria. He came to Shechem and they told him that they were also Jews. It is known that when it did not suit the Samaritans, they would deny that they were Jews. They wanted Alexander to visit their temple as well, and to also free them from paying the seventh year tax. He said he would have to wait on this, since he was not convinced that they were truly Jews. He took Sanballat's soldiers to Egypt, and there he gave them land and made them guards over Thebais.

After Alexander died, the temple on Mount Gerizzim remained. It became a place where Jews in Jerusalem would go when they were accused of breaking Jewish laws, and they would tell the Samaritans that they were unjustly accused. Jaddua the high priest died, and his son Onias became the high priest.

BOOK XII

FROM THE DEATH OF ALEXANDER THE GREAT TO THE DEATH OF JUDAS MACCABEUS

i

ALEXANDER, king cf Macedon, put an end to the kingdom of Persia and settled things in Judea. When he died, the areas he had ruled (Asia, Babylon, Hellespont, Macedonia and Egypt) were taken over by leaders who fought one another. Some of the wars lasted a long time and many people died. Syria in particular, ruled by Ptolemy, lost many people. Ptolemy came to Jerusalem on the Sabbath and pretended to be on the side of the Jews by offering a sacrifice. He took over the city when they weren't expecting it, and he ruled over them without mercy. Ptolemy took captives from Judea and from places around Jerusalem and Samaria and led them all to Egypt. He was aware that the Jews were faithful to keep their promises, so he allowed them equal status with the Macedonians in the forts. Some Jews moved to Egypt on their own, because of the good farms and the good terms of Ptolemy. There was trouble later with the Samaritans, however, over which temple to send their sacrifices: Jerusalem or Mount Gerizzim.

ii

ALEXANDER reigned for twelve years, and Ptolemy Soter reigned after him for forty years. Philadelphus reigned in Egypt for 39 years. He set free 120,000 of the Jews in Egypt from slavery.

Demetrius Phalerius, who was the librarian of the king, wanted to find all the books in the world for the king's collection. Ptolemy asked him how many he already had. He said, "Twenty times ten thousand," but he wished to have fifty times ten thousand. He wanted to include the many books of the Jews, but they would have to be translated from Hebrew into Greek. The king wrote to the Jewish high priest asking for these books.

The king had a good friend, Aristeus, who kept asking the king to free all the Jews. He spoke with the captains of the guards and asked for their help in this. He said to the king that, since they were collecting the books of the Jews, and hoping to translate them, it would be easier if they were not slaves. "Since you're good natured, this might be a good opportunity to free all of the Jews, since some are in a miserable condition. God gave them their laws, and we worship this same God, the creator of all things. We simply call him by a different name: "life" or Jupiter. They would prefer to worship their God in their own country. I'm not Jewish but I feel that God would be pleased with giving them favor."

The king was in a cheerful mood and asked him how many of them he thought needed to be free. He said, "A few more than ten times ten thousand." The king felt this was a big request, but those standing by said that he should remember with thanks that God had made him the king. He ordered that after the soldiers had received their pay, they should put aside 120 drachmae* from the king's money for every one of the slaves owned by his men. He promised to put this all in writing. He promised not only to free those who had been brought as captives by his father and his army, but those who had been brought there earlier. Their redemption money would be 400 talents*. "Draw up a list of people to be freed within three days and let them appear. Those who disobey this law to free the Jews will have their property taken and given to the king."

In the translation of the Hebrew law books, there were some copies which were not good enough. Demetrius asked the king to ask the Jewish priest to send six men from each of the twelve tribes, all of them good lawyers who understand the laws, in order to make a good, clear translation. A letter was written to Eleazar, the high priest, telling about the Jews who were freed. The king sent money for making large bowls, jars, cups and many precious stones. They could choose the stones they wanted to use. One hundred talents* were given for temple sacrifices and other uses.

Eleazar wrote a letter to King Ptolemy. He said that the Jews were pleased that he was honoring God and thanked him for the gifts. The king's two messengers were good men, he said. "We have offered sacrifices for you and your family, praying that your kingdom be at peace and that we will do a good job in the translation."

As for the gift items, there was a table sent to Jerusalem which was very large. It was thought to build one five times as large, but the king wanted his gift to be not only rich but useful, so it must not be too big. He had a table made of the same size but more beautiful. It was all of gold surrounded with a crown design. Precious stones were set into it in rows, and there were different fruits made from the jewels and set in gold. The stones shone out like rays from stars from the middle of the table. The feet of the table were like lily buds with leaves. There were also gold stems of ivy and grapevines so thin that they moved when the wind blew. The table was more than one half of a cubit* thick. The golden water pools had precious stones set in them. There were also lily-leaf and grape designs. The silver cisterns were like mirrors. The jars contained precious stones and were also engraved with ivy and vines. The king personally stood over all of this work and would not let anyone else see the work in process.

Ptolemy sent these items to Jerusalem and they were dedicated to God. Eleazar honored those who brought them and gave them presents in return. The king used to receive guests together with his own ambassadors, but he wanted to be alone when he received Eleazar's elders. The old men came in with the skins of parchment on which they had written the law in letters of gold.

The king was impressed that the pages were so thin. He thanked them for coming, for the one who sent them and he thanked God. The messengers cried out together wishing the king happiness. The king was moved to tears for the joy which he felt. He promised that he would proclaim this day as a yearly day to be remembered for the rest of his life. And it turned out to be the same day when he had won against Antigonus at sea.

The Jewish elders would eat with him and have the best place to stay in the upper part of the city. Those chosen to take care of foreign guests were told to give them whatever diet and provisions they were used to. The king ordered that each elder be given a double seat; half at the king's right hand and the other half behind his table. Eleazer, a priest who was there, was asked to bless the food (possibly the first example in history of a blessing being given at a meal). He stood and prayed, blessing the king and his people. The people all cheered with lots of noise and then ate. The king then began to talk to them about philosophy and asked each one a question. He was satisfied with their answers. This continued on for twelve days, and the questions and answers were written by Aristeus in a book.

The king and his philosopher, Menedemus, admired these guests. They said that God ruled over all, and that he was behind any strong or beautiful words which these men said. The king felt he learned things that would make him a better ruler. He gave each one three talents*. After three days, Demetrius took them over a bridge to an island where they would meet in a certain house. They would have a quiet place to talk about their work. They worked many hours a day, then relaxed and ate well. After 72 days they finished the interpretations which Demetrius requested. He came and read everything himself. The people themselves also approved of the interpretations of the law. The priests, elders and leaders said that since the interpretations were done so well, they requested that no one change them. If anyone would see something unnecessary or which needed correction, they would need to look at it again.

The king was happy in hearing the wisdom of the Law. He said he did not understand why poets or historians had not mentioned them before. Demetrius said that the laws were divine and anyone who had tried to use them in the past was punished by God. One man who tried lost his mind for more than 30 days. He had a dream and saw his error. He repented and God restored his senses to him. Another wanted to use information from the sacred laws in a drama, and suddenly he could not see. When he understood that God was allowing it, he prayed for mercy and was healed.

King Ptolemy was very pleased with the law books, and he wanted the interpreters to visit him now and then from Judea. The elders each received three sets of clothing, two talents* of gold, a valuable cup, and a piece of furniture from the feasting room Eleazar the high priest received ten beds with feet of silver with the matching furniture, a cup valued at thirty talents*, ten sets of clothing, purple, a crown and 100 pieces of the finest linen. In addition he received jars, dishes, pitchers and two golden water pools to be dedicated to God. The interpreters of the law were invited to visit at any time, and the king would share his riches with them. This king, Ptolemy Philadelphus, greatly honored the Jews and their holy writings.

iii

THE Jews also were favored by the kings of Asia. They have had equal citizenship with the Macedonians and Greeks to this day. The Jews were not to use oil prepared by heathens, and since it was a common item which replaced money, they had to receive the money instead of the oil. When Vespasian and Titus governed a large area, the Greek neighbors asked them to take away the privileges of the Jews. But although the Romans had suffered so much from the Jews, had fought against them and had not succeeded in taking away their weapons, they still allowed them to keep those privileges. Marcus Agrippa came out in the Jews' favor when most of the people in Ionia did not want them to have citizenship. Nicolaus of Damascus also had a part in helping them to be free to worship in their accustomed way and practice their own customs.

During the time when Antiochus the Great ruled over Asia, the Jews suffered greatly. Ptolemy, the king of Egypt, and his son Epiphanes also suffered. When Antiochus finally beat Ptolemy he took over Judea, and when Ptolemy was dead, his son sent out a large army against Celesyria under the command of Scopas and conquered many cities. Antiochus fought Scopas at the springs of Jordan and much of Scopas's army was destroyed. Antiochus took back the cities which Scopas had gained, including Samaria. The Jews went to his side and received him into the city of Jerusalem. They supplied both his army and his elephants with provisions. They helped him attack the fort in the city of Jerusalem, in which there were Egyptians. Antiochus was impressed and wrote to his army generals about how the Jews were behaving nicely towards him. He wrote to Ptolemy telling that he wished to help them rebuild Jerusalem. He wished to bring back those Jews who were scattered and give them animals for sacrifice along with wine, oil, frankincense, silver, flour, wheat and salt. "I want these to be paid to them as I have ordered. I would like to see them finish their temple as well as the living quarters. Wood can be brought from Judea and out of Libanus tax-free. I decree that the senate, priests, scribes of the temple and the singers be free from taxes for three years so that they can do the necessary repairs. Those who are slaves need to be freed, as well as their children. Foreigners are not to enter the temple. Jews who have not been purified may also not enter. No flesh of horses, mules or donkeys can be brought into the city. Other non-kosher animals are not to be brought in or bred in the city. Anyone not keeping these laws has to pay the priests 3,000 drachmae* of silver."

Antiochus also wrote to his father, Zeuxis. He had heard about rebellion in Lydia and Phrygia. "I wish to remove 2,000 Jewish families, with their belongings out of Mesopotamia and Babylon to guard these places. They can be trusted. It won't be an easy task but they need to be allowed to live by their own laws. I ask you to allow them to build houses and have land for animals and for planting vineyards. They will not need to pay tax for ten years on their produce. They need a supply of wheat for their servants until the first harvest. If we treat them well, they will cooperate with us. Take care that they will not be disturbed." Antiochus the Great was friendly with the Jews.

ANTIOCHUS and Ptolemy became friends, and Antiochus gave him his daughter Cleopatra to be his wife. Antiochus gave up Celesyria, Samaria, Judea and Phoenicia as a dowry. The kings divided the taxes between themselves. The Samaritans grew rich and bothered the Jews by taking their land and making some of them slaves. After the death of Eleazer, the high priest, his uncle Manasseh took his place. After he died, Onias became the priest. He was the son of Simon "The Just" and the brother of Eleazer. This Onias loved money and did not pay the tax of twenty talents* of silver as his forefathers had done. Ptolemy Euergetes was very angry and sent an ambassador to Jerusalem. He said that if they would not pay, he would take their land and put his soldiers on it. A young man named Joseph had a good name, and he reproved his uncle Onias for withholding the tax and endangering his nation. Joseph advised him to go to the king to settle the matter. Onias said that he would rather leave the priesthood, and he refused to go to the king. Joseph asked if he could go instead, and this was granted. Joseph went to the temple and spoke to many people. He told them not to fear for he would go to the king. The ambassador to the king was impressed by this young Joseph, and he promised to help Joseph solve the matter with Ptolemy in Egypt, which they did. Joseph gathered together borrowed money to pay the taxes, along with many garments, cups and animals to carry them. He went to Alexandria. The rulers in Syria and Phoenicia left their cities to receive taxes from the king. These men saw Joseph on the way and laughed because he looked poor. When

Joseph arrived in Alexandria, he heard that Ptolemy was in Memphis so he went there. The king was sitting in his chariot with his wife and his friend Athenion (the ambassador in Jerusalem who had been entertained by Joseph). Athenion saw him and told the king what a generous young man he was. Ptolemy saluted him and invited him to join him in the chariot. The king complained about Onias, and Joseph asked the king to forgive Onias since he was old. The king invited him to eat together with him daily in his palace. When the king came to Alexanderia, the chief men of Syria saw that he was friends with Joseph and they were upset.

On the day when taxes were to be given out to the highest bidder, the bid came to eight thousand talents*. Joseph said that the tax should be higher. He said he himself would give twice as much and for those who didn't pay, he would send their whole property. The king was impressed and allowed him to manage the taxes. Joseph promised the king that he would bring in all the taxes, and when the king asked what guarantee Joseph would give for this promise, Joseph offered the king and his wife as the guarantee. Ptolemy laughed but agreed to the plan. Those who came from the cities into Egypt hoping to win the bid went away to their own countries very disappointed.

Joseph took 2,000 soldiers from the king to help him collect the taxes. After borrowing 500 talents* from the king's friends in Alexandria, he quickly returned to Syria. When he was in Ashkelon they refused to pay, so he killed twenty leading men and took their property for the king. Ptolemy commended him for this action and allowed him to continue in this way. The Syrians were shocked to hear this, so they received Joseph and paid their taxes. When the people of Scythopolis refused to pay, he killed their leading men and sent what had been theirs to the king. Joseph gathered a lot of money in this way. He sent many gifts to the king privately as well, and to Cleopatra and their friends.

This went on for twenty-two years, and Joseph had a wife and seven sons. He had another son, Hyrcanus, by the daughter of his brother Solymius whom he also married. It happened this way:

Once he came to Alexandria with his brother; the daughter was with them because Solymius wanted to give her to a leading Jew to marry. Joseph ate with the king and fell in love with a beautiful actress and told his brother about it. A Jew was forbidden to even come near to a foreign woman. His brother wanted to save him, so he disguised his daughter and brought her to him at night and he slept with her. He was drunk and didn't know she was his niece. This happened many nights and he truly loved her. He was worried about losing her when he would have to leave. His brother told him not to worry, and told him the truth. Solymius said he would rather have his own daughter abused than to see Joseph publicly shamed. She was the wife who bore Hyrcanus.

This son was very smart already at age thirteen and was envied by his brothers. He was quick to learn and his brothers were not. Hyrcanus was given a test to farm some land with oxen which didn't have a yoke. He solved this problem in a clever way and returned with a good harvest, causing his father to realize that he had wisdom beyond his years. His brothers were jealous.

A son was born to Ptolemy the king, and all of the leaders of Syria and the conquered countries were called in to celebrate. Hyrcanus was chosen to go since his father was too old to attend. The brothers refused, saying that they were not good at talking. Hyrcanus said he would not need much money for the journey, only ten thousand drachmae*. He told his father not to give him presents to take, but to write a letter to Joseph's steward in Alexandria to give him the money to buy the best gifts there. Joseph wrote to Arion, his steward who managed his money in Alexandria, which amounted to 3,000 talents*. While Hyrcanus was away, his brothers wrote to the king's friends to kill him. When he arrived to Alexandria, Arion asked him how many talents* he wanted (hoping he would say ten). Hyrcanus wanted 1,000 talents*. The steward was angry and said that Joseph had worked hard for that money; Hyrcanus should be more careful with it. He agreed to give him ten talents* only. The son was upset and threw Arion into prison. Arion's wife told Cleopatra, and she said this young Hycanus should be punished. Ptolemy sent for him and asked why he had not yet come to see him but had already succeeded in sending a steward to prison. He gave a clever answer which made the king laugh; he was impressed with Hyrcanus's wisdom.

The steward saw that he could not win this argument, so he gave the child 1,000 talents* as he had asked, and then he was let out of prison. After three days, Hyrcanus came to the king and queen. He was treated well, since they respected his father. He came to the merchants privately and bought 100 boys and 100 girls for one talent* each. When he was invited to feast with the king together with the other leaders, he sat in the lowest place because he was so young. Those who sat with him made a pile of bones in front of Hyrcanus, filling the entire table. Trypho, the king's jester, stood by the king and called his attention to the bones, saying that Hyrcanus's father had made all of Syria as bare as these bones. The king asked Hyrcanus from where he had gotten so many bones. He answered, "There are dogs which eat flesh and bones together, like your guests have done – for they have nothing in front of them. I am a man who eats the flesh and throws away the bones." The king thought this was a good answer.

The next day Hyrcanus went to all of the most powerful men in the king's court to greet them. He asked their servants how big a present they would bring for the birthday of the king's son. They said twelve talents* or more. He pretended to be sorry he could not bring more; he said he only had five talents*. When they heard this, they told their masters and were happy thinking that Joseph's son would anger the king. When the day arrived, the gifts brought to the king were not over 20 talents,* but Hyrcanus, who had given one talent* to each of the 100 boys and 100 girls, had them give these talents* to the king and queen. Everyone was impressed. He also gave the king's servants gifts, since he was in danger of his life.

Ptolemy admired Hyrcanus and asked what he wanted for a gift. He wished only that Ptolemy would write to his father and brothers about him, which he did. When his brothers heard how he was honored, they went out to meet him in order to destroy him. Joseph was also angry with his son, but did nothing out of fear of the king. Hyrcanus killed two of his brothers and others who had come to fight him. The rest of the brothers escaped to Jerusalem to their father. No one would receive Hyrcanus, so he was afraid and went to live beyond the Jordan River, where he gathered taxes from the barbarians.

Seleucus, or Soter (the son of Antiochus the Great), was ruling in Asia. Joseph, Hyrcanus's father died. He was a good man who had raised the quality of life for the Jews. He received taxes from Syria, Phoenicia and Samaria for 22 years and worked on his farm. His uncle Onias died about this time and left the high priesthood to his son Simon. When Simon died, his son Onias became priest.

A letter was addressed to this Onias from Areus, king of the Lacedemonians. The letter said that they had discovered that the Lacedemonians were related to the Jews through the sons of Abraham. "We wish to know about you. Demotoles, who is delivering this letter, will return with your answer. This letter is square, and the seal is an eagle with a dragon in his claws."

After Joseph died, his older sons were elders. They made war against Hyrcanus, the youngest of Joseph's sons. The people were divided, but most of them were on the side of the elders, including Simon the high priest. Hyrcanus decided not to go to Jerusalem any more. He was also at war with the Arabians beyond Jordan. He built a strong castle entirely of white stone with pictures of animals carved on it. He dug a deep canal dug around the castle. He also dug many caves in a nearby rock and made large rooms inside for celebration, and for sleeping and living. He decorated the surroundings with water streams. Only one person at a time could enter the caves; these openings were narrow so that he could not be trapped there and killed. His courts were huge and had impressive gardens. He called this place Tyre, and it is between Arabia and Judea beyond Jordan, not far from the country of Heshbon. He ruled there for seven years while Seleucus was king in Syria.

After Seleucus died, his brother Antiochus Epiphanes became king. Ptolemy, king of Egypt died, who was also called Epiphanes. He left two young sons, Philometer and Physcon. When Hyrcanus saw that Antiochus had a large army, he feared he would be punished for what he had done to the Arabians, and he killed himself. Antiochus took everything Hyrcanus had.

V

AFTER the high priest Onias died, Jesus his brother took his place, since Onias's son was still a baby. The king did not allow Jesus to be the high priest since he was angry with him, and gave the job to his younger brother who was also named Onias. Jesus' name was changed to Jason and Onias was called Menelaus. Jason made trouble for Menelaus, and the people were taking sides. The sons of Tobias were on the side of Menelaus, but most of the people were with Jason. Menelaus and the sons of Tobias went to Antiochus and said they wanted to live like Greeks and forget their Jewish traditions. They asked that a gymnasium be built in Jerusalem, to which he agreed. They found a way to hide their circumcision in order to appear as Greeks in the gymnasium, where the men competed in the games naked.

Antiochus planned to conquer Egypt, since he felt that the son of Ptolemy was a weak ruler. He came with a great army and succeeded in Memphis, but he failed to take over Alexandria where Ptolemy lived. In the end, Antiochus was not only driven out of Alexandria but out of all of Egypt. The Romans told him to leave Egypt alone.

King Antiochus left Egypt and went against Jerusalem in the 143rd year of the Seleucidse kingdom. He was able to take the city without fighting. He killed many who opposed him, stole a lot of money and returned to Antioch. After two years he again came to Jerusalem and pretended to come in peace. He wanted all the riches in the temple. He broke the agreement that he had made, and took the temple's golden candlesticks, the altar of incense, the table of holy bread, the altar and the curtains. He took all of the secret treasures as well. The Jews were in great torment about this, and they were forced to stop offering their daily sacrifices. Antiochus continued to steal from the entire city, killing or taking prisoners as he went. He took about 10,000 men, women and children as captives. He burned down the beautiful buildings, and after he had destroyed the city walls he built a fort in the city with a tower that overlooked the temple and was strongly fortified. He put Macedonian soldiers there to guard it.

There were also some Jews there who had done evil things. The king built an idol altar on top of the Jew's altar and killed a pig on it. He forced the Jews to worship the gods which he worshipped, and he made them build temples and offer pigs daily on the idol altars. He did not let them circumcise their sons, and those who did were punished. He had officers to make sure that his commands were obeyed. Some Jews refused his demands, and they were whipped with rods, their bodies torn to pieces, and crucified. Those women who had circumcised their sons were strangled, and those who were crucified had their sons hanging around their necks on the crosses. If any holy Jewish book was found, it was destroyed along with its owner.

The Samaritans saw how the Jews suffered, and they wanted no connection with them. They claimed that the temple at Mount Gerizzim did not belong to Almighty God. They said that they were a colony of Medes and Persians. They sent ambassadors to Antiochus with a letter greeting him as a god, and saying that they were Sidonians. They requested from the governor Apollonius and from Nicanor not to punish them in the way the Jews were being punished. "We are aliens from their nation and customs. We want our temple, which has no name, to be called the Temple of Jupiter Hellenius. If we are left in peace, we will be more valuable to you." The king Antiochus wrote to Nicanor that the Sidonians who live in Shechem wished to live as Greeks. "We therefore declare them to be free from accusations and agree to rename their temple." He also sent a copy to Appolonius.

MATTATHIAS, living in Modin, was a Jew of the priestly line. He had five sons. One of them, Judas, was also called Maccabeus. Mattathias was so upset about the way Jerusalem was being abused that he said it would probably be better for them to die for the sake of their Jewish beliefs. When the officers appointed by the king arrived in Modin, they wanted Mattathias to offer the sacrifice, since others would follow the example of a respectable man in the community. Mattathias refused. One of the other Jews came forward and did as Antiochus had commanded. This caused Mattathias to run up and kill him with a sword, together with his sons. They also killed the king's general and a few soldiers. He broke down the idol altar and invited all who wanted to keep the worship of God to follow him. They escaped quickly into the desert, leaving everything behind. Entire families joined them, and they lived in caves. When the king's generals heard this, they left the fort in Jerusalem and came after them. They first gave them a chance to change their minds. The people did not change their minds and they were attacked on the Sabbath. The king's generals burned many people inside the caves, because some of the Jews refused to defend themselves on the Sabbath. About 1,000 men, women and children were smothered to death in the caves. Many who joined Mattathias realized it was better to fight on the Sabbath than to die. This rule continues to this day about fighting on the Sabbath if there is no choice. Mattathias went with his army and overthrew idol altars around the country and killed those who broke the laws of God. He also made sure that the boys were circumcised, and he chased away those who tried to stop the circumcisions.

After ruling one year, Mattathias got sick. He called his sons together and told them to continue what he had started. "Be ready even to die for the Jewish laws, and know that God sees all and will restore what you have lost and will give you freedom and peace. Your bodies are mortal, but there is the hope of immortality which you must follow. Even after going through many hard times, the loss of your life should not upset you. It's important that you get along with one another, and if one of you excels in something, recognize and learn each from the other. Simon will be like a father to you, and his advice should be honored. Maccabeus should lead the army, since he is strong and brave. Bring righteous and religious people to join you."

Mattathias then prayed to God to help them and to bring the people back to their peaceful life. He died shortly afterwards and was buried at Modin. He was greatly mourned by all the people. Judas became the governor and they chased their enemies out of the country.

APOLLONIUS, the general of the Samaritan forces, came against Judas but was killed along with many of his men. Judas took Apollonius's sword and killed and wounded many with it. They took much spoil. When Seron, the general of the army of Celesyria, heard about this, he came to fight against Judas since he was defying the king's laws. He gathered a large army, including Jews, and he came to Bethoron, a village in Judea. Judas knew that strength did not come from numbers and he encouraged his soldiers to be brave. He said that "innocence is the strongest army". They conquered Seron and beat the Syrians, who ran towards the sea after seeing that they lost their general. Judas killed about 800 of them.

When Antiochus heard about this, he was very angry and gathered his army, including those he had hired from the islands. In the beginning of spring he saw that he was lacking money for a war, so he first went to Persia and collected taxes. He appointed an officer, Lysias, to govern from Egypt to Lower Asia and the Euphrates River. He was to guard his elephants, and to bring his son Antiochus to conquer Judea, to take the Jews as slaves and completely destroy Jerusalem. But he did not carry out this plan.

Lysias chose Ptolemy to lead the army and gave him 40,000 foot soldiers and 7,000 horsemen. They came as far as the city of

Emmaus. Other soldiers came from Syria along with some Jews. Those who wished to buy slaves also came with their silver and gold. Again Judas saw their numbers, but he encouraged his men to put their hope in God, and to pray and wear sackcloth. He organized them in the way their Jewish forefathers used to fight, under captains of thousands. Those who were newly married were told they didn't need to fight, as well as those who had recently bought property. He gave a rousing speech that this was the time to regain their freedom to worship God in their own way. "The other choice is surrender to the enemy, which would also mean the end of our people. If anyone dies, they have gained everlasting glory. Be ready to fight against the enemy in the morning."

The enemy sent Gorgias with 5,000 foot soldiers and 1,000 horsemen to attack Judas and his army at night. Some of the traitor Jews were guides, but the son of Mattathias was aware of this plan. The enemies had eaten and left many fires in their camp. Gorgias marched all night and came to the Jewish camp at Emmaus, but he found no one there. Judas came to them in the morning with only 3,000 men, and they were no match for the enemy soldiers. But the Jews blew their trumpets and fell on the enemy suddenly. Many were killed and some were chased as far as Gadara and the plains of Idumea, Ashdod and Jamnia. About 3,000 were killed. Judas told them not to take the spoils from the Syrian camp, since they still needed to beat Gorgias. At this moment Gorgias's men looked down into their camp and saw that it was burned down. They started to run away when they saw Judas and his men ready to fight, so Judas's men then returned to the camp to take the spoils. They gained gold and silver, purple and blue and returned home singing songs to God for their success.

Lysias was surprised that Judas's soldiers had won the battle, so the next year he gathered 60,000 of his best men. He went to the hill of Bethsur, a village in Judea where they camped. Judas met him with 10,000 men. Again he prayed for God's help. He killed 5,000 of the enemy. The Jews fought with all their might and frightened away the enemy. Lysias's army returned to Antioch, where he hired foreigners for the next battle against Judea.

Seeing that the generals of Antiochus's armies had lost so many times, Judas gathered the people and told them that it was time to go up to Jerusalem to purify the temple and to offer sacrifices at the appointed time. When they arrived, they saw that the temple was deserted and the gates were burned down. Plants were growing inside the temple. The people were very sad and cried. Judas ordered some of the soldiers to fight against the guards in the fort until they could clean the temple for use. They brought in new curtains, the candlestick, the table of holy bread and the golden altar of incense. He hung up curtains at the gates and added doors. He took down the burnt offering altar and built a new one of stones. They lit the lamps and offered incense on the altar of incense. They laid the loaves on the table of holy bread and offered a burnt offering on the new altar. They restarted the offerings on the same calendar day exactly three years from the last time they had worshipped God in the temple. The worship had stopped since the time of Antiochus, which was the fulfillment of Daniel's prophecy given 480 years before: that the Macedonians would stop the worship of God for a time.

Judas celebrated with his people for eight days. They had a wonderful feast and God was honored. They sang hymns and psalms. They revived the Jewish laws and decided to keep this festival for years to come. This eight-day feast would be called the Festival of Lights to remember the restoration of the temple. "Our hope was restored; we were free again." This holiday is celebrated to this day. Judas rebuilt the walls around the city and built strong towers for their defense. Soldiers would guard them against their enemies. He also fortified the city of Bethsura for their protection.

viii

THE Jews were gaining strength, and the surrounding nations set traps for them and secretly plotted against them. Judas continued to try his best to defend the people from these attempts. He came to Idumea [descendants of Esau] and killed many of them and took spoil. He shut up the sons of Bean by burning their towers and killing those inside. He then went quickly against the Ammonites who had a great army under the leadership of Timotheus. He beat them and captured the city of Jazer, taking the wives and children captives. He burned the city and returned to Judea. The neighboring nations got together in the land of Gilead and came against those Jews living on the borders, who ran to Dathema. They told Judas that Timotheus was on his way to capture them.

At this time Judas also heard that the inhabitants of Ptolemais, Tyre and Sidon and strangers in Galilee were joining forces. Judas ordered his brother Simon to take 3,000 good soldiers and help the Jews in Galilee, while he and another brother, Jonathan, would go into Gilead with 8,000 soldiers. He left Joseph, the son of Zacharias to lead the rest of the army and to guard Judea carefully. He told them not to fight any battles until he would return. Simon won his battle, chasing the enemy to the gates of Ptolemais and killing about 3,000 of them. They took the spoil as well as captives, together with their baggage and returned home.

Judas Maccabeus and Jonathan crossed the Jordan River, and after three days they came upon the Nabateans. They met them peacefully and heard about the situation in Galillee. The Jews had been driven into forts, so Judas went quickly to save his people. He first took the city of Bosor, destroying all the men and those who could fight; then he burned the city. Even though it was night, he went from there to the fort where Jews were shut inside, surrounded by Timotheus and his men. In the morning when the enemies were breaking the walls and using ladders, Judas blew the trumpets and encouraged his men to cheerfully risk the danger for the sake of their brothers. He formed three groups of soldiers and attacked. Timotheus's men ran and Judas followed them, killing about 8,000 of them. He then turned aside to a city of foreigners called Malle and took it, killing all the men and burning the city. He conquered Casphom, Bosor and other cities of the Gilead.

Not long after this, Timotheus gathered an army, also hiring some Arabians by promising them rewards. They came to the city of Raphon, and he told them to block the Jews from crossing the brook. Judas heard that they were coming and went quickly against him. He crossed the brook and killed some of them. Others were scared; they gave up their weapons and escaped. Some ran to the Temple of Carnaim in order to save themselves; but Judas took the city, killed them and burned the temple.

Judas then gathered the Jews together with their children and wives and belongings, and they returned to Judea. When he came to Ephron, he asked them to open their gates to his men to pass through the city. They refused, so Judas surrounded the city and his men took it, killing all the men and burning it. His men walked over many dead bodies when passing through the city. They came to the Jordan, and arrived to a great plain near the city of Bethshan. When they returned to Judea, they sang psalms and songs which they liked to sing after their victories. They offered thanks to God for saving them, since not one of the Jews was lost in these battles.

Joseph, the son of Zacharias and Azarias, whom Judas had left to watch over Judea, did not obey Judas's order not to fight. They went against Jamnia and lost 2,000 of their army. Judas continued to pursue the Idumeans, taking Hebron from them, destroying its forts and setting all the towers on fire. The country of the foreigners and the city of Marissa was burned. They also took Ashdod, destroying it and taking the spoils. Afterwards they returned to Judea.

ix

KING Antiochus heard about a rich city in Persia called Elymais, which had the wealthy temple of Diana. Alexander of Macedonia had left many weapons and armor there. The king went there quickly and tried to take it over, but he was defeated. He was able to escape to Babylon, but many of his soldiers were killed. He also heard about his commanders in Judea who lost to the Jews. This bad news caused him to lose his mind for a long time. He called his friends to him and said that this was punishment for all that he had done against the Jewish nation. He had robbed their temple and cursed their God. After he said this, he died.

Before he died, Antiochus called for Philip, one of his friends and gave him his crown, robe and ring. He told him to give them to his son, also called Antiochus. He wanted Philip to make sure his son would have a good education to be a future king. Lysias told the people about Antiochus's death and appointed his son to be king, calling him Eupator.

The Jews were attacked in Jerusalem on their way to worship at the temple, by soldiers in the fort who were helped by traitor Jews. Judas decided to destroy those in the fort. This was during the period of the Seleucidae. He had war machines made in order to tear it down. Those inside asked for help from King Antiochus, arguing that they should not be attacked just because they had left Jewish worship. Antiochus, although he was only a child, was angry when he heard this, and he ordered his army to come together. They gathered 100,000 foot soldiers, 20,000 horsemen and 32 elephants. They quickly left Antioch, with Lysias as their commander, and came to Idumea.

They came to a strong city, Bethsura. It was a very fierce battle in which war machines were burned. When Judas heard about it, he left Jerusalem and came to meet King Antiochus. When Judas was 70 furlongs* from the enemy, the king's soldiers left Bethsura. He made the elephants pass through a narrow opening. Around every elephant were 1000 foot soldiers and 500 horsemen. There were high towers on the elephant's backs and archers in them. The army went up the mountains, his friends going first to shout and attack the enemy. They had gold and brass shields and looked impressive. Judas was not afraid of this and killed 600 of them. When his brother Eleazar saw the tallest of the elephants covered with royal armor plates, he knew the king was there and bravely attacked him. He killed many of the solders around the elephant, scattered the others and then killed the elephant under the belly, also killing himself. Judas saw how strong the enemy was and returned to Jerusalem. Antiochus sent part of his army to Bethsura, and the rest to Jerusalem. The people of Bethsura gave up, since they had no food and the king promised not to hurt them. Antiochus took the city and sent the people out naked. He set up a fort of his own in the city.

The siege of Jerusalem went on for a long time. The people ran out of food, because it was the seventh year when the land was to lie fallow, and many left Jerusalem. But Lysias, the army general and Antiochus, the king, left the siege when they heard that Philip was coming out from Persia to take over. They decided to go against him, but they did not want to tell their soldiers. The king told Lysias to instead tell them that the siege against Jerusalem was too hard, so they would try to make friends with the Jews and let them keep the laws of their fathers.

The king promised peace to Judas, and said he would let them live by their own laws. The Jews received this news gladly and left the temple. When Antiochus came to the temple, he broke his promise and ordered his army to destroy everything. All the walls were broken down to the ground, and they returned to Antioch. He took the high priest Onias (or Menelaus) with him. Lysius advised the king to kill him because he had made the people leave God's laws. The king sent Menelaus to Berea, a city in Syria, and there he was killed. He had been high priest for ten years. He had been wicked. Alcimus, from a different family, was made high priest in his place.

When Antiochus found out that Philip had already taken over the government, he made war against him and killed him. Onias, the son of the high priest, was a child when his father died. When he saw that the king had killed his uncle Menelaus and given the priesthood to Alcimus, who was not of the priestly line, he left for Egypt. There he was treated kindly by Ptolemy the king and his wife Cleopatra. He built a temple like the one in Jerusalem.

X

DEMETRIUS, the son of Seleucus, left Rome and took over Tripoli, a city of Syria. He made himself king and gathered soldiers and was welcomed by everyone. They took Antiochus and Lysias to him, and Demetrius had both of them killed. Antiochus had reigned only two years.

Certain traitor Jews came to the new king, together with the high priest Alcimus, complaining that Judas and his brothers had killed all their friends and had sent them away. They asked Demetrius to send someone to see what was happening there. Demetrius was very angry and sent Bacchides, a friend of Antiochus Epiphanes who had ruled all of Mesopotamia. Demetrius told him to kill Judas and gave him an army and the high priest Alcimus to join him. They left Antioch, and when Bacchides arrived he asked to meet with Judas to discuss a peace plan. Judas did not trust him, since he had come with a large army. Some of Judas's people went over to the side of Bacchides because they trusted Alcimus, who was one of them. The promises they and Alcimus made to one another were not kept by Bacchides, who killed sixty of them. He left Jerusalem and caught some of the deserters and killed them all. Those that lived in the country had to submit to Alcimus. Bacchides returned to Antioch to King Demetrius.

Alcimus won many people to his side by his kind words, but some in his army were wicked and deserters. Alcimus then went around the country killing Judas's people. Many good and holy men were killed. Alcimus needed Demetrius's help because he was losing the war, so he came to Antioch. Nicanor, Demetrius's best friend who fled with him from Rome, set out with a large army this time to beat Judas and destroy the entire nation. He arrived in Jerusalem and wished to make peace. He promised to do the Jews no harm. He only wished to tell them about Demetrius's intentions. Nicanor tried to trick Judas and gain his trust. While he was saluting Judas, Nicanor signaled to his soldiers when they were to attack Judas. Judas saw their wicked plan and escaped from them.

Now that his real plan was known, Nicanor prepared for an open battle at Capharsalama. He beat Judas, who ran to the fort in Jerusalem for safety. When Nicanor came into the temple, he was met by some of the priests and elders. They showed him the sacrifices which they had offered to God for the king. He cursed and told them that they needed to give Judas to him, otherwise he would destroy the temple. He left Jerusalem and the priests were very sad and asked God to save them from their enemies.

When Nicanor left Jerusalem, he set up camp in Bethoron. Another Syrian army joined him. Judas set up camp at Adasa, 30 furlongs* away with his 1,000 soldiers. He encouraged his men to attack the enemy bravely. They beat them in a hard battle, killing Nicanor and many of his men. The others ran, throwing down their weapons. Judas ran after them and killed them. He also had the trumpets blowing to tell all the neighboring villages of the victory. The neighbors quickly put on their armor and joined the battle, and all 9,000 of the enemy were killed. This victory is still celebrated as a festival day for the Jews on the 13th day of the month of Adar. There was peace for a while after this.

When the high priest Alcimus tried to pull down the ancient walls of the temple, which had been built by the holy prophets, he was struck down suddenly by God. He fell down and could not speak. He finally died after being high priest for four years. The people made Judas the new priest. After hearing that the Romans had conquered Galatia, Iberia, Cathage, Lybia, Greece and their kings Perseus, Philip and Antiochus the Great, Judas wanted to make peace with them. He sent two of his friends to Rome and he asked the Romans to write a letter to Demetrius telling him to stop fighting against the Jews. They wrote a decree and sent a copy of it to Judea. It was also engraved in brass and kept in Rome It made war unlawful between the Romans and the Jews. It was also unlawful to help a war against Jews by sending corn, ships or money. If any Jews or Romans were attacked, they would come to help each other. Eupolemus the son of John, and Jason the son of Eleazar wrote this decree when Judas was high priest, and Simon his brother was the army general. This was the first agreement made between the Romans and the Jews.

WHEN Demetrus found out that Nicanor was dead along with his soldiers, he sent Bacchides with an army from Antioch to Judea. They camped in a city in Galilee and caught the people who had hidden in the caves. He then went to Jerusalem. Judas Maccabee's army was camped in a village called Bethzetho. Judas had only 3,000 against Bacchides' 20,000 foot soldiers and 2,000 horsemen. Judas's soldiers were afraid and ran, leaving only 800 men with him. He encouraged them to attack, but they said that they were in danger and should pull back and save themselves. He said, "I hope the sun will never see me showing my back to the enemy. Even if it's my end, I should stand bravely and not run away, which would take away my former victories and their glory."

Bacchides put archers in the front and had horsemen on both sides of him. His trumpeter sounded the trumpet and the army shouted. Judas did the same. The battle lasted until sunset. The strongest part of Bacchides's army was on the right side so Judas ran to that side and cut through the line. Some ran away and he ran after them. Those from the other side came and surrounded Judas. He could not move and had to stand still. Judas killed many of the enemy but at last he was wounded and died. All of Judas's soldiers then ran away. His brothers Simon and Jonathan were able to take Judas's body and they carried it to Modin, where their father was buried. The Jewish people mourned for Judas many days and had the usual funeral. He had been a great warrior and had obeyed his father Mattathias's commands. He went through hard times to win freedom for his people. He had a great name and was remembered. He had delivered his people from slavery under the Macedonians. He was the high priest for the last three years of his life.

As you read the next Book XIII, and if it is difficult, skip to the next one and then return after you have finished the whole book.

BOOK XIII

FROM THE DEATH OF JUDAS MACCABEUS TO QUEEN ALEXANDRA'S DEATH

i

THE last book told of the fight of the Jewish people to gain their freedom from slavery to the Macedonians. Judas, the army general, fought many battles and finally died in one of them. After he died, many wicked Jews grew up in Judea who didn't care about God's laws. There was also a famine, so many left the country and went to the Macedonians. Bacchides gathered these Jews together who wanted to live like the Greeks, and he used them against the friends of Judas. These wicked Jews caught some of the other Jews, tormented them and killed them. It was suffering which they hadn't seen since their return from Babylon. The whole nation was in danger, so they came to Judas's brother Jonathan and asked him to lead them. He agreed to protect them and became their army general. He said he was willing even to die for them.

Bacchides heard this and set out to kill him. Jonathan and his brother Simon heard of this plan and ran into the desert, arriving at Lake Asphar [the Dead Sea]. When Bacchides found out where they were, he brought his army and crossed the Jordan River. Jonathan knew about this and sent his brother John (Gaddis) to the Nabatean Arabs. He asked them to watch over their belongings until the battle was over, since they were friends of the Jews.

But the sons of Ambri waited for John and took everything, killing John and his friends. They were punished by John's brothers.

Bacchides decided to attack Jonathan at his camp near the lakes of the Jordan on the Sabbath (since they would be resting). Jonathan prayed to God to give them the victory, and he killed many of the enemy. When he saw Bacchides coming boldly to him, he almost killed him but he missed. Jonathan ran to the river and swam over it, together with his soldiers, and they were not followed.

Bacchides returned to the fort in Jerusalem after losing about 2,000 of his army. He fortified many cities of Judea where the walls had been destroyed: Jericho, Emmaus, Bethoron, Bethel, Timna, Pharatho, Tecoa and Gazara. He built towers in all of them. The walls were very strong and he put soldiers in all the cities. The strongest citadel was in Jerusalem. He took sons of the leading Jews as hostages and kept them in the forts.

Someone came to Jonathan and Simon and told them that the sons of Ambri were going to celebrate a wedding. They were bringing the bride from Gabatha; she was the daughter of one of the leading Arabians. Lots of riches would be there. Jonathan and Simon said that this would be a good time to punish them for killing their brother. They waited in the mountains for the group to pass. As soon as they saw them, they came out and killed all of them, taking the spoil. About 400 died. Simon and Jonathan stayed by the lakes of the Jordan.

After taking over all of Judea with forts, Bacchides returned to the king. Judea was quiet for two years. Some of the wicked people, seeing that Jonathan lived peacefully, urged King Demetrius to send Bacchides to come and capture him. They felt it could be done in one night. Bacchides came and gathered support in Judea, but Jonathan heard of their plan and it failed. Bacchides was very upset and killed fifty of the Jews who had called him there.

Jonathan and Simon went to Bethagla, a village in the desert. Jonathan built towers and walls and posted guards. Bacchides again came to attack. This went on for many days. Jonathan bravely fought back. Later he escaped, leaving his brother Simon there. He gathered men together and they attacked Bacchide's camp at night. Many were killed. Simon saw this, so he left the fort and burned the Macedonian war machines. He killed many of the enemy. Bacchides saw that he was losing and blamed those whom the king had sent to help him. He wanted the battle to end so he could return to the king. Jonathan sent men to Bacchides to make peace, and to return the captives which had been taken from both sides. Bacchides agreed to this; he took his men with him and returned to the king at Antioch. He never again came to Judea. Jonathan lived in the city of Michmash and ruled over many people. The wicked and ungodly were punished and there was peace

ALEXANDER, the son of Antiochus Epiphanes, came up to Syria and took Ptolemais. The soldiers gave it to him because they were upset with Demetrius. Demetrius had shut himself up in a palace with four towers that was near Antioch. He wouldn't talk to anyone or do his job in ruling the people. When Demetrius heard that Alexander was in Ptolemais, he took his army against him and sent messengers asking Jonathan to join him. He was afraid that Jonathan would go with Alexander against him, so he let Jonathan form an army, make armor and receive the Jewish hostages back which he had been keeping in the fort of Jerusalem. Jonathan read the letter to the people in Jerusalem, and the wicked men in the fort were afraid. Jonathan sent the hostages back to their own families. He stayed in Jerusalem and built up the city and walls. The walls were built with square stones to protect them from their enemies. When those in the forts of Judea saw this, they all left and went to Antioch, except the wicked men in the city of Bethsura and in the citadel of Jerusalem.

Alexander heard about the promises which Demetrius had made to Jonathan, and he knew how well he had fought the Macedonians. He said that Jonathan would be the best one to help him because he also hated Demetrius. Alexander felt that now would be a good time to join forces, so he wrote him a letter asking for his friendship. He wrote: "Jonathan, you will be the high priest of the Jews, and you will be known as my friend. I have sent you a purple robe and a golden crown." Jonathan put on the robe at the time of the Feast of Tabernacles, eight years after the death of his brother Judas. After Judas died, there was no priest. Jonathan raised a great army and had armor made. Demetrius was very sorry when he heard this. He blamed himself that he had not moved faster to make friends with Jonathan. He also wrote a letter to Jonathan and to the people. He wrote, "You have been tempted by our enemies, but you will be repaid for not giving in. Continue in this way and you will receive rewards from us. You will be free from all of the taxes which you used to pay to our kings and to me. You no longer have to pay the tax on salt or for the crowns which you used to offer to me. There will be no need to offer fruits from the fields or the trees. There will be no poll tax on each person in Judea, Samaria, Galilee and Perea. And this means in the future as well. Jerusalem will be holy and free from the tithe and from taxes. Jonathan can take over the fort in Jerusalem and keep it for us. All the Jews who are captives and slaves in my kingdom shall go free. The beasts will also be free. People shall be free to keep the Sabbath, and three days before each festival they shall be free. I am also freeing the Jews who are living in my kingdom and ordering that no one is to harm them. Those who would like to join my army may do so, up to 30,000 men. They will be paid the same as my soldiers; some will serve in the forts, and some will be my bodyguards. They may keep their own laws. There shall be only the one temple for worship; the temple in Jerusalem. I will offer 150,000 drachmae* every year for the sacrifices, and if there is money left over you may keep it. I release the 10,000 drachmae* which the kings received from the temple, to be given to the priests. If anyone owes the king money, they shall be free of their debt. You may repair and rebuild the temple with my money. You may build the walls of your city and build high towers at my expense. If any town needs fortification, I will also pay for it."

King Alexander raised a large army of hired soldiers, and those who had run away from Syria, and he came against Demetrius. Demetrius chased part of the enemy, running after them and killing many. But the soldiers around Demetrius were beaten. He fought bravely, but while chasing them on his horse, the horse fell into a deep swamp and they could not get out. The enemy surrounded Demetrius and threw their darts at him. In the end he was so wounded that he could no longer stand. He died after being a king for eleven years.

iii

THE son of Onias the high preist, who had the same name as his father, ran away to King Ptolemy (also named Philometor) and was living in Alexandria. Onias saw that Judea was taken over by the Macedonians and their kings. He decided to ask Ptolemy and Queen Cleopatra to let him build a temple in Egypt like the one in Jerusalem. It would have Levites and priests from their own people. He was thinking of Isaiah's prophecy from more than 600 years ago, which told that there would be a temple built to Almighty God in Egypt by a Jew.

In his letter, he reminded them of how he had helped in the past wars. He said that the Egyptian temples were not built in the proper way, and there were too many differences in temple worship. "I found a place which already has a lot of materials and animals which can be used for sacrifice. I would like to tear it down, since it belongs to no one, and build a worthy temple the same size as the one in Jerusalem. It would be for the Jewish people, and when they come here to worship they will be a help to you." So Ptolemy and his sister (and wife) Cleopatra answered, "We are surprised that you wish to build a temple in Leontopolis, which is unclean, but we agree to it since you mention this prophecy. We would not want to offend God." Onias built the temple, but it was smaller and poorer than the one in Jerusalem. Onias found Jewish priests, and they began to serve there.

The Alexandrian Jews in Jerusalem and the Samaritans who worshiped on Mount Gerizzim argued with each other. The Samaritans felt that the Law of Moses justified their temple on Gerizzim. They wanted the matter to be discussed and settled before Ptolemy. The Samaritans had two people to argue their side and those from Jerusalem had one. Both sides took an oath before Ptolemy that those who were shown to be breaking the law should be punished by death. The king brought several friends to listen. The Jews in Alexandria sided with the temple in Jerusalem. Those representing the temple at Gerizzim let the man from Jerusalem, Andronicus, speak first. He told about the line of the high priests, and how the kings in Asia had brought their gifts to Jerusalem. Andronicus persuaded the king to rule that only the Jerusalem temple had been built according to the laws of Moses. Those speaking for the temple at Mount Gerizzim were put to death.

iv

AFTER Demetrius was killed in battle, Alexander ruled in Syria. He wrote to Ptolemy Philometor asking to marry his daughter. He said that Ptolemy's success was a reward from God. Ptolemy agreed and said that he would meet Alexander in Ptolemais. He brought his daughter, Cleopatra, from Egypt and gave her silver and gold for a wedding gift.

After the wedding Alexander wrote to Jonathan, the Judean high priest, inviting him to Ptolemais. Jonathan brought gifts and was honored by both of the kings. Alexander gave him a purple robe and made him part of the royal family. Jonathan was led through the city and it was declared that no one should speak against him. Some of those who were against this ran away. Jonathan became Alexander's best friend.

Then Demetrius, the son of Demetrius, came with many soldiers from Crete. Alexander was very upset. He left Phoenicia quickly and came to Antioch so that he could get ready before Demetrius arrived. A governor named Apollonius complained to Jonathan that he was not loyal to the king. He challenged Jonathan to meet the governor's army in a contest. Jonathan chose 10,000 soldiers and came with his brother Simon to Joppa. Joppa was closed to him because Apollonius had a fort there. Jonathan pressured them and they opened the city to him. When Apollonius heard this, he came with 3,000 horse riders and 8,000 foot soldiers to Ashdod. They quietly and slowly arrived in Joppa to surprise Jonathan's men, but Jonathan made clever plans. Simon had part of the army. They fought until evening, using their shields so well that they were able to stand against all of the enemy's darts. Jonathan killed many of them and chased them as far as Ashdod. The rest ran into the temple of Dagon, because Jonathan had already burned the city and the villages around it. Jonathan burned the temple and those inside; 8,000 were killed.

Jonathan then came to Ashkelon, and those people gave him gifts which he accepted. He came back to Jerusalem with much spoil. When Alexander heard that Apollonius had been beaten, he pretended to be glad. He rewarded Jonathan with the customary golden button and gave him the city of Ekron for his own. About this time King Ptolemy came to Syria, bringing his army by sea and land to help Alexander, his son-in-law. All of the cities received him willingly. When he got to Ashdod, the people complained about their destroyed temple. Ptolemy knew that Jonathan had done this but kept quiet. Jonathan went to meet Ptolemy in Joppa and received gifts from him and symbols of honor. Then he returned to Jerusalem.

When Ptolemy was in Ptolemais, he was almost killed by Ammonius his friend. He wrote to Alexander, asking that Ammonius be punished. When Alexander did not answer him, Ptolemy knew that Alexander was behind the plot and he was very angry. Alexander was on bad terms with the people of Antioch, since they had suffered much under his rule. Ammonius was killed later anyway, while he was pretending to be a woman.

Ptolemy was sorry he had given Cleopatra to Alexander for a wife, so he took her away. He told Demetrius he would give her to him as his wife. Demetrius agreed. The people of Antioch didn't want to receive Demetrius as their king, since they had suffered under his father. But they also hated Alexander because of Ammonius, so in the end Ptolemy persuaded them to put him out of Antioch. Alexander then went to Cilicia. Ptolemy came to Antioch and became king by the people and by the army. He had two crowns, one for Asia and one for Egypt. He felt that it would not be wise, however, and he persuaded the people to receive Demetrius. He told them that Demetrius would be a good governor and that they should forget their past troubles.

Alexander left Cilicia and came to Syria. He burned the country belonging to Antioch and ruined it. Demetrius came against him and beat him. Alexander ran to Arabia. But Ptolemy's horse heard an elephant call and threw the king off his back. His enemies saw him fall and gave him many head wounds. For four days he could not understand or speak. Zabdiel, a prince of the Arabians, cut off Alexander's head and sent it to Ptolemy, who by the fifth day was recovering. He saw and understood that Alexander had been killed. Not long afterwards, Ptolemy also died. Alexander had ruled over Asia five years.

When Demetrius, also called Nicator, took over, he treated Ptolemy's soldiers badly. The soldiers ran to Alexandria, but Demetrius kept their elephants. Jonathan the high priest gathered an army out of all Judea and attacked the fort in Jerusalem. Some Macedonians were in it, but a few escaped at night and came and told Demetrius. Demetrius came against Jonathan with an army, and wrote to Jonathan to meet him at Ptolemais. Jonathan stopped the battle and came to Ptolemais with elders and priests, bringing gold, silver, clothes and other presents with him. The king was no longer angry. Instead, Jonathan was again declared the high priest as before with the earlier kings. The Jewish deserters accused Demetrius, but the king did not listen. He instead wrote a letter freeing many places in Judea from paying taxes. He made a copy for Jonathan. He sent home many of his soldiers since there was peace. Some were upset because the earlier kings had paid them even during times of peace. The soldiers that Demetrius kept were foreigners from Crete and other islands. Some of the soldiers hated him for that.

(Part of this chapter is a repeat of what was stated in Chapter 2)

THERE was a commander in Alexander's army named Diodotus (or Trypho) who noticed that the soldiers were angry at Demetrius. He went to Malchus the Arabian, who had taken care of Antiochus, the son of Alexander, and told him this. Trypho asked Malchus to give him Antiochus, and he would make the boy king. At first Malchus didn't want to do this, but he later agreed.

Jonathan wanted to get rid of the soldiers who were in the fort in Jerusalem and in the rest of Judea. He sent messengers to Demetrius with presents, asking him to send all of these men home. Demetrius said that he was in a war now, but after it he would not only grant this request but more. Right now, though, Demetrius wanted Jonathan to send him some soldiers to help him. Jonathan chose 3,000 of his soldiers and sent them to Demetrius.

The people of Antioch hated Demetrius because of his father, and also because he was a harsh king. When they heard that Jonathan's soldiers were coming, they saw their chance. They surrounded the palace and tried to block the king from coming out. The king took his soldiers, together with Jonathan's, and attacked the people of Antioch. But he lost, because there were tens of thousands against him. The Jews went to the top of the palace and shot at the people without getting hurt. Later they set fire to the whole city, since the houses were close to one another and mostly built of wood. The people of Antioch had to run away from the fire. Demetrius saw that the people were trying to save their children and their wives instead of fighting, so he killed many of them. They had to surrender to Demetrius.

Demetrius forgave the rebels. He rewarded the Jews out of the rich spoil he got, because they had helped him win the battle. He then sent them back to Jonathan in Jerusalem. But he did not treat

Jonathan fairly afterwards. He broke his promises and demanded taxes from them which had not been paid to the earlier Syrian kings. He said he would make war unless they paid.

Trypho stopped the war by bringing the child, Antiochus, back from Arabia and making him king. Demetrius's soldiers who were not getting paid went with Tryphos and fought agains Demetrius. They captured the elephants and took over Antioch. Demetrius was beaten and went to Cilicia.

The child king Antiochus sent messengers and a letter to Jonathan to make peace. He gave him four areas in Judea to rule and sent him dishes and cups of gold and a purple robe. He also gave Jonathan the gold button and made his brother Simon general over the army, from the Ladder of Tyre to Egypt. Jonathan was pleased and promised to help Antiochus in a war against Demetrius, since his kindness to Demetrius was not returned but instead Demetius had hurt him.

Antiochus let Jonathan raise an army out of Syria and Phoencia to fight against Demetrius and his generals. Jonathan was welcomed in Askelon. In all the cities of Celesyria he told the people to join with Antiochus against Demetrius. When he came to Gaza, they shut the gates in his face, even though they didn't like Demetrius. Jonathan surrounded Gaza and ruined the land around it. When they saw that help was too far away, they agreed to join with Jonathan's army. This is to show that when people have suffered, they often change their minds about what is good for them. Jonathan took some hostages from Gaza and sent them to Jerusalem. He went around the country and came to Damascus.

When Jonathan heard that the generals of Demetrius had come to the city of Cadesh with a huge army (between Tyre and Galilee), he met them in Galilee with an army which he raised. He sent Simon to take over Bethsura, the strongest city in Judea, and he conquered it. When they saw Simon bringing his war machines, the people in Bethsura gave up. They asked to leave peaceably and return to Demetrius, which was granted. Simon then put his own men in the fort.

Jonathan left the Galilee, where he had camped at the waters of Gennesar, and came to Asor, not knowing that Demetrius's men were there. Jonathan realized just in time that they were waiting for his men, and they were able to get away. A few stayed with Jonathan (about 50), including Mattathias the son of Absalom and Judas, who were commanders of the whole army. They were able to chase the enemies back to their camp at Cadesh.

Jonathan killed 2,000 of the enemy and then returned to Jerusalem. He saw that God had blessed his work, and he sent messengers to the Romans wanting to renew the agreement of peace with them. He also wanted to make peace with the Spartans. The ambassadors came to the senate in Rome, and reminded them of their long friendship with the Jews. Jonathan's letters asked them to remember Onias, the Jewish high priest who had been their king. There was peace at that time (see the attached letter). Jonathan also wrote a letter to the Spartans: "It is time to renew our friendship. We remember to pray for your people's welfare and victory during our festival days when we offer sacrifices to God We have had to fight wars with the peoples around us who tried to take our land from us. We are looking forward to your reply." The peace was agreed to, signed and returned.

There were three sects among the Jews at this time: the Pharisees, the Sadducees and the Essens. The Pharisees believe that some actions are the work of fate, and some are within our power. The Essens say that fate controls all things. The Sadducees say that all events are within our own power, so that we bring on ourselves good or evil.

The generals of Demetrius came against Jonathan at Hamath. Jonathan sent out spies, and when he found out what he needed, he placed watchmen around his camp. He told them to be ready to fight at night in case they would need to. When Demetrius understood that Jonathan had found out their plans, they lit many fires to make him think they were still there, and then the army left. Jonathan could not catch them, since they had passed over a river and were too far away. Jonathan went instead to Arabia and fought the Nabateans. He took many captives and spoils and sold them in Damascus. At this time Simon his brother went over all Judea and Palestine as far as Askelon fortifying the forts. He took Joppa and filled it with soldiers, so that Demetrius's soldiers could not take it over.

Simon and Jonathan finished their work and returned to Jerusalem. There they began to restore the walls and to rebuild the wall around the temple. They built a wall inside the city to separate the market place from the fort, in order to keep the soldiers from getting supplies. Simon's job was to strengthen forts around the country.

Demetrius came to Mesopotamia and wanted to keep control of Babylon and the northern areas. Often the Greeks in the area would send messengers to him, promising that if he would come to them they would help him fight against Arsaces, king of the Parthians. Demetrius hoped to beat the Parthians and then to beat Trypho and drive him out of Syria. But when he fought against Arsaces, he lost all of his army and was captured.

vi

HEARING that Demetrius had been captured, Trypho decided to kill Antiochus so that he could take over the kingdom. But he feared Antiochus's friend Jonathan, so he planned to get rid of Jonathan first by tricking him. Trypho left Antioch for Bethshan, where Jonathan met him with 40,000 men. Trypho gave Jonathan many gifts and ordered his captains to obey Jonathan. He wanted to carry out his plan after Jonathan was convinced he was a friend. He even told Jonathan that he could send his soldiers home and keep only a few. Trypho asked Jonathan to go with him to Ptolemais; Trypho promised to give him the city and all the forts in the country. Jonathan thought all was well. He kept only 3,000 soldiers; 2,000 stayed in Galilee, and 1,000 went with him. The people of Ptolemais shut their gates as Trypho had told them to do. Jonathan was captured, and all of his soldiers were killed. Trypho sent his army to the 2,000 soldiers in Galilee to kill them, but they knew ahead of time and put on all their armor and escaped.

The people were very sad and fearful when they heard that their leader, Jonathan, had been captured and his soldiers killed. Simon called the people together in the temple and encouraged them. He reminded them of all of the times when his family had been willing to die for the sake of the Jewish laws and worship of God. "I am willing to pay back our enemies for the blood of my brothers, and I will deliver you and our wives and children with God's help. I will keep them from destroying our temple." All of the people cried out together that Simon should be their leader and that they would obey him. He gathered his soldiers, and they rebuilt the walls of the city and strengthened them with strong towers. He sent a friend to Joppa to empty the city so that Trypho would not conquer it, but he himself stayed in Jerusalem.

Trypho left Ptolemais with a large army and arrived in Judea, bringing Jonathan his captive with him. Simon met them with his army at the city of Adida, which was on a hill overlooking the plains of Judea. Trypho knew that Simon was the new leader, and he said that he would free Jonathan for 100 talents* of silver and two of Jonathan's sons. He needed a promise that Judea would not rebel against him as well. He said that Jonathan was a prisoner because of he owed money to the king. Simon knew that Trypho might not keep his promise but he feared the people would blame him if he didn't agree to the demand. He paid the money and gave him Jonathan's sons.

Trypho did not free Jonathan, but took his army all around the country. He intended to later take over Jerusalem by coming from Idumea [Edom]. The soldiers in the fort sent word to Trypho that they needed supplies, and Trypho got ready to come quickly. But there was a huge snowstorm, and the soldiers could not get to Jerusalem. Trypho came instead into Celesyria and attacked the land of Gilead and killed Jonathan. He ordered that Jonathan be buried, and he returned to Antioch. Simon sent for his brother's bones and buried him in the city of Modin. The people mourned him. Simon set up a very large monument for his father and brothers, made of white polished stone which could be seen from far away. It was surrounded by pillars, each one carved from a single stone – a wonderful sight. He also built seven pyramids for his father and for each brother, which were very large and beautiful; they are still standing today. Jonathan had been high priest for 14 years and also leader of his nation.

The people made Simon their high priest, and in the first year he freed his people from their slavery to the Macedonians. They no longer had to pay taxes. They had paid them for the past 170 years to the Assyrians. Simon tore down the cities of Gazara, Joppa and Jamnia. He broke down the fort in Jerusalem so that their enemies could no longer hide in it. He gathered the people and convinced them to work hard to tear down the entire mountain where the fort was. They worked day and night for three years and flattened the mountain, so that the temple was now the highest of all of the buildings in the city.

vii

SHORTLY after Demetrius was taken captive, Trypho his governor killed Antiochus, the son of Alexander, who was also called "The God." He had ruled four years. The death was blamed on the surgeons, but this was not true. He sent his close friends to the soldiers, promising to pay them a lot if they would make him king. He said that Demetrius's brother Antiochus would not be a good king; he would punish them for rebelling against his brother. The soldiers agreed to this. Trypho pretended to be good to the people, but he showed his real self to be wicked. The soldiers hated him and went to Cleopatra, the wife of Demetrius, who had been kept with her children in the city of Seleucia. Antiochus, the brother of Demetrius (Soter) was not allowed into any cities because of Trypho, so Cleopatra asked him to marry her and take the kingdom. Her friends persuaded her to do this, and she was in fear of her life if Trypho would take over Seleucia.

Antiochus came to Seleucia with his growing army. He chased after Trypho and drove him out of Upper Syria into Phoenicia. He trapped him in the strong fort of Dora. He sent messengers to Simon in order to make a friendly agreement and get help from him. Simon sent Antiochus a lot of money and supplies. Trypho escaped from Dora, but he was captured and put to death. He had ruled three years.

Antiochus forgot the kind help he had received from Simon. He sent an army, led by his friend Cendebeus, to attack Simon. Simon heard that Antiochus had broken the friendship, and although he was old, Simon led his army as the general. His sons joined him and were very strong. They set ambushes in the narrow valleys between the mountains and they beat all of their enemies. He made an agreement with the Romans.

When he had ruled the Jews for eight years, he was at a feast and his son-in-law Ptolemy killed him. He also caught his wife and two of his sons. Ptolemy intended to kill the third son, John (Hyrcanus), but he escaped to Jerusalem. Ptolemy tried to go after him and come in through another gate, but the people of Jerusalem didn't let him in.

viii

PTOLEMY went to one of the forts above Jericho, which was called Dagon. Hyrcanus had become the high priest; he went against Ptolemy in Dagon but it became very hard. Hyrcanus saw his mother and brothers, who Ptolemy had tormented in front of everyone. He told Hyrcanus he would throw the prisoners down from the wall if he did not stop the siege. His mother spread out her hands and begged him not to weaken, but to continue – she said even death would be sweet if she knew the enemy would be punished for their wickedness. Hyrcanus wanted to take the fort right then, but when he saw his mother beaten and torn to pieces, he lost his courage and the siege continued longer. The seventh year began when the Jews rest, so Ptolemy was freed from the war. He killed Hyrcanus's mother and brothers and then went to Zeno (Cotylas), who was the tyrant of the city of Philadephia.

Antiochus was upset about what Simon had done to him, so he invaded Judea in the fourth year of his rule. He burned the country and shut Hyrcanus up in the city and surrounded it with seven camps. The walls were very strong, so in the beginning they just waited. At one time those inside had no water, but God sent an early spring rain and they were saved. The king built 100 towers around the city three stories high, and he put soldiers in them. There were attacks against the Jews daily. He cut a deep double ditch which trapped the people inside like a wall. The Jews took every advantage to attack when the guards were away.

Hyrcanus knew that too many people inside meant there would be less food to go around, so he sent out the people who were not young and able to fight. But Antiochus would not let them leave the city. They wandered between the walls and died of starvation. When the Feast of Tabernacles came, the rest of these people were brought back into the city.

Hyrcanus asked for peace from Antiochus due to the festival, and it was granted. Antiochus even sent a large sacrifice: bulls with golden horns, sweet spices and cups of gold and silver. These were received at the gates and taken to the temple. Antiochus kept the feast with his army. He was very different from the earlier Antiochus – the one called Epiphanes who had offered pigs on the altar and done other acts hated by the Jews. They called this Antiochus "Antiochus the Pious."

Hyrcanus, seeing that the man worshiped God, took courage and asked Antiochus to give back the settlements which the Jews had received from their forefathers. Antiochus answered that if the Jews would give up their weapons, and pay the taxes for Joppa and the other cities bordering on Judea, and allow him to put soldiers in the city, he would make peace with them. The Jews were pleased, except for the demand of the soldiers, since they were not to live with foreigners. They were willing to give him hostages and 500 talents* of silver instead. They gave 300 talents* as a first payment and sent the hostages right away, which Antiochus accepted. One of the hostages was Hyrcanus's brother. Then Antiochus took down the war machines and left.

Hyrcanus opened David's tomb which had many riches in it. He took out 3,000 talents* and used the money to pay a foreign army. Hyrcanus opened the city to Antiochus and gave his army everything they needed. They went together against the Parthians.

HYRCANUS heard that Antiochus had died, so he went against cites in Syria. It took six months for him to take Medaba, and his army suffered greatly. They took some nearby places including the nation of the Cutheans: Shechem and Mount Gerizzim where their temple had been built. Alexander had permitted Sanballat to build it for the sake of Manasseh, son-in-law of Jadua the high priest. The temple was no longer used 200 years after it was built. Hyrcanus took Dora and Marissa and took over all of Idumea [Edom]. He let the people stay if they would be circumcised and obey the Jewish laws. They all agreed.

Hyrcanus wanted to sign a friendship agreement with the Romans, so he sent messengers to their senate. At the time, people from the Mentine and Falernian tribes were there. The Jews sent Simon the son of Dositheus, Apollonius the son of Alexander, and another man, all good, honest men. They asked the senate to give back to them Joppa, the harbor, Gazara, the springs of the Jordan and several other cities and places which Antiochus had taken in war. They wanted a promise that the king's soldiers would not pass through their country, and that decisions which Antiochus had made without senate approval be cancelled. They wanted payment for the places that he ruined. In turn the Jews would protect the kings and free captives. The senate answered that they would look into these matters when they had time to do so. In the meantime, the Jews were given money for their trip home and a guard so that they would get back to Judea safely.

King Demetrius wanted to fight against Hyrcanus, but he couldn't do it because he didn't have the support of the Syrians or his soldiers. He was a wicked man. When they sent ambassadors to Ptolemy (Physcon) asking the family of Seleucus to take the kingdom, he sent them Alexander (Zebina) with an army. There was a battle; Demetrius lost and ran to Cleopatra his wife, but she would not receive him so he went to Tyre. There he was caught and suffered much until he was killed. Alexander took the kingdom and made friends with Hyrcanus. But when Alexander fought with Antiochus the son of Demetrius (Grypus), he lost and was also killed.

X

AFTER Antiochus took the kingdom, he was afraid to come against Judea because he heard that his brother Antiochus Cyzicenus was gathering an army out of Cyzicum to fight him. He was the son of Antiochus Soter (who had died in Parthia) and the brother of Demetrius. (Cleopatra was married to two brothers.) Antiochus Cyzicenus fought against his brother in Syria for many years. This allowed Hyrcanus to live in peace, and he no longer paid the Macedonians any taxes or honor. Antiochus had no Egyptians to fight his war, and both he and his brother were weak.

Hyrcanus used his chance to go against a very strong city in Samaria, presently called Sebaste, which was later rebuilt by Herod. Hyrcanus was punishing them for the way they had treated the Jews in Marissa. He made a ditch and built a double wall around the city, and he made his sons Antigonus and Aristobulus commanders over the siege. The Samaritans were forced to eat things they didn't want to eat. They called for Antiochus Cyzicenus to help them, but he was beaten by Aristobulus. He escaped and the two sons of Hyrcanus returned to Samaria. The Samaritans were again trapped and they called a second time for Antiochus, who came with 6,000 men from Ptolemy Lathyrus. His mother did not agree to this. With these Egyptians Antiochus ruined Hyrcanus's country like a robber. He was hoping to get Hyranus to lift the siege of Samaria, but he failed and he lost many of his soldiers. He went to Tripoli and let Callimander and Epicrates fight the war.

Callimander was too bold in his attacks; he pulled back and was quickly killed. Epicrates loved money and he betrayed other cities to the Jews, but he was also not able to stop the siege of Samaria. After one year, Hyrcanus took the city and completely destroyed it. He brought water into it and soon there was no sign that the city ever existed.

This high priest Hyrcanus talked with God. He was alone in the temple on the day his sons fought with Antiochus Cyzicenus and was offering incense. He heard a voice that said his sons had just beaten Antiochus. When he left the temple, he told the people this and it turned out to be true.

The Jews in Jerusalem and Judea were doing well at this time, and so were the Jews in Alexandria, Egypt and Cyprus. Cleopatra was quarrelling with her son Ptolemy (Lathyrus). The two generals she chose were the sons of Onias who had built the temple in Heliopolis, similar to the one in Jerusalem.

The Jews themselves were jealous of Hyrcanus. The sect of the Pharisees had power with the Jews, especially if they criticized the king or high priest. They loved Hyrcanus who was one of their disciples. Once when he invited them to a feast and was a good host, he told them that he wanted to be a righteous man and please God. The Pharisees also had this goal. He said that if they saw him breaking any point of the law, that they should correct him. One guest named Eleazar liked to make trouble. He said, "If you really want to be righteous, be content to be the governor and let someone else be the high priest." When asked why he should do this, Eleazar said it was because Hyrcanus's mother had been a captive when Antiochus Epiphanes was king. This was not true, and Hyrcanus was very upset with this man. The Pharisees were also very upset with Eleazar.

Jonathan, a close friend of Hyrcanus, was from the sect of the Sadducees. He asked the Pharisees what punishment would be fitting for this troublemaker. The Pharisees said that he should be whipped and put in prison, but not put to death. Hyrcanus was angry with the Pharisees, thinking that Eleazar was speaking with their approval. Hyrcanus was so stirred up by what Jonathan did that he left the Pharisees and went with the Sadducees. He cancelled the laws which the Pharisees had put on the people, and he punished those who kept them. The two sides hated each other from then on. The Pharisees have many laws which are not written in the Law of Moses; the Sadducees reject these and say only the written Law should be obeyed. The Sadducees had the rich people on their side, but most of the people went with the Pharisees.

After Hyrcanus put an end to this uproar, he lived well. He ruled the government well for 31 years before he died. He had five sons. He was seen by God as worthy to be a governor, a high priest and a prophet. God was with him and enabled him to see the future. He foretold that his two oldest sons would not be involved in public affairs for long.

xi

AFTER Hyrcanus died, the eldest son Aristobulus crowned himself king. This was 481 years and three months after the people had returned from slavery in Babylon. Aristobulus loved his next brother Antigonus and treated him as his equal, but the others he kept in prison. His own mother was in prison because she argued with his way of ruling. He meant for her to starve to death. His brother Antigonus refused to believe the bad things others said about Aristobulus. Antigonus once returned from the army at the time of the Feast of Tabernacles. He was dressed richly and went with his soldiers to the temple. Aristobulus was sick and Antigonus meant to pray for him to get well. But wicked men told Aristobulus that Antigonus was showing off, and said that he was coming to kill his brother with armed men. Aristobulus ordered his guards to wait in a dark underground place (he was in the Antonia tower while sick). He ordered that if Antigonus came to him without weapons he could visit, but if he was armed he should be killed. The queen was part of the plot against Antigonus, and she gave him the opposite message. Since his new armor was special, she said, he should certainly visit his brother wearing it. Antigonus didn't suspect anything, and followed the queen's advice. When he came to a dark place called Strato's Tower he was killed. This shows what envy and slander can do.

It must be noted that Judas of the Essens never missed the truth in his predictions. When he saw Antigonus passing the temple that day, he said that it would be good if he (Judas) died now, because he had prophesied that Antigonus would be killed in Strato's Tower on this same day – but here he was, still alive. Judas thought he was in danger of being a false prophet, and he was sad. Then the news came that Antigonus had been killed in a place called Strato's Tower, and Judas was very upset.

Later Aristobulus was sorry he had killed his brother. He lost his mind from the guilt, and he had terrible stomach pains causing him to vomit blood. One of the servants who was carrying his blood away slipped and spilled some of his blood at the same place where Antigonus's blood spots still were. Those who saw this said that the servant was spilling it in the same place on purpose. Aristobulus heard this and asked what happened, but they would not answer him. Finally they told him about his blood being spilled on top of his brother's. He cried a lot and said that he should be punished for killing his brother and his mother. He then died, after ruling for one year. He loved the Greeks and made war against Iturea, adding a large part of it to Judea. He allowed the people to live there if they were circumcised and lived according to the Jewish laws. He was a modest person and kind to the Jews.

xii

AFTER Aristobulus died, his wife Salome (the Greeks called her Alexandra) freed his brothers from prison and made the oldest of them, Alexander Janneus, the king. This child had been hated by his father Hyrcanus from birth and had never been permitted to see his father. Hyrcanus loved his two oldest sons, Antigonus and Aristobulus, and when he asked God in a dream who his successor would be, Alexander's face appeared. So Alexander was sent away and was brought up in the Galilee. But God had shown Hyrcanus the right face; Alexander became the king after him.

Alexander Janneus went against Ptolemais and shut up his people in the city. There were only two seaport cities left to conquer: Ptolemais and Gaza, besides Strato's Tower and Dora which the tyrant Zoilus held. The people of Ptolemais asked for help from Ptolemy Lathyrus who was in Cyprus after being driven out of Egypt by his mother, Cleopatra. Ptolemy Lathyrus got his fleet ready, thinking that he would have help from the people of Gaza, from Zoilus and from the Sidonians.

Demetrius told the people of Ptolemais that it would be better to be under Jewish rule. To make Ptolemy their leader might cause a war from Egypt, since Cleopatra would not ignore an army raised by Ptolemy. She would bring her own army against him since she didn't want him in Cyprus. Ptolemy came with his fleet anyway, and landed at Sycamine. His soldiers and horsemen numbered 30,000. They marched to Ptolemais and set up camp, but the people of Ptolemais refused to speak to him.

Then Zoilus and the people of Gaza came to Ptolemy, since the Jews and Alexander had ruined their country. Alexander left them alone because he feared Ptolemy. Instead, he used deception. He privately invited Cleopatra to come against Ptolemy, but publicly Alexander made peace with him. He promised to give Ptolemy 400 talents* of silver for killing Zoilus and giving his country to the Jews. Ptolemy made a friendship agreement with Alexander and won against Zoilus, but then he found out that Alexander had sent for his mother. Ptolemy broke the agreement and attacked Ptolemais since the city would not receive him. Leaving his generals with some of the soldiers to continue the siege, he went to destroy Judea. When Alexander understood that this was Ptolemy's plan, he took 50,000 of his soldiers (some say 80,000) to meet him. Ptolemy attacked a city in Galilee, Asochis, on the Sabbath. He took 10,000 slaves and much spoil.

He tried to take Sepphoris, but he lost many men. Then he went to fight with Alexander, who met him at the Jordan River near Saphoth. Ptolemy had 8,000 army generals with shields of brass. Alexander's soldiers were not brave, but their leader encouraged them to cross the river to the army of the Jews. Many Jews ran away. Ptolemy's soldiers followed them and killed so many of them that their iron weapons became dull and their hands got tired. Around 30,000 men were killed (some say 50,000) Some were taken captive.

Ptolemy took over the whole country and stayed that night in a village in Judea. He ordered his soldiers to strangle the women and children, cut them into pieces, throw them into boiling pots and then eat them as sacrifices. He did this so that any deserters coming to them would think that their enemies were cannibals and be afraid of them. Ptolemy also took Ptolemais by force.

xiii

CLEOPATRA saw that her son Ptolemy had become very powerful. He had ruined Judea and controlled the city of Gaza. When he was almost at the gates of Egypt, she immediately sent out her army against him by sea and by land. She had two Jewish generals, Chelcias and Ananias. She sent her own possessions, her grandchildren and her will to a safe place on the island of Cos (near Egypt). Cleopatra told her son Alexander to sail with a great fleet to Phoenicia. Cleopatra came to Ptolemais but was not received, so she besieged the city. Ptolemy left Syria and came to Egypt, expecting the country to have no protection without an army. He tried to take it, but he failed. One of Cleopatra's generals died while chasing Ptolemy.

When Cleopatra heard that her son's attempt had failed, she sent part of her army against him and he was driven out of Egypt. He spent the winter in Gaza. At that time Cleopatra captured the fort in Ptolemais and took over the city. Alexander of the Jews came to her and gave her presents, because he had suffered from Ptolemy and could find help only from her. Some of Cleopatra's friends wanted her to capture Alexander and take over the whole country. Ananias, her Jewish general, disagreed and said, "Since this man is related to us, it would make all of the Jews your enemies." Cleopatra listened to him and left Alexander alone. She made an agreement with him in Coelesyria.

When Alexander was no longer afraid of Ptolemy, he went against Coelesyria and also took Gadara after a siege of ten months. He took a strong fortress, Amathus, belonging to the people above the Jordan River. There Theodorus, the son of Zeno, held his precious treasure. Zeno killed 10,000 Jews and took Alexander's supplies. Alexander was not worried. He went against the seaside parts of the country, Raphia and Anthedon (later king Herod called these areas Agrippias), taking them by force. When Alexander saw that Ptolemy had left Gaza and had gone back to Cyprus, and that his mother had returned to Egypt, he became angry with the Gazans since they had invited Ptolemy to help them. He came into Gaza and ruined everything. Apollodotus, the general of the army of Gaza, surprised the camp of the Jews by night with 2,000 foreign soldiers and 10,000 of his own. While it was night, the Gazans were winning since the Jews thought that it was Ptolemy attacking them. In the morning Jews found out the truth, and they came to Gaza and killed about 1,000 of them. The Gazans fought strongly. Aretas, the impressive king of the Arabians, encouraged them and promised that he would help them. Before he arrived, Apollodotus was killed by his brother who envied him and who gave up the city to Alexander.

Alexander came in quietly, but later he attacked and killed many in Gaza. The Gazans fought back with strength and courage. Many Jews were killed, and some Gazans burned their own houses rather than have their possessions taken by the enemy. Some even killed their own children and wives so that they wouldn't be taken as slaves. There were 500 Gazan senators who ran to Apollo's temple. Alexander killed all of them. After the city was overthrown, he returned to Jerusalem. The siege had taken one year.

At this time Antiochus (Grypus) died. He was betrayed by Hereacleon. He had lived 45 years and had reigned for 29 years. Seleucus his son then became king, and he fought against his father's brother who was called Antiochus Cyzicenus. Seleucus took Cyzicenus prisoner and killed him. After a while the son of Cyzicenus, Pius, came to Aradus and made himself king; he made war with Seleucus and drove him out of Syria. When Seleucus came to Mopsuestia, he took taxes from them. The people were angry and burned down his palace and killed him together with his friends. When Antiochus, the son of Cyzicenus, was king in Syria, Antiochus the brother of Seleucus made war on him, killing both him and his army. After him, his brother Philip crowned himself and reigned over part of Syria, but Ptolemy Latyrus took his fourth brother Demetrius and made him king of Damascus. Antiochus opposed both these brothers, but he died while trying to help Laodice, queen of the Gileadites, who was fighting against the Parthians. He fell at the time that Demetrius and Philip governed Syria.

The people were against Alexander. It was the fall festival when citrons (like lemons) are held as part of the celebration. As the king stood by the altar ready to sacrifice, the people threw their citrons at him. They said that he was from a family of slaves and was not worthy to be making a sacrifice. He was so angry that he killed about 6,000 people. He had a wooden wall built around the altar and temple so that only the priests could enter, and this kept the people from attacking him. He also hired foreigners from Pisidiae and Cilicia. He was at war with the Syrians, so he had no Syrian soldiers. He overcame the Arabians, such as the Moabites and Gileadites, and made them pay taxes. He took over Amathus. He fought a battle with the king of the Arabians and was thrown down into a deep valley due to the many camels at Gadara, a village of Gilead. He barely escaped with his life. He arrived in Jerusalem where the people insulted him. He fought against them for six years and killed no fewer than 50,000 of them. When he finally asked the people what he could do to win them, they all cried out that he should kill himself. They also sent word to Demetrius Eucerus and asked him to help them against Alexander.

DEMETRIUS came with his army and camped near Shechem. Alexander had 6,200 soldiers and about 20,000 Jews, and Demetrius tried to gain some of the Greek soldiers who were with Alexander. Alexander in turn tried to gain the Jews who were with Demetrius. But neither side succeeded, and they went to battle. Demetrius won, and all of Alexander's hired men were killed. Demetrius also lost some men.

Alexander ran to the mountains, and 6,000 of the Jews left Demetrius and came to him. Demetrius was afraid and left. The Jews later fought against Alexander, but many were killed in several battles. The strongest men were captured within the city of Bethome, and after taking over the city, Alexander brought them to Jerusalem. As Alexander was feasting with his women in the sight of everyone in the city, he ordered 800 of these prisoners to be crucified. Before they died, he ordered that the throats of their children and wives be cut before their eyes. This was in revenge for what the Jews had done to him. He did these inhuman acts because they had hired foreigners to help them against him. He was forced to give back the lands of Moab and Gilead to the king of Arabia, so that the Arabians would not join the Jews against him. They had done 10,000 other things to upset him. But still, this brutal act was not right. He was called a "Thracian" among the Jews, which meant a barbarian. The 8,000 soldiers who had fought against him ran away at night, and they hid until Alexander died.

Demetrius left Judea and went to Berea, where he besieged his brother Philip. He took with him 10,000 foot soldiers and 1,000 horsemen. Strato, the tyrant of Berea and a friend of Philip, called in Zizon the ruler of the Arabian tribes, and the king of the Parthians, who won against Demetrius. They came with their arrows and forced his army to give up from lack of water. They took much spoil and Demetrius himself with them. The people whom they took from Antioch were restored without a reward. Mithridates, the king of Parthia, honored Demetrius until Demetrius died of sickness. Philip then came to Antioch, captured it and ruled over Syria.

ANTIOCHUS (Dionysius), who was Philip's brother, took over Damascus. During the war against the Arabians, his brother Philip came to Damascus. Milesius, governor of the city and the people of Damascus, made Philip the ruler. But Philip did not show any gratitude or give Milesius any reward, so he had to leave Damascus. Milesius caught him marching into the Hippodrome and shut him up inside, and he kept Damascus for Antiochus who came back from Arabia. He also came against Judea with 8,000 armed foot soldiers and 800 horsemen. Alexander feared his coming, and he dug a deep ditch from Chabarzaba (now called Antipatris) to the sea at Joppa. He built a wall with wooden towers, which was 150 furlongs* long. He waited for Antiochus to come, but he burned all of the walls and his army passed through them into Arabia. The king of Arabia (Aretas) pulled back, but later he came suddenly with 10,000 horsemen. Antiochus fought hard against them and won. He was bringing some extra soldiers in to help when he was killed. After this battle, his army fled to the village of Cana and most of them died from lack of food.

After Antiochus died, Aretas reigned over Coelesyria. The people of Damascus wanted him instead of Ptolemy Menneus, whom they hated. Aretas went against Judea and beat Alexander in battle. But then he made an agreement and left. Alexander marched to the city of Dios and took it. He also took Zeno's treasures from Essa by enclosing the place with three walls. They took other places: the Valley of Antiochus and the fortress of Gamala.

He accused Demetrius, governor of those places, of many crimes and chased him out. Alexander made war for three years. When he returned home, the Jews were very happy for his success.

At this time the Jews ruled the following cities which had belonged to the Syrians, Idumeans and Phoenicians: Strato's Tower, Apollonia, Joppa, Jamnia, Ashdod, Gaza Anthedon, Raphia and Rhinocolura. In the middle of the country they held land near Idumea, Adora and Marissa. Near Samaria, he gained Mount Carmel, Mount Tabor, Scythopolis and Gadara. There were others gains in the country of the Gaulonites and Moab. Some cities were destroyed because those people refused to worship like the Jewish people. The Jews also had some major cities in Syria which had been destroyed.

After this King Alexander drank too much and was sick for three years. He still continued going out with his army, however. He died in Ragaba, a fortress beyond the Jordan. Before he died, Alexandra the queen came to him, crying and asking what would happen to her and the children. "You're aware of how the nation hates you," she said. He told her to not tell the soldiers about his death until later. Instead, she should go to Jerusalem as if there was a victory, and give some authority to the Pharisees. They would respect her for such an honor. He said that they had the power to hurt those whom they hated and to help those whom they liked. "The people believe them when they speak of others. They ruined my reputation among the people by what they have said. Show them my body and let them to do with it as they wish. Promise them that you will make no decision for the kingdom without them. Then I will have a grander funeral than whatever you would have made for me. If they do nothing bad to my body, you will be able to rule safely." He died at age 49 and had ruled 27 years.

xvi

WHEN Alexandra had taken the fortress, she did as her husband told her and spoke to the Pharisees. She put all things into their power, both his dead body and the affairs of the kingdom. So they let go of their anger against Alexander. The Pharisees spoke to the people that he had been a good king, and they were sad for his death. Alexander had a grander funeral than any of the kings before him.

Alexander had two sons, Hyrcanus and Aristobulus, but he gave the kingdom to his wife. The sons were not able to take care of public affairs. The older one, Hyrcanus, was quiet, and the younger, Aristobulus, was a bold man. Alexandra was popular because she seemed upset about the wrong things her husband had done.

Alexandra made Hyrcanus the high priest since he didn't like politics and he let the Pharisees do everything they wanted. She also ordered the people to obey the Pharisees. She restored the traditions of the Pharisees which her father-in-law, Hyrcanus, had cancelled. She seemed to be the ruler, but the Pharisees had the authority. They let exiles come back and set prisoners free, just like lords. The queen increased her own army so much that the enemies around Judea feared her. She also took captives from them. So there was peace – except with the Pharisees who wanted her to kill those who had persuaded Alexander to kill the 800 men. She let the Pharisees cut the throats of some of these.

Aristobulus and some of the most powerful men came and tried to stop her. They begged her to protect them, now that they had won over their enemies from outside, and not let enemies from inside kill them. They said that if their enemies would be satisfied with those who were already punished, they would keep quiet. If not, they asked the queen to send them away; and if she would not forgive them, they would die at her palace gates. The enemies would gladly take them on as soldiers, or they were willing to stay in her forts for the rest of their lives.

Aristobulus spoke before the people saying that they had caused their own fate by allowing a woman to rule over them, instead of young men who were better fit to rule. Alexandra didn't know what else to do, so she gave her forts over to these men, except the forts that held her treasures. Shortly afterwards she sent her son Aristobulus with an army to Damascus to fight Ptolemy (Meneus), but he did not do well and returned home.

News came that Tigranes, the king of Armenia, had invaded Syria with 500,000 soldiers (or less) and they were coming against Judea. The queen and everyone were very afraid. They sent many valuable gifts with messengers to him. Selene the queen (Cleopatra) who ruled over Syria, was against Tigranes, and the Jews begged him not to think that they were like her. Tigranes thanked them for the respect they showed him by coming so far, and this gave them hope. But as soon as Ptolemais was taken, news came to Tigranes that Luculus was ruining Armenia. So Tigranes returned home.

The queen became very sick, and Aristobulus decided it was time to take over the government. He left secretly at night with only one of his servants, and he went to the forts where his father's friends were living. He was afraid that if his mother died, they would all be under the rule of the Pharisees; his brother Hyrcanus was next in line as ruler, but he couldn't do the job. Only Aristobulus's wife knew where he was.

First he came to Abaga and met with Galestes, a powerful person. The queen found out that Aristobulus had left, but she didn't think it was important. Slowly reports came to her that he was taking over one place after another, and it wouldn't be long until he would be in full power. People were afraid that he would punish them for the way they had treated his family, so they decided to take Aristobulus's wife and children and keep them in the fort which was over the temple.

Many people came to Aristobulus from all over. In about two weeks, he had 22 strong places from which he could build an army. The elders of the Jews and Hyrcanus went to the queen for her opinion, even though she was ill. She told them to do what they thought was right. They had much in their favor, as well as enough money. She didn't care about public affairs, since she was too weak to tend to them.

After she spoke to them, she died. She had reigned nine years and died at age 73. Her sex was never to her disadvantage. She had ruled in a way which was strong and determined. But in not having the support of great men, she did great damage to her own family. On the other hand, there was peace in the land during her time of rule.

Book XIV

From the Death of Queen Alexandra to the Death of Antigonus

i

WE have told the story of Queen Alexandra's life and death. My aim is to write all the facts using the best words to describe everything. I hope that those who read my account in the future will be satisfied and find it a pleasure to read. The first aim of authors should be to speak accurately and truthfully.

Hyrcanus was high priest when Quintus Hortensius and Quintus Metellus ("Metellus of Crete") were consuls in Rome. Aristobulus began to make war against Hyrcanus in Jericho, and many of his soldiers left him and went to his brother's side. Hyrcanus ran to the fort inside Jerusalem where Aristobulus's wife and children were imprisoned by Alexandra, and he attacked and won against the enemies who were hiding in the temple. He offered a peace deal: Aristobulus would be king and he (Hyrcanus) would stay out of public affairs. They made the agreement in public, shook hands and hugged one another. Aristobulus went to the palace and Hyrcanus went to Aristobulus's former house as a private person.

But Antipater, a rich man and a friend of Hyrcanus, tried to make trouble with Hyrcanus against Aristobulus. This Antipater was Idumean. Nicolas of Damascus said that he came from leading Jews who had returned from Babylon to Judea, but he said this only to please Antipater's son Herod.

King Alexander had made the father of Antipater the general of all Idumea, and he made friends with the Arabians, Gazites and Ascalonites by giving them costly presents. Now this Antipater was suspicious of the power of Aristobulus, and he told everyone that Aristobulus had become king in the wrong way; the older brother Hyrcanus should have been king. He told Hyrcanus that his own life would be in danger. Hyranus did not take this talk seriously, since it was not his nature to speak against others. Hyrcanus appeared to others as weak. Aristobulus was the opposite, a more active person.

When Antipater saw that Hyrcanus did not take him seriously, he tried even harder to accuse Aristobulus of crimes. He convinced Hyrcanus to go to Aretas, the king of Arabia, promising that he would go together with him. Hyrcanus also felt he should go to Aretas. Arabia borders Judea. Hyrcanus sent Antipater to Aretas first, in order to know that he would be safe. Antipater returned to Hyrcanus in Jerusalem. Then he took Hyrcanus and left Jerusalem in secret. They arrived in Petra where Aretas's palace was. He persuaded Hyrcanus to return to Judea, promising presents. Hyrcanus promised Aretas that when he became king, he would give back the twelve cities which his father Alexander had taken from the Arabians.

ii

AFTER making these promises to Aretas, Hyrcanus went to war against Aristobulus with an army of 50,000 horsemen and soldiers, and he won. Many went over to Hyrcanus's side, leaving Aristobulus alone who ran to the temple in Jerusalem. The king of Arabia took all of his army and attacked the temple. Aristobulus was caught inside with only the priests on his side. Aretas, together with Jewish and Arabian forces pressed on against the Jews in the temple. This happened during the Passover celebration. The leading Jews ran to Egypt.

A righteous man named Onias, who had once prayed to God to end a drought and had his prayers answered, hid himself while the war was going on. The soldiers found him and ordered him to pray against Aristobulus. He refused to speak, but he was forced in the end to say something to the people. He prayed, "God, the King of the whole world, you see that those who are your priests under attack and those who are attacking them are all your people. I pray that you will not hear the prayers of either side." The wicked Jews standing around him stoned him to death.

But God punished them for this sin. During Passover, many sacrifices to God are to be offered, and the priests and Aristobulus did not have enough sacrifices. They asked the Jews outside the city to bring animals for the sacrifices, and they would pay whatever price was asked for them. They had to pay 1,000 drachmae* for each head of cattle. The money was let down over the walls. But when it was received, the sellers kept the money and did not bring the animals. When the priests found out that they had been cheated, they prayed to God to punish them. He sent a strong windstorm so that all of the crops in the country were destroyed. A modius* of wheat afterwards cost 11 drachmae*.

In the meantime Pompey sent Scaurus into Syria while he was in Armenia, making war against Tigranes. When Scaurus came to Damascus and saw that Lollius and Metellus had just taken the city, he came instead to Judea. Messengers came to him both from Aristobulus and Hyrcanus asking for his help. Aristobulus promised 400 talents* and so did Hyrcanus. Scaurus decided to help Aristobulus. He stopped the siege and ordered Aretas to leave or become an enemy of the Romans. Scaurus returned to Damascus and Aristobulus warred against Aretas and Hyrcanus at Papyron and beat them in battle. He killed about 6,000 of them, including Phalion, the brother of Antipater.

iii

POMPEY then came to Damascus and marched across Coelesyria. Messengers came to him from all over Syria, Egypt and Judea. From Egypt there was the gift of a crown valued at 4,000 pieces of gold. Aristobulus sent him a present from Judea, a golden vine that was worth 500 talents*. The Romans called it either a vine or garden named "The Delight." I saw the gift in Rome in Jupiter's temple with the inscription: "The Gift of Alexander, the King of the Jews. It is worth 500 talents* and Aristobulus. the Jewish governor, sent it."

Messengers came to Pompey: Antipater from Hyrcanus and Nicodemus from Aristobulus. Bribes had been taken, which made new enemies for Aristobulus. Pompey had invited those with complaints against each other to come to him during the spring He gathered his army and marched into Damascus and destroyed the fort at Apamea which Antiochus Cyzicenus had built. This was the country of Ptolemy Menneus, who was as wicked as his relative, Dionysius of Tripoli, who had been beheaded. But Menneus paid a bribe to escape punishment, and Pompey paid his soldiers with this money.

Pompey heard about the problems between Hyrcanus and Aristobulus. The people hated both of them and wanted the form of government of their forefathers, which was ruled by the priests. Hyrcanus complained that although he was the elder brother, he ruled over only a small part of the country, and Aristobulus had taken the rest by force. He also accused Aristobulus of piracy at sea and of stirring up trouble among the people because he was a violent man. There were 1,000 Jews who agreed with this, as well as Antipater.

Aristobulus answered that Hyrcanus was not able to rule, since he was not strong. Aristobulus had brought some supporters who were young and bold. They wore purple and jewels, had beautiful hair and were showing off. This was not right for appearing in the court of justice.

Pompey heard both sides and condemned Aristobulus for his violent ways. He told them that when he would visit their country he would settle the matter after he took care of the Nabateans. He told them to be quiet and treated Aristobulus with respect, in order to avoid a revolt which would make problems for his return. Aristobulus did make trouble and marched into Judea.

Pompey was angry. He took his army and went against Aristobulus. He came to Coreae, the first entrance into Judea after passing the midland countries. He came to a beautiful fort, built on the top of a mountain called Alexandrium, where Aristobulus was hiding. Pompey sent for him, and Aristobulus came when he was sure that he was not in danger. He still argued with his brother about who had the right to rule. Two or three times he met Pompey and was hoping that Pompey would support him as king. He pretended to obey Pompey, but he was afraid that Hyrcanus would get his support. Aristobulus was allowed to stay in the fort, and he had soldiers with him. Pompey told Aristobulus to give up the forts he held, and he obeyed. Then Aristobulus went to Jerusalem, planning to go to war. Some people told Pompey as he was on his way against Aristobulus that Mithridates was dead, killed by his son Pharmaces.

iv

POMPEY set up his soldiers in Jericho. In Jericho there are palm trees, and also balsam, which is gotten by cutting the wood with a sharp stone, after which it comes out like juice. In the morning he marched to Jerusalem. Aristobulus came to Pompey and promised to give him money if he would stop the attack. Aristobulus received Pompey in Jerusalem, and Pompey forgave him. He sent Gabinius and soldiers to receive the money and the city, but they were not given to him. Pompey became very angry and put Aristobulus in prison and came to the city. Jerusalem had strong walls except on the north side since there was a large, deep ditch, and a stone wall around the temple on that side.

There was a big argument in the city about whether or not to give up to Pompey. Aristobulus's supporters wanted the gates to stay closed. Some soldiers ran into the temple and cut off the bridge that went across the valley from the temple to the city. Others let Pompey come in through the city gate and gave up the city to him.

Pompey sent his lieutenant Piso with an army and put his soldiers in the city and in the palace. They also fortified the houses next to the temple. Pompey set his soldiers inside the city on the north side of the temple, and they built a bridge of earth across the ditch to the temple. They used whatever they could find to slowly make the bank of dirt higher. He brought his war engines from Tyre for this and battered the temple with big stones. The Jews rested on the Sabbath day, and although they were allowed to defend themselves from attack, they were not allowed to stop the enemy from doing other things on the Sabbath. The Romans used this against the Jews. They did not throw any stones or attack the Jews on the Sabbaths, but instead they worked on their earth bridge and their war machines. In spite of the battle, the priests kept offering the sacrifices in the temple twice a day. The time came, however, when the enemy got into the temple and attacked the priests and cut their throats. Even while others were being killed, the priests did not run away but continued with their godly duties.

The battering ram toppled the largest tower and broke the wall, which let the enemy into the temple. Many soldiers entered and people were killed in every direction. Some Jews were killed by Romans and some by one another. Some threw themselves down off the walls or burned their own houses. Around 12,000 Jews died, but very few Romans did. Absalom, who was both uncle and father-in-law to Aristobulus, was taken captive. Pompey entered into the temple and saw things which no one had seen before, as it wasn't lawful for anyone but the high priests. There was the golden table, the holy candlestick, the pouring vessels and many spices. There were 2,000 talents* of holy money, but Pompey did not touch any of these things. The next day he ordered those in charge of the temple to clean it and to offer the sacrifices according to God's law. He gave the high priesthood back to Hyrcanus because he had stopped the Jews from supporting Aristobulus against him. He had also rewarded Faustus and other soldiers who had climbed over the wall. Pompey made Jerusalem a city that served the Romans. Many cities around the country which the Jews had ruined were rebuilt and given back to their owners, including seaports. (Herod later rebuilt Strato's Tower in a grand way, and its name was changed to Cesarea.) Pompey made all those cities free and part of the province of Syria.

In this way the Romans took over Jerusalem, because Hyrcanus and Aristobulus had fought between themselves. They had to give back to the Syrians everything they had won in the wars. The Romans took from the Jews more than 10,000 talents,* and the right of the high priests to rule was given to private families. Pompey put Scaurus in charge of Coelesyria as far as the river Euphrates and Egypt, together with two Roman legions. Then he went to Cilicia and later to Rome. He took Aristobulus captive, together with his two daughters and a younger son, Antigonius. The older son ran away.

V

SCAURUS came against Petrea in Arabia. Since it was difficult to get to it, he burned all the places around it. His army was out of food, and Antipater gave them corn from Judea and all that they needed at Hyrcanus's command. Aretas was persuaded to give Scaurus money in order to prevent the burning of his country. So 300 talents* were given, ending the war.

Some time later when Alexander, the son of Aristobulus, came into Judea, Gabinius from Rome came against him because Hyrcanus could not fight him. Hyrcanus was trying to rebuild the wall of Jerusalem which Pompey had ruined, but the Romans who were there stopped him. Alexander gathered an army of 10,000 foot soldiers and 1500 horsemen and fortified Alexandrium, a fortress near Coreae, and Macherus near the mountains of Arabia. Gabinius and Marcus Antonius came together with the Jews who supported them, and they met Alexander. Alexander went to Jerusalem and afterwards the Romans came and killed about 3,000 of their enemies. They also took 3,000 captives.

Gabinius came to Alexandrium and asked the people to give up, promising that they would be forgiven. Many of their enemies were camping around the fort, and the Romans attacked them. Marcus Antonius fought bravely and killed many people. Gabinius left part of his army there to capture the place and went into other parts of Judea, giving orders to rebuild all of the ruined cities. They were rebuilt and filled with people after having been empty for a long time.

Gabinius then returned to Alexandrium to capture it. Alexander sent messengers to him asking his forgiveness; he gave up Alexandrium, which Gabinius destroyed, and some other forts. Alexander's mother, who was on the side of the Romans since her husband and other children were there, came to him and Gabinius gave her what she asked. He brought Hyrcanus to Jerusalem and gave control of the temple to him. Then he formed five councils, dividing up the nation into five parts. They were Jerualem, Gadara, Amathus, Jericho and Sepphoris in Galilee. The Jews were no longer under a king, but were ruled by a group of lords.

ARISTOBULUS ran away from Rome to Judea and began rebuilding Alexandrium, which had just been destroyed. Gabinius sent soldiers against him to take him captive again, but many Jews joined Aristobulus. An army officer in Jerusalem wanted to join him with 1,000 men, but Aristobulus took only those who had weapons. Still, he took 8,000 who were armed. The Romans attacked them and beat them. About 5,000 were killed and the others ran. Aristobulus was left with 1,000 soldiers, and they ran to Macherus and fortified it. After two days of siege, Aristobulus was badly wounded and taken captive to Gabinius with his son Antigonius, who had also escaped with him from Rome. Aristobulus had been both king and high priest for three and one-half years, and he had a great soul. He was imprisoned in Rome. But his children were freed, since their mother had asked for this when she gave up the forts to the Romans. They went back to Jerusalem.

Gabinius crossed over the Euphrates, but he changed his mind and returned to Egypt in order to restore Ptolemy to his kingdom. Antipater supplied his army with corn, weapons and money. He also had friends among the Jews who guarded the passes that led into Egypt. But when he left Egypt, he saw that there was uproar in Syria. Alexander, the son of Aristobulus, tried to be king again, and many of the Jews were supporting him. Alexander took a large army and killed all the Romans he could find, up to Gerizzim where they had run to hide.

Gabinius sent Antipater to Syria in order to see if he could calm them down, and this worked. He could not stop Alexander, however, since his army had 30,000 Jews. Alexander met Gabinius in battle and was beaten, losing 10,000 of his men at Mount Tabor.

Gabinius fixed things in Jerusalem in ways that Antipater liked, and then he went against the Nabateans and won against them. Gabinius was a war hero. When he got back to Rome he turned the government over to Crassus. Nicolaus of Damascus and Strabo of Cappadocia write about Pompey and Gabinius making war against the Jews, but nothing new is mentioned by them.

vii

CRASSUS, while going against the Parthians, came into Judea and took 200 talents* from the temple which Pompey had left. There were 8,000 talents* altogether. He also took a beam made of solid gold on which the curtains hung. The priest Eleazar gave it to him, after Crassus promised that if he could have this, he would not take anything else from the temple. It was worth many 10,000s of talents* [shekels]. The gold beam was inside a hollow wooden beam, and only Eleazar knew this. But Crassus broke his promise and took all the gold that was in the temple.

This wealth in the temple was from all the Jews around the world, including Asia and Europe, who had been sending gifts to the temple for hundreds of years. Strabo of Cappadocia wrote that Mithridates had gone to Cos to take money which Queen Cleopatra had put there, plus 800 talents* that belonged to the Jews. The Jews in Asia feared Mithridates and sent their money to Cos. In Cyrene and also in the city of Alexandria there were many rich Jews. They had their own judges and laws. Cyrene was ruled like Egypt.

When Crassus settled things, he marched into Parthia where he and his army were killed. Casius took over Parthia and then took some places in Judea, carrying about 30,000 Jews captive. He killed Pitholaus, the rebel who took over after Aristobulus (urged to do it by Antipater). Antipater was popular among the Idumeans and he married Cypros, the daughter of one of their leaders. He was also friendly with the king of Arabia, who took care of Antipater's children while he fought against Aristobulus. Cassius moved his camp and marched to Euphrates to meet those who were coming to attack him, as we wrote earlier.

Caesar set Aristobulus free and gave him an army to take care of Syria. But Aristobulus was not happy, and in the end his enemies poisoned him. Antony sent his body to Judea to be buried. Scipio was sent by Pompey to kill Aristobulus's son Alexander; he found Alexander at Antioch and cut off his head.

But Ptolemy, the son of Menneus, sent his son Philippion to Askelon to Aristobulus's wife, and asked her to send her son Antigonus and her daughters. Philippion fell in love with one daughter, Alexandra, and married her. Later his father Ptolemy killed him, married the girl, and took care of her brothers.

viii

CAESAR came to power after Pompey was dead. Antipater, who was in charge of Jewish affairs, helped Caesar in a war against Egypt, with Hyrcanus's support. Antipater came with 3,000 armed Jews, some chief Arabians and all of the Syrians to join with Mithridates of Pergamus, who came with his army to help Caesar. Mithridates took over Pelusium when they would not let him in. Antipater helped him by taking down part of a wall, and his soldiers rushed in and took over. The Egyptian Jews who lived in a country called Onion would not let Antipater and Mithridates pass them to get to Caesar with their soldiers. Antipater showed them some letters which Hyrcanus the high priest had written and persuaded them to be friendly with Caesar. He urged them to give him money and supplies. The Jews of Memphis invited Mithriates to join them as well.

After Mithridates passed the Nile Delta he came to the Jewish Camp. He was on the right and Antipater was on the left. Mithridates lost in battle but Antipater's soldiers came along the shore to save him, making some strong Egyptians run. Antipater took their camp and chased them. Mithridates lost 800 men, but Antipater lost only fifty soldiers. Mithridates wrote to Caesar telling him about Antipater's great deeds, and from that time, Antipater was chosen to fight the hardest battles for Caesar. At one point he was wounded.

Caesar finished the war and sailed for Syria. He gave great honors to Antipater, making him a citzen of Rome and free from taxes everywhere. He confirmed Hyrcanus as the high priest. (Hyrcanus and Antipater had gone to Egypt together to fight Caesar's battles.)

Antigonus, the son of Aristobulus, came to Caesar and blamed Antipater for his father's death by poisoning. His brother had been beheaded by Scipio as well, and Antigonus was looking for a place for himself. He said that Hyrcanus and Antipater were violent leaders. Antipater was there and spoke up. He told them that Antigonus and his people were always wanting new things and were rebels. He reminded Caesar of how he risked his life in Caesar's wars. He said that Aristobulus had been rightly taken to Rome, since he was an enemy of Rome. The beheaded brother, he said, deserved it for being a robber.

After Antipater's speech Caesar appointed Hyrcanus to be the high priest and allowed Antipater to choose where he wanted to rule. He chose Judea. Caesar gave Hyrcanus permission to rebuild the city walls which Pompey had destroyed. He wrote to Rome so that the message would be kept. He first listed those people who were there. It was a renewal of friendship between the Jews and the Romans. A shield of gold valued at 5,000 pieces of gold was brought by the Jews, and in turn they asked for letters to the kings and the free cities, ordering them to let the Jews live in peace. This was written in the ninth year of Hyrcanus's rule as high priest.

Hyrcanus also received honors from the people of Athens for helping them many times. A letter was written how he had welcomed them and then helped them to return home safely. They gave him a crown of gold, the usual reward according to their law, and put a brass statue of him in the temple of Demus and of the Graces. The crown was to be announced in the public theatre when the new plays would be performed, as well as in three other public shows. Messengers were chosen out of all of the Athenians to bring this decree to Hyrcanus and ask him to accept these honors.

CAESAR settled affairs in Syria and sailed away. Antipater left Syria for Judea and repaired the wall which Pompey had destroyed. He urged the people to support Hyrcanus so that they would have peace. The people agreed to this, because they did not want to have a tyrant for a leader.

Hyrcanus was slow and lazy, however, so Antipater made his own oldest son, Phasaelus, the governor of Jerusalem and its surroundings. Antipater's second son, Herod, ruled in Galilee from age 15 [sic – his age was more likely 25]. He was very smart, and he came against a robber who operated in the Syrian ports and killed him and some of his group. The Syrians were grateful and sang songs in Herod's honor. He became known to Sextus Caesar, who was related to the great Caesar and ruled over Syria. Herod's brother, Phasaelus, was jealous and worked hard to get the same honor from his people in Jerualem. Because of this, Antipater received respect and riches, and he was honored like a king. But he kept his friendship with Hyrcanus.

Some leading Jews were upset about the power of Antipater and his sons among the Jews. Antipater was friendly with the Roman emperors. Antipater urged Hyrcanus to send a gift of money to the Roman emperors, and he brought it to Rome himself and pretended it was his own gift to them. This made the Jews very upset. They came to Hyrcanus, accusing Antipater of taking over the nation. They were hoping that Hyrcanus would see how he was in danger. They also were afraid that Herod was a violent man. They said: "Our laws say that no one should be killed unless they are sentenced to death by the Sanhedrim [sic, Sanhedrin], yet Antipater's son killed Hezekiah the robber and those with him."

Hyrcanus agreed with this. Mothers of those whom Herod had killed also came every day to the temple, asking for Herod to be put on trial before the Sanhedrim. Hyrcanus brought Herod to trial. His father told him to come with a body guard. After settling affairs in Galilee, Herod came to the trial. Sextus Caesar, president of Syria, wrote to Hyrcanus asking him to let Herod go free, and threatening him if he did not. Sextus Caesar said that he loved Herod like a son.

Herod stood at the trial boldly, surrounded by his soldiers, making everyone afraid to speak against him. Finally Sameas, a righteous man, said that this was wrong and he had never seen anything like it. He gave a prophecy to the judges and said, "God is great. If this man who is on trial for murder is set free for Hyrcanus's sake, he will one day punish you and your king." This prediction came true; after Herod was king he killed all the members of the Sanhedrim and Hyrcanus himself. Herod did not kill Sameas because he persuaded the people to allow Herod into the city. He said this was punishment for their sins.

Hyrcanus saw that the Sanhedrin was ready to pronounce the death sentence on Herod. He put off the trial to another day, and then he secretly told Herod to leave the city and escape. Herod returned to Damascus. He decided that if he were called to another trial he would simply not come. The Sanhedrin was very upset with Hyrcanus, saying that he was hurting himself. Hyrcanus knew they were right, but he was too weak to do anything else.

Sextus made Herod the general of his army in Celesyria because Herod paid for it. So Herod came with his army to fight Hyrcanus, because he was angry about being called to the trial. But he was stopped by his father Antipater and his brother Phasaelus, who knew about Herod's awful temper. They told him that he should be glad that his trial ended the way it did. They urged him to think about the good side and not just the bad. God controls the results of war, they said, and Herod should not fight someone who had helped him. He had gotten bad advice and should not listen to it. Herod was persuaded by these arguments and he decided it was enough just to look strong before the people.

X

CAESAR came to Rome and got ready to sail to Africa to fight against Scipio and Cato. Hyrcanus sent messengers to him to renew the friendship between the Jewish people and Rome. It is important to write about the honors that the Romans and their emperors paid to the Jewish people. One should not believe what the Persians and Macedonians have written about us Jews, since those writings are not kept in public places. But no one can argue with the Roman decrees, because they are kept in public places in the cities, in the capitol and engraven on a brass pillar in Greek and Latin. Julius Caesar even made a brass pillar for the Jews at Alexandria which said that they were citizens of Alexandria. The following are decrees by Julius Caesar and the Roman senate, made for Hyrcanus and the Jews. The first was to the people of Sidon. "Hyrcanus, the son of Alexander, the high priest and ruler of the Jews, is to be honored for his faithfulness in peace and in war. He helped the Romans in the Alexandrian war with 1500 soldiers. When he was sent to Mithridates he was a brave soldier. His family should be rulers of the Jews and priests forever, and they will always be our friends. If there is ever a doubt about Jewish customs, Hyrcanus is the one to decide."

Other decrees:

"From Caius Caesar: Hyrcanus and his children are the rulers of the Jews. Our friendship with Hyrcanus should be recorded on a table of brass in the capitol, and in Sidon, Tyre and Askelon in the temple, in Roman and Greek letters. The decree should be made known to all of the cities, and presents should be given to the messengers."

"From Casius Caesar: The Jews shall be owners of Jerusalem and may close it with walls. Hyrcanus shall take care of it, and the Jews do not need to pay full taxes on their farmland. The tax should not be changed from year to year."

"Caius Caesar. Except for Joppa, all of the Jews should pay a yearly tax for the city of Jerusalem, except for the Sabbatical Year [the seventh] in which they do not eat from the fruit trees, nor do they sow their land. They are to pay the same tithes to Hyrcanus and his sons which they paid to their forefathers [the priests]. No Roman soldiers are to take money from them during the winter or bother them in any other way. Joppa is theirs as it was in the past. Export to Sidon is to be 20,675 modii* yearly, except the seventh year. Lydda should have the same conditions. In fights between single gladiators and those with beasts, Hyrcanus, his sons and his messengers may sit among the senators. If they wish to talk to the senate, they may do so and they shall receive an answer within ten days."

Hyrcanus sent messengers to Dolabella, the governor of Asia, to ask that Jewish men not have to serve in his army. This ruler wrote: "Greetings from the Ephesians. Since Jewish men are not to carry weapons or travel on the Sabbath, and cannot find the food which they are used to eating from the time of their forefathers, they shall be excused from the army. They may gather for religious purposes as their law requires. They also are allowed to collect what is necessary for their sacrifices. Write this to the cities under your authority."

A letter from the son of Caius asked the leaders of Cos to allow the Jews to pass safely through their country.

The son of Marcus wrote to the Sardians that the Jews had asked to practice their own form of law and justice. He ordered them to let them continue with these customs.

In another decree, many names were listed, and then a request to allow the Jews to observe their holy customs in Ephesus.

The Laodiceans wrote to the son of Caius that the Jews were asking to be free to keep the Sabbath and other holy practices according to the laws of their forefathers. "You have decreed that this should be done, so we are following your orders. They are our friends. The Trallians did not agree with this decision, but we will make sure that your decree is obeyed."

Publius Servilius, ruler of the Galban tribe, to the Milesians: "I hear that you are forbidding the Jews from keeping the Sabbath and their holy practices. I order you to let them keep their holy days without bothering them. They are also to farm their land according to their ancient customs."

From Pergamus it was decreed: "The forts and land and whatever else had been taken from the Jews should be given back. They may freely export their goods from their country, and any king or people who want to do the same shall pay a tax, except Ptolemy since he is our friend. We also order that all of their messengers be given a safe journey home. We heard from Theodorus about all the good deeds of Hyrcanus and his reward from Rome; this is in our public records. So because we are friends of Rome, we have made a decree like theirs, to do everything we can to help the Jews. Hyrcanus received a copy of our decree. Our ancestors were also friendly to the Jews even in the days of Abraham, the father of all the Hebrews, and this history is found in our public records."

The Sardians wrote a decree stating that the Jews are their fellow-citzens who have done good to them. "The Jews shall be free to gather together. They shall act according to their own laws, have their own buildings, and we will make sure that the foods they can eat will be imported into the city."

There were other decrees which I did not include, since they were too many. But it is clear from these that we Jews had good relations with the Romans in many places in those days.

THERE was a lot of unrest in Syria. Cecilius Bassus, one of Pompey's supporters, killed Sextus Caesar. He took over his army and started a war over Apamia. Caesar's generals came against him with an army of horsemen and soldiers, helped by Antipater and his sons. It was a long war. Marcus came from Rome to take Sextus's place, but in Rome Caesar was killed by Cassius and Brutus in the senate house. He had been emperor for three and one-half years.

The leading men went here and there to gather armies. Cassius left Rome for Syria and convinced Bassus and Marcus to join him. He collected weapons and soldiers and heavily taxed the cities. He was very hard on Judea, gathering 700 talents* in taxes. Antipater divided up this amount, so that his sons collected part of it and Malichus collected another part. Herod was liked by Cassius since he did everything that was ordered. Herod wanted to gain the favor of Rome; he saw that they made other cities into slaves. Cassius was so angry at Malichus that he almost killed him, but Hyrcanus sent him 100 talents* of his own through Antipater, to calm him down.

After Cassius left Judea, Malichus planned to kill Antipater, thinking that it would be good for Hyrcanus. Antipater knew about it and ran across the Jordan, and gathered an army of Arabs with his own men. Malichus denied that he was thinking of such a thing, and Antipater forgave him. Cassius and Marcus trusted Herod, making him general of the army in Celesyria, which had a fleet of ships, horsemen and soldiers. They promised that after the war they would make him king of Judea (a war had started between Antony and the younger Caesar). Malichus was afraid of Antipater and offered money to the butler of Hyrcanus to kill him by poison at a feast. After Antipater's death, his sons Herod and Phasaelus knew about the plot, but Malichus said he had nothing to do with it. Antipater had been a just man who loved his country.

Herod wanted to punish Malichus for their father's death and came against him with an army. But Phasaelus thought it would be better to trap him in politics, so he pretended to believe Mal-chus. He set up a nice memorial for his father, Antipater. Herod went to Samaria and cheered them up and took care of some problems.

Herod later came to Jerusalem with his soldiers at the time of a festival. Malichus told Hyranus not to let them into the city. Hyrcanus went along with this, saying that while the people were purifying themselves it was not right for strangers to enter. Herod came into Jerusalem anyway, at night, and surprised Malichus. Again Malichus denied he had plotted the murder of Antipater, and he cried over the death of his "friend". Herod and his friends did not argue with him, in order to avoid suspicion.

But Herod sent word to Cassius about the murder of his father, and Cassius answered that Herod should punish Malichus. He told his army commanders at Tyre to help Herod. After Cassius took over Laodicea, all the Judeans went to him with garlands and money. Herod thought that Malichus might be punished while he was there, but Malichus planned to get away and do a great thing. Malichus's son was a hostage in Tyre, so he hoped to steal him away, and then come to Judea and start a rebellion while Cassius was making his war against Antony, and take over the government for himself. But God stopped him. Herod knew about his plan and sent a servant to the army commanders. He asked them to go against Malichus with their daggers, and Malichus was killed by the seashore. Hyrcanus was shocked speechless to see that, and he asked who could have done this. Herod said that Malichus had been killed by Cassius's order, and Hyrcanus then said it was a good thing, since Malichus was a wicked man who was hurting his own country. This was the punishment of Malichus for murdering Antipater.

When Cassius marched out of Syria, Judea had problems from Felix, who came with his army to Jerusalem and tried to kill Phasaelus. Herod went to Fabius, the ruler in Damascus, to ask if he could go and help his brother, but then he got sick and could not go. Phasaelus beat Felix without help; he shut Felix up in a tower and took away his job. Phasaelus complained that Hyrcanus, despite all of the good things he had gotten, supported their enemies. Malichus's brother had started a rebellion in many places, and he kept soldiers in them, especially Masada, the strongest fort of all. Herod at last got well and came to help Phasaelus. He took over all the places which Felix had taken, and he took away his power.

PTOLEMY brought Antigonus, the son of Aristobulus, back into Judea. Antigonus gathered an army and made friends with Fabius by paying him money – he was also a relative. Marion also helped Antigonus; Cassius set him over Syria and he was a tyrant. Marion marched into Galilee which was near Tyre, and he took over three forts. When Herod came to Galilee, he took them back. But Herod sent away the soldiers in Tyre in a nice way and even gave some of them presents. He then went to battle against Antigonus and beat him, chasing him out of Judea. When Herod came back to Jerusalem, Hyrcanus and the people put wreaths on his head. Herod was also related to him; he was married to the granddaughter of Hyrcanus, who gave him three boys and two girls. (This was Herod's second wife; his first wife was Doris, from a low family of his own nation and from her his oldest son, Antipater, was born.)

Antonius and Caesar beat Cassius near Philippi. After that Caesar went into Gaul (Italy), and Antony marched into Asia. Messengers met him and accused Phasaelus and Herod of not letting Hyrcanus rule his people. But Antony respected Herod and wouldn't listen to them (because Herod paid him money). Antony came to Ephesus and Hyrcanus came with messengers, carrying a crown of gold as a gift. They asked him to free the Jews whom Cassius had made slaves even though they had not fought against him. Antony wrote a letter saying that he would help the Jews:

"I consider the Jews as our own people. We have punished those who did wrong to all of us. We beat Brutus and Cassius when they ran to Philippi in Macedonia, a city that welcomed them. Now I am ordering that all slaves taken by Caius Cassius or his officers are to be freed, and that the Jews' lands and cities be given back to them. I forbid the Tyrians to bother you. I have accepted the crown which you sent me."

Another letter was to Tyre. "The messengers of Hyrcanus met us at Ephesus and said that you have taken land from them. That land was taken from them by our enemies, so it is not considered yours – it was taken by force from the Jews, who are our friends. Those enemies have been punished. The places which belong to Hyrcanus must be returned, and you must live in peace with them. If there is any problem or lawful argument, this can be settled when we come. This decree is to be engraved on stones in the public placed in Roman and Greek letters: 'We have ended the madness of Cassius and we want to set things right again. So we give the order to restore what belongs to the Jews, either people or possessions. Those who do not obey will be punished.'"

Antony also wrote to the Sidonians, Antiochians and the Arabians. This shows how the Romans took care of the rights of the Jews.

xiii

ANTONY came into Syria and met Cleopatra in Cilicia and they fell in love. Then 100 important Jews came to accuse Herod and others before Antony. Messala contradicted them in the presence of Hyrcanus, Herod's father-in-law. Antony heard both sides and asked Hyrcanus who could govern the nation best. Hycanus said, "Herod and his friends." Due to his friendship with Herod's father, Antipater, Antony made Herod and Phasaelus rulers and said that they would take care of the Jewish nation. He put fifteen of their accusers in chains and would have killed them, but Herod forgave them.

Later 1,000 Jews came to Tyre to meet Antony, but he was not a fair judge because of the money which Herod and his brother had given him; Antony made trouble for the Jews. Herod and Hyrcanus met the Jews on the shore and told them to go home or they would get hurt. But they went on anyway, and the Romans killed many Jews with daggers. Some people afterwards complained loudly against Herod, and Antony was so upset that he killed the prisoners.

The Parthians took over Syria. Ptolemy was dead and his son Lysanias took over. The Parthian commander Pacorus made friends with Antigonus, who decided to use that. Antigonus promised to the Parthians 1000 talents* and 500 women if they would take the government away from Hyrcanus, give it to him, and kill Herod. The Parthians and their horsemen went into Judea with Antigonus. Jews in the Mount Carmel area also came to Antigonus and said they would help him take over Judea. At Drymi others met them and some men invaded Jerusalem quietly. Many others joined them and they came against the king's palace. There was a battle in the market place, and the young men beat their enemies, running after them into the temple. Armed men came to the nearby houses to keep those men trapped in the temple, but others came against them and burned them in the houses. Herod got even later by fighting and killing many of them.

There were small fights every day, and the enemy waited for many people to come for the Pentecost holiday. Lots of people came from the country to Jerusalem, and some guarded the temple. The king's palace was guarded by some of Herod's soldiers, and Phasaelus guarded the wall. Herod and his men went against many outside the city, chasing tens of thousands away into the city, the temple or forts nearby. Phasaelus helped Herod. The general of the Parthians was let into the city with some horsemen, pretending that he would help calm things down, but he really meant to help Antigonus take over. Phasaelus met him kindly, and the Parthians persuaded him to go as a messenger their general Barzapharnes. Phasaelus did not think anything was wrong, but Herod did not want him to go.

So Hyrcanus and Phasaelus left. Pacorus left 200 horsemen and ten men called freemen with Herod, and he went to Galilee. The governors met them. They came to Barzapharnes, who gave them presents at first, but later he planned to trick them. Then they heard that Antigonus had promised to give the Parthians 1000 talents* and 500 women to help him against them. Someone let them know that there was a trap set for them. He warned Phasaelus to escape and a rich Syrian offered to give them ships to get away. But Phasaelus did not want to leave Hyrcanus. He went to see Barzapharnes, saying that he could give him more money than Antigonus had given. He also said would be wicked to kill those who had given him their promises and had not made trouble. Barzapharnes said that there was no plot, and that they had heard lies.

But as soon as he left, some men came and caught Hyrcanus and Phasaelus. The servant who was sent to trap Herod had an order to take Herod outside the city walls and capture him, but Phasaelus sent messengers who warned him in time. Herod went to Pacorus, the leader of the Parthians, who said that Herod should go with them outside the walls and meet people who were bringing him letters which told about Phasaelus's success. Herod did not believe them, and the daughter of Hyrcanus also warned him. He considered her to be a wise woman.

The Parthians were waiting for a good time to catch Herod. So he decided to leave that night since it was clear he was in danger. He took his armed men, put his wives on horses, along with his mother and sister and Mariamne, the daughter of Alexander who was soon to marry him, and some other family members. He went to Idumea, and people felt sorry for them when they saw the women coming along with the babies, leaving their own land and their friends in prison, crying on the way.

Herod was brave in spite of everything and encouraged the others. But he almost killed himself when a wagon turned over and his mother was almost killed. As he drew his sword, others stopped him and begged him not to leave them alone. He was ashamed at what they said. They got safely to the fort of Masada. Herod was attacked on the way by the Parthains, but he beat them every time.

He was also attacked by Jews along the way. It was hand-to-hand fighting, but he beat them. Later he built a great palace at that place surrounded by a city, and called it Herodium. When he arrived in Idumea, his brother Joseph met him.

Herod met with friends to decide what to do. He had too many people with him to fit in the fort of Masada. He sent more than 9,000 away to find a place in Idumea to live, and gave them money to buy supplies. He took his closest friends with him to Masada, including his family, a total of 800 people. There was enough corn and water and other supplies for their needs. He then went to Petra in Arabia. The next day, the Parthians ruined all of Jerusalem and the palace, and left only 300 talents* that belonged to Hyrcanus. Much of Herod's money had already been sent to Idumea by then. The Parthians also took spoil from the surrounding country and ruined the city of Marissa.

The king of the Parthians brought Antigonus back into Judea, and gave him Hyrcanus and Phasaelus as prisoners. Antigonus was upset because the women escaped whom he had planned to give to the enemy for payment, together with the money. He was afraid that the Parthians might make Hyrcanus king again, so he cut off his ears to make sure that he could no longer be a priest (only those with all their body parts were allowed to be priests).

Phasaelus guessed that he would be killed. He wasn't afraid to die but he didn't want to be killed as a prisoner. He would rather kill himself. But he was tied up, so he crashed his head against a big stone to kill himself. Antigonus sent doctors to bandage his head, and he ordered them to put poison into the wound; in this way he died. But Phasaelus heard before he died that his brother Herod had escaped, so he was happy to think that Herod would punish them for his death.

xiv

HEROD went to Malchus, king of Arabia, to see if he could get a loan or a gift, since he had done good things for Malchus in the past. Herod, not knowing that his brother was dead, wanted to save him by paying his enemies 300 talents* for a ransom. He took the son of Phasaelus, a child of seven, with him to be a hostage until he repaid the money. But messengers from Malchus came to him and said that the Parthians had ordered him not to see Herod. This was an excuse; Malchus did not want to give him the money, which he really owed Herod. The leading Arabians also urged Malchus to cheat Herod of money which they had received from his father Antipater. Herod said he was only coming to speak with them.

Herod left for Egypt and stayed in a certain temple. The next day he heard that his brother had died. Meanwhile, Malchus changed his mind and ran after Herod, but he did not find him.

Herod ran into problems trying to sail to Alexandria, but finally he arrived and was given a place by Cleopatra. He did not stay long because he needed to get to Rome as soon as possible, even though it was stormy weather and Rome was in an uproar. He sailed to Pamphylia, and in a bad storm his ship almost sank, and lost all of its cargo. He managed to get to Rhodes with two of his friends. They saw how the city had been damaged by Cassius, so Herod helped them to rebuild. He built a three-decked ship there, and sailed with his friends to Italy.

In Rome he told Antony how his brother Phasaelus had been killed by the Parthians, and how Hyrcanus was a prisoner. They had made Antigonus king because he promised them 1000 talents* and 500 women. He (Herod) had rescued the women by escaping with them at night. He told Antony how he escaped from his enemies and survived the storm, in order to come to him, because Antony was now his only hope.

Antony was ready to help Herod because of his friendship with Antipater, and because Herod also offered money to make him king. He had also hated Antigonus since he viewed him as an enemy of Rome. Caesar also backed Herod, since he and Antipater got along well when they were at war in Egypt. The senate was formed, and Messala and Atratinus brought Herod in and said good things about him. They said that Antigonus was an enemy because he ignored the Romans and was helped in taking over the government by the Parthians. Antony said that if Herod were king in Judea, it would help Rome in their war against the Parthians. The senate agreed.

Antony thus showed his support for Herod by giving him a kingdom unexpectedly. Herod was not thinking to ask for the kingdom, since he was not of the royal family; he was going to ask it for his brother's son, the grandson of Aristobulus and Hyrcanus. So Herod left Italy as a king after being there only seven days. Herod later killed the grandson. Herod, Antony and Caeser went together to offer sacrifices after the senate meeting, and to set the new decrees in the capitol. Antony invited Herod to a feast in honor of the first day of his rule as king.

Antigonus besieged the Jews in Masada who lacked nothing but water. Herod's brother Joseph was thinking to leave Masada with 200 of his family to Arabia, since Malchus was again a friend of Herod. But God sent rain that night, filing their water tanks. Herod's friends were very encouraged that God was on their side. They came out of the fort and fought hand-to-hand with Antigonus's soldiers and killed many of them. The general of the Romans drove the Parthains out of Syria and came to Judea. He came there pretending to help Joseph, but he really wanted to get Antigonus to give him money. He did get a lot of money from Antigonus, and he left his commander Silo with his soldiers there. Antigonus still hoped that the Parthians would come to help him.

XV

HEROD sailed out of Italy to Ptolemais and gathered soldiers from his country, as well as strangers. He marched through Galilee against Antigonus. He was helped by Silo and Ventidius, who were sent by Antony to bring Herod back. Herod had a large army, and they were heading to Masada to free those relatives of his who were there. He had enemies in Joppa, so he took that city first. After winning a battle against some Jews who were attacking Silo, Herod continued on to Masada, gathering soldiers on his way. Some joined because they remembered that his father had been good to them; others because they felt that if he were ruling they would benefit later.

Antigonus tried to trap Herod's army but was he was not able. Herod took his family out of Masada and the fortress Ressa and went on to Jerusalem. Silo's soldiers were with him, as well as many people who feared him. They set up camp on the west side of Jerusalem. They were attacked from the wall by arrows and darts, and some came out of the city to fight hand to hand with Herod's best soldiers. Herod called out at the wall that he had come for the good of the people. He wanted to forgive all those who hated him in the past. Antigonus said that they should not let Herod be king since he was a common person, half Idumean and half Jew [not a proven fact]. The Jewish law stated that the king should be from the priestly family. Even if the people didn't want Antigonus, because Rome hated him, there were other men to choose from in his family. Antigonus then told his men to defend themselves, and Herod's soldiers were easily driven away from the towers.

Silo showed that he had taken bribes from Antigonus. He sent soldiers to complain that they needed leave to find food and somewhere to stay for the winter, since they were in a desert and Antigonus's soldiers had taken everything away. Herod told Silo not to leave, and he brought them all that they needed in supplies. He asked his friends in Samaria to send corn, wine, oil and cattle for those in Jericho. Antigonus heard of it and sent armed men around Jericho in order to take the supplies before they would arrive. Herod came to Jericho with a small group of soldiers and found it empty, except for 500 people living in the mountains with their families. The soldiers took everything that had been left in the city. The king left soldiers in Jericho, and sent the Roman soldiers to Judea, Galilee and Samaria for the winter. Antigonus gained a lot from the bribes he gave to Silo, so that part of the army could stay in Lydda in order to please Antony. So the Romans had a time of peace and plenty.

Roman soldiers using long hooks to reach inside the caves where the Jews were hiding, and kill them.

Herod became restless and sent his brother Joseph with 2000 armed soldiers and 400 horsemen to Idumea. He went to Samaria and left his mother and family there, and then to Galilee where he took some forts which Antigonus held. He went to Sepphoris and there was snow. Antigonus pulled his soldiers back. Herod killed all the robbers who lived in caves. Near Arbela he came out with his whole army and ran after the enemy as far as the river Jordan. He had many soldiers from Galilee, and he gave each one 150 drachmae* and more to the captains. He sent them away for the winter. Silo came to him because his men were no longer getting supplies from Antigonus. Herod gave this job to his youngest brother, Pheroras. After he made sure all the soldiers were supplied, they rebuilt Alexandium.

Antony was in Athens and Ventidius in Syria. They ordered Silo to help Herod in finishing the war. Herod continued against the robbers in caves and sent Silo to Ventidius. The families of the robbers lived with them in the caves, high in the mountains. Herod had special chambers hanging from chain pulleys which would be let down from the top of the mountains. Armed men with long hooks in their hands were trying to reach out and take the people from the caves and throw them down over the cliffs. They shot darts at the people, but some soldiers went into the caves as well and killed people inside. Some of the cave dwellers gave up and some didn't. The soldiers then set fire to some of the caves and the things inside burned easily. One old man with seven children and a wife would not give up, even when they begged him. Instead he killed each child one by one and his wife, throwing them down the cliff. Later he threw himself down rather than become a slave to the Romans.

Herod put Ptolemy in charge of these parts of the country, and he went to Samaria with 600 horsemen and 3000 foot soldiers to fight Antigonus. Ptolemy was attacked and killed, and his enemies ran to the lakes and hard to reach places, ruining the villages along the way. Herod returned and punished them, killing some of them and destroying their strongholds. All of the rebel cities were fined 100 talents*.

The Parthians were defeated. Ventidius sent Macheras to help Herod. Antigonus did not let Macheras into the city because he knew why he came; he threw stones at Macheras, so he left for Emmaus. He killed all Jews he met there, whether enemies or friends, because he was upset at what he had suffered. Herod was angry and went to Samaria. He decided he should speak to Antony and to tell him that he didn't need this kind of "help"; he could beat Antigonus on his own. Macherus begged Herod not to speak to Antony, so they made peace with each other.

King Herod went to Antioch on his way to help Antony. Others wanted to join Antony also, but it was dangerous along the roads. In a narrow pass there were barbarians waiting to attack them. The first part passed through, and then the barbarians attacked, chasing them. When Herod came from behind them with great strength, all of the enemies ran and his men who were running came back to fight. Barbarians were killed in all directions. Spoil and captives were taken, including many animals to carry things. Herod made the road safe for those who came after him, and they called him a saviour and protector.

Antony sent out his army to meet Herod because he heard of his victory. He hugged Herod and gave him honor. In a short time Antiochus gave up the fortress to Antony, ending the war. Antony ordered Sossius to go help Herod, and then he left for Egypt.

Joseph, Herod's brother, was killed in Judea. Macheras had given him five regiments, and he went to reap corn in Jericho. The Roman soldiers were from Syria and were new soldiers. They were attacked and many people were killed. Antigonus took Joseph's body and cut off his head, although Pheroras his brother would have given 50 talents* for it. After this defeat, the Galileans left their commanders and took Herod's people and drowned them in the lake. Macheras fortified Gitta in Samaria.

Messengers told Herod that his brother was killed but he had already dreamed about it. He raised an army of 800 men, having one Roman legion already with him, and he came to Ptolemais. He marched at night through Galilee. Enemies came against him but were beaten. Herod trapped them in their fort but he couldn't do more than that because of a big storm. The soldiers had to find shelter in surrounding villages. When Antony sent more soldiers to help Herod, the men in the fort ran away at night. So Herod marched to Jericho to punish those who killed his brother. He gave a feast for the main officers, and later he sent his guests away and went to bed. The upper part of the house fell in when no one was in it, so the people believed that Herod was loved by God since his life had been spared.

The following day 6,000 of the enemy came to fight the Romans. The king's guards were attacked with darts and stones and one dart hit Herod on the side. Antigonus sent Pappus his commander against Samaria to show the enemy their strength. But Herod took five cities, killing 2,000 who were in them and burning the cities. He then returned to fight Pappus. Many people ran to him and his soldiers. After a hard battle Herod's soldiers won, killing the enemies as they ran. Some ran to the tops of their houses, but his soldiers pulled down the roofs and soldiers were piled up inside. They threw stones on them and killed them. It was a terrible sight to see, with so many piles of dead men. Many people who came near left quickly after seeing this. The hard winter also put a stop to the war. Otherwise the king's army would have gone to Jerusalem, because Antigonus was ready to run away.

Herod ordered his men to have a late supper. He went to take a bath and was very tired. He had only one servant with him. Three men of the enemy happened to be hiding in that house, and they came through the door with their swords out. But they were so surprised to find the king taking a bath that they didn't try to kill him; they felt lucky just to get out of the house alive. The next day Herod cut off Pappus's head since he had already been killed. He sent it to Pheroras to punish him, because he was the one who had killed his brother.

Herod moved his army after the winter to Jerusalem. This was the third year since he had been made king in Rome. He found the weakest part of the wall, which was near the temple, intending to attack the city as Pompey had done. He built three ramps and towers. He cut down trees which were around the city. The army stayed there while he went to Samaria to marry the daughter of Alexander, the son of Aristobulus.

xvi

AFTER the wedding of Herod, Sosius came through Phoenicia. He had a large army, and Herod also came from Samaria with a large army of 30,000 They all camped north of Jerusalem. Sosius was sent by Antony to help Herod to take the government from Antigonus, who was an enemy of Rome.

The Jews inside the city fought hard against Herod. They stole supplies from the armies so that Herod had to bring more supplies from far away. Herod built three ramps; the work went fast because he had many workers and it was summer. The city walls were shaken from the war machines, but the Jews fought back. They came out of the city and burned some of the war machines. The Jews had less skill but they fought as bravely as the Romans. The two sides also fought in underground tunnels which they were digging. The Jews fought without enough food, because it was a Sabbatical year (when no crops were grown).

Twenty of the best men scaled the walls, followed by Sosius's officers. The first wall was taken in 40 days, the second in 15 more. Some of the rooms around the temple were burned. When the outer court of the temple and the lower city were taken, the Jews ran into the inner court of the temple and into the upper city. They asked to continue to offer sacrifices. Herod let them to do so because he thought they were ready to give up. But they opposed him in order to keep the kingdom for Antigonus. So Herod came with many Jews on his side, attacked the city, and it became full of dead bodies. The Jews and Romans alike fought like crazy men and killed everyone. The king tried to make them stop, but they kept killing babies, women and old people without mercy. Anti-gonus came down from the fort and fell down at the feet of Sosius who insulted him, calling him Antigone (the female form of the name). He was taken captive.

After Herod won over his enemies, he had to care for the for-eigners who had helped him. Many strangers rushed in to see all of the holy things in the temple. He tried to keep them out by force since it was against Jewish law. When the soldiers started ruining the city, he asked Sosius if the Romans meant to empty the city of money and men and leave him to be king of a desert. He said it wouldn't be worth it to rule the entire world knowing how many of his people had been murdered. Sosius replied that those soldiers who had helped him deserved a reward. So Herod gave them rewards from his own money. In this way part of the city was spared from being destroyed. Herod gave a rich present to Sosius, and he and his soldiers went away rich.

This destruction of Jerusalem happened when Marcus Agrippa and Caninius Gallus were rulers in Rome. The city had been taken on the same day twenty-seven years earlier under Pompey. Sosius dedicated a crown to God and then marched away from Jerusalem. He took Antigonus in chains to Antony. Herod was afraid that Antigonus would only be kept in prison by Antony and would someday prove to the Romans that he was of royal blood and that Herod was not worthy to be king. Therefore Herod gave Antony a lot of money to have Antigonus killed. With this, the rule of the Asamoneans finished 126 years after it had begun. They had been a noble family of priests who did much for the Jewish people. But because of their fights with each other, the kingdom had fallen to Herod, the son of Antipater who was of the common people.

BOOK XV

FROM THE DEATH OF ANTIGONUS TO THE FINISHING OF THE TEMPLE BY HEROD

AS I wrote in the last book, Sosius and Herod took Jerusalem by force and took Antigonus captive. Herod rewarded those on his side in Judea and daily punished those who had sided with his enemies. Pollio the Pharisee, and his disciple Sameas, received the greatest honor since they had told the people to receive Herod. Pollio was the one who had foretold to Hyrcanus and the other judges how this Herod, if allowed to escape, would later punish them all. These words were later fulfilled.

Herod took all of the royal jewels and took things from the rich men. He gave all of the silver and gold to Antony and his friends. He killed 45 leaders of Antigonus's supporters and put guards at the gates of the city, so that nothing valuable could be carried out with the dead bodies. Any silver, gold or other riches found on the bodies were given to the king. His greed made the people miserable, and it was also the Sabbatical year when there were no crops planted.

Antony wanted to keep Antigonus as his captive to show off his victory. But the Jews were rebelling – they hated Herod and still loved Antigonus. So Antony decided to behead Antigonus at Antioch in order to quiet the Jews. Antony may have been the first man who beheaded a king. This was in order to force the Jews to forget Antigonus, and to bend their minds to hate Herod less.

HYRCANUS, the high priest who had been taken captive by the Parthians, came back to Jerusalem when Herod was king. The Parthians had treated him well. There were many Jews in Babylon and Hyrcanus was given a home there. But Hyrcanus wanted to go back to Herod, thinking he would reward him, since Hyrcanus had saved his life in the past. The Jews in Babylon wanted him to stay with them. They reminded him that Antigonus had maimed him and so he could no longer be a high priest in Jerusalem. Apart from this, Herod might not remember a favor he had received when he was a common person; he was probably changed now that he was an important man.

But Herod wrote to the Parthian king to not keep Hyrcanus from coming to him. He wanted Hyrcanus to rule with him, since Herod had been brought up by Hyrcanus and later had been saved by him. Herod also sent him many gifts. Herod's motives were out of fear, however. Since he himself did not have a clear right to be king, he wanted Hyrcanus in his power.

So Hyrcanus came to Jerusalem, with his trip paid for by the Jews of Babylon, and was received well by Herod. Hyrcanus received the seat of honor at public meetings and feasts. Herod was trying to cover up his plans to get rid of him. He brought an unknown priest out of Babylon, Ananelus, and he became the high priest.

Alexandra, the daughter of Hyrcanus and wife of Alexander (the son of Aristobulus the king), could not accept that this unknown man should be high priest. Her son Aristobulus was handsome. Her daughter Mariamne, already married to Herod, was known for her beauty. She felt that only Aristobulus should be the high priest. She wrote to Cleopatra so that Antony would help her gain her request.

Antony did not answer. Antony's friend Delliu came to Judea, and he admired the young Aristobulus, who was very tall and handsome, and Mariamne, who was beautiful. He convinced their mother to have pictures drawn of the children to send to Antony. Dellius said that the children must not have been born of human seed but from some god. He meant to tempt Antony into sleeping with them. Antony decided not to try for Mariamne so as not to anger Cleopatra. But he did ask for Aristobulus. Herod did not want to send 16-year-old Aristobulus to be abused by Antony; everyone knew Antony's sexual habits. So Herod said that if the boy left the country, the people would rebel.

Herod thus kept Aristobulus away from Antony. But his wife Mariamne nagged at him to restore the high priesthood to her brother. Herod decided this would also keep Aristobulus at home. He called his friends together and said that Alexandra had plotted against him, trying to make Aristobulus king with the help of Antony. She had been unjust, but he, Herod, would still do the right thing and make Aristobulus high priest. He said that he had only put Ananelus in the position because Aristobulus was too young at the time. Alexandra saw that she was suspected, and she cried and apologized. She said that it would be good enough for her son to be priest – she never wanted him to be king, even if the people wanted it. She said that she would submit to Herod from now on, and so the suspicions cleared up and they made an agreement.

iii

HEROD sent Ananelus away from being high priest, in order to quiet his family. Ananelus was one of tens of thousands of Jews carried away captive beyond Euphrates. He was from a priestly family and had been an old friend of Herod's. Herod broke the Jewish law by sending him away. Once a man became priest, no one was to remove him. The only others who had dared to do this were Antiochus Epiphanes, who removed Jesus as high priest for Jesus's brother Onias; and Aristobulus, who had taken the honor from his own brother Hyrcanus.

At Herod's request, his acquaintances drown
Aristobulus (Herod's son) in the pond in Jericho.

Herod's family seemed to be content for now, but he feared that Alexandra might try more tricks in the future, so he commanded her to live in the palace and not be involved in public affairs. She had body guards and no privacy. Little by little she began to hate Herod. She decided she would rather speak than live like a slave, so she complained to Cleopatra and asked for help. Cleopatra told her to take her son and to come to Egypt. Alexandra had two coffins made for her and Aristobulus, which would help them to escape the palace. She ordered her servants to carry them out at night to a ship that was waiting to take them to Egypt. One of her servants made a mistake and told the plan to another servant named Sabion. This Sabion had been an enemy of Herod and was thought to be one of those who poisoned Herod's father, Antipater. He needed to gain Herod's favor, so he told Herod the news. Herod caught them in the act of escaping. But he forgave them because he didn't want Cleopatra to hate him more. He wanted to look like a generous, moderate person. He decided he needed to get rid of Aristobulus, but not openly.

It was the feast of tabernacles. Aristobulus was 17 years old and went to offer sacrifices dressed in the priestly clothes. The people showed too openly how much they liked him, and they remembered that his grandfather, Aristobulus, had once been the king. Herod became very jealous. Later, when he was feasting in Jericho with Alexandra, Herod brought the young man out to a lonely place and they played like children. It was very hot and they stood by the large fish ponds. Herod and Aristobulus watched the servants swimming in the water to cool off, and Herod convinced him to join them. Some of Herod's servants in the pond had been told to drown Aristobulus. As it was getting dark, Herod's servants pushed him under the water, pretending that it was a game, and they held him there until he died. He had been high priest only one year. Ananelus again became high priest.

When the women of the family heard of Aristobulus's death, they were full of grief. All of Jerusalem grieved as if they had lost one of their own family. But Alexandra guessed that her son had not died by accident. She was so upset that she thought to kill herself, but she decided to keep living in order to punish the unjust murder. She didn't let anyone see what she was thinking. Herod made sure that no one connected the deed with himself. He cried a lot over Aristobulus, and maybe inside he did feel sorry that such a beautiful boy was dead. He arranged a very rich funeral, with a grand tomb, many spices and treasures buried with the body. This helped to comfort the women.

Nothing could comfort Alexandra. She wrote to Cleopatra about the murder, and Cleopatra told Antony that the murderer must be punished. This was even more important since Antony had made Herod king when he was not of royal blood, and now he had murdered a royal son. Antony told Herod to come to him and defend himself from the charge. Herod was afraid but had no choice. He left his uncle Joseph to manage the public affairs, and said that if Antony would kill him, Joseph should also kill Mariamne. Antony had fallen in love with her because of her beauty, and Herod did not want him to take Mariamne for a wife after his death.

Joseph took care of the kingdom, which required seeing Mariamne often. He would mention the king's goodness to her, but the women made fun of that idea. Thinking to make the king look good, he told her how Herod could not live without her, and that if something should happen to him, he had ordered that Mariamne be killed. The women did not take this in a positive way! It was understood that they could not escape abuse by life or by death, and what Joseph had told them made them very suspicious of Herod later.

The enemies of Herod said that Antony had tortured Herod and killed him. Alexandra told Joseph that they should leave the palace and join the soldiers who were guarding the city under Julius, where they would be safe. She also thought that if Antony could see Mariamne, they could receive the kingdom since they were a royal family.

Then letters came from Herod, showing that he was alive. He had given many presents to Antony which made him ignore Cleopatra's opinions. Antony told Herod that it wasn't good to make a king explain his actions; otherwise he wouldn't be a king at all. He said the same to Cleopatra, saying that it would be best for her not to be involved in the king's government. Herod wrote all of this down, including the discussions he had with Antony and how they ate. He enjoyed being there in spite of Cleopatra's accusations. Cleopatra, said Herod, was wanting to rule Judea, but she should be happy that Antony had given her Coelesyria instead.

The women had thought to go to the Romans only because they thought that Herod was dead, so they changed their minds. Herod went against the Parthians with Antony and then returned to Judea. Mariamne and Herod's sister Salome didn't like each other, and Salome told her brother that Mariamne and Joseph were sleeping together. Herod was upset at Mariamne but he did not punish her. When she was questioned about Joseph, she denied it, and after a while he believed her. They made peace as lovers do, crying and hugging. Then she told him what she had heard: that if he had died, he had wanted her to die as well. The king was so shocked that he tore out his hair and decided that Joseph really had been sleeping with Mariamne. He almost killed his wife, but he held himself back. This troubled him for a long time, and he ordered Joseph to be put to death without seeing him. Alexandra was put in prison as the one who caused all this trouble.

iv

CLEOPATRA continually tried to get Antony to remove princes from other countries and give them to her to rule. She had a great influence on him and Syria was in confusion. She had poisoned her brother because he was to be king of Egypt, when he was only 15 years old. She had her sister Arsinoe killed by Antony when she was at Diana's temple in Ephesus. Cleopatra would also steal treasures from temples and tombs. Because of her Antony killed Lysanias, son of Ptolemy who ruled Syria, saying that he had brought the Parthians into those countries. Cleopatra wanted Judea and Arabia too. But Antony knew there was a limit, and he would take only part of a country to give to her. She received cities below the river Eleutherus (separating Syria and Phoenicia) as far as Egypt, except for Tyre and Sidon which were independent cities.

Cleopatra went with Antony to Armenia as far as Euphrates. She then came to Apamia, Damascus and then to Judea. Herod met her there and gave her parts of Arabia and money from the area around Jericho. Balsam grows in this area and nowhere else. There are also many palm trees there. She tried to sleep with King Herod and might have actually fallen in love with him. Herod knew that it could be a trap, and that he needed to avoid her advances. He thought it might be good to kill her since she was trouble for everyone. He asked his friends what they thought about this idea. He thought he would even be doing Antony a favor, knowing that she would not be faithful to him. His friends told him that it would be too dangerous, and Antony would not see things that way. Cleopatra was the most honored woman in the world at the time. They talked Herod out of the idea; he could lose his life and his kingdom. So he treated Cleopatra kindly, gave her presents and sent her back to Egypt.

Antony took over Armenia and sent the son of Tigranes as a captive, together with his family, to Egypt as a present to Cleopatra, together with all the royal treasures. The oldest son, Artaxias, had escaped and became the king of Armenia. He was later put out by Archelaus and Nero Caesar when they restored Tigranes his younger brother to the kingdom. Herod had to pay Cleopatra money for the land which Antony had given her. He paid 200 talents*. Later the payments were slower in coming and much smaller.

V

HEROD was planning to go against the king of Arabia due to his ingratitude and injustice towards him. The Roman war of Actium would soon take place, which was the 187th Olympiad when

Caesar and Antony were to fight to be the top ruler of the world. Herod was rich after receiving much tax money and having a great army and many supporters. He wanted to help Antony, but Antony said that he did not need his help and told him to go punish the king of Arabia. Cleopatra was behind this too, hoping that the two kings would hurt each other. Herod took his army to Arabia and the Arabians were prepared for the battle, but the Jews won. Later they got a larger army together. Herod already knew about this. He came to the enemy near Cana and set up a defense wall, to wait for the right time to attack. But all his men said not to waste time but to attack now. Herod took this advice and they fought with great success, with Herod in his armor standing at the front. Most of the Arabians ran away. But Athenio, Cleopatra's general, suddenly attacked the Jews after they thought the battle was won. Athenio had decided that if the Arabians looked like they were winning, he would be still. He saw that they were beaten, so he attacked the Jews from behind and killed many of them. The Arabians saw this and came running back to the battle and killed many. Only a few Jews escaped and returned to the camp. Herod saw that his army was losing and came to help them, but it was too late. The Jewish camp was taken, which the Arabians could not have done without Athenio. Herod became like a robber, making sudden attacks in Arabia and then running into the mountains. He took care of his soldiers.

In the seventh year of the reign of Herod, the fight between Octavius Caesar and Antony took place in Actium. The worst earthquake ever also happened at that time in Judea. Many cattle were killed, and 10,000 men were killed by falling houses. The army was out in the field and was not hurt. When the Arabians heard about this they were happy; they thought that all of Judea was ruined, and there was no one left to fight them. They took the Jewish messengers who had come to make peace with them and killed them. The Jews lost their hope, since things were so bad at home and they had no one to help them. Herod gave a speech to encourage them.

"In the past there were many problems to overcome. This war was a just one, which needed to be fought because our enemies were being unfair. You know the wickedness of the Arabians. They are barbaric and don't know God. It's because of their envy of us that they have attacked us suddenly. They were afraid of being slaves to Cleopatra, and we saved them – we and Antony who was my friend. Even when Antony took some of our land and theirs to give to Cleopatra, I gave presents from my own money in order to keep our nations free. I gave 200 talents* and promised another 200 that were owed. So they have cheated us when we were supposed to be friends. We shouldn't have been forced to pay taxes in the first place, but we saved the Arabians and have been good to them.

"God declares that the unjust should be punished. They have killed our messengers, something that the Greeks and even the barbarians would never do. Angels and messengers are holy; they have made God known to mankind and have made peace between enemies. What can be more wicked than to kill messengers of peace? How can these people live in security or win a war? I think it is impossible. What is holy and righteous is on our side. Some may say that the Arabians have more men and are braver than we are. But where God is, there can also be courage and numbers. Think about what happened in the first battle we won. In the second battle, they did not fight bravely, and it was Athenio who helped them in an unfair way. Then there was the earthquake, but accidents happen. If it was the will of God, then the earthquake also ended by his will. If He had wanted to hurt us, he could have done so."

Then Herod offered sacrifices to God. The people were ready to fight again and went against the Arabians by passing over the Jordan. They thought to attack a castle, but the Arabians also had that idea. More and more soldiers joined the battle, but the Arabians were beaten and ran away. Herod went to destroy their defense wall. There was hand-to-hand fighting, and many were lost on each side. In the end the Arabians gave up and ran.

They were killed by their enemies and also by trampling on one another. In the end 5,000 men died, and the rest ran to the fort. There was no water there. The Jews surrounded them and kept them from leaving.

The Arabians sent messengers out to Herod asking to make an agreement and begging for water. But Herod was angry and would not help them; he wanted them to completely give up. After five days 4,000 of them came out and were taken prisoner. Others fought but they were so weak they just wanted to be killed, and 7,000 were killed. They were surprised at Herod's strength even after what he had been through, and they made him ruler of their nation.

vi

HEROD'S position was secure. But after Antony was defeated by Caesar (Octavian) in the battle of Actium, there was a certain fear that Herod would be punished for having been friends with Antony. Herod felt that Hyrcanus might be made king in his place, since Hyrcanus was from the royal family.

Hyrcanus wanted to just be the high priest and was not interested in ruling human affairs. But Alexandra, his daughter, still wanted their family to get back the kingdom. She told her father to punish Herod for his bad treatment of their family. She wanted him to write a letter to Malchus, then governor of Arabia, to receive them and to protect them until Herod would lose his place as king, which seemed about to happen.

Hyrcanus didn't listen at first, but he finally sent the letter and asked Malchus for some horsemen to meet them at Lake Asphaltites. Hyrcanus gave the letter to his servant Dositheus, who already hated Herod since he had killed his relative Joseph. Dositheus was also a brother of those who had been killed in Tyre by Antony. But Dositheus decided it would be better to stay on Herod's good side, so he showed both Hyrcanus's letter and the answer to Herod. Malchus said that he would receive Hyrcanus and protect them on their journey. When Herod saw this letter, he sent for Hyrcanus and accused him of plotting with Malchus. When Hyrcanus denied it, Herod showed the letter to the Sanhedrim and put Hyrcanus to death immediately.

This is the way Herod told what happened, but others did not agree. One told that Herod asked Hyrcanus if he had received any letters from Malchus. He answered that they had only been letters of greeting. Had he received any presents? "No, only four horses to ride on." Then Herod had accused him of bribery and treason, and had given orders to have him killed. But Hyrcanus was not the kind of man to plot against him. He was a gentle man even when he was young, and as a king he had given the management of public affairs to Antipater. He was now over 80 years old and had no reason to fight Herod. He had come over the Euphrates and left those who greatly honored him, in order to be under Herod's government. These writers believe that Herod made the whole thing up.

So the life of Hyrcanus ended. He had been through many hard times. He became high priest of the Jewish nation from the beginning of the reign of his mother, Alexandra. She had reigned nine years, and he became king after her for three months. He lost the throne to his brother Aristobulus, was restored by Pompey with great honors, and served forty years until Antigonus wounded him and he became a slave to the Parthians. Herod gave him hope and he returned, but Herod didn't keep his promises. Hyrcanus did not deserve this cruel trap. He stayed away from the public eye and wasn't clever enough to govern a kingdom. Both Antipater and Herod became great because Hyrcanus took the back seat. His end was unjust and unholy.

After Herod had killed Hyrcanus, he went to Caesar to try to be friends with him. He put matters into the hands of his brother Pheroras. He sent his mother Cyprus, and his sister Salome and the family to stay in Masada. Because his wife Mariamne could not live together with his sister and his mother, Herod sent Mariamne to live in Alexandrium with Alexandra her mother. His treasurer Joseph and Sohemus of Iturea took care of that fort.

These two had been faithful to him from the beginning and they would guard the women. Herod told them that if anything bad happened to him, they were to kill those two women, so that the kingdom would be kept for his sons or his brother Pheroras.

Herod then went to Rhodes to meet Caesar. He took his crown off but did not beg or cry for mercy. He said that Antony was a great friend of his and that he was glad to have helped him. He had sent him both money and corn for the war, and wished he had done more. "I did not leave him after his defeat at Actium. I have been his counselor and told him that if he wanted to keep his authority he would have to kill Cleopatra, and he should be friends with you. But Antony did not take my advice. He was not wise, but this has turned out to be in your favor. If you want to punish me for being a good friend, remember that I would now do the same for you."

In this way Herod gained Caesar's friendship by the very thing that had made him look bad. Caesar gave the crown back to Herod and asked him to be as good a friend to him as he had been to Antony. He also remembered that Herod had helped him in an affair with the gladiators. Herod then brought men to go with Caesar for his trip to Egypt and gave him presents. He asked Caesar not to kill Alexander, Antony's friend. Herod then returned to Judea with confidence, much honor and the feeling that he had God's favor. He got ready to receive Caesar on his way from Syria to invade Egypt. He made great feasts for him at Ptolemais, giving presents and many supplies to his army. He rode along with Caesar with his 150 men. When crossing the desert they had plenty of wine and water. He gave Caesar 800 talents* which was more than he could afford to give. When they left Egypt he again gave them as much as before.

vii

HEROD came home to trouble. Mariamne and her mother Alexandra, living in the Alexandrium fort, felt that it was not for their safety but to keep them prisoners. Mariamne felt that Herod did not really love her, and if something happened to him, he would make sure that she would die also. She remembered what Joseph had told her. She made friends with Sohemus, the guard of Herod, who told her what his orders were from Herod. Sohemus was thinking that this would pay off in the end. He figured that Herod might die, and even if he returned alive, he would never refuse the wishes of his wife since it seemed he truly loved her. Mariamne knew that she was in danger from Herod, and she said she no longer wanted to live with him.

Herod came back from Caesar proud and happy. He told his wife first about his surprising success, but she was upset instead of happy for him. He went back and forth from being angry with her to loving her. Sometimes he thought to punish her for her rebellion, but he didn't. He was torn between love and hate, and thought he ought to kill her, but then he worried that without her he would be more miserable than before.

Herod's mother and sister saw the trouble, and added to it by telling Herod long stories and accusations against Mariamne, making him hate her more. But Herod still didn't want to kill her. Then Herod heard that Caesar had won the war in Egypt, and that Antony and Cleopatra were both dead. He went to meet Caesar. Mariamne told Herod that Sohemus had done a good job guarding her. She asked Herod to make a place for him in the government, which he granted. Herod received great honor from Caesar when he arrived in Egypt. He received 400 Galatian guards who had been Cleopatra's guards. He also got back the country that Antony had taken from him, as well as Gadara, Hippos and Samaria and the seacoast cities. Herod took Caesar to Antioch.

When he returned home, Mariamne continued to treat him badly. She was also mean to his mother and sister due to their more humble birth. Both sides became worse for an entire year after Herod's return. Once when Herod was having a nap at noon he called for his wife to come to him since he loved her. She came in but would not lie down by him. She accused him of causing her grandfather's and brother's deaths. Salome, Herod's sister, saw that he was upset and sent his cupbearer to tell lies about Mariamne. He told the king how Mariamne had persuaded him to help make a love-potion for him. He said that only Mariamne knew what was in the potion, and that it was meant only for Herod. The servant said he wasn't sure it was safe. The king was very angry and ordered that Mariamne's closest servant be tortured to find out more about this potion, since he must know about it. But even when tortured, the servant could only tell him that Sohemus, the guard, had private talks with Mariamne, and that she hated Herod because of what Sohemus had told her. Herod shouted that Sohemus, a faithful servant to him in other matters, would not have told Mariamne of Herod's orders unless he was having an affair with Mariamne. He ordered the death of Sohemus. Then he had a trial for Mariamne and accused her about the love-potion, even though there was no proof. The court passed the death sentence on her. But Herod was still not sure about killing her, and he felt that she be put in prison for a while instead. Salome and her friends urged him that she should die right away, and this was the final decision. They convinced Herod that he had to do it quickly in order to avoid a riot by many of the people who loved Mariamne.

Alexandra saw the same fate waiting for her and tried to change her behavior. She joined in the accusations against her daughter. She cried out in front of the crowd that Mariamne was a bad woman and ungrateful to her husband, and that she had deserved to be punished. She even tore out her hair, but everyone knew she was just pretending and many in the crowd said so. Mariamne went to her death without crying.

Mariamne was beautiful and talked like a queen. But she was too free in speaking against Herod, thinking he would never hurt her since he was truly fond of her. If she had forgiven him for the crimes against her family she would have been better off. She also upset his mother and sister until they became her enemies.

After Mariamne's death Herod could not be at peace. He would sometimes call for her or cry for her in an abnormal way.

He tried to forget her by planning feasts and meetings, but it did not help. He was so sick over missing her that he had to stop his duties as king. At this time there was a disease which killed many people. Some felt that this was God's punishment for Mariamne's death. Herod went to the desert and pretended to hunt, but he went there to torture himself. He got sick from this habit; he had pain in the back of his head and began to go mad. All medicines were useless. Many doctors were with him, but he wasn't eating healthy food; he ate whatever he wished. He was in Samaria, now called Sebaste.

Alexandra was in Jerusalem and knowing he was sick, she tried to take over the fortified places around the city. The one by the temple decided whether or not the Jews could offer their sacrifices, so whoever controlled it took over the nation. She told the guards that she was keeping the kingdom safe for the sons of Herod, who would need to take his place. They hated Alexandra, and also felt it was too soon to think of Herod as dead, since they were his friends. One of them, Achabus, was his cousin. So they told Herod about Alexandra's plan and he gave orders to have her killed. He was sick in mind and body, and killed anyone who worried him, even a few of best his friends.

Costobarus was an Idumean. He was married to Salome, Herod's sister. He was proud of his success and told Cleopatra that he would rather be in her kingdom than obey Herod. Salome fought with her husband and decided to divorce him. She told Herod that she left Costobarus out of loyalty to him, and told him about some men, the sons of Babas, who Costobarus kept alive after Herod had told him to kill them. While Antigonus was king, Herod's army besieged Jerusalem. Costobarus was supposed to kill the enemies of Herod as they came out the gates, but he hid the sons of Babas, a powerful family honored by the people. He denied this to Herod, and Herod searched for them but never found them. His sister now showed him where they were hiding. They were found and Herod had them killed, which ended all the family of Hyrcanus. Herod felt he would now be free to ignore Jewish laws.

HEROD changed the old customs of the Jews and started for-eign practices. Worship of God was neglected. Every five years he would arrange games to honor Caesar. He built a theatre in Jerusalem and a huge amphitheatre in the valley. Both were very costly. People came from the surrounding countries to play and to watch. There were wrestlers and prizes were given to the winners. Some sports were played while naked. There were also musicians. There were chariot races drawn by two, three or four pairs of horses. Herod copied shows and games from other countries, and didn't mind the great cost. He had stones made with writing of Caesar's victories and prizes from the nations which he had got-ten in the wars. All were of gold and silver and were on display in the theatre. The costumes for the games were costly, including precious stones. He brought many lions and wild animals that were very strong or rare. They would fight one another or attack men who were prisoners. Foreigners were surprised and happy to watch these things, but the Jews were disgusted; it was far from their way of life. It was horrible to throw men to the wild beasts, but it was also terrible to display the images which were like gods, since the Jews were not to honor images.

Herod argued with the Jews about the statues which were in the theatre. He brought the leaders there and asked them what they thought. They said that the statues looked like men, so he removed the clothes and they saw only pieces of wood under them. The Jews laughed. Some of the people calmed down, but others were still angry and believed God would punish the Jews for this change.

Ten men plotted to kill King Herod, and they had daggers under their clothes. There was a certain blind man went with them who couldn't help but greatly encouraged them. They went into the theatre and agreed that if they missed Herod, they would kill others around him, even if they should die themselves. A spy whom Herod had ordered to listen for such plans told the king of the plot even before they entered the theatre. Herod went to his palace and called the accused men to come forward by name.

They were not ashamed, nor did they deny their plan. They felt they were doing a holy thing by standing up for their Jewish customs. They were tormented to death. The spy was then killed by a group of people and pulled apart limb by limb and given to the dogs. Many people saw this but no one would tell who did the deed. Herod was so intent on finding them that he tortured women to make them tell. Then he killed the entire families of those who had done it. But the people still hated Herod, and he worked hard and watched the people all the time in order to put down any plan of rebellion.

Herod fortified his palace in Jerusalem and rebuilt the fort of Antonia. He made a fort in Samaria called Sebaste which was one day's journey from Jerusalem. He also built a fort for the people once called Strato's Tower, which he renamed Cesarea. He had horsemen in the valley at a place called Gaba which was in Galilee. He had guards all over the country to keep the people quiet. He had spies all over to prevent plots against him. He built the wall of Samaria (Sebaste) with the help of his soldiers and local people. All were made citizens. He wanted to build a temple there and expand the city; it was to be a monument in his honor. He also gave some land to the Samaritans. The wall of the city was very strong, and ran for twenty furlongs* around it. The sacred place was richly decorated. The temple was large and beautiful. There were many decorations throughout the city as well.

ix

IN the 13th year of the reign of Herod many calamities hit the region. Were they God's judgment or natural events? There was a severe drought. There was hunger and disease with no cure. Anything which had been stored was used up. The people had no seeds for planting. Herod did not get help from others because no one had any food to sell. He cut up his expensive furniture and sold the best silver and gold parts, and sent the money to Petronius in Egypt. He was Herod's friend, so he sent the Judeans corn. Petronius was the only one who tried to help. Herod gave the impression that the food came from himself, and so he turned enemies into friends. He was caring for the needs of the people including the elderly and sick. He also got winter clothing for them since the sheep and goats had died and no wool was available. He gave planting seed to the Syrians, whose soil was rich. He sent 50,000 men to help in their harvest. It turned out that the harvest was plentiful both for them and for Herod's country. Herod supplied the needs of the multitudes, so the Jews felt less hatred towards him for having violated their customs.

Herod sent 500 good soldiers to Caesar who served him well by the Red Sea. Herod built a huge palace. The furniture was gold with marble seats and beds, and the rooms could contain many people. One apartment was called Caesar's; another Agrippa's. He fell in love again and married another wife.

Simon, a citizen of Jerusalem, was made a priest because of his daughter, who Herod wanted to marry. She was considered the most beautiful woman of that time. He didn't want to just take her, because people would think he was violent and abusive, so he married her. Herod removed the priest Jesus and made Simon the priest, in order to make the family more honorable.

After the wedding Herod built a fort in the place where he had conquered the Jews while Antigonus had been king. It was 60 furlongs* from Jerusalem. It was in the shape of a woman's breast and had circular towers. There were steps of 200 polished stones. The apartments were both secure and beautiful. Water was brought from far away.

Herod didn't expect any trouble with his people, since he ruled them with a strong hand. He also gave impressive speeches to them. He was friendly to all of the governors and gave them presents. At the same time, whoever disobeyed would be severely punished. He stayed friends with Caesar and the most powerful men in Rome, but this meant breaking some of the Jewish laws. He built many grand cities and temples at great cost. There were no idols in Judea, like the Greek statues of animals elsewhere; he put them other places.

Herod built a huge city of white stone at Strato's Tower on the sea. There were huge palaces and buildings and he built a special harbor which was protected from the waves of the sea. It was as large as the Pyraeum in Athens and had a double port for ships. Much of the stone was brought from far away at great cost. The city was in Phoenicia in the passage by sea to Egypt, between Joppa and Dora which were not good ports due to the strong south winds that roll sand up on the shore. Herod used stones more than 50 feet long and no less than 18 wide and nine deep, sinking them into 20 fathoms* of water, which prevented waves from coming in. He also built a wall and several towers, one of which was named after the son-in-law of Caesar who died young, Drusus. The sailors lived under the arches. There was a nice walking path around the entire harbor, the entrance being on the north where there was less wind. A temple was built along with buildings of polished stone. The temple could be seen from far away, and there were two statues; one of Rome, and the other of Caesar. The city was called Cesarea. There were vaults and tunnels underneath as well, some to float the cargo back and forth, and others to carry sewage and rainwater. The city was kept clean by the changing tides. Herod built a theatre of stone and a huge amphitheatre facing the ocean. It took twelve years to build the city, and Herod kept up with the project and paid the bills on time.

x

AFTER Herod rebuilt Sebaste (Samaria), he sent his sons Alexander and Aristobulus to Rome to be in the company of Caesar. They stayed at the house of Pollio, but could have stayed in Caesar's palace if they had wished. Caesar gave to Herod certain places to rule. One of Caesar's men, Zenodorus, was very corrupt and took money unjustly in Syria. There were many robberies taking place and Caesar ordered Herod to take over and bring peace. These robbers had no way to make a living and even lived together with their cattle. They did have a way to keep water and kept corn which they guarded carefully against theft. They were hard to catch since they lived in caves with narrow entrances. There were also rocky trails that were hard to find. But Herod found them by hiring skillful guides. He put an end to the robberies, and there was finally peace in the neighborhood.

Zenodorus was sorry he had lost control, and he envied Herod who had gotten it. He went to Rome to complain about Herod, but he got nowhere. Agrippa was set up to succeed Caesar in the countries beyond the Ionian Sea, and Herod went to see him. Some of the Gadarens came to Agrippa and accused Herod, but Agrippa didn't listen to them; he sent them as prisoners to Herod. Then the Arabians made trouble for him over a piece of land which Herod controlled; Zenodorus had sold the same land to them for 50 talents*. They felt cheated and tried to attack him in court. They also tried to get the people to rebel, but Herod was aware of this and was able to calm them down.

Herod had ruled for 17 years and Caesar came into Syria. Most of the people in Gadara were against Herod, saying that he was a tyrant. The people wanted to be under Caesar's rule and not Herod's. The Gadarens were not afraid to complain, since those who had accused Herod before Agrippa had been set free without being punished. Herod had a strange custom of being easy on others while being harsh with his own family. The Gadarens accused him of hurting and robbing them and ruining their temples. Caesar obviously did not believe them, and they gave up. They even feared the punishment for their accusations, so some of them cut their own throats at night or threw themselves over cliffs. Others drowned themselves in the river. Caesar cleared Herod from all of the crimes he was accused of. Zenodorus also became so sick that he lost a lot of blood; he died in Antioch in Syria. Herod became the ruler of this large country.

At this point there were only two men who ruled the huge Roman Empire: first Caesar and then Agrippa, his favorite friend. And Herod was friends with both. Herod decided to ask for a kingdom for his brother Pheroras. Herod gave him 100 talents* in order that his brother would be safe, and his sons might not overrule their father. Herod went with Caesar to the sea, and he went home. He built a beautiful temple of white stone in Zenodorus's country near Panium. It is a cave in a mountain located over a crater. There is a deep water in the crater, and the river Jordan begins from here.

Herod reduced the people's taxes by one third in order to restore their loyalty, which was lacking due to his disrespect of the Jewish religion. He made sure the people kept too busy to criticize him and he would not let them gather in meetings. They couldn't even walk together or eat together without being punished. Many were brought to the fort Hyrcania, both openly and secretly, and killed there. There were spies everywhere. Sometimes even Herod would go out in disguise and mix with the people at night, just to hear what they were saying about his government. He required people to take an oath of loyalty to him, and they obeyed out of fear. Those who refused were killed. He tried to convince Pollio the Pharisee, Sameas, and most of the scholars to take the oath but they refused. They were not punished since he respected Pollio.

The Essens were also excused from this oath, and here's why. One of them, Manahem, was a prophet. He had seen Herod when he was a child going to school. Manahem saluted him as king of the Jews, but Herod did not know who he was. He slapped him on the backside with his hand, saying that Herod would begin his rule happily since God considered him worthy. The slap was a sign of change, he said. "If you stop doing right, you will be punished." Herod did not pay attention to what Manahem said, but later when he was a great king he sent for Manahem and asked how long he would reign. Manahem would not tell him. He asked, "Ten years?" Manahem said, "20 or 30 years." So from this time Herod honored all of the Essens. I mention this because many Essens have been thought worthy to receive words from God due to their great righteousness.

xi

IN the 18th year of Herod's reign, he wanted to build God's temple higher. It would be his biggest project up to this time, and a lasting memorial to himself. But in order to get the people's support, he made a speech. He stressed, "The buildings which I built up to now were not for my own glory but to offer security to you. I believe that I've brought the Jewish nation to a new level of happiness. You don't need to hear the details, since you already know. But now I want to raise God's temple higher. The size of the second temple were set by Cyrus and Darius. Now I am your governor, and by God's will since we have been at peace and since we have the resources and are well regarded by the Romans, who are rulers of the whole world, I will complete the task."

Some people were afraid that the project was too big, believing that after pulling the temple down he would not be able to rebuild it. Herod promised that he would finish the work. He brought 1000 wagons for carrying the stones. He chose the most skillful workers and brought 1000 garments for the priests. Some of the priests were taught to work as stonecutters and carpenters.

All of the old foundations were removed and the new temple was built on a new foundation. It was 100 cubits* long and in the beginning was 20 cubits* higher than the present temple, because 20 cubits fell down when the foundation sank. (It was this part which we Jews wanted to rebuild during Nero's reign.) The strong white stones used were 25 cubits* long, 8 cubits* high & about 12 cubits* wide. The middle part of the temple was higher and could be seen far away, but other parts were lower. The temple had doors at the entrance which were the same height as the temple. There were embroidered curtains with purple flowers interwoven with pillars. There was a beautiful gold vine decoration hanging down from the high ceiling.

Solomon had by God's wisdom built a great wall which supported the hill, and Herod did the same. It separated the temple area from the deep valley. The rocks were held together with lead and rocks on the inside were held together with iron, making them immovable. All of the holes were filled up. A wall 4 furlongs* square surrounded the entire hill, and a smaller wall for reinforcement was built on the east side. In the open space along the wall there were many gifts from past kings, spoils of war from the nations, and spoils Herod had taken from the Arabians.

There was a strong square fort on the north side built by the Asamoneans who were high priests before Herod's time. In this tower the high priest's holy clothes were kept, including the garment which was worn each year for the festivals. After Herod died the Romans protected these garments until the time of Tiberius Caesar, who restored their keeping to the Jews. They were later passed back to the Romans, and under Claudius Caesar were given back into the Jewish King Agrippa's control. But the clothing stayed in this tower. The Jews went the day before their festival and showed their seal to the Roman captain of the temple guards. The garments were given to them and returned after the holiday. This tower Herod named Antonia in honor of the Roman ruler Antonius.

There were four gates in the western quarter of the temple. One led the king's palace through a walkway over the valley. Two more led to the suburbs of the city, and the fourth led to the other city where a road went down into the valley with many steps and up the other side. The city was like an amphitheater facing the temple. There was a deep valley south of it. The fourth side of the temple on the south had gates, and three paths which reached from the east valley to the west. The valley was so deep that someone looking from the top would become dizzy.

There were four rows of pillars in the temple's first court, and the fourth row was a part of the stone wall. Three men surrounding a pillar could touch hands. The length of the pillar was 27 feet with a double spiral base. There were 162 pillars in all. The top of them was cut in the Corinthian style. There were wood carvings on the roof. The front wall had beams resting on interwoven pillars and the front was all of polished stone. A few steps up led to the middle part, which had a sign forbidding foreigners to enter on punishment of death. There were three gates, and on the east side (the side of the sunrise) was the gate where the purified worshippers would enter with their wives. The women were not allowed further than here. And in an innermost room only the priests could enter. The temple was here, and in front of it was the altar for burnt offerings. Herod was not allowed into any of these three rooms since he was not a priest. He took care of the other parts of the building, and he finished them in eight years.

The priests built the temple in one and a half years. The people praised God and celebrated. Herod sacrificed 300 oxen to God. It was also the anniversary of Herod's reign as king, so it was a huge event. There were so many sacrifices offered they could not be counted. There was a secret passage built for the king which led from Antonia to the inside of the temple at the eastern gate. He built a tower over this so that he would be protected from any uprising. It was said that during the time the temple was built there was never rain during the daytime; rain fell only at night so that the work was not hindered. Is this not God's blessing?

BOOK XVI

FROM THE FINISHING OF THE TEMPLE BY HEROD TO THE DEATH OF ALEXANDER AND ARISTOBULUS

HEROD punished criminals in a different way than was done in the Jewish tradition. He simply put them out of the country forever. The Jewish laws said that a thief should return what was stolen four times as much if he could. If not, he would become a slave, but only to a Jew; and these slaves were released after six years. Instead of acting as a king it was said that he was a tyrant who didn't care about the people. It is no wonder the people hated him.

Herod sailed to Italy to meet with Caesar and to see his sons who lived in Rome. They finished their studies in the sciences and returned to Judea. Everyone was impressed with the way they looked. Salome, the king's sister, became jealous. Those who hated Mariamne spread a rumor that they might conspire against Herod since he had killed their mother. It didn't seem proper that they would get along with him. After hearing what was being said by the people, Herod started to hate his sons in time, but for now his love for them as a father was stronger, so he respected them. He gave them wives when they were old enough. Aristobulus married Salome's daughter, Bernice, and Alexander married Glaphyra, the daughter of Archelaus, king of Cappadocia.

HEROD heard that Marcus Agrippa had sailed from Italy into Asia, so he invited him to come to Judea. He took him to his new cities and fed him the best food at Sebaste and Cesarea. He also showed him Alexandrium, Herodium and Hyrcania. The people greeted them in Jerusalem wearing holiday clothes. Agrippa offered sacrifices to God, and there was a feast of the best food available. He stayed many days but left before winter, returning to Ionia. Herod gave him many presents.

After the winter Herod went to meet him at the Bosphorus. He sailed by Rhodes and by Cos and thought he would find Agrippa there, but the ship was unable to stop so he sailed on for many days. Whenever people came to him, he gave them valuable gifts. The portico (covered walkway) of the city had been destroyed during the Mithridatic war. The portico had been very big and beautiful, and Herod offered to pay for it to be rebuilt. Sailing on, he finally caught up with Agrippa. Agrippa was very impressed with Herod's efforts, seeing this as a sign that their friendship was more important than Herod's affairs back home. Herod gave him advice about war and ruling the people. They traveled together for a while on land, and afterwards sailed from Ephesus to Samos. King Herod contributed money to every city which he visited, together with Agrippa's support. The people of Ilium had been upset and he made peace with them. The people of Chius owed money to Caesar, but Herod helped them pay it back.

Many Jews living in cities in Ionia came to Agrippa and Herod to complain about being wronged. They were unable to keep their laws in their own way, and they were not free on their own holy days. They were deprived of their money for religious purposes and they were forced to serve in the Roman army. Herod asked Agrippa to hear their side and chose his friend, Nicolaus, to speak for the Jews. The leaders of the country were called together. Nicolaus gave a long speech.

"If one were to ask Gentiles which of two things they would part with if they had a choice: life or the customs of their forefathers, they would choose to suffer rather than to stop their traditions. Many have chosen to go to war for this reason, and we're the same. It's obvious that Rome has brought the greatest blessing to everyone. Compared with the previous kingdoms, everyone feels free now. We are prosperous but so is everyone else. All we want is to keep our religion without any problems. Our customs are merciful and just. By not working on the seventh day we are able to learn our customs and laws. Our sacred money has been confiscated and we are also brought to court on our holy days, and this is deliberate.

"Agrippa, this was not happening in the past, and the laws are written on stones in the capitol. We could speak a long time about the prosperity you have brought about everywhere. We are not unworthy of all that we have received. I remind you of the father of one of our judges here, Antipater, who helped Caesar with 2,000 armed men when he went to war in Egypt. He was honored and we also remember the sacrifices which you offered to God and how you held a feast for our people."

After Nicolaus's speech, the Greeks did not offer any argument. Agrippa answered that due to Herod's good will and friendship, he would grant the Jews all that they had asked. And if there were any other requests, they would be granted as long as they would not be against the Romans. He sent everyone home, and Herod thanked Agrippa. They hugged and said goodbye. Herod sailed home, landing in Cesarea in a few days since the weather was good. He gathered all the people in Jerusalem and told them about his trip and about the Jews in Asia, and how they would live free to be Jews. He was in a happy mood and gave everyone a fourth of their taxes back from the last year. The people were happy and wished the king well.

TROUBLE was growing in Herod's house. Salome hated Alexander and Aristobulus since they were the sons of Mariamne. She feared that they would punish her for hating their mother. The young men didn't hide their hatred of her; Salome's hatred was more subtle. The family fights became the number one item for gossip around the city. The people were sorry for the sons who weren't smart enough to see what Salome was doing. She laid traps for them while they openly complained that they had to live with their mother's murderers.

Things got worse when Herod was away, and when he returned the sons thought it would be good to speak Archelaus, the king of Cappadocia, and with his help accuse their father to Caesar. Herod heard about this and he was very upset. It was strange how he could have such success in his outward life but have so much trouble at home.

Herod decided to bring his sons to behave better by raising another son, Antipater, to a higher position. In time he spoiled this son, giving him more than he deserved. Herod hoped his older sons would see that if they didn't show him respect, Antipater could take the throne instead of one of them when the time came. But Antipater used the situation to turn Herod against his other sons.When Agrippa had been ruling Asia ten years, he returned to Rome. Herod sailed from Judea, together with Antipater whom he brought to Agrippa, together with presents, with the hope that he would become Caesar's friend. It looked like Antipater would beat Herod's other sons in taking the throne of Judea.

WHILE Antipater was in Rome he had mixed feelings. He was highly regarded, but at the same time he worried because he couldn't make trouble for his brothers in Judea. He sent many letters to his father, repeating any stories he heard of how his brothers had behaved in ways that would make his father angry. Herod by now hated the sons of Mariamne, but in order not to appear as a lawbreaker, he sailed to Rome to accuse them before Caesar instead of killing them himself. He was in such a hurry that he met Caesar in the city of Aquilei instead. There Herod brought his sons before Caesar and told him that they were plotting to take his life. Herod had done everything for them, even marrying them to honorable wives. They should be punished.

The sons were afraid to speak before Caesar and they cried and groaned because they didn't know what to answer. The audience was crying for them, and even their own father had to hide his feelings for them. As the two sons saw this, Alexander called to his father and said that he knew Herod had the right to kill them. The fact that he brought the case to Caesar to make a judgment showed that he truly cared for them. "No one who planned to kill a man would bring him to the temples and altars here. We can't live with ourselves any longer, knowing how we have hurt our father. It would be better to die than to have everyone to be suspicious of us. But gossip is not proof. Can anyone show that we have prepared poison? Have we plotted with friends, bribed servants or written letters against you? How can accusations be based on only gossip? If we are fit to be kings, why should we need to fight for it? If we should kill our father, the people would never let us be kings. How would we even be allowed to enter the temple which you have built? Can a murderer be free of punishment so long as Caesar is alive? Our mother is dead, but this is a lesson to us to be cautious. We wish to say before Caesar, the lord of all, who is now our mediator, that if you, our father, can be free of all suspicions about us, only then can we live our lives."

Caesar was impressed, and looked seriously at Herod, who was confused. Most of the people believed the young men, since they were handsome and it seemed impossible for them to want to kill their father. They had cried and fallen to the ground. It seemed that Herod had no proof to accuse them with. Caesar waited, and then said that they were completely innocent but that they should have have humbled themselves before their father and not let things get this bad. He told Herod to stop suspecting them, and said he hoped that they could fix their relationship with one another. Herod hugged the crying sons while the audience, both free people and slaves, were crying.

They thanked Caesar and left, together with Antipater who pretended to be happy with the reconciliation. Caesar received 300 talents* from Herod. Caesar gave Herod half the profits of the copper mines in Cyprus and gave him to manage the other half, as well as other gifts and income. He left it up to Herod to appoint the son of his choice as the next king, or to divide it into three parts so that each would have a part.

Herod returned to Judea. While he was gone there was a rebellion in Trachon, but his soldiers stopped it. Herod sailed with his sons and came to the island of Eleusa (later called Sebaste) where he met the king of Cappadocia, Archelaus. The king received him kindly and was glad to know that the accusation against Alexander, who had married his daughter, had been dropped. They exchanged gifts. Herod came to Judea. He made a speech before the people in the temple. He told about Caesar's kindness to him and other details. He told the people that all three sons would rule after him; Antipater first, then Alexander and Aristobulus. They were to respect him as king and lord of all in the meantime, since he was still healthy and was old enough to rule wisely. He intended to rule over his household wisely as well. Not everyone was comfortable with this speech, since there were still some who wanted to see his sons rule.

V

IN the 28th year of Herod's rule, the building at Cesarea Sebaste was completed. The dedication was grand, including music and games to be performed naked. There would be gladiators fighting each other and beasts, horse racing and sports which were already known in Rome and elsewhere. The games were in honor of Caesar and Herod ordered them to be celebrated every five years. He sent some of his own furniture to be on display. Julia, Caesar's wife, sent some of her most valuable furniture from Rome. The value of the furniture came to 500 talents*. Herod paid for the visits of some of the guests who came from other lands, and made feasts for them in the public inns. There was plenty of food. There were fights in the daytime and expensive parties in the evenings. He had to show the world that he could do a better show than anywhere in the known world. Caesar and Agrippa had said that Herod's kingdom was too small for his soul; he should also have Syria and Egypt.

After this festival Herod built a city in the plain of Capharasaba, where there was plenty of water and rich soil. A river surrounded the city and there was a grove of trees. He called it Antipatris, in honor of his father Antipater. He also built a city above Jericho called Cyprus, in a good location. The finest monuments were dedicated to his brother Phasaelus, including a tower. He also built a city called Phasaelus in the valley of Jericho to the north. The land there became more fruitful as the people worked on it.

Herod helped many cities in Syria and Greece which lacked money for building public places. His most impressive project in Greece was the temple of Apollo at Rhodes. This came from his private money, and he also gave them much silver to repair their ships. In Antioch in Syria he had public courtyards built along the main street and made a road of polished stone. He also helped them celebrate the Olympic Games. He helped them often and was thanked as a manager of the games.

One can only stand amazed at Herod, who seemed to be the most generous person on earth, and yet terribly cruel. In my opinion, he was fighting to be honored above all others, and so he was cruel to anyone who opposed him. A friend could turn into his enemy to be punished, as soon as he disagreed with Herod. He paid honor to those higher than him, like Caesar and Agrippa, and he expected the same from those who were below him. But the Jews, preferring righteousness to glory, could not honor him with statues, temples or performances. To me this explains

Herod's crimes towards his own people and advisors, and his favors toward foreigners and those not related to him.

THE Jews were treated badly in Asia and Libya which joined Cyrene. Earlier kings had given them equal rights as citizens, but the Greeks began to take away their money set aside for the temple in Jerusalem, and they caused trouble in other ways. The Jews sent messages to Caesar, who sent letters to set things right.

One letter written by Caesar Augustus as "high priest and commander of the people" stated that the Jews had been grateful to the Romans now and in the past. "Hyrcanus, the Jewish high priest under my father [by birth his uncle], was given a law that the Jews should be free to practice the customs of their forefathers. Their sacred money should not be touched but sent to Jerusalem. They should not be forced to appear in court on the Sabbath, and anyone stealing their holy books will be punished, with his possessions going to the public treasury of Rome. Those not obeying this decree will be severely punished." This was inscribed on a pillar in the temple of Caesar. Agrippa also wrote on behalf of the Jews to the Ephesians. "The sacred money should only be kept by the Jews themselves. They should also not be forced to come to a trial on the Sabbath."

A ruler wrote to the leaders of the Sardians with Caesar's agreement that the Jews should be allowed to gather together to keep their customs. Another leader wrote to the Ephesians, with the approval of Augustus and Agrippa, that the Jews in Asia be permitted to offer their first fruits offerings to God by carrying them as a group to Jerusalem. "The Jews have shown proof that in the past they were able to follow their customs in their worship of God."

I am giving these examples to end the hatred between ourselves and other peoples, since it is unreasonable. Justice is good for everyone, including Greeks and barbarians. Our laws teach us to be kind and friendly to all men, and we would like to receive the same treatment in return. Doing right and accepting others are keys to the preservation of life.

HEROD spent great amounts of money building cities, both in his kingdom and outside of it. Hyrcanus, who was king before him, had opened David's tomb and taken out 3000 talents* of silver. Since he heard that there was still more inside, Herod went there secretly at night with his friends. He didn't find money, but there was gold furniture and other valuable items, all of which he took out. He wanted to go in farther, even as far as the bodies of David and Solomon. Two of his guards had been killed there by a flame which suddenly burst out, so he was too afraid. Herod built an expensive white stone monument in memory of this frightening experience, and he set it at the entrance of the tomb. Nicolaus, who recorded events for Herod, mentions this monument but does not tell why he built it, since everything he wrote about Herod had to be positive. He also wrote about the death of Mariamne and her sons in a way which made it their fault rather than due to Herod's cruelty. Nicolaus had no choice because he was serving the king. As for me (Josephus), from a family close to the Asamonean kings, also being priests, we have to be truthful. We honor Herod's family but we know the truth, and this makes some people upset.

Herod's family troubles could have grown from his attempt to rob David's tomb. It was as if civil war broke out in his palace, and it fed much hate between everyone. But Antipater was smarter; he accused his brothers many times but he would also apologize for them, to give Herod the impression that he was concerned for his father's safety.

Herod recommended Ptolemy to Antipater as an important manager in his kingdom. He also consulted with his mother about public affairs. They were able to turn Herod against the others while promoting themselves. Herod's sons grew worse and worse, and did not hold high positions. The women didn't get along at all. The king's brother Pheroras married a woman who was a servant even though he was engaged to marry Herod's daughter. This was a great insult to Herod, but he tried to make peace by offering his second daughter. Pheroras agreed to put away his wife and marry her, but he loved his wife and in the end he did not keep his promise. Herod became very angry every time Pheroras's name was mentioned.

With all the family fights, he was never at peace. His sister Salome urged her own daughter, who was married to Herod's and Mariamne's son Aristobulus, to treat her husband badly. She made gossip out of anything her daughter told her. The daughter said that the men hated their father, and that one day they would make Herod's sons by his other wives become teachers in the country, since they were more fit for that work. When the women saw Mariamne's sons in rich clothes, they said that someday they would be dressed in rags and would never see the sun. Salome took all of this gossip to Herod who started to believe that everyone was against everyone. The sons defended themselves, and made Herod's mind easier for a time, but later it became more serious.

Pheroras told Herod's son Alexander that Herod was in love with Glaphyra his wife. Alexander was very upset and confronted his father, and when Herod heard of it he was even more upset, because it was not true. Herod felt it was very unfair since he had been so good to everyone. He confronted Pheroras and accused him of being ungrateful and trying to get his own son to poison him for revenge. He told Pheroras to go away.

Pheroras blamed Salome, saying she had started the rumor; but when she heard this she cried out and denied it. She said everyone was trying to make the king hate her, even though she was trying to save him from the plots against him. She had persuaded their brother Pheroras to divorce his wife and to take the king's daughter, so this is why he hated her. When she spoke, she tore her hair and beat her chest trying to get Herod to believe her, but some who were watching thought she was faking. In the midst of the confusion, Herod sent his brother and sister away. He was pleased with the behavior of his son and that he came to Herod. He went out in the evening to get some fresh air. In this fight, Salome got the blame for starting the trouble, and she was not trusted by the king's wives. They said she could suddenly turn from a friend to an enemy.

Obodas, king of Arabia, was a lazy man but Sylleus managed most of his affairs. He was clever, young and handsome. When he came to Herod he saw Salome and fell in love with her. He heard that she was a widow. Salome, now on bad terms with her brother, was willing to marry Sylleus. King Herod's wives laughed about it and told Herod. After seeing their behavior at the supper table, he could see that they were truly in love. Sylleus left for two or three months and then asked Herod if he could marry Salome. This way, he said, there would also be a stronger link with Arabia, which was already under his control. Herod spoke with his sister about it and she agreed. But when Sylleus was told he would have to become a Jew, he refused, saying that the Arabs would stone him. Pherorus was upset with Salome for her loose behavior with Sylleus. Meanwhile, Salome asked that the daughter of Herod, who had been engaged to Pheroras but then rejected, be given to her son. But Pheroras talked him out of that. In the end Herod decided to give her to Pheroras's son instead. So she became his wife, and she received 100 talents* from Herod as a wedding present.

viii

HEROD had servants who were very good looking. One would bring him drinks, one his supper, one would put him to bed, and the other had a high position in the government. Someone told Herod that his son Alexander paid them money to plot against him. When the servants were questioned, they said they did not know of any plots against Herod. They were mercilessly tortured on a rack. Then they finally confessed that Alexander hated his father. He had told them that Herod didn't have long to live, and in order to hide his age he colored his hair black. Alexander was sure he would take his father's place as king, and he had the support of many rulers and friends.

Herod feared a plot to kill him more than ever. He sent out spies and in the end suspected innocent people. Many of his servants were killed, since they began accusing one another and they were all trapped by the accusations, even if there was no truth in them. Herod was sorry he had started it, but he never repented; when people were killed by mistake, he killed their accusers.

Herod even told his friends to stay away from the palace while this was going on, because he didn't want them to stop him. He sent away two old friends who had been his advisors in kingdom affairs and also tutors to his sons. One was expelled because his son was Alexander's friend. The other was expelled because he was a friend of Alexander when he was in Rome.

Antipater was the cause of all this. He would urge Herod to suspect innocent people because they did not confess anything when they were tortured. One of the young men tortured said that when Alexander walked with Herod he would shorten himself so that he would not look taller than the king. And when they were hunting together, Alexander would miss the mark on purpose since he knew how Herod needed to win. This man said that Alexander had plotted with his brother Aristobulus, that while hunting they would kill Herod and then run to Rome and ask for the kingdom. There was also a letter found, written to Alexander complaining that Herod shouldn't have given Antipater a country that earned 200 talents* a year.

Because of this evidence, Herod put Alexander in chains, but he wasn't convinced that it was true. He thought the story didn't make sense, and that he might be wrong to send his son to prison. Herod tortured Alexander's best friends and put many to death. One of the youngest while being tortured said that Alexander had asked Caesar to invite him to Rome to tell him of a dangerous plot. The king of Parthia was plotting with his father Herod against Rome, and he had a poison already prepared in Askelon.

Herod searched for the poison but never found it. Alexander was so angry with his father that he sent four letters to Herod saying that he didn't need to torture any more people; he would "confess" to even greater crimes. Alexander wanted to make his father ashamed of so quickly believing every rumor. He started accusing everyone he could think of. He had Pheroras as a partner in his plans, and Salome came at night and slept with him even against his will. The most faithful friends of the king, Ptolemy and Sapinnius, were accused, and all men everywhere agreed to kill Herod as soon as possible. There was no way to discover the truth, and everyone expected to be killed. Herod didn't trust anyone. He was beginning to lose his mind, thinking that his son was attacking him or that he stood by him with a sword in his hand.

Archelaus, king of Cappadocia heard about Herod and was worried about his daughter who was married to Alexander. He came for a visit but didn't try to argue with Herod, seeing that he was beyond hope. Instead he sided with Herod to make him calm down. He wanted to end his daughter's marriage with Alexander, since Alexander must be guilty as Herod said. When Herod heard this, he pleaded on Alexander's side. Archelaus then said that Herod's brother probably made Alexander turn bad. Herod was then angry with Pheroras, who had no one to speak for him. Archelaus said some well-chosen words, and saved everyone. Pheroras was forgiven and Alexander was declared innocent. Herod now saw Archelaus as his best friend and gave him many presents. Herod went on a trip to Rome, having written to Caesar about these events. Archelaus went with him part of the way, and Herod brought peace between Archelaus and Titus, the president of Syria. Then he returned to Judea.

ix

AFTER Herod returned from Rome, the Arabians started a war against him. As I wrote before, Caesar took the country of Trachonitis away from Zenodorus and gave it to Herod. The robbers there had to stop living from stealing; they had to work the land

and live peacefully. The hard work did not make them happy, and with Herod being away, the people went back to their old ways. The Trachonites spread a rumor that Herod had died, but Herod's governors punished the robbers. About forty of the chief robbers ran away to Arabia. Sylleus helped them since he was unable to marry Salome. They overran Judea and all of Coelesyria, taking much spoil. Herod returned and was unable to catch the robbers, so he killed their families in Trachonitis. The robbers had a law to get revenge for that, so they set out to destroy Herod's kingdom. By now there were 1000 robbers. Herod was demanding that the Arabian king Obodas return a loan of 60 talents* and give up the robbers, but Sylleus said he didn't know where the robbers were, and he put off paying the money. The two presidents of Syria were asked to settle the argument.

Sylleus went to Rome and didn't pay the money. Herod got the approval of the presidents to take care of the problem himself. He attacked the Arabian fort and destroyed it after taking all of the robbers. The Arabians came and fought against them, and Herod lost a few soldiers. The captain Naceb and some soldiers fell, and the rest escaped. Herod put 3000 Idumeans in Trachonities to control the people. After this, Herod sent a report to the captains, showing that he did nothing beyond punishing the guilty.

Messengers brought the news to Sylleus in Rome, and made it sound worse than it was. Sylleus went in to Caesar wearing black. With tears in his eyes he said that 2500 of his leading men had been killed, including the captain Nacebus, his friend. "All of the treasures in Raepta were taken and Obodas, who was sick, was unable to fight. I have come knowing that you will help us to live in peace." Caesar only asked if Herod had led this army. When Herod's friends admitted that he had, Caesar became very angry and wrote a harsh letter to Herod. Sylleus's letter to the Arabians made them so happy they refused to give up the robbers, pay the money they owed, or pay the rent for their land, since Caesar became angry and the king of the Jews was in trouble. The

Traconites rose up against the Idumean fort and robbed them like the Arabians.

Herod was very sad and afraid because Caesar had believed Sylleus. Obodas died and Aeneas (Aretas) became king. Sylleus wanted to be king and promised to give Caesar a lot of money. Also Caesar was angry that Aretas didn't ask him before he took over. Aretas sent a letter to Caesar, and a gold crown which weighed many talents*. He wrote that Sylleus had been a wicked servant who had poisoned Obodas, abused the Arabian women and had debts. Caesar did not believe these accusations and he sent Aretas's presents back.

Things in Judea and Arabia were getting worse and worse. Of the two kings, one had not yet received permission to rule. The other, Herod, had to accept Caesar's anger because he had no choice. He decided to send messengers to Rome again, to see if he could get Caesar to listen to him. He sent Nicolaus of Damascus.

X

A leading person from Lacedemonia, Eurycles, came to Herod with gifts and became a trusted friend. He lived at Antipater's house, but he made friends with Alexander and pretended that Archelaus, the king of Cappadocia (the father of Alexander's wife) was his friend. He was friendly with everyone but he was using them; after getting information out of one, he would tell the other and receive rich presents from all of them. Alexander was young and Eurycles convinced him that Alexander could trust him alone with his complaints. When Eurycles spoke with Antipater, he told him that Alexander was plotting to kill him. Antipater gave him gifts and told him to tell Herod. Herod believed the gossip, and to show his thanks he paid Eurycles 50 talents*. After receiving them, Eurycles went to the king of Cappadocia, Archelaus, saying that he had helped Alexander make peace with his father Herod, so he received money from Archelaus as well. But Eurycles was sent out of his own country because of all the lies he told.

Herod wanted to believe everything bad about his sons that people told him. When he heard that Eurastus had plotted with Alexander, it was good news to him.

Herod had two tall and strong guards whom he had sent away. They were now riding with Alexander and he would give them gold and other gifts. The king thought they were plotting against him, so he tortured them; at last they confessed that Alexander wanted them to kill Herod when he was hunting wild beasts, so that it could be said that he fell off his horse onto his own spear. This had actually happened once before. They also told where money was hidden in a stable. The chief hunter had given them the hunting spears and weapons at Alexander's order. For this the commander of the fort at Alexandrium was caught and tortured, since he had allowed the young men into his fort and helped them with the king's money. He did not admit to this, but his son came and brought a letter asking to enter the fort, which looked like Alexander's handwriting. Herod believed that his sons had plotted against him. But Alexander said that someone had faked his handwriting, and that Antipater was behind this. The scribe who did this was later found guilty of the same thing and was put to death.

Those who were tortured were brought to a crowd in Jericho. They were stoned to death. When the crowd wanted to kill Alexander and Aristobulus also, Ptolemy and Pheroras stopped them. Instead they were kept in jail and treated like condemned criminals. Aristobulus brought Salome, his aunt and mother-in-law, to help them. He said that she was also in danger, because she had told their plans to Sylleus when she was hoping to marry him. She immediately told this to her brother and he had the men bound and separated from each other. They were told to write down everything they had done against Herod and bring it to him. They wrote that they had not planned anything against their father, but that they had just wanted to leave and to live far away from accusations.

Melas, an ambassador from Cappadocia under Archelaus, came and Herod called for Alexander. Alexander, still in chains, said that he wished to go to Archelaus who had promised to send them to Rome. Herod then questioned Archelaus's daughter, Alexander's wife, to see if she was aware of Alexander's plot against his father. When she saw Alexander a prisoner, she beat her head and groaned. Alexander cried. They were unable to speak for a while. Ptolemy asked if his wife was aware of what he did. He said that he loved her more than his own soul and had children from her – how should she not know everything that he did? She said that she knew of no wicked plans, but if accusing herself falsely would save his life, she would do it. Alexander replied that he hadn't thought of any bad deed; they only intended to see Archelaus and then go on to Rome. Herod decided they were guilty, and he sent a letter to Archelaus saying that he had proven the accusations against them.

Meanwhile, Herod and Caesar were friends again, thanks to Nicolaus, who accused Sylleus before Caesar. Many of Obodas's friends were killed by Sylleus, partly because they had letters proving that Sylleus was guilty. Nicolaus said Sylleus lied about what had happened in Arabia. In the presence of Aretas's messengers, he said that Sylleus had killed King Obodas and other Arabians, he owed money, and he was guilty of adultery with Arabian and Roman women. Most important, he had turned Caesar against Herod by telling lies. Caesar stopped Nicolaus and asked him to explain about Herod, and prove that he had not led an army into Arabia, slain 2,500 men there, taken prisoners and ruined the country. Nicolaus answered that if any of this were true, Caesar should have been even angrier with Herod than he was. Caesar was listening, and Nicolaus said that there was a debt of 500 talents* due Herod, with a contract saying that when the time was up and the debt was not paid, part of the Arabian country could be taken for the debt. There was no army, only a group sent out to collect the money which was due. A promise had been given in Caesar's name that the money would be paid within 30 days, and that the robbers would be handed over, but Sylleus broke his promise. Herod's trip to Arabia was not a war. As for the robbers, they were from Trachonitis and were only forty in the beginning. They escaped Herod's punishment by running to Arabia. Sylleus received them and gave them food and received payment from their robberies. He promised Herod that he would deliver these men to justice. When the Arabians came against Herod's people and one or two died, only then Herod fought back in defense; their general and about 25 others fell. Sylleus counted every soldier as 100 soldiers and ended up with the report of 2,500.

Caesar looked at Sylleus in anger and asked him how many Arabians were killed, really. Sylleus said that he had been forced to lie. Nicolaus read out the records about the borrowed money, and letters from the presidents of Syria about the damage done in the cities by those robbers. Sylleus was condemned to die and Caesar was again friendly to Herod.

Caesar was still upset that Aretas had taken over the kingdom without his consent, since he had intended to give Arabia to Herod. After reading Herod's letter complaining about his sons, however, Caesar decided that Herod was too old to take over another country. He also had too many problems in his own family. Aretas's messengers were brought in, and in the end Aretas was confirmed as governor of Arabia.

xi

CAESAR wrote to Herod that he was sorry about Herod's sons behaving badly toward their father. He said they should be punished if they had plotted to kill him; but if they were only trying to leave, Herod should not be too hard on them. He told Herod to do whatever he thought best. He should gather an assembly near Berytus, a Roman city, and bring together the region's leaders to advise him what to do for their punishment.

Herod was happy that Caesar was again friends with him, and that he had complete control over his sons. Archelaus was not

invited to the court, because he might upset Herod's plans. His
sons were not there, but were in a city close by, in case he needed
to bring them. There were 150 judges present, and Herod read out
the confessions his sons had written, which he was sure proved
that they plotted against him. The letters only said that they had
planned to escape, and they had no plots to kill him. Herod told
the judges that in his land there was a law that if parents put their
hands on accused children, the bystanders were required to throw
stones at them and kill the children. Since the sons were not there
they could not defend themselves, and the judges gave Herod
the right to do what he thought best. Saturninus, who had been
a ruler, said that he condemned the behavior of Herod's sons but
that they should not be killed. He had three sons of his own, and
they agreed with their father. Volumnius's opinion was to kill
them. Herod left with his sons to Tyre, where Nicolaus met him.
Herod asked Nicolaus what his friends in Rome thought should
be done. He said that some felt the sons should be kept in prison,
but their punishment should be fair and not from anger. Most of
his friends in Rome felt that Herod should forgive them; otherwise his life would never get any better.

The main talk in Cesarea was Herod's sons. The people felt
sorry for them, but everyone worried about their own safety if
they should say the wrong thing out loud. Tero, an old soldier of
Herod's, had a son who had been Alexander's friend. Tero often
spoke out the truth without fear. He said loudly among the people that truth had died and that there was no justice; only lies and
misunderstandings. Tero was someone people listened to, because
he said what they were thinking.

Tero asked to speak to Herod alone and when he had the
chance he spoke very plainly. "You have done great things during your time, but isn't your soul empty? How can you kill your
queen's two sons who have succeeded in life? Do you want be left
alone in your old age? The very silence of all of the people should
speak to you. The whole army and officers are on the side of the
sons." The king was calm until Tero mentioned that Herod's army

favored his sons. Tero went too far and didn't know when to stop talking. So Herod had Tero and all those people he named arrested and put in prison.

Trypho, the king's barber, told Herod that Tero had tried to get him to cut Herod's throat, promising that he would be Alexander's friend and receive rewards from him. At this Herod gave an order to torture Tero, his son and the barber, which was done. Tero's son saw how badly his father was suffering and said he would tell the truth if Herod would let them both go free. The son said that Tero was willing to kill Herod by himself, and even if he would die for it he was willing, since it would be done as a favor to Alexander. No one was sure whether Tero's son said this because he was forced, or because he hoped to free his father from the torture.

Herod then had no doubt that his sons were guilty. He brought 300 officers who were accused of being against him, including Tero, his son and the barber before a large crowd. He accused them all, and the people stoned them to death. Alexander and Aristobulus were brought to Sebaste and strangled at Herod's command. Their dead bodies were taken at night to Alexandrium where their uncle on the mother's side and most of their ancestors were buried.

Who was to blame for this sad end – the father or the sons? How did the situation get past the point of no return? How could Herod be alone and immovable? Aren't all men accountable for their actions? The young men were vain and full of pride in their family line. But who can excuse Herod, who never saw concrete proof of their intentions to kill their father? The sons were handsome, charming, expert hunters and great soldiers. Alexander was the most outstanding. Couldn't they have just been sent away from their father, who was continually surrounded by his Roman soldiers who could have guarded the king? Herod had put off carrying out the murders time and again. He finally carried them out, which shows the evil of his heart. And in time, all of his best friends were killed as well.

BOOK XVII

FROM ALEXANDER AND ARISTOBULUS'S DEATH TO THE BANISHMENT OF ARCHELAUS

THE people hated Antipater more than ever, because of the part he had in getting his brothers killed. Even the soldiers who were responsible for guarding him hated him, and this was a bad situation for a king. Antipater still ruled along with Herod, but he was looking for a way to kill Herod and take the kingdom. He lived in fear that his father would find out that Antipater was only pretending to be protecting his father, and that he really hated Herod as much as his brothers. If Herod stayed alive, he could become a powerful enemy to Antipater. In order to make himself stronger, Antipater sent gifts to Herod's friends in Rome and especially to Saturninus, the president of Syria. He also gave rich presents to the brother of Saturninus and to Salome, the king's sister who had married one of Herod's best friends. He was able to fool the others that he was their friend, but Salome knew him too well and was not fooled. Even though they were related by marriage, she hated Antipater.

Herod cared for his two sons' children. Alexander had two sons by Glaphyra, and Aristobulus had three sons by Bernice (Salome's daughter) and two daughters. He paid for the best education for them. He also found good marriages for them with noble families. Herod promised a daughter of Aristobulus to another son of his by a high priest's daughter, also named Herod. (It was allowed for a man to have more than one wife.) Antipater hated these children as much as he hated his brothers. He argued against Herod's plans, and instead Antipater himself married Aristobulus's daughter, and his son marrying Pheroras's daughter. Herod went along with this but didn't really like it.

At this point Herod had nine wives. One of his wives was a Samaritan and she gave him three children.

ii

HEROD wanted to have stronger control of the Trachonites. He built a city for the Jews in the middle of the country in order to have a place to attack from. He heard that there was a Jew who had left Babylon who had 500 horsemen who could shoot arrows as they rode on horseback. He also had 100 in his family who had crossed the Euphrates and lived in Antioch where Saturninus ruled. He had given them a place called Valatha. Herod met this man and promised to give them all another place to live, tax-free. The leader agreed and built forts and a village, calling it Bathyra. The Jews continued to gather there, since they felt safe and they could offer sacrifices in Jerusalem. When Herod died and Philip became king, they had to pay small taxes for a while. Philip was followed by Agrippa the Great and his son who bothered them but didn't take their freedom. Then the Romans took heavy taxes from the people, but still let them be free. This Babylonian, Zamaris, died leaving honorable children behind him. One was named Jacim, who was an expert horseman. He trained a troop and they became guards of their leaders. His son Philip was outstanding and he became a good friend of King Agrippa. Philip's army was as strong as that of the king.

Antipater was the chief ruler at this time, and he was able to keep his wicked, secret plans from his father Herod. His friend Pheroras, Herod's brother, was very dedicated to his wife. Antipater kept women around him like guards, and the women of the family advised him and Pheroras. The two men pretended before

Herod to hate each other, but when they were alone they were very close and plotting against Herod together. Salome found out everything and told her brother about their true plans. He knew it was true, but he couldn't believe Salome because she had lied before.

The Pharisees were known for opposing kings. When all of the Jews had given their promise to obey Caesar and his government, more than 6,000 of these Pharisees refused; and when they were fined, Pheroras's wife paid their fine for them. These Pharisees claimed to see the future, that Herod's government would end and the kingdom would come to her and Pheroras. Salome heard about this and told Herod. He killed the Pharisees who were accused of giving the prophecy, including Bagoas the eunuch and Carus. He also killed all in his own family who believed that prophecy. Bagoas had been hoping for rewards from the future king, and a good marriage.

iii

HEROD blamed Pheroras's wife for fines that had not been paid by the Pharisees. He said she was also responsible for the problems between Herod and Pheroras. Herod told Pheroras to divorce her because his relationship as brother was more important. Pheroras said that he would die before he could do this, and Herod backed down. But Herod forbade Antipater and his mother to speak with Pheroras, and told the women that they could not meet together. But Pheroras and Antipater kept meeting secretly, and word went out that Antipater also been intimate with Pheroras's wife in a meeting arranged by Antipater's mother.

Antipater was afraid of his father and wrote to his friends in Rome, asking them to send for him to come to Caesar. Herod sent him with gifts and also his will, which stated that Antipater would be king after Herod died. If Antipater would die first, then his son, Herod Philip, would become the ruler. Sylleus the Arabian was in Rome also. He was accused by Antipater of the same crimes that Herod accused him of: he had killed many leading Arabians at Petra, and also Fabatus, a friend of Herod who had saved him from a plot. Sylleus had persuaded one of Herod's guards to kill the king by giving him a lot of money. When Fabatus heard about this, he told Herod who had the guard tortured until he confessed. The traitor and two others who were going to help were sent to Rome.

Pheroras and his wife were sent far away from Herod, and Pheroras promised that he would not come again until he heard that Herod was dead. But Herod wanted to see Pheroras as he had become ill, and he did come. Herod took care of Pheroras's funeral and had his body brought to Jerusalem and buried there. This was going to cause trouble for Antipater, who had already sailed for Rome. God would punish him for all of the murders he had done.

iv

AFTER the death and funeral of Pheroras, two of Pheroras's freed slaves came to Herod and told him that he needed to avenge his brother's death. They said that Pheroras had eaten with his wife the day before he became ill, and that a poison was put in his food. This poison had been brought from Arabia as a love potion, but the purpose was to kill Pheroras. Arabian women were skillful in making these poisons, and the woman who made it was a good friend of one of Sylleus's lovers. Both the mother and the sister of Pheroras's wife had been at her home, and had asked her to sell them this potion. The king was very angry and tortured the women slaves. No one confessed, until one who was tortured greatly prayed that God would send the same trouble on Antipater's mother who had caused them such misery. Herod increased the tortures until all of their secrets were revealed. So Antipater's hatred towards Herod was found out.

Herod had told Antipater to keep secret the gift of 100 talents* to him for not speaking at all with Pheroras, but the women knew about it. Antipater had also complained about how long Herod was living; he was getting old and now it was almost too late to be a king. If Antipater died, his brother was to be king instead of one of Antipater's children. Antipater had also accused the king of great cruelty and the slaughter of his sons. He feared for himself and this is why he wanted to go to Rome.

These confessions agreed with what Herod's sister had told him. Herod freed her from the accusation of being unfaithful to him. He punished Doris, Antipater's mother, took away all of her costly jewelry and sent her away. He became friends with Pheroras's women.

Herod was very upset to hear that Antipater had prepared a deadly poison and had given it to Pheroras. Pheroras was to poison Herod while Antipater was away, so no one would think that he was behind the act. One of Antipater's friends, Antiphilus, brought it from Egypt, and it passed through the hands of family members until it came to Pheroras, who gave it to his wife to keep. When the king asked her about it, she went to bring it, but instead she threw herself down from the top of the house. She did not die because she fell on her feet.

Herod said he would forgive her if she would tell him all the truth, but if she should hide anything she would truly suffer. She said that a physician had found the poison and that Antipater prepared it for Herod. But when Pheroras was ill and Herod came to take care of him, Pheroras felt terrible about the plot. She told Herod: "Pheroras was surprised that you loved him, and so he called me to him and said that Antipater was wicked to talk him into trying to murder his own brother. He understood that he was going to die from his sickness, so he told me to burn up the poison in front of him." His wife obeyed and burned most of his potion. She kept a little so that after Pheroras's death, if the king treated her badly, she could poison herself and escape suffering. At this she brought out the poison which was in a box.

Another brother of Antiphilus and his mother were also tortured and confessed that this box was the one which had been brought from Egypt. The high priest's daughter, the king's wife, was aware of all of this but kept quiet, so Herod divorced her and cut her son from his will. He also took the high priesthood from his father-in-law Simeon, and gave the job to Matthias the son of Theophilus, who was born in Jerusalem.

Bathyllus, Antipater's freed slave, came from Rome, and when he was tortured he confessed that he had another poison to give to Antipater's mother, in case the first one didn't kill Herod. There were letters from his friends in Rome, which they wrote as Antipater asked; these accused his brothers Archelaus and Philip as blaming their father for the deaths of Alexander and Aristobulus. The letters said these two were afraid that when they would leave Rome and return to Judea they would also be killed. Antipater also wrote to Herod and accused them of awful things, but then he said it wasn't their fault, since they were young. Antipater also wrote that he had been busy dealing with Sylleus. He bought presents for the leaders in Rome costing 200 talents*.

How did Antipater not know that for seven months there were great accusations against him in Judea? The reason was that the roads were heavily guarded, and that the men hated Antipater. No one cared to risk his life in order to warn him.

V

ANTIPATER wrote to his father Herod that he was on his way home. Herod hid his anger and wrote back to him not to delay. Herod made a little complaint about his mother but promised that he would not mention this when he came. Herod didn't want Antipater to suspect something was wrong and run away. Antipater heard about Pheroras's death, and he was sad – not because he liked Pheroras, but because he had died without keeping his promise to kill Herod. Some of his friends advised him to wait for more news; others said that he should go home right away in order to stop any suspicions against him. He sailed on and landed at Sebastus. No one greeted him.

Varus was in Jerusalem as he was to replace Saturninus as president of Syria; he came to advise Herod. Antipater came home when they were sitting together. He came dressed in purple. The door keepers let him in but kept his friends outside. He greeted his father and was pushed away. Herod called him a murderer of his brothers and one who wanted his father dead. Herod said Antipater would be judged the next day by Varus.

Varus and Herod, with their friends, family and Herod's sister Salome, all gathered to accuse Antipater. They had found a letter from his mother before it was sent; it said that his father knew all about his plots and that only Caesar could deliver him and her from his father's hands. Antipater fell down at his father's feet and wanted to be heard. Herod first complained about how he had suffered so much from his children, and now Antipater was causing him grief in his old age. He mentioned how he had given his children all that they needed, but in spite of this they were trying to take the kingdom from him instead of letting nature take its course. He wondered why Antipater was trying to kill him when he had already been named as the next king, and was receiving 50 talents* a year, besides another 30 for his journey to Rome.

Herod began to weep and could not speak, so Nicolaus of Damasacus, the king's friend who was his partner in all matters, spoke. He talked about Herod's goodness to Antipater, and the evidence against him. Antipater defended himself by naming all the honors he had given to his father. He had shown many times that he was protecting his father from plots against him. He already had half of the kingdom, so why would he ruin his chances by wanting the other half? He was the one who uncovered the plot of his brothers and brought about their punishment. The letters that accused him may have been forged. As for torturing people, it didn't necessarily bring out truth – people often said whatever would please the torturer in order to ease the suffering. He offered himself to be tortured.

Herod was affected by Antipater's weeping but tried to hide this. Nicolaus praised the king's good points, like how he had paid for the best education. They were young and had been ruined by the wrong advisors. They had tried to rise to power before they were ready. Antipater was like a serpent which could not be tamed. He was as guilty as his young brothers of barbaric behavior. "You pretended to love your father as you were getting rid of his sons. At one time you called him a wild beast and sent poisonous accusations around to members of his family in order to protect yourself. You say that those who were tortured have lied, yet you are willing to be tortured yourself. Antipater, you are the bloodiest butcher of all."

Nicolaus added a summary of his mother's gossip about predictions and sacrifices relating to Herod. Besides the information gotten by torture against Antipater, some of his friends became his accusers because they were afraid that they would be punished if they kept quiet. Also Antipater was not kind to his friends, and they felt he deserved to be hated. Many people in the audience who had kept quiet out of fear now spoke against Antipater – not to make friends with Herod, but because they knew the truth and didn't owe Antipater any favors.

Antipater's turn came to defend himself. He fell on his face and appealed to God, saying he was innocent and that God would show a sign. Up to now he had acted if there was no god in the world, but now suddenly he expected God to defend him against the accusations. Varus asked that the poison be brought before the court to see if it still worked. One person who was sentenced to die was told to drink it, and he died right away. Varus left the court and the following day went to his home in Antioch.

Antipater was put in chains, and Herod sent letters to Rome to Caesar about him. Antipater got a letter from Egypt from Antiphilus, which the king opened. It was wishing him success and said another letter was sent with it. The king asked about the other letter, but the slave of Antiphilus said that he never saw it. One of Herod's friends saw the slave hiding the second letter in his inside coat of the slave. The king opened the other letter. This one was from Acme, the servant of Julia, Caesar's wife. She wrote about a fake letter from Herod's sister Salome, which made it sound like she was plotting against Herod. Antipater had written it himself. Acme was a friend of Antipater because she had received lots of money from him. This was proof of Antipater's wicked plots against his father and his aunt.

Herod was amazed and was ready to have Antipater killed immediately. He was not only plotting against his father but also against his sister. He was also ruining Caesar's servants. Salome beat her chest and told Herod to kill her if he really believed that she was guilty. Antipater could not say anything for himself when Herod questioned him. Herod wanted to send him to Caesar in Rome, but he changed his mind thinking that Antipater might escape. He sent more messengers and letters to Rome, this time writing about Acme's part in the plot.

vi

HEROD'S messengers hurried to Rome to tell Caesar about what had happened. They had all of the letters with them. Herod became very sick and he wrote his will. He passed the kingdom to Antipas his youngest son, since he hated Archelaus and Philip (who had been accused by Antipater). He gave 1000 talents* to Caesar, 500 to Caesar's wife Julia, his children and friends. He divided up more money, income and lands among his sons and grandsons. Salome, his sister became very rich, since she had remained faithful to him. Herod was now seventy years old. He would often go into a rage because he felt that people were happy about his misery. There was also an uprising.

Two Jewish men who spoke well and were popular with the people were teaching every day. They knew the Jewish law well after studying it all their lives. When they heard that Herod had a fatal disease, they urged the people to tear down everything which Herod had built contrary to Jewish laws. It was because he had broken the law that he now had this horrible, rare sickness. They pointed out the large, very costly golden eagle which Herod had placed over the gate of the temple. It should be taken down, they said. It didn't matter if those doing it would be killed, since they would be honored for years to come because they were brave for the sake of their beliefs.

A report came that Herod was dead, so in the middle of the day a crowd pulled the eagle down and cut it into pieces with axes. Many people were in the temple. The king's captain came with many soldiers, and they caught 40 young men who didn't try to escape. Herod [who was still alive] asked how they had dared to pull down something which had been dedicated to God. They answered that they put Moses's laws above the king's commands, and that they were willing to suffer punishment or death for these beliefs. Herod ordered that they be bound and they were sent to Jericho. The people were gathered in a theatre and Herod lay on a couch since he could not stand. He bragged about how he had made the temple beautiful, and that in the 125 years that the Asamoneans had been ruling, they had not been able to honor God with any project like his. He had given valuable treasures to the temple and wanted to be remembered for it. He cried out that these men had insulted him in the daytime, in the sight of everyone, by falling on the eagle and destroying it. But they also had insulted God.

The crowd felt that the young men should be punished, but nothing more. Herod took away the high priesthood from Matthias and appointed Joazar, Matthias's wife's brother in his place. Herod burned Matthias and his companions, and there was an eclipse of the moon that night.

Herod's disease gave him an endless appetite. He had pain in his colon and his feet were very swollen with fluid. It was so awful it seemed to be God's judgment. His male organ was rotting and full of worms, and he had a hard time breathing. His bad breath was made worse by vomiting. He was shaking in all parts of his body. He sent for doctors and was willing to try whatever they advised. He even went beyond the River Jordan to bathe in warm baths in Callirrhoe. One could also drink the water. This water runs into Lake Asphaltitis [the Dead Sea]. At one point he took a bath in oil and he was better for a time. He gave 50 drachmae* to every soldier and their commanders and his friends, since he thought he was nearing the end. He came to Jericho and called all the leaders of the Jews to come to him. Those who refused would be put to death. They were all shut up in the theatre. He sent for his sister Salome and her husband Alexas, and said that he would die in a short time since he was in a lot of pain. He was afraid that the people would not be sad about his death or honor him like a king. The Jews had already tried to rebel and they ruined the donations he had dedicated to God. So he commanded that when he died, before anyone should hear about his death, all the leading Jews held prisoner in the theatre were to be killed with darts by his soldiers. This way he would be properly mourned by the whole nation, rather than people making fun of him. His sister and her husband promised to carry out what he requested. This showed Herod's great wickedness: he commanded that one person from every family should be killed, even though they were innocent. Normally, people who are dying try to do one last good deed.

vii

AS Herod was giving commands to his family, the messengers returned from Rome with letters from Caesar. Acme had been killed by Caesar since she had joined Antipater's wicked plot. Caesar said that Herod could either banish Antipater or kill him, whichever he decided was best. Herod felt better after hearing this news. He became faint and asked for an apple and a knife. He looked around and thought to stab himself, but his cousin stopped him and cried for help. Many thought the cry meant that Herod was dead. Antipater thought if Herod was dead he could be freed from prison and take over the kingdom. He asked the jailor to let him go, promising him great things. The jailer would not listen to him; instead he told the king. Herod heard from the jailer of many plans which Antipater had against him, and he beat his head although he was already almost dead. He raised himself on his elbow and sent for the guards ordering them to kill Antipater right away, and to bury him in a careless way in Hyrcania.

HEROD then changed his will, making Archelaus king of Judea. Galilee and Berea would be ruled by Antipas. Gaulonitis, Trachonitis and Paneas were given to his son Philip. His sister Salome received Jamnia, Ashdod and Phasaelis along with 500,000 drachmae* of silver. He gave much money and income to other family members. He gave Caesar ten million drachmae* of coined money as well as gold and silver vessels. Julia, Caesar's wife, received costly clothing. Herod died five days after Antipater was killed. He had behaved in a barbaric way towards everyone and was a slave to his anger. But he was very lucky as a common man who had become a king. He escaped 10,000 dangers and lived until a very old age. He thought he was fortunate with his family, but in my opinion [J Flavius] he was very unfortunate.

Salome and Alexas opened the theatre and told the leaders that Herod had told them to go to their own lands and continue to care for their own affairs. Herod's death was made public. They gathered all of the soldiers in the amphitheatre in Jericho, and they read Herod's letter to them thanking them for their faithfulness to him and asking them to be loyal to his son Archelaus as king. After this Ptolemy read the king's will and Archelaus came forward. The soldiers came by groups with their commanders and promised to serve him and prayed for God's blessing on him.

When this was over, they prepared for Herod's funeral. Archelaus brought out many ornaments. The body was carried on a golden couch set with lots of very precious stones. It was covered with purple as well as the body itself. Herod had a gold crown on his head and a scepter in his right hand. His sons and many family members walked alongside, followed by soldiers from different countries. The guards went first, followed by the Thracians, the Germans, the Galatians and the rest in their battle uniforms. His servants carried spices. They walked eight furlongs* to Herodium, since that is where he said he was to be buried. It is said that it must have taken at least 25 days for them to arrive there. Archelaus and the people mourned Herod for seven days as the custom is in the Jewish law. Archelaus gave the people gifts and went into the temple. The people praised him loudly wherever he went, even trying to outdo each other. He took a very high seat on a gold throne and spoke nicely to the people. He was thankful that they did not remember the harm his father had caused them. He asked them not to call him king yet. Caesar needed to confirm the will and this was why he had refused to be crowned at Jericho.

Seeing that Archelaus was being kind, the people started asking for things. Some asked for lower taxes. Others asked him to release people who Herod had imprisoned. Others wanted him to cancel taxes on items sold and bought. Archelaus agreed to all of these requests in order to make his kingdom quiet. He offered a sacrifice to God and then went to feast with his friends.

ix

THE Jews were angry about the death of Matthias and his friends whom Herod had killed for pulling down the golden eagle from the temple. At the time the people were too afraid of Herod even to mourn for them. They got together and asked Archelaus to get revenge for them and punish those whom Herod had honored. They also asked that another high priest be chosen to replace Herod's choice, one who was stronger in the Jewish beliefs and more pure. Archelaus sent a general to speak for him. He was to agree to this request but explain that Archelaus needed to go right away to Rome in order for Caesar to approve him as king. The people needed to wait on these issues so that they would not be accused of causing trouble. After all, their friends had been killed lawfully for their crime.

Archelaus sent the general, but the Jews would not allow him to speak, and they were so angry he was afraid for his life. They were very upset that their loved ones had been killed and the killers had never been punished while Herod was alive. Archelaus sent others to speak to them, but they wouldn't listen to anyone. A rebellion was forming.

The feast of Passover was coming when there would be many sacrifices offered. Many Jews would be gathering, even from far away. The rebels were mourning for Judas and Matthias. There was no lack of food. Archelaus was afraid of a rebellion so he sent a regiment of soldiers together with a captain of a thousand to keep order. The people attacked the soldiers by stoning most of them. Some ran away wounded, including the captain. The people went back to their sacrifices. Archelaus sent the whole army out against the people this time, along with horsemen, with the orders to kill those inside and outside the city who tried to escape. At least 3000 were killed while some escaped to the mountains. Archelaus sent the crowds home before the end of the festival.

Archelaus, his mother, Nicolaus and Ptolemy and many friends went to the seaside, leaving Philip his brother in charge. They also had Salome, Herod's sister and her children and family with them, who pretended to help Archelaus but they were secretly against him for what he had done in the temple. Sabinus, Caesar's steward of Syrian matters, and Varus, president of Syria, met with Archelaus in Cesarea. Sabinus let Archelaus keep Herod's treasures until Caesar would decide what to do with them. But after Archelaus sailed for Rome, Sabinus went to Jerusalem and took over the king's palace. He required the servants to give him a list of all Herod's possessions, and he gave orders about the things in the castles as he saw fit. But the servants obeyed Archelaus and kept everything as it was; they said it was all being kept for Caesar.

Antipas, another son of Herod, sailed to Rome at this time in order to take the kingdom. His mother Salome told him that he was far more fit to rule, and he had been chosen as the next king in Herod's earlier will, which was more valid than the present one. Antipas brought his mother to Rome with him and Ptolemy the brother of Nicolaus, who had been Herod's best friend. Irenaeus the orator encouraged him as well. He had support from some relatives who hated Archelaus. They really wanted to be under Roman rule, but if the people would not accept this, they would prefer Antipas over Archelaus. Sabinus also accused Archelaus to Caesar in letters.

Archelaus had sent the official papers to Caesar which presented his right to the kingdom, his father's will, the accounts of Herod's money and Herod's seal which Ptolemy brought. After Caesar had read these papers, along with Varus's and Sabinus's letters, he saw that Antipas also had letters to claim the kingdom. Caesar gathered his friends together as well as Caius and Julia, the son and daughter of Agrippa whom he had adopted, to hear their opinion. Antipater, Salome's son was a very good speaker and a bitter enemy to Archelaus. He said that it was ridiculous for Archelaus to ask for the kingdom since he had already taken it before Caesar had given it to him. He said that Archelaus had killed many people at the Jewish festival, and this was not authorized by Caesar. If he was acting as a common man, this was a great crime. He had replaced many army commanders and ruled in lawsuits before he had the right. He had released prisoners who had been held in the Hippodrome, and other things which a young person would do out of a desire to be a king. He was also charged with not mourning for his father and with having parties the very night of Herod's death, ignoring all of the benefits he had received from his father. In the daytime he pretended to be sad, but like an actor on the stage; at night he celebrated his victory in taking over the kingdom. He danced and sang as if an enemy had fallen. The greatest offense was what he did in the temple, killing thousands of worshipers were as if they were sacrifices, and some of them were foreigners. The temple was full of dead bodies, not because of a stranger but rather the king of that land. Herod his father knew Archelaus was a wicked man, and when Herod was in his right mind he had not chosen him to rule, but rather Antipas. His father had only changed the will when he was dying, and then he was sick in his mind as well.

Antipater brought witnesses from among Archelaus's own relations, who also spoke against him. Then Nicholaus began his defense of Archelaus. He blamed the killing in the temple on those people themselves for resisting the authority of Archelaus. They had been opposing the authority of Caesar himself by attacking those who were sent by Archelaus to keep order. Such people did not have respect for God or the festival, and they only wanted to hurt Archelaus. They were forcing those who came to punish them to defend themselves. Archelaus had been chosen by Herod, and it was wrong to accuse Herod as a madman. Nicholas was sure that Caesar would not oppose Herod's last will, since Caesar's virtues and righteousness were known around the world. He would not refuse the wishes of Herod, a man Caesar had shared his power with. Herod had given the kingdom to a good son, who had come to Caesar himself to confirm it.

After hearing this, Caesar felt so warm towards Archelaus that he raised him up after he had fallen down at his feet. He said that Archelaus deserved the kingdom and that he would honor Herod's last will. Caesar gave his word that Archelaus could depend on him, but he would make his final decision later. Caesar was wondering to himself whether Archelaus should be king, or whether he should divide the kingdom up among all Herod's sons.

X

MEANWHILE Archelaus's mother, Malthace became ill and died. Letters came from Varus, the president of Syria, informing Caesar of a revolt by the Jews while Archelaus was away. Varus had to stop them by punishing the leaders. He then left for Antioch, leaving one legion of his army to keep order in Jerusalem. This did not help, since Caesar's representative Sabinus continued to upset the Jews. He used some of the Roman legion as guards to take over the forts by force and search for the king's money, in order to take it for himself.

When Pentecost arrived, tens of thousands of men got together in Jerusalem, not only for the feast but because of the evil of Sabinus. There were many Galileans, Idumeans, those from Jericho and others who had crossed the Jordan. They organized themselves into three groups in order to attack Sabinus. Some surrounded the Hippodrome, some were on the northeast side of the temple, and the third group held the western part of the city where the king's palace was. They intended to trap the Romans from all sides. Sabinus was afraid and sent a letter to Varus crying for help. He went up to the highest tower of the fortress of Phasaelus, built in honor of King Herod's brother. Sabinus gave a signal to the Romans to attack the Jews. It was a terrible slaughter. The Jews got up on the roof which surrounded the outer court of the temple and threw stones at the Romans, both with their hands and with slings, something they were good at. The Roman archers were not able to hit them; they were below, so when they sent up arrows they did not reach the Jews. The Romans decided set fire to the courtyard roof while those standing there could not see it. The wood on the roof was full of tar and wax which burned easily, and the gold covering was attached with wax as well. The whole huge and costly roof was destroyed together with the people. Some fell to their death when the roof fell down, and others were killed by their enemies. Some even threw themselves into the fire or onto their own swords to escape the Romans. All those who tried to run were killed by the Romans because they no longer had weapons. The Romans ran through the fire and took the treasure which included the sacred money. The soldiers got most of it, and Sabinus got 400 talents*.

The Jews were very upset about the death and also the stolen money. The rebels who were left surrounded the palace and intended to set fire to it and kill all those inside. They offered a promise to anyone who surrendered that they would not be hurt, and most of the king's soldiers came out. Rufus and Gratus, who had 3,000 of Herod's most warlike soldiers with them, went over to the Romans. The Jews continued the siege and dug tunnels under the palace walls, warning the others not to stop them – they were hoping to make the country free again. Sabinus wanted to leave, but he was afraid of the Jews after all the bad things he had done. So he put up with the siege, expecting that Varus would return.

There were 10,000 other rebellions going on in Judea at the same time.

Some 2,000 of Herod's old soldiers got together in Judea to fight against the king's soldiers. Judas, who was the son of a leader of robbers, gathered wicked men and attacked the palace in Sepphoris; he took the money and weapons, arming his men with them. He destroyed all who came his way, just to prove that he should be given a chance to rule - not because he was a skillful warrior, but because he was so cruel.

Simon, who had been Herod's slave, was tall and handsome; he put a crown on his head and had a few followers. He burned down the royal palace in Jericho and stole everything. He set fire to many of the king's houses around the country, completely destroying them. He gave things away to others, and he would have continued to destroy if he had not been stopped. Gratus took some Roman soldiers and met Simon in battle. Simon's soldiers fought hard but without skill. Simon escaped through a certain valley, but Gratus found him and cut off his head. The royal palace at Amathus by the Jordan was burned down by Simon's group and others.

Things were out of control in the nation, since there was no king to keep order. The foreigners who tried to stop them only added to the Jews' anger.

Athronges was a shepherd and unknown, but because he was tall and had strong hands he made himself king. He had four tall brothers and each of these men had a group of followers who obeyed them as commanders and made them powerful. Many Romans and the king's soldiers were killed, since these men hated both sides. Some were killing people out of habit, while others wanted to gain something, but they became more and more cruel. Once they attacked some Romans at Emmaus who were bringing corn and weapons to the army. They killed the centurion Arius and forty of his best foot soldiers. The Romans were afraid and ran away, escaping with the help of Gratus who was in the area. These four brothers caused trouble to the Romans but also to their own people. They were finally stopped, one of them in a fight with Gratus and another with Ptolemy. Archelaus took the oldest one prisoner, and the youngest had no choice but to surrender to Archelaus since his army was sick and weak from overwork. Archelaus promised to save him alive.

So Judea was full of robbers, with each group looking for a leader to be like a king to them. They bothered the Romans in a small way, but they murdered their own people for a long time.

Varus heard about all this from Sabinus, and he feared for his soldiers who were left there. He took two other legions (there were a total of three legions in Syria), four troops of horsemen and other soldiers, and he headed for Judea. Another 1500 men from Berytus, a city they were passing through, joined the legion. Aretas, the king of Arabia Petrea, out of his hatred to Herod and in order to gain the favor of the Romans, also sent soldiers. Part of the soldiers went with Varus's son to Galilee near Ptolemais, where they attacked the enemy and took Sepphoris, making slaves of the people and burning the city. Varus continued with his army to Samaria and camped at Arus, which the Arabians burned out of their hatred for Herod. Then they arrived at another village which the Arabians also burnt and spoiled, even though it was strongly defended. Everywhere they went, the towns were destroyed by fire and filled with the dead. Emmaus was burned by Varus's order. When Varus came with his army to Jerusalem, the Jews there said that it was strangers who were responsible for the war, and that they had been on the side of the Romans. Joseph the cousin of King Herod, together with Gratus and Rufus and their soldiers, met Varus. Sabinus did not come to meet Varus; he left the city quietly and went to the seaside.

Varus sent soldiers to capture those who had led the revolt, and some of the most guilty ones were punished. Around 2000 were crucified. He dismissed his soldiers since they were no help to him; they were not disciplined and only wanted to find loot. He heard that 10,000 Jews had gotten together and he meant to capture them, but on the advice of Achiabus they surrendered to

Varus. Varus forgave the whole group for the crime of revolting, but he sent several commanders to Caesar. Many of these Caesar sent home, except for several relatives of Herod who were involved in the war. They were punished because they had fought against their own relatives.

VARUS set things right in Jerusalem and set his former legion there, and he returned to Antioch. Archelaus was having problems in Rome with messengers sent by the Jews to Rome at the permission of Varus, in order to ask for more freedom to live as Jews. There were 50 Jews sent, and there were 8,000 Jews in Rome already. Caesar gathered his friends and the leading Romans in the temple of Apollo, which he had built at great cost. Archelaus came, but several of his relatives did not come because they hated him. Philip came at Varus's urging to help his brother Archelaus, since Varus was his good friend.

The Jews accused Herod of having been a terrible and cruel king. Many of their people had been killed due to his tyranny, and those who survived were more miserable than those who had died. They were in danger of losing even their homes. He improved cities but foreigners came to live in them. When he began ruling, the nation was rich; now it was poor. He took away the houses of important men whom he had killed. He took gifts for himself and his friends, and everyone had to pay money to live in peace. Young virgins were abused and wives were accused of being unfaithful whether it was true or not. Herod had behaved like a wild beast. "We have gone through many changes in our history, including abuses, but Herod's rule was the worst suffering ever for our nation."

They said they had been ready to welcome Archelaus, since anyone would be nicer by far than Herod. They had joined with him in mourning his father in order to please him. But, they said, Archelaus seemed eager to show that he was just like Herod, even before Caesar had made the decision regarding the next king.

When Archelaus killed 3000 of his own countrymen at the temple, how could they not hate him? They wanted Caesar to add them to the government of Syria, under the authority of a president and not a king. They would show Rome that they were not rebels; they could behave in an orderly manner if they were ruled by a moderate leader.

After the Jews had spoken, Nicolaus stood up for the two kings. He said that Herod had never been accused of these crimes in his lifetime, and that it wasn't right to accuse him now that he was dead. He said that Archelaus was not to blame – the Jews had brought the punishment on themselves for not obeying the laws, but rather wanting to be above them.

Caesar ended the meeting. A few days later he made Archelaus ruler over half of the area which Herod had ruled. Caesar said he would be made king if he showed that he could govern that part wisely. The other half was divided between Herod's other two sons, Philip and Antipas. Antipas (who had asked to rule the whole kingdom) received Perea and Galilee, and received 200 talents* a year in taxes. Philip was to receive 100 talents* from the part he ruled. Archelaus would be paid taxes of 600 talents*. from Idumea, Judea and Samaria; but Caesar lowered taxes by one fourth for the people who had not joined the revolt.

Herod's sons received a large amount from their father's inheritance. Salome received from her brother 500,000 drachmae* of coined silver. Caesar also gave her a palace in Askelon. Altogether she received 60 talents* yearly. She lived within Archelaus's territory. The rest of Herod's family received what he had written in the will. Caesar gave a present to two of Herod's unmarried daughters, besides what their father had left them (which was 250,000 drachmae* of silver), and Caesar married them off to Pheroras's sons. He gave the 1500 talents* that Herod had willed to him to the king's sons, and he kept only a few items which were reminders for him of the king.

AFTER Caesar had settled who was to rule what, a certain young Jew who had been brought up by a Roman citizen in Sidon claimed to be Alexander the son of Herod. Many people had told him that he looked like Alexander, which gave him ambition to play the part, so he found a mentor who had known the real Alexander, but was otherwise an evil man. This man invented a story that when Herod gave the order to kill Alexander, he was hidden away and someone else was killed in his place. Supposedly Aristobulus had also escaped death. In Crete, this man convinced all the Jews that he was Alexander. He received a lot of money from them. In Melos they also believed him, and gave him money in hopes that as part of the royal family he would give them something in return. He fooled many others along the way, and they paid for his trip to Rome. He arrived in Rome accompanied by a crowd of supporters. Many Jews said that it was God's will that he had miraculously escaped death, and they were happy for his mother's family. When he arrived he was carried through the streets on a royal platform with many decorations. The crowd gathered around him and shouted their praises.

When Caesar heard about this he did not believe it, since it would have been hard to fool Herod about it. He asked his servant, who had known the real Alexander, to bring him to Caesar, but the servant was no more certain than the others. Then Caesar saw that this Alexander had the rough hands and strong body of a worker, not the soft body which the true Alexander had from his pampered life. He asked "Alexander" about Aristobulus. If they were hidden away together, where was he? The clever boy said that his "brother" had remained in Crete so that the children of Mariamne might not be lost if there should be any accident at sea. Then Caesar took him aside and asked who he really was, and who had taught him this story. He told Caesar the truth, and Caesar allowed him to row with the seamen since he was strong, but he killed the one who had convinced him to be an imposter. As for the people of Melos, Caesar felt it was punishment enough that they had thrown away so much money on this false Alexander.

WHEN Archelaus began ruling in Judea, he accused the high priest Joazar of helping the rebellion. He took the high priesthood away from him and put his brother Eleazar in his place. Archelaus also rebuilt the royal palace at Jericho at great cost and diverted half of the water from the village of Neara onto the valley in order to water palm trees which he had planted. He also built a village which he called Archelais by his own name. He broke the Jewish law and married Glaphyra, the daughter of Archelaus who had been the wife of his brother Alexander, by whom she had three children. It was not acceptable among the Jews to marry a brother's wife. Eleazar was soon replaced by Jesus, the son of Sie.

After Archelaus had ruled ten years, the leaders of Judea and Samaria accused him before Caesar. Caesar had told him to rule with moderation but he had become a tyrant. Caesar was angry and called for Archelaus's steward, who was also named Archelaus, and ordered him to Judea to bring Archelaus back with him to Rome. When he arrived in Judea he found Archelaus feasting with his friends. He took him away to Rome, and after hearing accusations against him, Caesar sent him away to Vienna, a city of Gaul, and took his money from him.

Before Archelaus left for Rome, he had a dream which he told to his friends. He saw 10 ears of perfectly ripe corn which were eaten by oxen. He sent for someone to interpret it, since he felt it was very important, but the interpretations did not agree. Then Simon of the Essens asked to give his interpretation. He said that the oxen meant that he would suffer, and that his affairs would change in the way that land ploughed by oxen changes. The ten ears of corn represented years, since an ear of corn grows in one year. The message was that his rule was over. On the fifth day after this dream, the other Archelaus arrived to bring him to Rome, where the dream came true.

Archelaus's wife, Glaphyra, also had a dream that came true. She had been married to Alexander the son of Herod, and after Alexander's death she was married to Juba the king of Libya. After he died, she lived as a widow in Cappadocia with her father. Archelaus divorced his wife Mariamne in order to marry Glaphyra. And during that time, she had this dream. She thought she saw Alexander sitting next to her, and she hugged him warmly, but he complained and said that women can't be trusted. "Didn't you marry me when you were a virgin? And didn't we have children together? But you forgot my love since you wanted a second husband. Even worse, you were married a third time – to Archelaus your husband and my brother. But I will not forget your love for me, and you can be mine again." She told this to her friends and then died within a few days.

I [Josephus] wrote about these events since I am writing about kings, but it shows that the soul lives on after death, and that God watches over human affairs. If someone doesn't choose to believe this, fine, but don't let him stand in the way of another who would be convinced by these stories to live a life of virtue. Archelaus's country was joined with the province of Syria. Cyrenius, who had been a governor, was sent by Caesar to manage Syria and to sell the house of Archelaus.

BOOK XVIII

FROM THE BANISHMENT OF ARCHELAUS TO THE DEPARTURE OF THE JEWS FROM BABYLON

i

CYRENIUS, a Roman senator who had held other important jobs in the Roman government, came to Syria with some others, sent by Caesar to be a judge there and to check on money matters. Coponius was to be governor of the Jews. Cyrenius visited Judea which was to be ruled with Syria, to see how money would be used there. The high priest, Joazar son of Boethus, told the Jews not to object to giving the Romans this information, even though it meant being taxed. But Judas of Gamala, together with a Sadduc and a Pharisee, tried to cause a revolt against the tax, complaining that they were being treated as slaves. The trouble which they started became worse and worse, turning into a violent war. Many Jews were killed, robbers increased and Jewish leaders were killed. There was also a famine at this time. Entire cities were ruined, and the temple was burned down. Judas and Sadduc formed a sect and had many followers, particularly young people.

By this time the Jews already had three sects: the Essens, the Sadducees and the Pharisees. The Pharisees ate simply and showed respect for the elderly, never disagreeing with them. They believed that man has a free will to do right or wrong. The soul lives on after death, and rewards in the next life will be based on how they chose to live. The wicked would be held in an everlasting prison.The Pharisees were respected leaders in their communities, and the people obeyed them in matters of worship, prayers and sacrifices.

The Sadducees believed that the souls die with the bodies. They saw it as a virtue to argue about issues with their teachers. The greatest leaders held this view but not many others; most people followed the Pharisees. When the Sadducees wanted to lead the people, they were forced into saying the same as the Pharisees, so as not to lose their standing in the eyes of the people.

The Essens taught that the soul would live forever. One must be righteous in order to gain the rewards. They did not offer sacrifices in the temple because they offered their own sacrifices somewhere else; so they were not allowed in the court of the common people. They had a good life and spent a lot of time farming. Neither Greeks nor barbarians were able to live as righteously for as many years as the Essens did. They had everything in common so that no one was rich, nor was anyone poor. There were about 4,000 of a special group of men who didn't marry or keep servants. They took care of one another. They collected what came from their farms and turned it over to trustworthy men and priests who prepared corn and other food for them.

The fourth sect, led by Judas of Gamala, was like that of the Pharisees, except that they loved their freedom most of all. They said that God was their only ruler and Lord. They did not care about their own death, or the death of relatives and friends; nothing would make them call anyone Lord. In the days of Florus, this sect went wild and grew strong across the nation, because Florus abused his authority and made them rebel.

ii

CYRENIUS finished taxing the people and handing over Archelaus's money. He took the high priesthood away from Joazar, whom most of the people liked, and replaced him with Ananus, son of Seth. Herod [one of Herod's sons was also called Herod] and Philip were governing in their areas. Herod built a wall around Sepphoris, the main city in the Galilee and the strongest. He also built a wall around the city of Julias, named after the emperor's wife. Philip built Paneas at a source of the Jordan and called it Cesarea. He also built up Bethsaida which was at Lake Gennesareth. He later called it Julias, the name of Caesar's daughter.

Coponius, governor of Judea had come with Cyrenius. As the Jews were celebrating Passover at the temple, it was traditional for the priests to open the temple gates just after midnight. Some Samaritans secretly entered Jerusalem and threw dead men's bodies into the courtyards. After this the Samaritans were forbidden ever to enter the temple, and the Jews guarded the gates more carefully. Then Coponius returned to Rome and Marcus Ambivius took his place. After Salome, Herod's sister died, Caesar's wife Julia took over Jamnia, Phasaelis in the valley, and Archelaus where many palm trees grew. Annius Rufus was the next governor; he served under the second emperor of the Romans who reigned for 57 ½ years. The third emperor was Tiberius Nero, Julia's son, and he sent Valerius Gratus to rule Judea. Gratus replaced Ananus the high priest with Ismael son of Phabi. After a short time Eleazar, son of Ananus, was high priest for a year. Simon was then given the priesthood for one year, followed by Joseph Caiaphas. Gratus returned to Rome after serving in Judea eleven years. He was replaced by Pontius Pilate.

Herod built Tiberias in the best part of Galilee at the lake of Gennesareth. There were warm baths close by in a village called Emmaus. Strangers came and lived in this city as well as Galileans. Some people were forced by Herod to live there, including poor people and slaves. Herod freed the slaves and encouraged everyone to stay by building them nice houses from his own money. He also gave them land. He needed to convince people to live there because many graves were there, which were taken away to make room for Tiberias. This was against Jewish law; after touching graves the inhabitants would be unclean for seven days.

Phraates, king of the Parthians died because of his illegitimate son. Julius Caesar had sent an Italian maidservant to Phraates, Thermusa. She was beautiful and became his concubine. When she gave him a son, Phraataces, he married her. She could convince him to do anything, and she wanted her son to rule Parthia. She needed to get rid of the legitimate sons first, so she persuaded Phraates to send them to Rome, and he agreed. Then Phraataces together with his mother (whom he also slept with) plotted to kill his father. The people were angry, since both sins were equally evil, and they rebelled and sent him out of the country. He later died.

The Parthian leaders realized that they needed a king and they would only accept a man from the family of Arsaces (especially after the trouble with the Italian concubine). They called Orodes to be their king, even though the man was cruel and had a temper. The people plotted against him and killed him, either at a celebration while offering sacrifices or on a hunting trip. They sent messengers to Rome and asked Caesar to send them a son of Phraates as a king. Vonones was sent since he was considered the best. But the lawless Parthians soon changed their minds and decided that Vonones had been a slave in Rome (they could not bear the idea). So they invited Artabanus, king of Media, to be their king since he was also from the line of Arsaces. He agreed and came to them with an army. Vonones met him to fight for the throne. The Parthians stood on his side and the army was gathered for battle, but Artabanus was beaten and fled to the mountains of Media. Shortly afterwards he gathered a large army and again fought with Vonones, and this time Artabanus beat him. Vonones fled on horseback with some of his men to Selucia on the Tigris River. After Artabanus had killed many people he ruled over the Parthians. Vonones went to Armenia and wanted to rule there, so he sent messengers to Rome asking to be made king. Tiberias refused. Vonones was not a brave man, and the Parthian king threatened him, so he surrendered to the Syrian president, who allowed him to stay there since he had been educated in

Rome. Artabanus gave Armenia to Orodes, one of his own sons. Antiochus the king of Commagene died, and the people asked to become a Roman province. The senate needed to decide who the new leader would be, and they sent Germanicus. But the people formed a plot to kill him; after Germanicus had settled various matters Piso poisoned him.

PILATE the governor of Judea moved his army from Cesarea to Jerusalem for the winter. He wanted to cancel the Jewish laws by bringing images of Caesar on the Roman banners into the city. He did it purposely at night so the people would not know it. When the Jews saw the images, crowds of them came to Cesarea to beg him to take them away. He refused, but they kept coming back every day. On the sixth day, Pilate again came to his judgment seat which was in an open area in the city. The army was standing nearby but hidden. As they started again with their request, Pilate gave a signal and the army came out of hiding. He told them they would die right then if they did not leave. They threw themselves on the ground and said they would rather die than have to give up their beliefs which were against any images. With this Pilate was moved, and ordered that the images be returned to Cesarea.

With holy money belonging to the temple Pilate built a water conduit to Jerusalem which was 200 furlongs* long. But 10,000s of people were upset about this and yelled insults at him. He sent his soldiers into the crowd with daggers under their clothes to threaten them. They kept yelling, so at a certain signal from Pilate the soldiers attacked them. But the soldiers were more cruel than Pilate had intended; they attacked those who were yelling and those who were quiet, and many died. Some ran away wounded. In this way the revolt was put down.

Jesus, a wise man (he can be called a man, since he did miracles) was teaching those who liked to hear truth. He gained support from many Jews and Gentiles. He was the Christ and Pilate condemned him to be crucified as suggested by the Jewish leaders. His followers who loved him were together with him, since he appeared alive to them after having been dead three days. The Jewish prophets had foretold this and 10,000 other wonderful things regarding Jesus. As of this writing the Christians, so named because they are followers of Christ, are still alive.

At this time another disaster upset the Jews. But first I must tell about the evil done in the temple of Isis. There was a woman in Rome, Paulina, who was righteous and also very rich. She was modest but beautiful and was married to Saturninus, also a good man. Decius Mundus fell in love with her, a horseman high in the ranks. She rejected his many presents, which only made him want her more. He offered her 200,000 Attic drachmae* for only one night with her. When she refused, he decided he would starve himself to death. Mundus had a common woman for a friend, Ide, who had been freed by his father. She was upset at how he was punishing himself, and she gave him hope that he might succeed with Paulina. She said that she wanted 50,000 drachmae* in order to trick Paulina, and Mundus gave her the money.

Ide knew that Paulina was very devoted to the worship of the goddess Isis. She met with some of Isis's priests and bribed them with 25,000 drachmae* (and more to come) to trick Paulina to come alone to the temple. The oldest of the priests went to speak to Paulina alone. He said that he had been sent by the god Anubis, who had fallen in love with her and wanted her to come to him. Paulina received this message well and considered it an honor to join Anubis. She even told her husband, and he agreed since he believed that she was pure in her desire. She went to the temple, and after she had eaten and it was time to sleep, the priest shut the doors. The lights were put out and Mundus came out of hiding. She was at his service all night because she thought he was the god. He went away in the morning, before the priests came who didn't know anything about this. Paulina came early to her husband and told how the god Anubia had favored her. Her friends weren't sure whether to believe her or not.

Three days after this, Mundus met Paulina and said that she had saved him 200,000 drachmae*. "I had much pleasure while taking the name of Anubis." When she realized what a horrible thing she had done, she tore her clothes and told her husband about Mundus's wicked deed. She pleaded for his help. Saturnius told the emperor, and Tiberias looked into the matter. He questioned the priests and ordered them to be crucified, as well as Ide who had planned the whole thing. He tore down the temple of Isis and ordered that her statue be thrown into the river Tiber. Mundus was only sent away, since Tiberius decided he had only been carried away by his love.

A Jew was living in Rome who had been sent away from Judea for breaking the Jewish law. He and three other men made themselves into teachers of the Law of Moses. They persuaded Fulvia, a great woman who had converted to Judaism, to donate purple and gold to the temple in Jerusalem. It was later discovered that the four men took the gifts for themselves. When Tiberius heard about this from Fulvia's husband, he ordered all of the Jews to be sent out of Rome. The records show that 4,000 of them were sent to the island of Sardinia, but even more were punished because they refused to become soldiers on account of the Jewish faith. In this way all of the Jews were sent out of Rome due to the wickedness of four men.

iv

THERE was one man of the Samaritans who gathered the people together on Mt. Gerizzim, which to them was the most holy mountain. He said that he would show them holy vessels which Moses had buried there. They came armed and they were staying in Tirathaba. They all wished to climb the mountain together, but Pilate stopped them by blocking the roads with horsemen and foot soldiers. Some of the people were killed and others fled. Pilate ordered that some of the strongest who got away be killed.

The Samaritan senate sent messengers to Vitellius who had been a consul and was now president of Syria. They accused Pilate of the murders. Vitellius sent a friend of his to check the complaint, and he ordered Pilate to go to Rome and answer to Caesar. After Pilate had been in Judea for ten years he went to Rome; he did not dare refuse. But before he arrived, Tiberias died.

Vitellius came to Judea and went to Jerusalem during the feast of Passover. He was well received and he freed the people from taxes on the produce of their fields. He also let them take care of the high priest's garments, a duty which was formerly kept by the Romans. These holy clothes were kept in the citadel of the tower of Antonia.

One of the high priests long before, Hyrcanus, had built a tower near the temple in which he lived. He kept garments there with him, and so did his sons who took his place. When Herod became king, he took the garments in order to make sure the people would not rebel against him. Archelaus continued in this way as well. When the Romans took over control, a captain of the guard would hand them over to the priest seven days before a festival, so that he could purify them before wearing them. The day after the festival they were to be returned to the guard. This was repeated for each of the three yearly festivals and on the fast day. Vitellius now ordered the captain of the guard not to worry about getting them back, giving control back to the priests. Vitellius wanted the people to be at peace with him. He also removed Joseph Caiphas from being the high priest, and replaced him with Jonathan son of Ananus the earlier high priest. He then returned to Antioch.

Tiberias sent a letter to Vitellius ordering him to make friends with Artabanus, the king of Parthia. Artabanus had taken Armenia away from him, which made him afraid. Vitellius sent many presents and asked the king of Iberia and the king of Albania to fight against Artabanus. They didn't want to fight, but they did give the Scythians permission to come through their country, opening the Caspian gates. So Armenia was taken back from the Parthians and there was war. The leading men were killed, including the king's son and 10,000s of soldiers. Vitellius sent much money to Artabanus's father's family and friends, and with this bribe he made a plot with them to kill Artabanus. Artabanus saw that he had fallen into a trap, so he fled to the upper provinces. Later he raised a large army and held off the enemy in his region.

Tiberias heard about this, and wanted Artabanus to be his friend. Vitellius and Artabanus went to the Euphrates; they each crossed the river with their guards and met in the middle of the bridge. They made a peace treaty, and Herod put up a rich tent where they feasted. Artabanus sent his son Darius as a hostage to Rome with many presents, including a giant Jewish man who was seven cubits* tall, by the name of Eleazar. Vitellius went to Antioch and Artabanus went to Babylon. Herod told Caesar all about the event. Vitellius's letters came later and Caesar said he had already heard the news. Vitellius was angry about this, and he waited to take revenge on Herod.

Philip, Herod's brother, died after he had been ruling Trachonitis, Gaulonitis and the country of the Bataneans for 37 years. He was a moderate and quiet leader and had a few good friends. He was quick to hear complaints and set things right. If the guilty needed to be punished, he did not delay. Those who had been unjustly accused were freed. He died at Julias and was buried in a grave which had already been prepared. He had an impressive funeral. Tiberius took over his land since he had no sons. The territory was added to the province of Syria, but the taxes were to be used in the land itself.

V

AT this time Herod the king and Aretas had a fight. Herod had married the daughter of Aretas, the king of Arabia- Petrea, and he lived with her for a long time. When he was in Rome, however, this Herod (called Herod-Antipas) lived with Herod-Phillip who was his brother by a different mother (the son of the high priest Simon's daughter), and he fell in love with Herodias, Herod-Phillip's wife – who was also the daughter of Aristobulus their brother and the sister of Agrippa the Great. He spoke to her about marriage, and Herodias said that he had to divorce Aretas's daughter. Herod-Antipas agreed and sailed to Rome. But when he came home after taking care of business there, Herod-Antipas's wife (the daughter of Aretas), who found out about the agreement he had made with Herodias, asked him to send her to Macherus, a place on the border of the territories Aretas and Herod ruled. She made her way to Arabia and told her father of Herod's intentions. Aretas and Herod were already quarreling about territory, so they raised armies on both sides and prepared for war. All of Herod's army was destroyed by people from Phillip's area who had joined Aretas's army. Herod wrote to Tiberius, who was very angry and wrote to Vitellius to take Aretas alive and bring him as a prisoner, or to kill him and to send him his head.

Some of the Jews felt that the destruction of Herod's army came from God as a punishment for what Herod had done to John the Baptist. He had been a good man who had taught the people to live righteously and to be good to one another. They were to be baptized in water as a purification of the body – not for forgiveness of sins but as a symbol showing that the soul had been purified by righteousness. He grew great crowds, and Herod feared that the people might rebel since they were ready to follow whatever he said. John was sent to prison in the castle in Macherus and he died there.

Vitellius had two legions of armed men and horsemen, and they set out against Aretas. They were on the way to Petra and stopped at Ptolemais. As they marched through Judea, the leaders met him and did not want the army to cross their territory since they were bringing Caesar's images with them which the Jews found offensive to look at. So Vitellius ordered the army to march along the plain, while he, together with Herod the tetrarch and his friends, went to Jerusalem to offer sacrifices to God. The Jewish festival was approaching. They stayed for three days and were well received. During that time, he removed Jonathan from the high priesthood and gave the job to his brother Theophilus. But on the fourth day letters arrived informing him of the death of

Tiberius. The Jews were asked to promise to obey the new Caesar Caius. The army was sent home, since Caius was not the one who had ordered this war. When Aretas heard that Vitellius was coming to fight him he consulted with his fortune-tellers, who said that this army would never enter Petra because one of the Roman rulers would die. Vitellius went to Antioch.

Meanwhile, Agrippa the son of Aristobulus went to Rome a year before the death of Tiberias, to ask for help with his affairs. Now it's time to look at the family of Herod. Over a hundred year period we see that Herod's many children did him no good – almost all of them were all destroyed. This could have been punishment for the incest, since they were marrying their own nephews and nieces. In contrast Agrippa, a man who was not in line to be king, moved into a place of great power and authority.

Herod the Great had two daughters by Mariamne, the granddaughter of Hyrcanus. One was Salampsio, who was married to her first cousin, and the other was Cypros, also married to a first cousin. After a few generations, there were only three sons left from their line. Aristobulus, the third brother of Agrippa, married the daughter of the king of Emesa and they gave birth to a deaf daughter. The descendants of Alexander son of Herod left the Jewish religion and went over to that of the Greeks. The rest of the daughters of Herod the king died childless. This was the family of Herod when Agrippa the Great came on the scene.

vi

BEFORE the death of King Herod, Agrippa lived in Rome and was friends with Drusus, the son of the emperor Tiberius. He was also friends with Antonia, the wife of Drusus the Great, and also admired Agrippa's mother Bernice and wished to see her son do well. Agrippa wanted to give his friends many presents, but while his mother was alive he was careful not to make her angry by wasting money. After Bernice died, Agrippa wasted all his money giving rich presents and he became poor. He could not live in

Rome any longer. After Drusus died, Tiberius refused to see his son's friends because they made him sad.

Agrippa sailed to Judea but could not get away from the people to whom he owed money. He went to the tower of Malatha in Idumea, and he was so ashamed that he thought about killing himself, but his wife stopped him. She sent a letter to his sister Herodias, who was now the wife of Herod the tetrarch, and she asked for help. So Agrippa was given a place in Tiberias and even became a judge in the city. But he couldn't stop spending money. At a feast in Tyre where Herod was present, Agrippa and he insulted each other. Herod shamed him by reminding him that Agrippa was getting all his needs met by Herod. Agrippa then went to Flaccus who was now the president of Syria.

Flaccus received both Agrippa and Aristobulus, Agrippa's brother who was also living there. Aristobulus didn't like Agrippa and turned Flaccus against him. The Damascenes had an argument with the Sidonians, and when Flaccus was to judge between them they saw that Agrippa was able to influence him. The Damascenes bribed Agrippa to speak in their favor. Aristobulus found out and told Flaccus about the bribe. Flaccus was angry and stopped being friends with Agrippa.

Agrippa came to Ptolemais and wanted to sail to Italy, but he couldn't go further because he had no money. He asked his freed man Marsyas to find someone who would loan him money. Marsyas went to Peter, the freed man of Bernice Agrippa's mother, but Peter gave him less than he asked for, because there was an old debt Agrippa hadn't paid back. Agrippa was ready to sail but suddenly the ruler came with soldiers and demanded the money he owed Caesar. He pretended that he would pay it, but at night he cut the ship's cables and sailed to Alexandria, where he asked Alexander to lend him 200,000 drachmae*. Alexander refused, but then he changed his mind because Agrippa's wife Cypros was so loyal to him. Still, he gave him only part of the loan in Alexandria and promised the rest later at Puteoli, because he was afraid that

Agrippa would spend it all right away. Cypros watched Agrippa leave for Italy, and she and their children went back to Judea.

Agrippa wrote to Tiberius Caesar at Puteoli telling him that he would like to visit him in Capreae where he was living. Tiberius treated him well when he arrived. But the next day Caesar received a letter telling about the 300,000 drachmae* which Agrippa had borrowed and not paid back on time. The governor told how Agrippa ran away out of reach of those who were owed the money. Caesar said that Agrippa would not be allowed in his presence until the debt was paid. So Agrippa begged Antonia, mother of Germanicus and Claudius (who later became Caesar), to lend him those 300,000 drachmae* so as not to lose Tiberius's friendship. Antonia did so for the sake of her love for Agrippa's mother Bernice. Tiberias Caesar then received him, and even wished that he would always take his grandson abroad when he would be travelling.

Agrippa and Caius, the grandson of Antonia, were good friends, and once when they rode in the same chariot Agrippa spoke about Tiberius, saying that he wished that he would die so that Caius could take his place, since he was more worthy. Eutychus, Agrippa's servant who drove the chariot, heard these words. Agrippa later accused him of stealing some of his clothes, and when he was caught and had to appear before Piso the governor, he spoke up, saying that he needed to tell Caesar about a danger to him. He was bound and sent to Capreae. But Tiberius took a very long time to call him and hear what he had to say. Tiberius was very slow about receiving anyone who came to see him, whether they were prisoners or messengers from his governors. When his friends asked him why, he made the excuse that hearing the requests of governors too quickly would only make it harder for the people. If they were sent home right away, they would have more time to squeeze money from their subjects in the long run. He gave the example of flies landing on the wounds of a wounded man. It was thought better not to shoo them away, since these flies were already full and not bothering him so much, whereas new, hungry flies would take their place to suck blood and wear him down. The people who had their leaders for a long time were better off than they would be with newer ones. Tiberius followed this rule himself; he was emperor for 22 years and sent only two different governors to the Jews; namely, Gratus and Pilate. As for delaying the hearings of prisoners, he said it was good for those who were worthy of punishment, because it would cause them more suffering.

For this reason Eutychus was not able to get a hearing. Finally Tiberius came to a town about 100 furlongs* from Rome. Agrippa asked Antonia to request that Tiberius call Eutychus to a hearing. Antonia was highly respected by Tiberius since she had been the wife of his brother Drusus, and because she was a widow who refused to remarry. She had also helped Tiberius when there was a plot against his life. Tiberius was able to find them and kill them after she heard of it and wrote to him about it in detail.

Antonia found her chance when Tiberius was relaxing after dinner at the same time that her grandson and Agrippa were present. So she asked Tiberius to call Eutychus. Then Eutychus told about the time when Agrippa said to Caius that "one day this old man will die and you will be ruler of the whole earth." Tiberius believed Eutychus and he ordered a servant to bind the wicked man. But the servant wasn't sure which man Tiberius meant. They walked around the hippodrome and saw where Agrippa was standing. Caesar told him to bind this man. Agrippa was put in chains. He was very thirsty and needed to drink, and finally a slave of Caius gave him a drink. Agrippa told the good man that after he was free he would free this water carrier from Caius, who didn't even try to help him. Later Agrippa kept this promise and made him a steward over his treasures, and even left him to serve his son Agrippa and his daughter Bernice. The man was honored for years and later died.

Agrippa was bound and standing by the royal palace. He leaned on a tree and a bubo bird (an owl) was above him. A German prisoner asked a soldier who the man in purple was. He was told that this was Agrippa, a Jew and one of the leaders in that nation. He asked to speak with him in order to ask him something about his country. This German told him that he would rise out of his grief soon. "I must tell you this prediction of the gods at my own risk. You will be delivered and will hold a position of power, but notice this bird and realize that the next time you will see him you will live only another five days. It would be unjust for me to conceal this. So when you are able, do not forget the misery I am in and try to free me." Agrippa laughed at him but later he remembered this prophecy.

Antonia took Agrippa's troubles to heart. She couldn't ask Tiberius to free him, but she requested that Agrippa eat together with the centurion over him and that he be free to bathe daily. She also made sure that his friends would be able to visit him. Silas came to him and other men who brought him his favorite food. They brought clothes as if to sell them, but they were to make a bed for him to lie on. This went on for six months.

When Tiberius returned to Capreae he became ill. He asked that his children come to him. He had no living sons, and he prayed to his country gods for a sign of who should take over the kingdom. He decided that whichever child would come to him first the next day would be the next ruler. He tried to make sure it would be his grandson Tiberius, but when the servant went out, there was only Caius at the door. Tiberius was very sorry that this grandson would not take over, and he feared for his safety if there would be a fight for the throne. Tiberius had studied astrology and was interested in predictions coming true, even more so than those who studied the subject. When Galba came to him he said to his best friends that here was someone who would one day be head of the Roman Empire. Now Tiberius was sorry that he had asked for this sign since he would die knowing how his own loved ones would die. He didn't want to speak to Caius, but against his will he said, "Although Tiberius is more nearly related to me than you are, I put into your hand the Roman Empire. Remember my kindness to you. Take care of Tiberius your relative. He will take care of you, both as a ruler and personally. If he dies, it will be a hardship to you, since you will be alone with great burdens. Be aware that any unjust actions you do will be punished." Caius promised to be just, but he killed this Tiberius (as the emperorTiberius had predicted), and within a short time Caius himself was killed in a plot.

A few days later Caesar Tiberias died, having ruled for almost 22 ½ years. Caius was the fourth emperor. The Romans were happy to hear Tiberias was dead, but they were afraid to show their joy in case it was not true. Tiberias had troubled even the best families of the Romans – he was hot-tempered and did not forgive others. He hated men without reason and punished people by death for small things.

Marsyas, Agrippa's servant ran to tell him while he was on his way to the bath. He said in Hebrew, "The lion is dead." Agrippa replied, "Thanks and happiness be to you for this news if it is true." At the feast that evening Agrippa and the centurion who guarded him were celebrating with drinks, when someone came and said that Tiberius was still alive and would return to the city in a few days. Agrippa was taken off the couch and put in chains again and guarded all night. The next day the rumors grew that Tiberius was truly dead, and some were offering sacrifices. Letters finally came from Caius which told them of Tiberius's death. Agrippa was sent back to the house where he lived before, and although he was still a prisoner he was free to take care of his affairs. Caius came to Rome with Tiberius's dead body, and a rich funeral was held. Antonia advised Caius not to free Agrippa that day (which he wanted to do) so it would not look like a celebration of Tiberius's death. So Caius waited a few days. Then had Agrippa change his clothes, put a crown on his head and named him king of the region that had belonged to Philip. He received a golden chain in place of his iron prisoner's chain. The people were surprised when Agrippa returned Judea to rule as a king. His poverty had been exchanged for joy and prosperity.

HERODIAS, Agrippa's sister and now the wife of Herod the tetrarch of Galilee and Perea, was envious of Agrippa since he was honored more than her husband. He had run away because he could not pay his debts, and now he returned with riches and honor. She would not see him marching among the people as if nothing had happened. She urged Herod to go to Rome and receive the same honor. Agrippa was only the son of Aristobulus who had been condemned to die by his father, and he had come to her husband while in poverty and expected to be cared for daily. He returned as a king. She urged Herod, "We should go to Rome no matter what the cost and get the whole kingdom for you."

Herod opposed her request knowing that it wouldn't be easy for him in Rome. She nagged him until he agreed. He got ready to travel to Rome along with her, spending a lot of money for the journey. When Agrippa found this out, he also decided to go to Rome. Agrippa sent Fortunatus, one of his servants, with presents to give to the emperor and a letter against Herod. They arrived about the same time in the little city of Campania where they found Caius. They were staying in royal palaces built over a natural warm-water health spa. Caius greeted Herod and met with him. Later he read Agrippa's letters accusing Herod of being against the rule of Tiberius and Caius. As proof, Agrippa wrote that Herod had the armor to equip 70,000 soldiers. When questioned, Herod admitted that he had the armor, and Caius took his kingdom away. He gave it to Agrippa as well as Herod's money and ordered him to move to Gaul. When Caius heard that Herodias was Agrippa's sister, he gave her a present. But she refused the gift, saying that she would stand with her husband not only in good times but also in times of trouble. Caius was angry at this answer, and both Herod and his wife were sent away. Her house was given to Agrippa. In this way God punished her for envying her brother, and punished Herod for listening to the gossip of a woman. Caius had the support of the Romans during the first two years of his reign since he was fair. Later he became corrupted by the power which he held over a large territory, and he made himself into a god.

THE Jews and Greeks were arguing with each other in Alexandria. Three messengers were chosen from each side to go to Caius. Apion was very harsh against the Jews and accused them of not honoring Caesar because they did not tolerate the altars and temples which had been built in honor of Caius, nor would they swear in his name. He had intended to make Caius angry against the Jews. Philo, a leading philosopher wanted to defend the Jewish people, but Caius wouldn't let him speak. Philo told the Jews to be brave, because God was on their side.

Caius made Petronius as president in Syria in place of Vitellius, and gave him an order to invade Judea. They were to put Caius's statue in the temple, and if the Jews would not allow it, there would be war. Petronius took two Roman legions with him and stayed for the winter in Ptolemais, planning to go to Jerusalem in the spring. But 10,000s of Jews came to him in Ptolemais begging him not to force them to break the law of their people. They would rather die than give in to this Roman order. Petronius said that he had no choice; he had to follow the orders of Caesar. The Jews answered that they feared the anger of God who was higher than Caius. Petronius saw that there was danger of war, and he went to Tiberias. Many thousands of Jews met him there also. They threw themselves on their faces and stretched out their throats, saying that they would not fight, but they would rather die than see Caius's statue in their temple. They did this for forty days and left their farming, even though it was the time to plant crops.

King Agrippa's brother Aristobulus and other Jewish leaders came to Petronius, pleading with him to stop the plan. They said that Caesar would be wiser not to destroy the people. With no one to to farm their land robbery would increase, and the people would have no money to pay their taxes. Tens of thousands of

Jews were gathered in Tiberias, and Petronius said that he would send word to Caius of their request. He saw that they were telling the truth; they were being loyal to their God above all. He said that if Caius would be angry with him, he would rather suffer himself than to see so many people die who had been behaving well.

"Go back to your farming and I and my associates will go to Rome," he told the leaders of the Jews, and he encouraged them to be hopeful. As soon as Petronius finished speaking, there was a sign from God of His blessing. Suddenly heavy rain came down on a clear day, and this during a year that had seen almost no rain at all. Petronius saw that God was truly caring for his own people. Petronius wrote to Caius about this sign and pleaded with him not to bother this great crowd of people, for he would lose their taxes and would also be cursed by them for all time.

King Agrippa, who was now living in Rome as a great favorite of Caius, was treating him with a rich meal. After drinking, Caius was in a very good mood, and he promised Agrippa that he would reward him with a rich gift. He expected that Agrippa would ask to rule over some large country or receive the money from certain cities. Instead Agrippa asked him to cancel his plan to put the statue in the Jewish temple. Agrippa could have been killed for asking this. But Caius, seeing Agrippa's simple and brave goal to keep the peace among the Jews, and knowing that many people had heard him promise Agrippa to give him whatever he asked, agreed. He wrote to Petronius, telling him that if the statue was not already in the temple, he could forget about it and send the army home. But then he received Petronius's letter telling him that the Jews refused to obey, and Caius got angry; he sent another letter saying that since Petronius honored the Jews more than Caesar, he should judge himself worthy of death.

Petronius did not receive this letter until after Caius was dead, since the ship which carried it sailed slowly. He first received a letter telling him that Caius was dead, and later Caius's letter which ordered Petronius to kill himself. Caius was killed by his senators,

Petronius sees the miracle of rain after agreeing not to force the Jewish people to place the Roman idol of Caius in their temple.

because he had been harsh with them. Petronius saw how God protected him after he had put himself in danger for the sake of the Jews. This was a sign of God's power and a reward for honoring the temple of God and standing up for the Jewish people.

THERE was a very large city in Babylonia called Neerda. It was well protected by walls and was surrounded by the Euphrates River. Further down the river was a city called Nisibis. The Jews living in these cities collected the half-shekel tax to send to Jerusalem for God's work, and the money was held there until it would be taken to Jerusalem. 10,000 men were sent to carry the offering safely to Jerusalem and to prevent attacks from the Parthians. Two brothers, Asineus and Anileus, lived in Neerda with their mother, and they learned how to weave curtains. The man they worked for was not happy that they came to work late, and he punished them. In return they stole all the weapons that were in that house, and ran away. They came to some farmland good for cattle and sheep, where there was also a storage place for fruit which would be used in winter. There were some poor young men who joined the brothers, and this group built a fort. They told all the farmers in that place that they would protect the cattle of those who gave them meat for food and helped them. Those who refused would have their cattle killed. The farmers agreed because they had no choice. The group grew in numbers and power, and the king of Parthia heard about them.

The Parthians joined forces with the Babylonians to attack them. They thought that they would be able to beat them easily, since they intended to attack suddenly on the Sabbath when the Jews would be resting. Asineus heard their horses and sent someone to see if enemies were really coming. They reported that there was a large army coming their way. Asineus told the people to defend themselves and be willing to die even though it was the Sabbath. They took up their weapons and killed many of the soldiers, and chased away the rest of them.

Artabanus the king of Parthia heard about the boldness of the Jews and wished to speak with them. He sent his guards to them and said that even though he had been treated badly by the Jews, he admired their bravery and wanted to make friends with them. He asked the brothers to come and see him, and he would guarantee their safety and give them presents. Anileus came and brought him presents. Artabanus asked why his brother Asineus was not with him, and he understood that he was afraid and stayed by the lake. The king then gave Anileus his right hand as a promise that he wanted peace, which was a sign among the barbarian tribes that they would keep their promise. Artabanus told Anileus to convince his brother to come and see him. The king did this because he didn't want his own governors or his enemies to join with the Jews in a rebellion.

So Asineus agreed to come when he heard of the king's good will and promise. Artabanus admired Asineus for what he had done. Asineus was a small man who did not look as strong and brave as he was. Artabanus told his friends that Asineus's soul was greater than his body. One of Artabanus's generals wanted to kill Asineus as a punishment for what he had done to the Parthian government, but the king wouldn't allow it. He said he had given Asineus his right hand and made a promise. If the general wanted to kill Asineus, he would have to do it without the backing of Artabanus. He then called Asineus and said that he needed to return home, since his generals might try to murder him. Artabanus also gave Babylonia into his care and asked Asineus to repay his kindness by keeping the land free of robbers. He gave him presents and sent him away. When Asineus arrived home he built forts and had great success within a short time. He was greatly respected by the Parthian governors and succeeded in taking good care of Mesopotamia for 15 years.

A certain Parthian army general came to the area and had a wife who was very talented and beautiful. Anileus fell in love with her, and after her husband was killed in battle he married her. She caused him a lot of trouble by bringing her foreign gods into their home. She used to worship her gods privately, but after they married she worshipped them openly as she was used to doing with her first husband. Anileus's friends accused him of leaving his Jewish faith and said that as a result he would lose God's blessing. One who accused him was killed by Anileus for speaking up, and as he was dying he pronounced punishment on his murderer, his brother Asineus, and their friends for not helping the murdered man. The friends came to Asineus and told him that the woman's worship of her gods needed to be stopped before they would all die. They reminded him that they had not approved of the marriage, and this idol worship was dishonoring the God they worshipped. Asineus favored his brother above their advice and forgave him for his crime. When their uproar grew stronger, he told his brother Anileus to send the woman home to her people. The woman became aware and was afraid for Anileus, so she poisoned Asineus's food and killed him.

Anileus led an army against Mithridates, the leader in Parthia who had married king Artabanus's daughter. They found a lot of money, sheep, took many slaves and ruined the villages. Mithridates was very upset, since he had done nothing to deserve this, so he gathered as many horsemen and soldiers who were fit for war and came to fight Anileus. He intended to attack Anileus on the Sabbath, the following day, since the Jews would be resting. A Syrian stranger informed Anileus where Mithridates would be feasting. Anileus and his army attacked the Parthians, killing some while they were asleep, and chasing the others. Anileus took Mithridates alive and made him ride naked on a donkey, which was a great insult for the Parthians (Whiston writes: Today in Damascus the Turks don't allow the Christians to ride horses but only donkeys when they tour the country.)

When the army came to the forest, they wanted to kill Mithridates, but Anileus said that it was not right to kill a man from a leading family of the Parthains who was honored by being married into the royal family. He warned them that if they would kill Mithridates, Artabanus the king would kill all of the Jews living in Babylon. So they freed Mithridates. But his wife was upset, saying that a son-in-law to the king needed to take revenge – it was shameful that he was content to have been captured and set free by the Jews. She told him, "Go back and show your courage," or she would swear by the gods of their royal family and that she would end their marriage. Mithridates did not want to fight Anileus, but he was afraid she would really leave him. So he got an army together and marched along with them, thinking that he should not give credit to the Jews as a Parthian for his saving his life.

Anileus heard about the huge army marching his way, and he left the area of the lakes to go and meet him, hoping to beat him as before. They began to march and many joined Anileus in order to share in the victory. But after they had marched 90 furlongs* they were very thirsty, and that was when Mithridates attacked them. Anileus and his men were tired and thirsty, while Mithridates's men were strong and rested, so they killed 10,000 of Anileus's men. Many of Anileus's men ran away into the woods, and Mithridates beat his army. Anileus escaped, and many bad men came to him, who didn't fear death if they could gain some temporary pleasure. With these men, Anileus destroyed the villages of the Babylonians. The Babylonian soldiers sent messengers to the Jews in Neerda, telling them to hand Anileus over to them. The Jews could not do this, but they did want peace. So some Jews went with the Babylonians and they came secretly to Anileus where he was hiding. They killed him and his men when they were drunk and asleep.

The Babylonians were now free from the heavy rule of Anileus, which had kept them from showing their hatred of the Jews. Now the hatred between the Jews and the Baylonians came out in the open. The Jews could not fight it or live with it, so they moved to Seleucia, the city which Seleucus Nicator had built. There were many Macedonians, Grecians and Syrians living there. The Jews lived there peacefully for five years. In the sixth year, a disease broke out in Babylonia and the Babylonians also moved to Seleucia, and they made trouble for the Jews again.

Because of the living habits of the different groups in Seleucia, there were many fights among them. The Greeks and Syrians could not get along, and the Greeks were stronger. The Jews, who were ready to fight for any reason, sided with the Syrians and made them stronger. The Greeks went to the Syrians to try to make peace and become the leaders again. This time the Syrians and Greeks agreed to fight on the same side, based on their common hatred of the Jews. They attacked the Jews and killed about 50,000 of them. Only a few escaped with the help of friends or neighbors. These few went to a Greek city near Seleucia where the king of Parthia spent the winter every year, and where his treasures were kept. All of the remaining Jews feared both the Babylonians and the Seleucians since all of the Syrians joined with the Seleucians to fight the Jews. These Jews escaped to Neerda and Nisibis since they were strong cities and fighting men lived there.

BOOK XIX

FROM THE JEWS' DEPARTURE OUT OF BABYLON TO FADUS THE ROMAN PROCURATOR

CAIUS had done great evil beyond Jerusalem and Judea. His murders went from land to sea and included those in his own city of Rome. It didn't matter that they were noble leaders from great families or that they were from the army of the horsemen who were equal to the senators (many of them became senators). Caius often had people killed so that he could take their wealth. He went to the temple of Jupiter in the capitol and called himself the brother of Jupiter. He built a bridge from the city of Dicearchia to Misenum measuring thirty furlongs* over the ocean, just because he didn't want to row across in a small ship. He felt he was lord of the sea, so he closed the whole bay inside his bridge and drove his chariot over it. He ruined Greek temples and ordered that their most beautiful treasures be taken from them and given to him. He felt that the best things should only be kept in Rome. He put some of these in his own house and gardens, and put a few in his other houses around Italy. The statue of Jupiter Olympius, made to honor the Olympic Games by the Greeks, Caius ordered to be moved to Rome. But the Greek architects told the one who was to remove the statue that it would be ruined if it were moved. So this Roman wrote to Caius explaining that it could not be moved, and for this he was in danger of death. But Caius died, so he was saved from punishment.

Caius was so crazy he took his newborn baby daughter to the capitol and put her on the knees of the statue of Jupiter, and said that the child had two fathers, Jupiter and himself. He allowed slaves to accuse their masters of any crimes they could think of. Claudius, the uncle of Caius, was accused by his slave, and Caius was not ashamed to be present at the trial of his own uncle. Caius made life miserable for many people due to the false accusations made by the slaves and others. Many more would have died if Caius had not come to a sudden death himself.

There were at least three leading men to make plans to get rid of Caius. One was by Regulus, a man from Spain, one organized by the army commander Cherea, and a third by Minucianus another respected man. Regulus hated injustice, and being bold and free he told others what he thought. Minucianus joined him because a friend of his had been murdered by Caius. Cherea was considered a friend of Caius but felt that he was in danger. The tribune had an advantage in being the closest of the three as a personal guard to Caius, so he could more easily kill him.

The time came for the horse races called the Circensian games. All of the people of Rome looked forward to this and people also used the games as a time to ask favors from Caesar, who was in a mood to grant them. This time they were complaining about the taxes. Caius's answer was to send soldiers to catch those who were yelling and put them to death. Many people were killed in this way, those who saw the result got quiet. This event made Cherea more certain than ever that he needed to kill Caius. He was only waiting for a time when he could not fail.

Cherea had been in the army a long time and was tired of being around Caius. Caius had told him to gather taxes but he had pitied some of the people whose debts had doubled. Caius became very angry and said that Cherea acted like a woman. Cherea received passwords every day from Caius for the soldiers, and Caius would choose feminine words that were insulting to Cherea, and the commander was forced to repeat them to his soldiers as the password, which made them laugh at him. Caius would also dress in women's clothes in front of him, and Cherea took this as an insult. For these reasons some others joined him in their hatred of Caius.

A senator named Pompedius had an enemy called Timidius. This Timidius told Caius that Pompedius had insulted Caesar, and that Quintilia, a beautiful woman who attended the theatre, was a witness. But Quintilia and Pompedius were lovers, and she refused to be a witness. Caius ordered that this woman be tortured until she admitted that her lover was against him. He gave Cherea the job of torturing her, and he was very harsh because he did not want to be insulted again by Caius for being weak. When this woman was brought to the rack, she stepped on the foot of one of her friends and told him not to worry about her. Cherea tortured Quintilia cruelly but she refused to say anything. When he brought her to Caius, it was Caius who felt sorry for her because she had once been so beautiful. She was freed as well as her lover, and Caius gave her money to make up for her torture.

Cherea was very upset about this, since he had forced himself to torture Quintilia for nothing. He told Clement, the army general, that by guarding their emperor from all the conspiracies against him, they were helping Caius to do evil. Clement said nothing because he was afraid, but his true feelings showed on his face. Cherea became braver and continued, "We can pretend in words that Caius is guilty of all these crimes, but it is I and you, Clement, who are guilty since we have the power to kill someone who is making life miserable for many citizens. We are only tools of his cruelty, using our weapons to keep him safe; the one who has enslaved the Romans in body and mind. We are made unclear with all the innocent shed blood. He doesn't keep us because he likes us, but because he suspects us. Later we will get the same treatment from him and be killed also. Instead we should free all of the people from danger, and at the same time free ourselves."

Clement agreed but told Cherea to be quiet so that the word would not get out. Clement went home, and Cherea went to speak with Sabinus one of the tribunes. Sabinus had the same idea as Cherea, and they asked Minucianus to join them, whose friend had been killed by Caius. This third man, Minucianus asked what Caius's password was for the day; the way Caius insulted Cherea by these passwords was known around the city. Caius was happy to find out that Minucianus agreed with him, so he told Minucianus about his plan to end the slavery of a once free country by killing Caius.

Minucianus hugged Cherea and wished him good luck. When Cherea entered the court where Caius was, together with many senators, soldiers and horsemen, there was a voice either from God himself or from someone in the crowd, telling him to carry out his plan. Nearly everyone in that crowd was ready to kill Caius.

One man who served Caius, called Callistus, was a wicked man who took bribes and was very rich. He was almost as bad as Caius himself, but he also was afraid that one day Caius would kill him for his money. He hoped that if Caius was removed, he would rule in his place. Caius once ordered Callistus to poison Claudius, but Callistus made excuses and never carried out the plot. In this way, God protected Claudius from the madness of Caius.

There were many chances to kill Caius, like when he went up to the capitol to give offerings to the gods for his daughter, and when he stood on his royal palace and threw gold and silver coins out to the people. It would have been easy to simply throw him down from that high place. Cherea was angry with his partners in the plot because he felt they had already missed some good opportunities. They told him to be patient a bit longer. There were shows held in the palace in honor of Caesar, and the senators and their families would come. Caius would come to see these shows together with 10,000s of people, and in the narrow entrances it would be easy to kill him even if the guards around him wanted to save him.

Three days of the shows passed, and only one day remained. Caius told his friends that time was running out and that after this Caius would leave by ship to Alexandria to see Egypt. He said to them, "Why should he be allowed to be victorious on land and also at sea? Or maybe some Egyptian will kill him instead of us. I will do the right thing today and risk the danger."

The other partners in the plot were encouraged, and they agreed to do the deed that day. In the morning they arrived at the palace, and Cherea had his horseman's sword on him and was due to receive the password from Caius. There were no seats set aside for the senators or the horsemen; everyone mixed together, the leaders with the common people. Caius offered the sacrifice to Augustus Caesar, the one being honored by the show. A certain priest fell and his blood splashed on the clothes of a senator named Asprenus, causing Caius to laugh. This was an omen, since Caius and Asprenus would be killed at the same time. Caius was in an unusually good mood. He sat down with his closest friends. When the people had quieted down, one senator asked another if he had heard any news. He continued, saying that "the game of the slaughter of tyrants" would be played today. The other told him to be quiet.

Fall fruit was thrown out to the audience and rare birds were freed into the crowd. The birds were fighting for the fruit, and the people were trying to catch the birds. The plays were about a leader of robbers who was crucified and about a father and daughter who were killed. A lot of fake blood was used. This was the same day that a friend of Philip, king of Macedonia, had killed the king as he came into the theatre. Caius was not sure if he should stay until the end of the plays or if he would take a bath and eat dinner, and return later. Cherea had already gone out. Minucianus, one of the plotters, got up to look for Cherea, but Caius asked where he was going. To show respect to Caesar he sat down. But a few minutes later, he got up again and Caius thought he was going to relieve himself. Asprenus, another plotter, convinced Caius to go bathe and have dinner and return later, because he wanted to get the deed done.

It was getting late and the conspirators were getting worried. Caius left the theater and went into a private narrow passage on his way to the baths. He also wanted to see the Asian boys who would be singing and dancing. Cherea met him and asked him for the password, and Caius gave him a silly, insulting word. Cherea drew his sword and stabbed him, but the wound was between the shoulder and neck and did not kill him. Caius did not cry out for help; he groaned and tried to run away. But by then the other plotters were around him with their swords. One pushed him down on his knees, and they took turns stabbing him with their swords. Aquila gave him the final stroke that killed him, but Cherea was the one who gave them all the courage to carry out the plot.

Now the plotters were trapped, and they knew that the emperor's soldiers would soon find them in that narrow passage. They came to the house of Caius's father and were out of danger for a while, but they knew as soon as the news got out, there would be a search for Caius's killers. Caius's guards were Germans, and when they found Caius dead, they were sorry and angry. They had no understanding about public affairs but judged everything only by the good it brought to themselves. Sabinus, a former gladiator, led the Germans to hunt for the murderers. The first senator they found was Asprenas, whom they cut to pieces. He was the one with the priest's blood on his clothes, a sign that his meeting with the soldiers would turn out badly. The Germans killed two other senators who they found in the place, not caring it they were guilty of Caius's death or not.

When news got to the crowd in the theatre, most of the people refused to believe it. Some were hoping it was true but were afraid to say so. Others thought that no one had the power to kill Caius. There were soldiers who were afraid, because they had mistreated the best citizens in order to gain honors for themselves from Caius. The women and youth and been kept content by shows, gladiator fights and fresh meat, so they had learned to ignore Caius's cruelty and madness. The slaves were sorry because Caius had let them accuse their masters falsely, and they had received rewards from their master's money along with their freedom. The reward for informers was fixed at one eighth of the criminal's possessions. The nobles knew that maybe Caius really was dead, since they either knew of the plot or they wished it would happen. They hid their joy, however, in case the rumor would turn out to be false and they would be punished. Another rumor was that he was wounded and was being helped by a doctor. Others said that he was wounded but he was still able to go yell at people in the marketplace. No one left their seats in the theater, since they feared that they would look guilty because they were leaving.

The Germans surrounded the theatre with swords drawn. When the people saw them, they were afraid to leave and afraid to stay. They begged the soldiers not to kill them since they were innocent. They cried to God with tears and beat their faces. The soldiers calmed down and decided not to kill them; instead they put the heads of the senators they had killed up on the stage. So the people had no pleasure from Caius's death because they were so afraid that they might die as well.

There was a public crier in the market with a strong, loud voice. He pretended to mourn despite the hatred he had towards Caius. He entered the theatre, and with a great show of sadness announced Caius's death. He and the Roman commanders told the Germans to put away their swords, since Caius was dead. This was what saved the people from the German soldiers. The Germans understood that their zeal to kill Caius's enemies was in vain; there would be no rewards for their effort, and they might even be punished in the end.

Cherea was afraid for Minucianus, so he told all of the soldiers to keep him safe. Clement, the army general said that Caius was his own enemy; he was so wicked that even his closest friends could only see him as an enemy. The people tried to leave the theater, but there was an uproar because people were leaving too fast. A doctor sent people out to gather supplies he would need to treat the wounded, but he did this just to help them escape with him. The uproar came about as the people tried to find Caius's murderers. The senators only pretended to look for them. The people were upset that they couldn't find the killers. The Roman governors wrote an accusation against Caius and told the people to go home and they would be rewarded. They promised to reward the soldiers also if they would keep quiet, since they were in fear that more people would be injured and that the temples would be ruined. In the end the senators got together, especially those who had plotted against Caius, and they began to take control of the government with great confidence.

ii

THE soldiers met together and decided that a democracy would not be good for them, and that Claudius, the uncle of Caius, should be the new emperor. His family was very respected and he had the proper education to be king. But a senator who heard of this plan, Cneus Sentius Saturninus, stood up in the senate and told everyone they must not go back now that tyranny had been ended. "Only the old men among us remember a time when we were free. The young men hardly know what it is to do right and follow laws. Democracy was ended by Julius Caesar, and every Caesar after him did more damage to our ancient laws. These tyrants were responsible for breaking the spirits of the most righteous people. And of all those emperors, Caius was the worst; he terrorized whole families, friends and everyone with undeserved punishments. These men wanted to ruin the homes and wives of their enemies. All lovers of freedom are enemies of tyranny, and we owe much to Cherea, who was helped by the gods to free us by killing Caius. This man risked his life for all of us. Cassius and Brutus killed Julius Caesar, but that started rebellion and civil wars in our city. In this case, the death of Caius has freed us."

The senators and the soldiers of the horsemen who were there were happy with this speech. One of the men quickly went to Sentius and took the ring off of his finger, since the stone had the image of Caius on it. Sentius had forgotten to take it off, so this man broke the ring. It was late at night and Cherea received the password "Liberty" from the governors. Democracy had been unknown in Rome for 100 years. The people all left happy and full of hope and courage. There would no longer be an emperor.

Cherea was worried that Caius's daughter and wife were still alive, so he sent Lupus, one of Clement's family, to kill them. Some felt this was too cruel, since Caius did not take his wife's advice in any case. Others said that she had given Caius poison, and when he went mad she gave the orders in place of Caius. So it was decided that she must die. Lupus found her lying beside her husband's dead body in the palace on the floor. She was covered with blood from his wounds and crying. Her daughter sat beside her. She complained that Caius had not listened to her warnings, and those who heard her argued about what this meant. Some said the "warnings" were to treat people in a righteous way or his cruelty would come back to punish him. Others said the "warnings" were to kill all those who had plotted against him, and she was upset that he had acted too slowly. She showed Lupus his dead body and urged him to come closer, but then she understood why he was there. She stretched out her throat and urged him not to fail. Lupus killed her as well as the daughter and left to report to Cherea.

Caius had reigned four years and four months. He was a pleasure-loving man who used his power against innocent people on purpose. He became rich by way of murder and injustice. He valued shame and punishment above doing right. He listened to the crowd and didn't care about his closest friends if he had ever become angry with them. People would be punished for the smallest offense. He was guilty of incest with his sister, and when this became known, the people truly hated him for it. The only great project he did for Rome was building the ports of Rhegium and Sicily in order to receive the corn brought from Egypt. Even this project was left unfinished. He could speak well and knew

Greek and Roman well. He was clever on many subjects and was persuasive. Since he was the grandson of the brother of Tiberius, he was encouraged to study. But the learning did not teach him not to be a tyrant. He was at first surrounded with worthy friends, but when he became wicked he lost their confidence; and in the end, their hatred towards him brought about his death.

iii

CLAUDIUS spent his life out of sight and studied Greek literature; he did not want to be involved with all the unrest in the government. When the uproar started after Caius's death, Claudius hid in a dark place. The praetorian, the most righteous part of the army, got together to decide what to do. The Germans were hunting for the murderers of Caius, and they killed people mainly to satisfy their fierce tempers rather than for the public good. One of the palace soldiers, Gratus, found Claudius and took him away by force. Claudius begged to be kept alive, but Gratus said that he would become the new Caesar. Gratus said, "Accept the throne of your ancestors." Claudius was not able to walk so they carried him.

Gratus had some guards around him, and more of the soldiers gathered around him, but the crowd ran away, not understanding what was happening. Claudius was carried on a chair and was very weak. They came to the court of the palace and then to the public treasury. Many soldiers were happy to see Claudius and felt he should be emperor, since they had loved his brother Germanicus. They also knew about the many serious mistakes the senate had made when they held power. If a single person would be in charge, they would be in danger, but if Claudius were king, he would reward their kindness.

The senate and the people were not agreed about Claudius. The people wanted to stay free of all kings, but the senate felt that an emperor was needed to keep the people under control and prevent a civil war, like the one in the days of Pompey. When the senate saw that Claudius had been brought by the soldiers into the camp, they sent their best men to warn him not to take the government by force. He should work with those in the senate to rule by the laws, and if he brought peace and righteousness, he would have great honor. If Claudius were to act foolishly as Caius had done, he would be punished for it since the senators had weapons and slaves who would fight. They also said that the gods would not help anyone who did not work for the liberty of the country. The two men sent to speak, who were tribunes, made this speech to Claudius and they fell on their knees and begged Claudius to take the kingdom with good-will and not force, and to protect the city from wars and disaster.

CLAUDIUS followed the advice of the senate to be gentle, and with the encouragement of the soldiers and of King Agrippa that he should be Caesar, he took the throne. Agrippa had been Caius's friend, so he hugged Caius's dead body, covered it and told people that he was still alive and needed a doctor. When Agrippa heard that Claudius had been brought by the soldiers by force, he came to him. He told Claudius that he should be king, and then he returned home.

Agrippa put oil on his head and went to the senate to ask what Claudius had decided. They told him and asked him what he thought they should do. Agrippa said that he was loyal to the senators, but if they were going to fight the soldiers who wanted Claudius as king, they would need a trained army and not one made up of freed slaves who might not obey. "Skillful soldiers on the side of Claudius, and so I am willing to go and ask him to give up the government."

The senate agreed with this and sent Agrippa with their messengers. Privately Agrippa told Claudius that the senate was not decided, and he needed to speak to them with dignity and authority. Claudius told them that he understood they were not happy about another Caesar, since they had seen a lot of bad leaders. But he promised them that his rule would be fair and right, with the authority to be shared. After the senate's messengers left,

Claudius's soldiers promised to be loyal to him, and he gave each of the guards, captains and all of the soldiers 5,000 drachmae* each.

The governors called a meeting of the senate in the temple of Jupiter the Conqueror, even though it was night. Some of the senators did not come, and instead hid. Some went to their farms and preferred to be slaves rather than risk the unknown in running a government. Only 100 senators came to the meeting. The soldiers who came wanted the senate to choose an emperor instead of having lots of rulers. So the senators were in a bad position; they could not agree to rule the country together, and some feared Claudius. Some senators wanted to be king since they had married into the royal family, for example Minucianus, who was married to the sister of Caius. Even gladiators, night watchmen and ship rowers thought they might have a chance to join the government. But they gave up the idea, either for the sake of keeping peace in the city or in fear for their lives.

Cherea came in the morning and tried to deliver a speech to the soldiers, but they did not allow him to speak since they desired a king. Cherea said he would give them an emperor, if anyone would bring him the password from Eutychus. Eutychus was a charioteer from the green-band group and a great friend of Caius who used to bother the soldiers with building stables for horses. Cherea brought up Eutychus's name to curse the soldiers. Cherea told them that he would bring them the head of Claudius, calling him a fool. But the soldiers did not listen; they went to Claudius to promise loyalty to him. So the senators were left with no one to protect them, and they started blaming one another. One of Caius's murderers came and said he would kill himself if Claudius became emperor and put the people into slavery all over again. He blamed Cherea for not being willing to also kill himself, even though he was the first to hate Caius. If the freedom he risked his life for was not going to happen, Cherea should not want to live.

The debates continued in the senate, but others were surrounding Claudius and promising loyalty to him as Caesar. One governor came there who left the senators, and he was almost killed by the soldiers. But Claudius saved him. But others who came later were not given mercy, and one went away wounded. Then Agrippa went to Claudius and told him to treat the senators more gently, since he would need them in order to rule the country. Claudius agreed and called the senate to the palace. He was carried through the city by the soldiers, but the crowd was angry because two of Caius's murders, Cherea and Sabinus, were marching in front even though they had been ordered to stay out of public places.

When they arrived at the palace, Claudius gathered his friends together and asked them what they thought about Cherea. They said that Cherea had done a good deed but he did it through betrayal, so he should die. So Cherea was put to death, along with many other Romans. Lupus, the man who killed Caius's wife and daughter, was also killed. Cherea went to his death bravely, and he made fun of Lupus when he complained about the cold, saying that the cold should not bother a "lupus" (wolf). When Cherea arrived at the place of execution, he asked the soldier if this was the first time he had ever used that sword to cut off a head. He asked that he use the same sword which he had used to kill Caius, which was very sharp. He was happily killed in one stroke. Lupus had to be cut many times, because he did not boldly stretch out his neck.

A few days later, when the Romans made offerings to their ghosts, they put things into the fire in honor of Cherea and begged him to be merciful to them and not to be angry if they had been ungrateful. Sabinus was freed by Claudius and again became an army commander, but he felt bad about his fellow soldiers; so he fell on his own sword, and the wound reached up to the handle of the sword.

V

CLAUDIUS killed all soldiers whom he suspected were against him. He then repeated that the kingdom which Caius had given

Agrippa would be kept by Agrippa, as well as Judea and Samaria which Agrippa's grandfather Herod had ruled over. This was all confirmed by an oath at the forum in Rome. He took away territory from Antiochus and gave him something else. He freed his mother's servant who had been imprisoned by Caius. Agrippa gave the widow of Alexander's son, Marcus, to his brother Herod to marry, and asked Claudius to make Herod a king.

Trouble arose in Alexandria between the Jews and the Greeks after Caius was dead. Under Caius, the Greeks were allowed to mistreat the Jews, and now the Jews got ready to fight back. Claudius sent an order to the president of Egypt to quiet things down. "Caius had no understanding and tried to make the Jews call him a god, which is against their religion. Let everyone now keep the laws that Augustus Caesar made, and I want no more trouble from either side."

King Herod and King Agrippa then asked Claudius to give the same rights to all Jews in the empire as he had given in the order to Alexandria. Claudius wrote: "It is right for the Jews to be free to keep their customs. Our old public records show that the Jews had all of these rights since the time of Augustus. I grant this favor to the Jews who have asked me, since they have been faithful in their friendship with the Romans. I ask that the Jews show the same respect and not bother those with other customs.This decree is to be written on tables by the judges of all the cities and colonies in the public places, both inside and outside Italy. These decrees are to be displayed for 30 days in places where they can be read from the ground."

vi

CLAUDIUS Caesar sent Agrippa home to rule in his own territory, and he sent letters to the presidents and leaders in the region that they should treat Agrippa well. Agrippa returned a rich man and came to Jerusalem to offer sacrifices according to the Jewish laws. He ordered that the Nazarites should shave their heads. He took the gold chain which Caius had given him which was the same weight as the iron chain he wore as a prisoner in Rome, and he hung it over the temple treasury as a reminder of what he had suffered, and that God had raised what had fallen. Even King Agrippa had once been chained for a small reason, but afterwards he received better things. Agrippa gave the priesthood to Simon, after removing Theophilus the son of Ananus from being high priest.

Agrippa freed the people in Jerusalem from paying taxes on their houses. He put Silas in charge of the soldiers. At this time, some young men in Doris carried a statue of Caesar into a Jewish synagogue, greatly upsetting Agrippa. He went immediately to the president of Syria accusing the people of Doris. Petronius, president of Syria, wrote with anger to the city of Dois, telling them that this act was a serious crime against the Jews and the emperor himself. "The men who have done this are to come to me and explain themselves, since they have acted against Augustus's order. This needs to be stopped right away, in order not to give an excuse for the Jews to get revenge and cause problems." Petronius dealt with this and upheld the Jewish law.

King Agrippa again changed the high priest, giving the job back to Jonathan, the son of Ananus. But Jonathan refused it, saying once was enough for him, and he asked that his brother Matthias receive it since he was a worthy person. Agrippa was glad and took Jonathan's advice. Marcus later became president of Syria.

vii

SILAS had been a very good friend of King Agrippa, who put him in charge of his horses. Silas had rescued him from danger many times. But Silas thought this made him equal to the king. Silas talked too much and bothered Agrippa by continually reminding him of how good Silas had been to him. Finally in anger the king took his job away from him and sent him back as a prisoner to his own country. When Agrippa was celebrating his birthday, however, he recalled that Silas had been a good friend to him and he suddenly invited Silas to come to him. The messengers came to Silas, but the silly man promised that he would speak even more loudly than before about all that he had done for the king, especially now that he had been mistreated. Silas said he would never forgive Agrippa for this offence. They told this to the king, and as a result Agrippa kept Silas in prison.

King Agrippa repaired the walls of Jerusalem next to the new city called Bezetha. He used public money and made the walls wider and higher. In a short while, they would have been so strong that no one could destroy them. But the president of Syria, Marcus, wrote to Claudius Caesar, who worried about a rebellion. So he ordered Agrippa to stop the project, which he did.

Agrippa gave many gifts to people and had a good reputation. Herod had been very different, since he severely punished people and had no mercy on those he hated. Herod was friendier to the Greeks than to the Jews and donated money which was used in foreign cities, including baths, theatres, temples and porticoes. He never gave any money to a Jewish city. But Agrippa gave many gifts and also treated foreigners well. He preferred to stay most of the time in Jerusalem and he carefully observed the Jewish laws, making a sacrifice every day.

Simon was a man living in Jerusalem who knew the Jewish law well. He gathered people while the king was away in Cesarea, and he accused Agrippa of not being worthy to enter the temple. One of Agrippa's soldiers told the king. Simon was called to the king and invited to sit beside him in the theatre. He asked Simon what there was about the place which was contrary to the law. Simon was sorry and asked the king to forgive him. Then the king gave him a small present and sent him home. King Agrippa felt that gentleness was better and more effective than anger in a king.

King Agrippa built in many places, and he built a theatre for the people of Berytus. It was large and grand and cost a lot of money. He also built baths and walkways for them. The dedication of this theater was an expensive and big celebration, with lots of musicians which performed. Agrippa also sent lots of gladiators: 700 men fought against 700 other men, and all of them were criminals. He combined the need for warlike punishment with a peace-time recreation, and the criminals were all destroyed at once.

AFTER Agrippa finished the work at Berytus, he moved to Tiberias. He was respected by many kings, and he invited them to Tiberias and treated them well. Then Marcus the president of Syria came to visit. King Agrippa went seven furlongs* out to meet him, to show honor to him as a Roman. But Marcus was suspicious to see Agrippa taking all these other kings with him in his chariot. Marcus thought there might be a plot to rebel against Rome, and he sent some servants to each one of those kings and ordered them to go home. Agrippa was upset and became Marcus's enemy. Agrippa also took the high priesthood from Matthias and gave the job to Elioneus.

After Agrippa had ruled in Judea for three years he arrived in Cesarea for a performance honoring Caesar. Many important people arrived. On the second day he wore a silver garment and arrived at the theatre early in the morning. Those who saw him were frightened to see the sun's reflection on him, and they decided that he was a god. The people shouted that they needed his mercy since they now realized he was immortal. Because King Agrippa did not stop them from saying this, he was punished by God. He looked up and saw an owl on a rope over his head, and he remembered that this bird was a sign of bad news just as before it meant good news. At that moment, he felt strong stomach pains. He told the people that he, whom they called a god, was going to die. He said that he would have to accept whatever God was bringing him.

The pain became worse, and he had to be carried into the palace. The crowd heard that he would soon die, and they all sat in sackcloth and asked God to spare him. The king was on an upper floor and saw the people lying on the ground praying for him. He had pain for five days and afterwards he died. He was 54 years old and had ruled seven years. The taxes he received from all the lands he ruled came to 12 million drachmae* (425,000 sterling, Agrippa's yearly income, which was ¾ of his grandfather Herod's income), but he still had to borrow money. Agrippa was generous and always spent more than he had. Before the people were aware of his death, one of the king's faithful servants killed Silas as if King Agrippa had ordered his death.

ix

KING Agrippa died and his children remained: a son aged 17 also named Agrippa, and three daughters. One daughter, Bernice was married to Herod, his father's brother and was 16. Mariamne and Drusilla were ten and six, respectively. There is a story that after Agrippa died the soldiers of Cesarea and Sabaste forgot his kindness, and they even stole the statues of these two young girls and abused them. (One author says that it was actually the young girls who were abused by the soldiers.) It is said that many of the people were so happy about Agrippa's death that they feasted with flowers on their heads and drank for joy. They did not remember the good which Agrippa had brought them, or the good of his grandfather Herod who had built their cities.

Agrippa, the son was in Rome and had been raised with Claudius Caesar. When Caesar heard about Agrippa's death and that the people had reacted in a disgusting way, he was very upset. He wanted to send the young Agrippa back to rule. But his advisors said that he was too young for the job, which was hard even for a grown man. Caesar sent Cuspius Fadus to be governor of Judea and the rest of Agrippa's kingdom. He ordered that those people in Cesarea and Sabaste be punished for their disrespect and for abusing the daughters. Those groups of soldiers were to be sent to another place, and a different group from Syria was to come to replace them. But some of the soldiers did not leave, and they became troublemakers for the Jews in the future when Florus became the governor. They were only removed when Vespasian came to power.

BOOK XX

FROM FADUS THE ROMAN PROCURATOR TO FLORUS

i

AFTER King Agrippa died, Claudius Caesar sent Lassius Longinus to replace Marcus, out of respect for Agrippa (who was opposed to the president of Syria, Marcus). Then there was trouble in Judea on the border of Perea, in a place called Mia. The Jews of Perea killed many of the Philadelphians. Fadus the governor was upset since they had not asked him to judge the case. He took three of the Jewish leaders and had one killed and the others sent away. A fourth man, who had robbed people and caused trouble in Idumea and Arabia, was finally brought to Fadus and afterwards killed. Fadus succeeded in stopping all robberies in Judea.

Fadus also ordered that the clothing of the high priests be kept in the tower of Antonia to be guarded by the Romans as in the past. The Jews asked to send messengers to Caesar to ask if they could keep the clothing. When the messengers came to Rome, the young Agrippa, who was still living with Claudius, asked Caesar to grant their request. So Claudius sent a letter stating that Agrippa was his friend whom he had raised. "Agrippa, who knows how I have acted on behalf of your nation, has asked me to grant this favor. I want everyone to be allowed to worship God according to their own country's laws. I grant the wish of King Herod and Agrippa who have asked me to let the high priest's clothing remain in the power of the Jews. They are both my good friends and men of good character." He then named those who brought him the letter.

Herod, the brother of the dead Agrippa asked Claudius Caesar to give him authority over the temple, the money and the choice of the priests. Herod took out the last high priest and gave the job to Joseph the son of Camus.

HELENA, queen of Adiabene, and her son Izates became Jews, and this was how it happened. The king of Adiabene, Monobazus, fell in love with his sister Helena, married her and had a child. One night when Monobazus had his hand on Helena's belly, he heard a voice that the child would be fine. He had another son by Helena before this, and he had other sons by other wives, but he loved Izates more than the others. Izates's brothers envied him because he was a favorite of his father. The king feared that they would harm him, so he sent Izates to live with the king of Charax-Spasini. This king loved the boy and he later married his daughter. He gave Izates a country to rule, and he became rich.

When Monobazus was old, he called for his son Izates and was very happy to see him. He gave him the country called Carrae which had rich soil containing amomum (the spice cardamom). There were also remains of Noah's ark in that country. Izates stayed there until after his father died.

The day he died, Helena gave a speech to all of the armies and said that Monobazus wanted Izates to be the next king. "I await your decision, however, since it is better that a majority decide rather than one person." They all agreed to this but felt that all of the brothers should be killed in order to make Izate's position more secure. Helena asked them to wait on this idea until Izates would come. Queen Helena chose Monobazus, the oldest son (named after his father) to be king, crowning him and giving him his father's signet ring. He was to rule until his brother arrived.

During the time that Izates lived in Charax-Spasini, a certain Jewish merchant, Ananias, taught some of the king's women to worship God according to the Jewish religion. He met Izates and taught him also. At the same time Helena was taught by another Jew about the Jewish religion. After Izates came home and saw his brothers and other relatives in prison, he was unhappy. But he didn't want them to be free either, because they could do him harm. He sent some of them together with their families to Caesar in Rome, and others to Artabanus the king of Parthia.

Both Izates and his mother kept the Jewish customs. Izates wanted to be circumcised, but his mother talked him out of it. She said that since he was the king it would not be wise, since their people might not want to be ruled by a Jew. Word got to Ananias and he agreed with Izates's mother; he said it would not be wise. Ananias stopped teaching Izates because he was afraid that people would think he was making trouble. He told Izates that circumcision is not necessary, but rather worship of the true God is the main thing. Izates would have God's forgiveness for not being circumcised.

Eleazar from Galilee arrived, and when he saw Izates reading the laws of Moses, he told him it was a shame since he was not obeying what he read. Eleazar told him that he needed to be circumcised. Izates sent for a doctor who did the circumcision. Later he sent for his mother and Ananias and told them what he had done. They were in shock and afraid that others would find out, and that he would no longer be king. But God kept Izates safe as well as his sons; although they saw dangers, they were saved from them. They were rewarded for their righteousness and faithfulness.

The kingdom of Izates was a peaceful one, and Helena felt it was time for her to go to Jerualem in order to worship God in the temple and offer thank offerings. Izates gladly gave her permission to go and gave her a lot of money for the trip. Izates also went part of the way with her. The people of Jerusalem were suffering from a famine, and many had already died. Queen Helena sent some of her servants to Alexandria to buy corn and to Cyprus to buy dried figs. She gave these out among the people and they had great respect for her. When Izates heard about this famine, he also sent a lot of money to the leaders in Jerusalem.

ARTABANUS, the king of the Parthians, feared that some of the governors in his land had plotted against him. He went to Izates to ask for help. He brought 1,000 of his family and servants with him, meeting him along the road. He came humbly and bowed to him according to his custom. He pleaded for help with tears. Izates jumped down from his horse and encouraged him, promising his friendship. He said that either he would help Artabanus get his kingdom back or he, Izates, would lose his own.

He put Artabanus on his own horse and followed him by foot. Artabanus did not feel comfortable with this, and he said that if Izates did not get back on his horse, he, Artabanus, would get off. So they rode together on the horse. They arrived at the palace and Izates treated Artabanus with the honor of a king. Izates wrote to the Parthians, asking them to receive Artabanus again and to forget the past. They wrote back that they had a new leader, Cinnamus, and that they were afraid that a civil war might break out if Artabanus came back. Then Cinnamus himself wrote to Artabanus, the man who had brought him up, and asked him to come back. Artabus returned and when Cinnamus met him he bowed and saluted him as the king. He took the crown off his head and put it on the head of Artabanus.

So Izates restored the kingdom of Artabanus. Artabanus honored Izates by letting him wear his crown with the tip of the cone straight up [an old custom of great kings] and giving him a gold bed sleep in, customs which were unique to the kings of Parthia. Artabanus also gave Izates some fruitful land in Armenia. This area was called Nisibis, which contained the city of Antioch.

After Artabanus died, his son Bardanes ruled. He came to Izates and wanted him to join Bardanes's army to fight against the Romans. Izates would not agree; he knew how powerful the Romans were. He had also sent his five young sons to study the

Judean language and his mother had been to worship God at the temple. These were more reasons not to rebel against Rome. Izates told Bardanes about the great army of the Romans, in order to discourage him. The Parthian king was upset and said he would make war against Izates. But the Parthians killed Bardanes when they heard about his plan to fight the Romans, since they knew it would fail. His brother Gotarzes became king, but he was killed in a short time, replaced by another brother, Vologases. He in turn gave two of his brothers two of the provinces. Parcorus received the country of the Medes, and Tiridates received Armenia.

iv

IZATES believed in God and was a popular leader. The king's brother Monobazus and his other relatives also wanted to become Jews. Some of Izates's leaders were upset about this and felt they deserved punishment. They wrote to Abia, king of the Arabians, and offered him a lot of money if he would come and fight against Izates. The king of Arabia came with a large army, and Izates was left to fight alone. He had been betrayed but he did not panic. Instead he stopped fighting and found out who the plotters were, and he got rid of them; then he went back to the battle the following day. He drove the Arabian king into a fortress called Arsamus, and Izates eventually took it over. He took all the treasures and then went back to Adiabene. But he did not capture Abia, the Arabian king; when he was surrounded in the battle, he killed himself.

The enemies of Izates then wrote to the king of Parthia, asking him to kill Izates and replace him with someone from a Parthian family. Izates was troubled and saw that only God could help him. He took his wives and children to a very strong fort, together with a supply of corn. He set the hay and grass on fire, and then he waited. The Parthian king came with his large army of footmen and horsemen, sooner than expected. Izates had 6,000 horsemen on his side. A messenger came to Izates from the Parthian king and warned him that he would be punished, and that the God he worshipped would not deliver him out of the king's hands. Izates answered that his God was stronger than all men. Izates pleaded to God, throwing himself on the ground and putting ashes on his head. The whole family fasted. With tears in his eyes, he called upon God as the highest of all beings. He asked for his help against his enemies, for his sake and also because they had lifted up their proud and arrogant tongues against God. God heard his prayer. That very night the Parthian king received word that he should return since some enemies came and ruined his land. In this way Izates was left unharmed.

Izates died at age 55 and had ruled 24 years. He had 24 sons and 24 daughters. He gave orders that Monobazus would take his place, to repay his brother for keeping the kingdom for Izates years ago. When Helena head about Izate's death, she was very upset but was thankful to know that her oldest son would rule in his place. She went to see him in Adiabene, but she did not live much longer. Monobazus sent her bones and Izate's bones to Jerusalem and ordered that they be buried in the pyramids which Helena had built. There were three pyramids less than three furlongs* from Jerusalem. (One of these pyramids or pillars could have been what we now call Absalom's Pillar.)

V

WHILE Fadus was governor of Judea a certain magician, Theudas, convinced many of the people to take their things with them and follow him to the river Jordan. He said that he was a prophet and that he would divide the river, making an easy way across for them. Fadus did not allow them to try this idea, however, but brought horsemen against the people; he killed many of them and took some captive. They took Theudas alive and cut off his head and carried it to Jerusalem.

Tiberius Alexander took the place of Fadus. He was the son of another Alexander, from a wealthy family. There was a famine in Judea, which was when Queen Helena brought corn from Egypt and gave it to those in need. The sons of Judas of Galilee had also been killed. This Judas had caused the Jews to revolt. Then Cumanus took the place of Alexander as governor.

Many were gathered in Jerusalem for the feast of Passover. Cumanus was afraid of a rebellion and put soldiers in places around the temple courtyards in order to stop any possible uprising. On the fourth day of the feast, a soldier took his pants down, exposing himself to all of the people. The people were furious and called it an offense against God. Some felt that Cumanus was to blame. Cumanus was upset at the soldier, but he had to calm the people down. He gave orders for the whole army go to the fort of Antonia by the temple. When the people saw the soldiers, they tried to run away quickly, but the passages were too narrow. Afraid that they were being chased by the soldiers, 20,000 of the crowd went into a panic and were crushed to death. What was to be a joyful holiday turned into a day of mourning. The prayers and sacrifices were forgotten. There was much crying and all because of a single action of an obscene soldier.

While some of the people were going along a road about 100 furlongs* from the city, someone robbed a servant of Caesar named Stephanus. Cumanus heard about this and sent soldiers right way, ordering them to rob all the villages in that area and to bring him the governors in chains. In the meantime, one of the soldiers took the laws of Moses which were in one of the villages and brought them out; then he tore them to pieces in the sight of everyone, yelling and cursing. The Jews became furious. They came in great numbers to Cesarea where Cumanus was, and said that God's honor must be avenged. They were very offended and said that they would no longer be able to continue living. Cumanus's friends advised him to kill the soldier to avoid a riot. The man was beheaded and there was calm.

vi

THE Jews would walk to Jerusalem for the festivals, and those living in Galilee would take a shortcut through Samaria. One time they passed through a village called Ginea and many of the

Galileans were killed by the Samaritans there. Some of the Galilean leaders went to Cumanus and asked him to avenge the murders, but he did nothing since the Samaritans bribed him with money. This caused the Jews to organize for battle. They asked for the help of Eleazar, a notable robber who was already robbing Samaritan villages. Cumanus heard about this and he took some soldiers, together with Samaritans, and marched against the Jews. Many were killed and others taken captive. Leaders in Jerusalem put on sackcloth, put ashes on their heads and mourned the dead. They tried to stop the Jews from fighting, warning them that even the temple was in danger of burning if they would not lay down their weapons. The people then went home, but robberies continued all over Judea.

The leader of the Samaritans went to Quadratus, the president of Syria who was in Tyre at the time, and accused the Jews of burning their villages and taking spoil. They said they were upset that the Romans had not been asked to bring justice, and they were now asking for their help to set things right. The Jews then came with the opposite claim, and the Jews and the Samaritans were blaming each other. The Jews said that Cumanus had been bribed by the Samaritans and was silent in regards to the first killings. At this Quadratus said that he would hear the case when he came to Judea and could find out more. Quadratus came to Samaria and heard that the Jews whom Cumanus had imprisoned had caused trouble, so he ordered them to be crucified. Later he came to Lydda and heard about a certain Jew, Dortus, and four others who had convinced the people to rebel against the Romans. He ordered them to be put to death. He also sent Ananias the high priest and Ananus the commander in the temple to Rome as prisoners to account for what they had done to Claudius Caesar. He then ordered the leaders of the Samaritans and Jews, as well as the governor Cumanus and the tribune, to go to Italy to the emperor in order to let him judge their case. He came to Jerusalem, and finding the people at peace and celebrating their festival, he returned to Antioch.

Cumanus and the others arrived in Rome and the day was fixed for them to speak. Caesar's friends were on the side of Cumanus and the Samaritans, but the young Agrippa, who was still in Rome, begged the emperor's wife to convince her husband to hear and understand who the real rebels were. When Claudius learned that the Samaritans had started the fight, he ordered that they all be killed and that Cumanus be sent away. He ordered that the tribune be carried back to Jerusalem, taken through the city for the people to see, and then killed.

vii

CLAUDIUS sent Felix to take care of matters in Judea. After Claudius had reigned for twelve years, he gave Agrippa Philip's kingdom and other countries. After receiving this gift from Caesar, Agrippa gave his sister Drusilla to the king of Emesa, Azizus, since he agreed to be circumcised. She had been offered to the son of King Antiochus after he promised to be circumcised, but he changed his mind so the marriage did not take place.

Felix fell in love with Drusilla, since she was the most beautiful woman in the area. He sent her a Jewish friend of his named Simon from Cyprus who pretended to be a magician. He tried to convince her to divorce her husband Azizus and marry Felix. Drusilla wanted to get away from her envious and mean sister, Bernice, so she was convinced to ignore the laws of her forefathers. She did marry Felix and they had a son named Agrippa. This son died when the volcano at Vesuvius erupted in the days of Titus Caesar.

Bernice lived as a widow long after the death of Herod, king of Chalcis, who was both her husband and her uncle. She had slept with her brother Agrippa junior, and to stop the rumors about this she convinced Poleme, the king of Cilicia, to be circumcised and to marry her. He agreed mainly because she was rich. This marriage did not last long, and she left Poleme and also left the Jewish religion. At this same time Mariamne left Archelaus and married Demetrius, the leading Alexandrian Jew since he was wealthy. They named their son Agrippinus.

CLAUDIUS Caesar died after reigning thirteen years. It is said that he was poisoned by his wife Agrippina. Agrippina had been married to Domitius who had killed his first wife, by whom he had two children, Britannicus and Octavia. Agrippina and Domitius had a son, called Domitius, after his father. She was a widow for a long time and later married Claudius. One of the daughters of Domitius, Octavia, was married to Nero, the name which Caesar gave to Domitius after adopting him.

Agrippina may have poisoned Claudius because she was afraid that her son Nero would lose the kingdom to Britannicus. Nero poisoned his rival Britannicus in a secret way and later put his own mother to death. He also killed his wife Octavia and other prominent people, saying that they were plotting against him.

I, Flavius Josephus, will not write more about Nero, since there is much written about him. Indeed, some wrote lies because they received benefits from him. Others hated him so much that they have lied and deserve to be punished. Many have no regard for the truth about any history; they write whatever they wish. I will relate what happened to the Jews carefully, whether it shows our sufferings or the crimes we have been guilty of.

During the reign of Nero after Azizus died, his brother became king of Emesa. Aristobulus, the son of Herod king of Chalcis, became governor of Lesser Armenia. Agrippa ruled part of Galilee, Tiberias and Taricheae. He also received a city of Perea called Julias and fourteen surrounding villages.

The Jews suffered more and more from robbers and pretenders who tricked the people. Felix killed many pretenders and robbers daily. He caught Eleazar the robber by promising him that he would not hurt him. After he came, Felix put him in chains and sent him to Rome.

Felix was also against the high priest, Jonathan, since he would tell him how the Jewish affairs should be managed better. Felix convinced one of Jonathan's faithful friends, a citizen of Jerusalem called Doras, to bring robbers to attack and kill him for a lot of money. Doras agreed. The murderers would arrive in Jerusalem as if to worship God while hiding daggers under their clothes. They killed Jonathan and were not caught. They became bold and continued to kill their enemies, both in the temple and in parts of the city. They mingled among the crowds and no one noticed. Some of the murders were done for money. They felt no guilt, and this is why God allowed the temple to be destroyed by fire, as if to purify the place. "God brought the Romans and slavery on us and our wives and children, in order to make us wiser."

Some pretenders drew the people out into the desert promising to do wonders and signs from God. Felix brought them back and punished them.

There was a man from Egypt who claimed to be a prophet. He persuaded the people to come with him to the Mount of Olives which was five furlongs* from Jerusalem. He promised that he would order the walls of Jerusalem to fall down and they would all go into the city. Felix ordered his soldiers to take their weapons and stop this man. They killed 400 of the people and took 200 prisoners. The Egyptian escaped and no one saw him again. The robbers tried to get the people to rebel against the Romans, and when they would not agree they set fire to their villages and took spoil.

There was trouble in Cesarea between the Jews and the Syrians. The Jews claimed that since Herod their king was a Jew by birth and had built their city, they were more worthy. The Syrians said that Cesarea had previously been called Strato's Tower, and that there were no Jews living there at that time. The leaders of the fighting on both sides were whipped. The Jews had more money and they looked down on the Syrians. The Syrians, although poorer, were proud that most of the Roman soldiers from Cesarea or Sebaste were Syrian. The two groups threw stones at one another and some were wounded, but the Jews won.

Felix suddenly came there and told the Jews to stop. They refused, so he sent his soldiers to fight them; many Jews were killed and some were taken captive. He permitted his soldiers to rob some of the homes which contained riches. Leading Jews who were less extreme begged Felix to spare them and send the soldiers away; he granted their request.

King Agrippa gave the priesthood to Ismael the son of Fabi. The high priests and the leaders in Jerusalem were fighting and throwing stones at one another. The city was wild, as if there was no government. The high priests even sent their servants into the threshing floors in order to take tithes which were due them. Because of this, some of the poor priests died from hunger. There was no justice.

Porcius Festus was governor after Felix. The Jewish leaders in Cesarea went to Rome to accuse Felix, and he would have been punished, but his brother who was a great friend of Nero begged for mercy. Two leading Syrians bribed Nero's teacher to convince Nero to take away the equal rights of the Jews which were given them by Rome. Nero wrote a letter to the Syrians to do this, and when Jews in Cesarea heard about it the unrest turned into a war.

When Festus came to Judea, robbers were setting fires in all of the villages and robbing them. One group of robbers, called the Sicarii, used small swords which were curved like sickles. Many were killed by these men in Jerusalem when they came for the festivals. Festus sent horsemen and foot soldiers to kill one pretender who had promised the people freedom if they would follow him out to the desert. The Romans succeeded in killing all of them along with the leader.

King Agrippa built a large dining room in the royal palace in Jerusalem near the temple. The palace had been built by the Asamoneus and was high, offering an impressive view over the city. The king could lie down and eat and at the same time see what was being done in the temple. The chief men in Jerusalem were upset about this, since the ceremonies in the temple, especially the sacrifices, were not to be seen by others. They built a wall on the highest building in the inner court of the temple on the west side, blocking the view from the palace and also from the soldiers' fort.

King Agrippa and Festus were very upset, and Festus told them to take the wall down. The Jews asked to take the matter to

Nero to decide, saying they could no longer live knowing that any part of the temple would be torn down. They sent their leaders and Ismael the high priest to Nero, as well as the keeper of the holy treasure. Nero forgave them and let them keep the wall. This was done to satisfy Nero's wife, who was religious. The ten messengers were sent home, but the keeper of the treasury and Ismael the priest were kept as hostages with Nero's wife. When Agrippa heard his, he gave the priesthood to Joseph, son of Simon, who had been high priest before.

CAESAR heard that Festus had died and sent Albinus to Judea to take his place. Agrippa took Joseph from the high priesthood and gave the job to Ananus. Ananus's father, also called Ananus, had five sons who had all been high priests. This young Ananus one of the Sadducees who were strict in dealing with those they thought of as breaking Jewish law. He gathered the Sanhedrim of the judges and brought the brother of Jesus named James, and accused him of breaking the Jewish laws. The more fair-minded Jews wrote to King Agrippa, saying that they did not approve of some of the punishments of Ananus. They also sent messengers to Albinus, who was on the way to Judea, complaining that Ananus had gathered the Sanhedrim without the governor's consent. After three months Ananus was sent home by King Agrippa, and Jesus, the son of Damneus, became the high priest.

Albinus came to Jerusalem and he tried to bring peace by killing many of the Sicarii. In the meantime, Ananias (Ananus the father) had favor with the people. He had a lot of money and gave Albinus presents. He had wicked servants who went to threshing floors and took tithes that belonged to the priests by force. Some of the poor people were even beaten. Some of the older priests died since they had no food.

Some of the Sicarii came to the city at night before the festival and caught Eleazar, a scribe of the temple who was a son of Ananias, keeping him as a hostage. They told Ananias that they would release Eleazar if Ananias would convince Albinus to free ten Sicarii prisoners. The request was granted. The Sicarii continued to cause trouble, taking Ananias's servants as hostages to free more of their friends.

Agrippa enlarged Cesarea Philippi and in honor of Nero called it Neronias. He built a theatre at Berytus at great cost, and there were yearly shows which cost 10,000 drachmae*. He gave out corn and oil among the people. He put valuable and beautiful statues all around the city which he had from other places, and the people hated him for taking their treasures away to put in a foreign city. Some were rare and very old.

Jesus, the son of Gamaliel, took the place of Jesus, the son of Damneus, as the high priest. With all the changes of the high priest, there were fights among the priests, causing them even to throw stones at one another. Ananias was rich and so he remained the strongest in these fights. Costobarus and Saulus were also favored by some wicked people because they were related to Agrippa, but they were violent and robbed the weaker people. The city of Jerusalem was full of violence and things got worse from day to day.

Albinus heard that he would be replaced by Gessius Florus, and to gain favor with the people he emptied the prisons. He put to death the prisoners who seemed to deserve death, but those who had done smaller crimes were freed after paying a fine. So the prisons were empty, but the country was filled with robbers.

Many of the Levites sang hymns and they asked Agrippa to gather the Sanhedrim and to let them wear linen clothing along with the priests. This was something new which they said King Agrippa would be remembered for. So he allowed it. He also allowed them to sing some new music. But all this was against the Jewish laws, and it was sure to bring punishment.

The temple was finished, and there were now more than 18,000 people who had worked on the building who had no jobs. The people came up with an idea to build up the east court of the temple, which was above a deep valley, using huge white stones.

King Solomon had first used these stones which were 20 cubits* and 6 cubits* high. King Agrippa felt it would take too long and cost too much so he refused. But he did let them build pavement in the city from the white stones. The king replaced Jesus the son of Gamaliel with Matthias as high priest. He was priest when the Jews began their war with the Romans.

HERE is the line of Jewish high priests. Aaron, the brother of Moses, was the first high priest. The high priests after him were to be only from the family of Aaron. There were 83 in all. Thirteen of them were priests during the time the Jews were in the wilderness and the tabernacle was standing, a total of 612 years from the time the Israelites left Egypt until the temple was built by King Solomon in Jerusalem. From the days of Solomon's temple until Nebuchadnezzar king of Babylon burned the temple and took the Jews captive to Babylon, 18 more high priests ruled; the time was 466 and a half years. When the captives returned from Babylon after 70 years, Jesus the son of Josadek became the high priest. There were 15 priests in all until the time King Antiochus Eupator began to rule; he and his general Lysias killed Onias (also called Menelaus) the priest, and chased away his son Onias. They replaced him with Jacimus, who was from the family of Aaron but not of the family of Onias. Onias, a nephew of the previous Onias who was priest, came to Egypt and made friends with Ptolemy Philometor and Cleopatra his wife. He convinced them to make him the high priest of the temple which was built in Egypt, a copy of the one in Jerusalem.

Jacimus was a priest for three years, and after he died there was no priest for seven years. When the sons of Asamoneus began to rule the Jewish nation, having won the war with the Macedonians, Jonathan was made priest. He ruled for seven years, but was killed by the wicked Trypho; Simon Jonathan's brother took his place as priest. Simon was killed at a feast by his son-in-law, and his own son Hyrcanus became priest. Hyrcanus was priest for

30 years and died an old man. He was succeeded by Judas (also called Aristobulus), who was the first to be both priest and king. Judas died from a disease, and his brother Alexander took his place. Alexander was both king and high priest for 27 years, and when he died his wife Alexandra named the next ruler. She chose her son Hyrcanus as priest but Alexandra herself ruled the kingdom for nine years until she died. The brother of Hyrcanus, Aristobulus, fought against him and took both the priesthood and the kingdom.

After three years, Pompey came and took Jerusalem by force, and he sent Aristobulus away to Rome together with his children. He made Hyrcanus priest again, and governor of Judea, but he was not allowed to wear a crown. He was priest for another 24 years, until the Parthians took him prisoner. Antigonus the son of Aristobulus became king, but only for three years before he was killed by Herod and Antony. The Romans then made Herod the king, and from this time onward the high priests were no longer from the family of the Asamoneus but from common families, perhaps not even priestly families. Herod did choose one, Aristobulus, the grandson of Hyrcanus who was liked among the people, and Herod married Aristobulus's sister Mariamne to get favor with the people. Later he feared him and caused him to drown at Jericho, and from that time Herod did not trust any of the family of Asamoneus. Herod's son Archelaus followed this rule, and so did the Romans who later ruled over the Jews. From the time of Herod until the day Titus took the temple and the city and burned them, there were 28 priests over a total of 107 years. Some were political rulers under Herod and his son Archelaus. After their death the government became an aristocracy, and the priests had a certain share in the authority.

xi

ALBINUS was replaced by Gessius Florus to rule Judea under Nero. His wife was Cleopatra, a friend of Nero's wife, and this was how he got the job. Both Florus and his wife were very wicked, and Florus was so cruel to the Jews that Albinus seemed like a good ruler in comparison. Florus became friends with the criminals and was open with his totally unjust punishments that were taking place constantly. Many Jews had no choice but to leave the country and take their chances with foreigners. Floris pushed the Jews to go to war against the Romans despite the risks, since life was becoming unbearable. The details are given in my book called "The Wars of the Jews."

Here I conclude my book which began with the creation of man until the twelfth year of Nero. I have shown not only what happened to the Jews but also events which took place in Egypt, Syria, Palestine and the suffering which the Assyrians, Babylonians, Persians, Macedonians and last of all the Romans brought upon us. I have written about our high priests which served for around 2,000 years. I have written about our kings and rulers.

No other person, whether Jew or foreigner, has made the effort to give this accurate account to the Greeks. Being Jewish myself, I was the most qualified to write about my own nation. At the same time I spent much effort to learn the knowledge of the Greeks, including their language. I can't speak their language perfectly, but we Hebrew-speaking people are not encouraged to learn foreign languages. The Jews consider this a goal for common people like their servants, to learn other languages as they feel the need. The only wise men they admire are Jews who not only know our laws but who can interpret them. Not many have succeeded at this, however; only two or three and only they were well rewarded for their efforts.

This history of the Jews is contained in twenty books and 60,000 verses. If God allows me I will briefly write about the wars again. I am 56 and we are in the thirteenth year of the reign of Caesar Domitian. I also wish to write three books about our Jewish opinions about God, His essence and about our laws.

TABLE OF EQUIVALENTS

Shekels	600 shekels = 15 pounds or 6.9 kilograms
Talents	666 talents = 25 tons or 23 metric tons
Cubits	1 cubit = 18 inches or 46 centimeters
Furlongs	1 furlong = one-eighth of a mile or 0.2 kilometers
Drachmae	1,000 drachmae = 8.5 kg
Modius	In ancient Rome, a measure of dry capacity approximating closely to a modern peck.
Fathom	unknown
Attic drachmae	unknown

ACKNOWLEDGMENTS

The following people made it possible for this book to "see the light" (as we say in Hebrew): Hannah Weiss, Mark A. Stephens, Chris O'Byrne, Debbie O'Byrne, Baruch Maranzenboim, Dr. Chris Macosko, Rev. Kathleen Macosko, M. Div., Mark Malatesta and Dvora Hemstreet. I can never thank them enough for helping me to see a dream of years come true.

ABOUT THE AUTHOR

Originally from California, Miriam Maranzenboim has lived in Israel since 1977. Miriam has always loved writing. Her screenwriting teacher at Cal State L.A., the famous David Dortort of the Bonanza series, once told her, "Miriam, you have a way with words." Over the years, her friends and family agreed that expressing herself in writing was a particular talent.

Once in Israel, Miriam was fascinated by all she learned about Judaism and the Hebrew language. Particularly interested in history, Josephus was her obvious choice of reading material. Finding it to be very difficult reading, Miriam often said, "Someone has to make this easy to read. This is important stuff."

Josephus - The History of the Jews Condensed in Simple English encapsulates Miriam's passion for the Bible, Israel/Jerusalem, archaeology, and ancient history.

A musician, writer, and lover of history, Miriam and her husband, a former refusenik, live in Haifa, Israel.